Pilgrim Church

Pilgrim Church

A Popular History of Catholic Christianity

WILLIAM J. BAUSCH

FIDES PUBLISHERS INC
NOTRE DAME INDIANA

Bausch, William J.
Pilgrim church.

Includes bibliographical references.
1. Church history.   2. Catholic Church—History.
I. Title.
BR145.2.B37   282'.09   73–6608
ISBN 0–8190–0598–3

Contents

For ANN
who also serves

Introduction

How can I disarm the professional historian and critic except by admitting right off that this is a book written by a parish priest for the average, educated parishioner? That as the work of an amateur it has large gaps in it, the loss of certain insights and all the faults of popularization? Yet, with all of these admissions I wish to justify the book on the grounds of adult education. The more I listen to people, the more I lecture, the more I realize how wide is the gap between the people's understanding of the Church and that Church's historical realities. Some of the people seem to view the Church as a massive entity moving unchanged and unalterable down the corridors of time. They are really only aware of *their* Church which, unbeknown to them, turns out to be the Tridentine Church, hammered out by the French Revolution and molded by the reactions of the popes from Pius IX to Pius XII.

Little do they know, I have found out, that the Church has had many life styles, many variations in liturgy, ministry and structure. Little do they know what is behind the legitimate (and illegitimate) happenings in the Church today that so confuse and infuriate them. Many of the Catholic people have so little context, background, perspective or prophetic stance from which to view the chaos and consolidations of the Church after Vatican II. Yet there are many things they should know that only history can supply.

Here are some samplings, all covered in this book, that should help the average Catholic of today to assess his Church: the origins of Christian antisemitism, the rich variety of ministries in the early Church, the real role of the pope; the rise, fall and recent reinstatement of the deacon, the role of women in the Church, the origins of the various liturgies, vestments and popular devotions; the beginnings of priestly celibacy and modern day Pentecostalism; the journey of the Church from local community to universal imperial kingdom, the effect of the first Church councils, the causes of the split between East and West; who was "Pope Joan," who elected the bishops for over a thousand years; what caused the Reformation, what are the bases for ecumenism, why the modern Church is decentralizing; how the Church got its reputation for conservatism, why Pope John XXIII was so popular and what is behind all the new theologies.

These, of course, are teasers. They are indications of the sweep of this book. I have made a sincere effort to be objective and I have made the effort to be selective on the basis of adult education. This accounts for the omissions of several great events such as the conversion of Moscow (the "third Rome"), the contributions of Spain, the glories of the Moslem empire and so forth. I have kept names and dates to a minimum and have tried to keep the book within reasonable limits—about 500 pages or so (and 2000 years into 500 pages gives an indication of what has been left out). I have included footnotes and references to the best popular books that I could find and urge the reader to follow them up. What I did not find and did not include in this book I may never know. But what I did find and did record has been exciting and enlightening to me. I hope it will be helpful and informative to the Catholic who wants the long-range view of his Church and an understanding of the origins of what is happening in the Church today.

I wish to thank all those people who attended my lectures and who gave me the hints and the questions that have aided in the shaping of this book. I wish to thank Ann DeVizia who worked so hard and so long in preparing the manuscript. Finally, I wish to thank all those scholars and authors on whom I have relied and who help us all to know history better so that we shall not be condemned to repeat it.

I

Background and Beginnings

TRIUMPH AND CHALLENGE

The great world religions are, as it were, great rivers of sacred tradition which flow down through the ages and through changing historical landscapes which they irrigate and fertilize. But as a rule we cannot trace them to their source, which is lost in unexplored tracks of the remote past. It is rare indeed to find a culture in which the whole course of this religious development can be traced from beginning to end in the full light of history. But the history of Christendom is an outstanding exception to this tendency. We know the historical environment in which Christianity first arose: we possess the letters of the founders of the Churches to the first Christian communities in Europe, and we can trace in detail the successive stages by which the new religion penetrated the West.[1]

Thus wrote the great historian of religion and culture, Christopher Dawson, some twenty-five years ago. He was only pointing up what Christianity has always boasted about: that it is a historical religion open to the full light of investigation. Being a historical religion, however, is not only Christianity's boast but also its challenge. Boast because records and documents are accessible and do provide the foundation for Christian claims; challenge because each year, it is no exaggeration to say, something new turns up in Christianity:

5

some new document or manuscript, some new artifact, some new monument, building or wall painting that goes back to the very beginnings. The result of all this modern scholarship and discovery is the challenge to broaden and even revise our understanding of the nature of the Church. The challenge is to harmonize the new insights with Christianity as it has historically developed over the last two thousand years.

Naturally in the process of harmonization many sacred and vested traditions are going to be questioned. As theory and controversy trickle down from the scholar to the average person there will be open distress over any tampering with his religion. This distress has been most evident for the Catholic living after Vatican II Council. Having very little historical background he has no defense or explanation as to what is happening in his Church. He only knows that change is its modern hallmark and that change seems to be based on the whim or the crass insensitivity of those seemingly out to destroy his Church. Yet we would maintain that history holds the key for such a person. For example: the average Catholic will never understand the changes in the liturgy unless he appreciates the discovery of the liturgical forms of the ancient Church. He will never understand the current controversies over the structures of the Church, the revival of the diaconate, etc., unless he has really read that first history book of the Church, *The Acts of the Apostles.* He will not understand why Pope Paul VI created the Synod of Bishops or why he has given the layman a share in the nomination of bishops unless he has some appreciation of the centralizing process of the Middle Ages. He will not understand the impact of the pastoral pope, Pope John XXIII unless he knows the histories of Pius IX, Pius X and Pius XII. He can never understand the rationale behind ecumenism unless he knows something of the issues of the sixteenth century Reformation. He will never be more than shocked at the calculated titles of controversial books by modern theologian Hans Kung like *Infallibility? An Inquiry* (1970) and *Why Priests?* (1972) unless he finds out the background to these issues. He cannot understand the long road from a totally religious society of the Middle Ages to the almost totally secular society of today unless he knows his history.

Franklin Roosevelt uttered his famous phrase that there is nothing to fear except fear itself. St. Pius X (with an irony that will be evident as one reads his times) proclaimed the same sentiment when he said that the only real enemy of the Church is ignorance. He was right and is right. For the educated Catholic of post-Vatican II it is necessary that he dispel some of that ignorance and acquire a new confidence in the historicity of his religion. "It is rare indeed to find a culture in which the whole course of this religious development can be traced from beginning to end in the full light of history." Rare indeed, but true for Christianity. As average people looking for directions and identity in our modern Church let us begin our investigation. Let us start at the beginning, with Judaism.

JEWISH HISTORY

The average Catholic has some vague memories about Jewish history before the time of Christ. At best he can recall only a few things he has learned in school or read. But more than a vague memory is needed if he is to understand the beginnings of Christianity for Christianity is an Oriental religion imported to the West. It takes its roots from Judaism. Its early theology and liturgy are grounded in Jewish terms and ways and in the cultural context of Palestine, an

Eastern country, not a European one. Thus, we must refresh our memories about ancient times, at least in broad terms and in simple outlines for there are many gaps in Jewish history and the Bible is not always complete, accurate nor unbiased.[2]

The Hebrews or Jews as they were later called after Judah, the fourth son of Jacob, whose tribe along with that of Benjamin made up the kingdom of Judea, began as a grouping of small tribes. They were consistently overawed, overshadowed and overcome by the Big Powers around them and it was only when these great and ancient empires were rising and falling—in the interludes as it were—that the Jews were able to gain political independence.

We recall that it all began with Abraham: his call, God's promise to him and his son Isaac that they would father a great nation. Isaac's son, Jacob (later called Israel) had twelve sons who were to head the Twelve Tribes of Israel and after whom the Twelve Apostles as leaders of the New Israel were fashioned. Among the twelve, Joseph (he of the multicolored coat) having been sold by his brothers into slavery became in time the Prime Minister of Egypt. During a period of famine the Hebrews were forced to seek food from their southern neighbor and it was at this time that Joseph, now fully Egyptianized and older, revealed himself to his eleven brothers exclaiming with tears, "I am Joseph, your brother!" (Genesis 45:4). These famous words were used by Pope John XXIII in receiving a delegation of rabbis to the Second Vatican Council and the warmth and ecumenical significance of the words were not lost on them. Through Joseph the Hebrews settled in Egypt and there they went from years of prosperity and peace to ones of slavery. From such slavery they were delivered by Moses. They wandered in the Sinai desert wilderness and after forty years of trial and discipline, having received the Law from Moses, they emerged as a people, the Chosen People, armed with a ritual, a moral code (the Ten Commandments) and a covenant—the "bargain" of mutual love and obligations between them and God. At last, in the early twelfth century B.C., they invaded Palestine or Canaan, the "Promised Land."

PERIOD OF THE KINGDOM

There were people living there already, of course, including the Canaanites and later on, around the time of Jewish kings, the Philistines who gave the name Palestine to the country. From the Canaanites the nomadic Jews learned the ways of agriculture and urban life. With the Canaanite language they meshed their Aramaic tongue to produce the classical Hebrew in which most of the Old Testament is written. Later they were to return to the original Aramaic and this was the tongue that Jesus spoke. In fact, their language and their writings, the Scriptures, were to be the one great Jewish contribution to history. They left nothing else, not even their famous Temple. But their writings of religious genius were to shape the world for ages to come.

A serious threat from the invading Philistines made the Jewish tribes clamor for a united front under a king and the prophet Samuel reluctantly conceded to their wishes with the anointing of Saul. (It must be mentioned, however, that the new unity was more apparent than real as the northern and southern parts of the kingdom continued to be rivals. When the Philistine threat was allayed the kingdom lost no time in separating.) These kings from Solomon onward worked hard to make little Palestine a part of the larger international life among the Great Powers in Asia Minor and Egypt. In this they were acting contrary to the Jewish prophets who, fearing the contamination of foreign ideas and religious customs, vigorously preached an isolationism. If the Jews copied much from their Canaanite neighbors there was one thing that they refused to assimilate, namely, religion, and the prophets wanted to keep it that way. Yet, with Solomon, even though he built the first great Temple, Jerusalem was internationalized and the prophets' fears were realized as foreign religions and cults permeated the life styles of the Jews. Under Solomon's son civil war split the always uneasy north and south. In 721 B.C. the fierce Assyrians overcame the northern kingdom of Israel (with its Ten Tribes). The Assyrians scattered the Jewish elite while leaving the peasants and the natives to mix with themselves. However, a group called the Samaritans claimed to be direct descendants of the members of the Ten Tribes who stayed. As a matter of fact, they regarded the Jews of the Two Tribes in Judea as heretical because they accepted all the books of the Old Testament whereas they (the Samaritans) only accepted the Pentateuch (the first five books). In addition, the Samaritans held that God's chosen place on earth was on Mt. Gerizim in their territory; therefore they regarded the Jewish Temple as an apostate Temple. Naturally the Jews in turn looked on the Samaritans as half-breeds and heretics and so the hatred was mutual. Hence we see the force of Jesus' reference to the *Good* Samaritan and his conversation with the Samaritan woman at Jacob's well and her references to worshiping at Mt. Gerizim rather than Jerusalem. (John 4: 3-42).

THE EXILE

The southern part of the Jewish kingdom, the kingdom of Judea, lasted longer but in 587 B.C. the new world power of Babylon conquered it and carried off the Jews into captivity and razed the famous Temple of Solomon. Here was a major crisis. The great symbol of their religion, the Temple, was destroyed and the Jews were exiled to foreign lands. This catastrophe was to have fundamental results in many ways both for Judaism and Christianity. First of all, the tragedy caused the defeated and exiled Jews to rethink their basic questions concerning their covenant with God and the problem of evil. No longer was the thought of political liberation. Now the aspirations of the exiled Jews took on a universal character. They were looking for spiritual deliverance, restoration and a Messiah who would achieve all this. Secondly, the "Babylonian Captivity" as it is called changed the quality of the Jewish religion. For one thing since the Temple was now destroyed, the city of Jerusalem inaccessible, the priesthood scattered, Jewish piety and religious life began to shift. They began to be focused on the Torah, that is, the Law as found in the Pentateuch. The Law became all important. It was studied, explained, commented on. All this commentary eventually became the great Jewish Talmud or the body of civil and canonical law for the Jews.[3] It was also probably around this time that, since the Temple was no more, the synagogue arose as the place to meet, to worship and to get instruction in the Law. We might recall that when as a visiting rabbi Jesus went into the synagogue he was allowed to comment on the Scripture read that day and to give instruction, even though, as it happened, his talk infuriated the congregation. (Luke 4: 16ff). Finally, the Babylonian captivity was to have great effects for Christianity. Jews were now spread all over the world. In time they would acclimate themselves in their respective countries and even form great Jewish centers. It would be to these communities that the first Jewish Christians (such as St. Paul) would go on their missionary rounds.

After seventy-two years the exile was over and under new world rulers, the Persians, the Jews in 538 B.C. were allowed to return to Palestine. Many Jews stayed in their adopted lands but some returned and under men like Nehemiah and Esdras the Law was restored and in 516 the Temple was rebuilt. From this point on it seems that a kind of semiisolation of those who returned lasted some two centuries.

> This is virtually all the information available regarding the lot of the Jewish people between the time of Nehemiah and the invasion of Alexander the Great. On the other hand, it is certain that this was a period of intense religious consolidation and, as it seems, of remarkable intellectual activity. It was then that the forms of postbiblical Judaism evolved and acquired their profound hold on Jewish life in its every aspect. It was in that period that what was to be rabbinic Judaism struck its roots, that the synagogue emerged as an established institution, that the liturgy began to assume its definitive shape and that the works comprising the Old Testament assumed, as it seems, their present form and were assembled in an authoritative fashion. It was thus one of the great formative ages in Judaism, and therefore in the history of the Jewish people, which emerges from this period equipped with the literature, the outlook and the institutions thereafter to be so characteristic of it and the main secret of its endurance.[4]

CONTACT WITH THE GREEK-ROMAN WORLD

When in 331 B.C. Alexander the Great defeated the Persians Palestine was annexed to Egypt where Greek ideas were able to penetrate the Jewish religion. This Greek-infiltrating process or "hellenization" process via Egypt was especially successful among the Jews who remained and flourished in exile, the Jews of the Diaspora or Dispersion as they are called in contrast to those who went back to Palestine. For example, the Jews in Alexandria perhaps numbering a million or so made that city the center of Jewish intellectual thought and later on people like the famous Jewish philosopher Philo would make great efforts to reconcile Greek and Jewish thought. In fact, so thoroughly hellenized did the Jews of the Diaspora become that at the beginning of the third century B.C. a translation of the Bible was rendered in Greek (the Septuagint) for those Greek-speaking Jews who no longer could speak Hebrew.

After Alexander's death his kingdom passed to the Ptolemies of Egypt who were tolerant of their Jewish subjects as regards customs and religion. However, when the rival Seleucid family of Antioch, Syria, overcame the Ptolemies they proved less tolerant. In fact they were bent on making the empire uniform including culture and religion. Into Jerusalem accordingly they introduced Greek gymnasiums whose naked athletes scandalized the Orthodox as it enticed the more liberal Jew. The injury to Jewish sensibilities did not stop there. A pig was sacrificed on the very altar of the Temple and a statue of Zeus was set up on the high altar becoming truly the "abomination of desolation" for the Jews of which the prophet Daniel spoke (Daniel 11:31). Such insults could only produce revolt and eventually the Hasmonaean or Maccabee family drove the conquerors from the Holy City. The Temple was purified of the abominations perpetrated there and in 165 B.C. it was rededicated, an event which to this day is celebrated among the Jews as the feast of Hanukkah.

Still, the Jews were not at all united over the paganizing or hellenizing process. They divided into two camps. There were those who were quite conservative, the Sadducees, and consequently heavily nationalistic and isolationist. They revolved their lives around the Temple and its ritual. The other party, the Pharisees, was more willing to flirt with the cultural mainstream. They centered their lives on the Law (the Torah). The tension between the two fostered a civil war over rival claims to the Hasmonaean throne. This broke out in 63 B.C. causing the new world power, the Romans, to intervene. General Pompey placed Jerusalem under Roman imperial power and sold thousands of Jews as slaves to Rome. The Jews, as a matter of fact, proved to be poor slaves since they would not work on the Sabbath and would not eat certain foods but they were excellent companions and rose to positions of influence in Rome as time went by. It was this influence that led the Pharisees to force Pilate to condemn Christ, else they would put pressure on in Rome. Although Jerusalem became a Roman protectorate it was allowed some autonomy and a unique exercise of religion under its own high priest and local religious council of the Sanhedrin. Some thirty years later Mark Anthony gave the wily Herod the Great the throne of Palestine. Herod built many palaces and, above all, he rebuilt the Temple on a grander scale. When he died Rome partitioned Judea into several protectorates and finally in 6 A.D. placed it under a procurator or governor (v.g. Pilate).

To carry this history past our time of interest: in 70 A.D. the Jews revolted from Rome. The emperor Titus came in and destroyed Jerusalem and, for the last time, the great Temple (and we might mention also the infant Christian Church there). He left only the foundation standing[5] and on his triumphal arch in Rome may be seen portrayed the Menorah or the holy seven branch candelabrum which he took from Jerusalem. Also, at the time of this second destruction of the Temple a Jewish hero, Rabban Johanan, fled taking with him all the sacred texts and commentaries. Since the Temple was no more, these texts provided the rationale for the permanent synagogue which had emerged the first time the Temple was destroyed. We might mention here also that as the Temple gave way to the synagogue so the rabbi displaced the Jewish priest. There was no more Temple in which to offer sacrifice, only a synagogue in which to expound the Law. The rabbi became *the* scholar and the studious rabbi became the new traditional Jewish folk-hero. The emphasis was now placed on knowledge and indeed the Jewish prayer was that the Jew be delivered from three things: from being a Gentile, from being a woman and from being ignorant. The Jews became the "people of the Book" and started their tradition for earnest study and academic excellence.

A second insurrection in 132-135 A.D. during the reign of the emperor Hadrian brought in the Roman army once more, sealing the fate of the Jewish state altogether.[6] Jerusalem became little more than a Roman military campsite. Gradually, however, legal disabilities were removed and the Jews were allowed to resume normal life. But the state had disappeared and was not to be restored until modern time with the creation of the State of Israel on May 14, 1948. Significantly, the new state's Declaration of Independence reads, "The State of Israel will be open for the immigration of Jews from all the countries of their dispersion. . . ." But from 135 to 1948 the "Wandering Jew" and the people without a country would be a painful reality for God's Chosen People.

At the time of our immediate interest, however, it is about 4 B.C. Herod the Great is ruling, the Romans are in power. The Jews are in Palestine and dispersed throughout the world. They are looking for deliverance, both national and spiritual and looking forward to the Messiah who would achieve both, a sentiment which was still reflected at the Ascension of Jesus when his disciples asked him, "Lord, are you going to restore the rule to Israel now?" (Acts, 1:6).

The Jews are divided along conservative and liberal lines. There are also other subgroups such as the Essenes living strictly ascetical and celibate lives in small communes. They seem to be the forerunners of Christian monasticism and to have had an influence on St. Luke's Gospel.

PAGAN CULTURE

Meanwhile, what about the non-Jewish world? This world abounded in religions, cults and cultures which had crossed and recrossed during many centuries of warfare and conquest. To simplify the situation we might say that in the time of the Roman Empire as it existed at the time of Christ there were, outside of the official Roman gods and emperor worship, three main categories of religious expression. At one end, there were the intellectual philosophical pantheisms of the aristocracy; at the other end there were the many various local cults of the masses. In between these two there stood the so-called "mystery" religions. They were "mysterious" in the sense that they were secret, their teachings and rituals being revealed only to the initiated. These mystery religions gave great emphasis to the after-life and many of them had their types of deliveries, saviors and heroes who died and brought life by that death.

To a restless people at a restless time all three types fed their anxious minds and hearts causing a rather intense period of religious interest. In particular the mystery religions were appealing because their main motif was deliverance after death:

> Despairing of true happiness for themselves in this life or the triumph of peace, justice and prosperity on earth, men turned their thoughts to a future life beyond the grave or to a spiritual life detached from the material world. In the

mystery religions . . . the dominant motif was to seek assurance for a life after death. As Attis was slain and rose again, so those who gained mystic communion with him and learned his secrets would live in blessedness after their earthly death. As Osiris was torn in pieces and brought to life, so those who were instructed in the ancient lore of Egypt would know the password to the world beyond. Souls purified by his mysteries Mithras would escort through the seven planetary spheres to the highest heaven, where they would live for ever in eternal light. . . .[7]

CHRIST

Into this mainstream of Oriental mysticism, Hellenistic culture, Roman rule and deep Judaic longing for deliverance plus their fierce devotion to monotheism came the Jew, Jesus Christ. He was born in Bethlehem in Judea, a puppet state of Rome but with some independence for the high priest and Sanhedrin within certain limits. He would grow up in this conquered state and come into contact and conflict with the conservative party of the Sadducees and the liberal party of the Pharisees and live among the constant undercurrents and aspirations for political freedom. The life of Jesus need not detain us here. We know that he preached the immortality of the soul (as against the Sadducees who said there was no resurrection and who tried to trap him on this point, Luke 20:27ff), renunciation and charity. His moral code was not nationalistic, but universal, commenting that God would look more kindly on the repentant Samaritan than on the selfish Jew. Jesus did not deal with the great social issues of the time but rather gave a law that goes beyond all law: the love of God and the love of neighbor. In fact, all that was necessary for salvation was summed up in his own person for he and he alone was "the way and the truth and the life." From this point on a man's destiny and eternal salvation would be determined by his attitude to Christ and his acceptance of his message.

During his public ministry, Jesus ran into more and more conflict with the leaders. He was brought before Pilate, charged with the ever sensitive political crime of treason and was crucified as a common criminal. But on the third day he arose from the dead, was seen by the Apostles he had chosen and by many others and on this one overwhelming root experience the early Church was built. The one indisputable conviction for the Apostles and other disciples was that Jesus rose from the dead:

> The theme of the Kerygma was the resurrection of Jesus. This event was an act of God: "God raised him up." This unheard-of statement the Apostles justified in three ways. First, by their own evidence; they took full responsibility for it. In essence, their evidence was that they had seen the risen Christ. The appearances of the risen Christ between Easter and the Ascension here take on their full meaning: their purpose was to establish the Apostles' faith. St. Paul was later to show that they were one of the essential points in the tradition he received from the Apostles. To have witnessed the risen Christ was the condition for being an Apostle and as the last to whom the risen Christ appeared, Paul belonged with the Twelve. It is this evidence of the Apostles which the Church will transmit: the tradition is "Apostolic tradition".[8]

This unshaken belief would be the source of the unflagging motivation urging the followers of Christ towards a new attachment, a new way of life and eventually to a new Church apart from the synagogue. All that Jesus said, all that he did, all that he was would be the radical inspiration of the new Church. "Jesus proclaimed the message, the Church proclaimed *him*".[9]

But here we enter uncertain territory. In the history of the

Church the vaguest decades are the period between the death of Jesus in 30 A.D. and the writing of the last Gospel about 90 A.D. After this latter time we know considerably more about the Church; the six decades mentioned are less revealing. What we do know comes from a close source, not from outside contemporary sources. For instance the Jewish historian Josephus who lived during this time (from 37 to about 93 A.D.) has a distinct reference to Christ. In fact, it was reported in February of 1972 that two Israeli scholars had found an authentic text of Josephus (whose former reference to Christ in Greek was always suspect as the work of Christian forgers) giving evidence from a non-Christian source of the existence and life of Jesus. The newly authenticated text from a tenth century Arabic manuscript goes like this:

> At this time there was a wise man who was called Jesus. And his conduct was good, and he was known to be virtuous. And many people from among the Jews and other nations became his disciples. Pilate condemned him to be crucified and to die. And those who had become his disciples did not abandon his discipleship. They reported that he had appeared to them three days after his crucifixion and that he was alive; accordingly, he was perhaps the messiah concerning whom the prophets have recounted wonders.[10]

Pliny who died in 112 had but one indirect reference to Christ. Tacitus around the year 115 mentions that Christ was killed in the reign of the emperor Tiberius. And that is it. But we said that we do know some things from sources close to Christ. St. Paul was a contemporary to the events. He was converted around the year 35 A.D. and he wrote his first epistle to the church-community at Thessalonia in 49 or 51, some twenty years after Jesus' death. The Gospel of St. Mark was formerly thought to have been written about 65 or 70, but again modern scholarship may date it back to the year 50, only fifteen years after the death of Jesus. In March of 1972 a Spanish priest, an expert on ancient papyrus scrolls, had perhaps dated a fragment of Mark that does go back to the year 50.[11] By the end of the first century we have all of the New Testament. We must remember, however, that the Gospels (at least the first three) are merely a setting down in writing the word-of-mouth traditions that were necessarily very active from the beginning. Such oral traditions became systematized enough in due time to appear in little sayings, stories, narratives until many (though not all, cf. John 21:25) surfaced in the Gospel texts. But there was more in these early decades. There were specific outlines of a baptismal rite, a common eucharistic meal, a forming organizational structure and the common Christian slogan proclaiming that Christ was Lord and Master. The final content that defined the Church in these vague early decades was the common expectation that Jesus would return to earth again very soon in judgment and redemption. Thus, basically the early Church (as the Church of today) was an "eschatological" community; that is, it was a community always looking ahead towards ultimate fulfillment in Christ. The Church of the first decades, as the Church of today, is a community united by baptism, rooted in the Scriptures, nourished by the Eucharist and awaiting Christ's second glorious visit to earth. The only difference between then and now is the time element. The early Church thought Christ was coming immediately. When Christ did not come the Church had to make adjustments and in the process it had to meet three immediate and very severe crises. Two of these crises were external: they concerned Judaism and the Roman Empire. One was internal: it concerned heresy. Let us take a look at the first external crisis, reserving the others for the next chapter.

JUDAIZERS

We can get some appreciation of the serious problem Judaism presented for the early Church if we recall that the first Christians all were Jews: Jesus, his mother, his friends and disciples. The Christian religion began in Palestine and was centered in Jerusalem, the Holy City where Jesus did much of his preaching, where he celebrated the Last Supper, where he died and where Pentecost took place. With the new religion being born in so much "Jewishness" how would it, how could it, differ? If the new religion did differ, could it separate itself from the mother religion without pain and conflict? The inevitable answer to this last question had to be in the negative especially if we recall that the Jews themselves ran the gamut from the conservative Aramaic speaking Orthodox kind to the Greek-speaking liberal kind. The very presence of chronic tension between them would have to produce not only the antagonism of the old religion against the new but also conflicts with the newly-born Christian Church itself.

In the very first days, although the followers of Jesus did not have a strong identity they were aware that they were a special community. Even though they still continued to attend the Temple worship certain novel things were present. For one thing new converts were taken into the group by the initiation rite of baptism. There were secret eucharistic meals in private homes in addition to the Temple obligations. Right here was something to make the Orthodox Jews suspicious. The suspicions tended to break out into open hostility when more of the Greek-speaking liberal Jews took up the new way. The traditional tensions between conservative and liberal Jews were heightened thereby. In any case the upshot was that the conservative Jews drove the Greek-speaking

Jewish Christians out of Jerusalem. Naturally these Greek-speaking Jewish Christians gravitated to the hellenized Jewish communities scattered throughout the East. Particularly they fled to Antioch in Syria with the result that Antioch became the mother Church of the foreign missions. It was from here that St. Paul and Barnabas (hellenized Jews) and others were sent as the *Acts of the Apostles* tells us (Acts 13: 1-3). In fact, it was Paul, the most dynamic hellenized Jew of them all, who became the main target of the anger of the Orthodox Jews. And they were hostile to Paul more for political reasons. A revolt against the Romans was brewing and the Jews needed all the loyalty and solidarity they could get and Paul by his de-Judaizing was threatening that unity. Thus they followed him constantly and stirred up opposition to him and local persecutions.

At Antioch the first Christian community was founded and for the first time the name "Christian" is used to describe the followers of Christ. Other communities were quickly founded at Cyprus, Athens, and Corinth. From such centers as these Christianity spread and thanks to the hellenized Jewish communities of the Diaspora the Christian message carried by the Jews had a natural place to go. The clear result of such activity was that no longer will the new religion be Oriental, taught in Aramaic. Now it will be Mediterranean and taught in the cultured, world-wide languages of Greek and Latin. Spearheading much of the missionary activity was, of course, St. Paul, who next to Christ himself was to shape Christianity for all time. He above all others was responsible for rejecting the specifically Jewish features of Christianity and making it truly catholic or universal.

Besides external persecution from the staunch Orthodox Jews who remained in Judaism the question of "Jewish features" was a most acute personal problem for the early Jew-

ish Christians. After all, for these people, just how did their
new religion stand in reference to the old one? Was it a
continuation or a replacement? What *should* be the life style
of the new Jewish converts? Should they continue as they
had been doing to observe the Mosaic laws and the kosher
food and dietary precepts? Should they continue with circumcision? The ancient Scriptures? Temple worship? Answers to all such questions among the Jewish Christians were
by no means unanimous. There was a marked division in
response. One faction centered around James the Apostle
the head of the local Jerusalem church-community and his
staunch Orthodox group in Jerusalem which favored the re-
tention of Jewish customs and traditions (Acts 2:26; 21:10).
Opposed to them within the Church were the Greek-speaking
or hellenized liberal missionary party which came to be
identified with Paul and, to a lesser degree, with Stephen
and Philip. The struggle became aggravated when Gentile
converts were accepted into the Church. Should Jewish customs and traditions (especially circumcision) be imposed on
them? After all such Gentile converts could hardly be expected to have the same emotional allegiance to Jewish practices such as circumcision. It came down to this: "For the
Jewish Christians, the question of continuity was the question of their relation to their mother; for Gentile Christians
it was the question of their relation to their mother-in-law."[12]
This question not unexpectedly arose in Antioch which sent
the problem to the Apostles who gathered in the Council of
Jerusalem (Acts 15). It seems, moreover, that it was not just
a question of Jewish customs such as circumcision, but of
nationalism. Once more Judaism was coming into political
conflict with Rome and therefore it was especially important
that non-Jews be circumcised, not for religious reasons, but
for the sake of being identified with the Jewish national state.

In any case the answer that came from the Council was in favor of freedom for the Gentile from Jewish customs but certain compromises were made. Gentile converts were only to observe the prescription of not eating food sacrificed to idols and to perform certain sexual purifications. This decision did not please the strict Orthodox Jewish Christians and it marks the first break between Christianity and the Jewish community. They opposed it vehemently and caused considerable dissension at Antioch, Galatia, Corinth, Colossae and Rome—in fact, wherever the liberal St. Paul went. He and his kind thus continued to be harassed not only by the traditional Orthodox Jews who never left Judaism but also by those conservative Orthodox Jews who turned Christian.

Understandably the conflict grew worse when in 70 A.D. Jerusalem was destroyed and the Temple was razed to the ground. This tragedy led the Jews more than ever to hold on to their traditions. At the same time the tragedy more than ever opened the door to the Gentile converts. As a matter of fact what was most distasteful of all about Christianity to outsiders were the things it inherited from the generally suspect and disliked Judaism. Once Christianity shucked off both the kosher food laws, Jewish religious ritual and circumcision, it moved apace among the non-Jews. Paul, on his part, had lost no opportunity to quicken that pace by his emphasis on justification as a pure gift of God and obtained by faith, not by Jewish external Law observances. Thus the fall of Jerusalem put an end to the pressure Judaism had put on Christianity. Still, the early Church had been too deeply engaged in the Jewish world to be able to free itself from it in one stroke. That is why the years between 70 and 140 constitute a period of search. The Jewish forms of thought will persist until they will be recast in a Greek framework later on.

TEMPLE AND CHURCH

We have now examined the first tension in the early Church. Before we close this chapter we must make some pertinent observations from this initial conflict with Judaism for to this very day there exists the ambiguity of the relation-ship of the Church to the Temple. In fact it will be interest-ing to see how the early Church tried to resolve the problem in the first five centuries and how its efforts have bequeathed to us today the very uneasy solutions they arrived at. One trend of thought that soon developed among the early Chris-tian writers was to try to demonstrate that the Christian Church was indeed connected with Judaism but only in the sense that it had now taken over not, unfortunately, that it had organically arisen from it. The Church was the new and the true Israel replacing the old. Other writers (such as Philo and Origen whom we shall meet later) saw in the Old Testament types and preview of Christ and the Church. We can see the trend to this sort of allegorizing even in the Gos-pels such as St. Matthew's who goes out of his way to show that Jesus is a fulfillment of all that Moses and the prophets spoke of. So, taking this clue, the early Christian writers made the psalms apply to the resurrection of Jesus. The Red Sea crossing under Moses became a symbol of the passage of Christians through the waters of baptism (thus explaining the many allusions in the Holy Saturday night's blessing of the baptismal water and in the rite of baptism itself). Jesus was seen as the suffering servant of Isaiah (chapter 53) whose book became a kind of "fifth Gospel." This sort of in-terpretation took the steam out of Judaism and came to rep-resent a complete victory of Christian over Jewish thought. It must be admitted, however, that this victory was won to some degree by default since the Jewish community had become weak, out of touch with contemporary trends and thus unable to meet Christian interpretations effectively.

The Old Testament was fulfilled in the New and so the early Christian Church in its worship, songs and liturgy filled them with allusions and references to the Old Testament. In short, the Church simply out and out appropriated the Jewish Scriptures and St. Irenaeus of the second century would claim, "the writings of Moses are the words of Christ." Even if all this were legitimate, it did not solve the problem of Judaism itself. Judaism did not and has not phased out and still has its Scriptures. The question would remain which asked what should be the relation of the Church to the Temple besides one of tolerant isolation and estrangement?

> Not only the Jewish Scriptures and the Levitical priesthood, but other prerogatives and claims of the chosen people were consistently transferred to the church—a practice which was both an index to and a cause of the isolation of Gentile Christian thought from the Judaism contemporary with itself as well as from the Jewish Christianity out of which it had originally come.[13]

In later times, most unfortunately, the intellectual conquest of the Christians over the Jews moved them to a position of indifference. The Christians tended to forget the holy history that had organically preceded them in Judaism and ever so gradually Christians began to equate Judaism and paganism as if they were on the same level. Christian writers would go even further and claim that the Jews did not understand their own Bible anyway, else they could see that it clearly pointed to Christ. If they could not see, they were blind. If they were blind then obviously they were deliberately blind—hard-hearted and stiff-necked as always. From this attitude and from the desire to show their difference rather than harmony, a distinct anti-Jewish bias sprang up which remains to this day. A whole theology grew up centering on exclusiveness and irreconcilability rather than upon the common patrimony of the two religions. A typical example would be that in 325 at the first General Council of the Christian Church the new Christian emperor, Constantine, would stand up and declare that the Christian date of Easter should be changed from the Jewish Passover date for "It is unbecoming beyond measure that on the holiest of festivals we should follow the customs of the Jews. Henceforth let us have nothing in common with this odious people; our Savior has shown us another path. . . ." Constantine's anti-Jewish legislation was restated in the Theodosian Code of 438 and woven into the legal framework of the later Roman Empire and medieval Europe. The cry of "God-killer" would haunt the Jews through the centuries. Other Church Councils would condone anti-Jewish legislation and Christian Crusaders in the Middle Ages would slay tens of thousands of Jews on their way to the Holy Land and in 1099 would burn Jews alive in their synagogues. Twenty centuries of such bias would culminate in the terror of Auschwitz and Dachau. The non-Jewish world (and a measurable degree of apathy from American Jews themselves) would be mute as six million Jews were exterminated in a massive holocaust.

> When the chips were down, very few non-Jews came to the aid of the Jews during the holocaust—which for us was an eyeopener with sad—not angry but sad—connotations . . . the sincere Christian knows that what died in Auschwitz was not the Jewish people but Christianity. . . . They were shooting thousands and thousands of Jews—entire communities, with machine guns, directly. There was a direct contact. And they had Ph.D.'s and some of them were theologians, and some of them, many of them, went to the priest, to confession and so forth. So John the XXIII understood it . . .

And therefore he opened the doors. And therefore he liberalized the church. That explains Vatican II, the ecumenical movement.[14]

In past years the Catholic Church has begun to repudiate any anti-Jewish bias. Pius XII deleted references made about the "unfaithful" Jews in the Good Friday liturgy. John XXIII was greatly influenced by Jules Isaac's book *Jesus and Israel* which led him to denounce antisemitism. The Second Vatican Council said that "what happened in His passion cannot be blamed upon all the Jews then living, without distinction, nor upon the Jews of today. Although the Church is the new people of God, the Jews should not be presented as repudiated or cursed by God. . . ." Vatican II might have said more but fear of Arab reprisals against Catholics was a consideration. Still, theological questions remain:

The partnership between Judaism and the God of Israel is not questioned in the decree of the Council. The Catholic Church, it may be thought, admits that the ancient covenants of God with the ancestors and tribes of Israel, with various individuals of the Old Testament and with the primary heir, Judaism, have not been revoked. . . . But the question remains as to whether this type of ecumenical thinking can bring about a just verdict on Judaism, in view of its long and independent development, externally so far from Christ, and in view of its actual concrete type of existence today and its diverse interests.[15]

SUMMARY

We have seen Jewish background and Christian beginnings. We recalled the promises made to Abraham and his descendants. We saw the long history of the Chosen People, their setting up of a kingdom, civil war and foreign conquest which sent the Jews all over the world. We saw that the

Persians allowed them to return and how Alexander brought Greek culture to bear on them. We took note of the Seleucids who profaned the Temple and the Romans who took Jerusalem under its protection. Christ was born into all of this Jewish-Greek-Roman history. He died in 30 A.D. and left his disciples with the feeling that he would soon come again. When he did not return his nascent Church had to deal with the problem of their parent, Judaism, and its Temple worship and rituals and traditions. Inevitable and immediate conflicts between the new Orthodox Jewish Christians and the liberal Greek-orientated Jewish Christians (plus the additional Gentile converts) led to a breaking away under men like Paul from Judaism and gave Christianity its catholic thrust. Predictably the axis of activity shifted from Jerusalem to Antioch, especially after Paul's death, when in the year 70 Jerusalem and its Temple were destroyed. Shortly thereafter the Gentile Christian converts would predominate and Judaism would recede more and more into the background and indeed become an enemy to be treated with polemic and finally indifference. Meanwhile Christianity began to spread with remarkable rapidity and in its wake, frequent and often fierce persecution from the imperial power of Rome.

NOTES

1. Christopher Dawson, *Religion and the Rise of Western Culture,* p. 12. Image Books edition, 1958.
2. Lest anyone be scandalized let him be reminded that the Bible does not pretend to be complete and that some of the books were written by men with a point of view to present thereby causing them to omit certain other items or outlooks of interest.
3. This commentary was called the Midrash (sermon) and came into vogue about 200 B.C. Soon oral customs and traditions were added as supplements to the Torah. During the first and second centuries

of the Christian era this combination of Torah and supplements was in turn commented on and thus was born the Talmud.

4. Encyclopedia Britannica, vol. 12, p. 1063, edition, 1971.
5. The present Wailing Wall in Jerusalem is said to contain some original stones from the Temple of Solomon, stones no doubt included in the foundations left by Titus.
6. For a fascinating account of this uprising and its hero, Bar-Kokhba, read the book, *Bar-Kokhba: The Rediscovery of the Legendary Hero of the Second Jewish Revolt* by Yigael Yadin, Random House, New York, N.Y., 1971.
7. A. H. M. Jones, *Constantine and the Conversion of Europe*, p. 41. Collier Books, New York, N.Y. New Revised Edition, 1962.
8. Danielou and Marrou, *The Christian Centuries,* volume I. p. 5. McGraw-Hill Book Company, New York. 1964.
9. Rudolf Bultmann, *Primitive Christianity in Its Contemporary Setting*, quoted in *A Short History of Christianity* by Martin E. Marty, p. 26. Meridan Books, The World Publishing Company, Cleveland and New York. 1959.
10. *The New York Times,* Sunday, February 13, 1972.
11. If this is true that Mark goes back to the year 50 then the whole Bultmann school of criticism which holds that the Christian communities wrote the Gospels a half a century later is discredited. However, most modern scholars do not accept the findings of this Spanish priest.
12. Jaroslav Pelikan *The Emergence of the Catholic Tradition,* p. 14. The University of Chicago Press, Chicago and London. 1971.
13. *Ibid.*
14. U.S. Catholic magazine, p. 29, September, 1971.
15. *Sacramentum Mundi,* volume III, p. 228. Edited by Karl Rahner, Cornelius Ernst and Kevin Smyth. Herder and Herder, New York, N.Y. 1969.

II

Expansion and Its Problems

Christianity spread with amazing rapidity in the first decades after Christ's death. First, as we have seen, during apostolic times Christianity spread to Asia to cities like Antioch in Syria, Ephesus, Lystra, Derbe, Cyprus, Miletus, Smyrna, Philippi, Thessalonia, Athens, Corinth, and in Europe to cities such as Pozzuoli and Rome and all those other exotic towns mentioned in the *Acts of the Apostles*. In the second century it spread to cities in France such as Vienne and Lyons (the home of Irenaeus) and Spain. There are sections in old Persia and Edessa that boast of second century Christian foundations. In all, the network of Christian church-communities in the first two centuries spanned from Spain to Germany and the Yugoslavia of today to the Black Sea. Many cities would pride themselves on their early foundations. In an age of theological competition it was important for the larger and prominent cities to lay claim to being founded by one of the Original Twelve Apostles themselves or persons who lived in Christ's time. Thus Alexandria lays claim to being founded by St. Mark himself. There are more fanciful claims. Lazarus whom Jesus raised from the dead was supposed to be the first bishop of Marseilles in France. The boy who had the loaves and fishes in the Gospel story turns up as another first bishop in that century. Such legends reflect the desire of the cities to lay claim to a title of dignity. We should take special note that the Church spread to Africa in the first century and that its chief city, Alexandria, had a major role in the early Church. Alexandria (Alexander the Great's city) had become the main center of the Graeco-Roman or Hellenistic culture. It was at the crossroads of civilization. It was at Alexandria in the second and third centuries that Christianity, which came from a Semitic people, got its Hellenistic coloring. ". . . At the level of ordinary Christian life it is in Alexandria that we find Christian morals, inherited from the Christian Church, breaking free from their Jewish forms and putting on what was best in Hellenistic humanism. . . . The important point about the Alexandrian movement is the alliance of the gospel and Greek culture."[1] Later on this great Christian center and the whole African Church were completely destroyed by the Moslem invaders but not before they gave to the Church (and civilization) Tertullian and Cyprian and the great St. Augustine.

Beyond the necessary missionary activity there were many reasons for this amazing spread. For one thing adversaries were impressed with the courage of the Christian martyrs and grudgingly showed their admiration. Tertullian was right: the blood of martyrs *is* the seed of the Church. Secondly, in a time of competing religions and conflicting anxieties Christianity offered the virtue of cutting right through it all and presenting one safe, sure road to salvation. Its very intolerance of other religions, its very sureness of its own abilities and powers attracted many. Finally we might mention a third cause of the victory of Christianity in the hearts of men. Let us listen to the professedly agnostic scholar, E. R. Dodds:

But lastly, the benefits of becoming a Christian were not confined to the next world. A Christian congregation was from the first a community in a much fuller sense than any other corresponding group. . . . Its members were bound together not only by common rites but by a common way of life and, as Celsius shrewdly perceived, by their common danger. Their promptitude in bringing material help to brethren in captivity or other distress is attested not only by Christian writers but by Lucian, a far from sympathetic witness. Love of one's neighbor is not an exclusively Christian virtue, but in our period the Christians appear to have practiced it much more effectively than any other group. The Church provided the essentials of social security: it cared for widows and orphans, the old, the unemployed, and the disabled; it provided a burial fund for the poor and a nursing service in time of plague. But even more important, I suspect, than these material benefits was the sense of belonging which the Christian community could give. . . . Within the community there was human warmth: some one was interested in them, both here and hereafter. It is therefore not surprising that the earliest and the most striking advances of Christianity were made in the great cities—in Antioch, in Rome, in Alexandria. Christians were in a more than formal sense "members one of another": I think that was a major cause, perhaps the strongest single cause, of the spread of Christianity.[2]

Fraternal love, it seems, was the most powerful force.

PERSECUTION

It was inevitable that this sudden world-wide (at the time) spread would attract the notice of the imperial powers. It is customary to speak of the Ten Persecutions of that power; actually it was all the ebb and flow of one general persecution. Moments of peace (during which the Church grew considerably) alternated with moments of hostility of varying degrees for some two hundred years. There were many reasons for the persecutions. Sometimes the Jews themselves instigated them because although, as we have seen, some of them were converts to Christianity, others were not and those of the Diaspora (in exile) were quite willing, wherever they were, to obey the prescription handed down by the Sanhedrin against the Christian sect. More often, however, it was the empire itself that took a hand.

It had to take a hand. For one thing, the Roman authorities were always quick to check the formation of a political or religious club that did not have their official sanction. They felt that not only did such new cults tend to undermine Roman morals but they feared that rebellion could get an easy toe-hold in the secrecy of any group that met under the pretext of divine worship. That was the first ground for Roman intervention. Secondly, as the contemporaries Suetonius and Dio Cassius tell us, there was the most natural error in identifying the (Jewish) Christians with the Jews who were never held in high esteem. Of course, as long as the confusion existed the Christians could also reap a benefit: they could get in on the official protection that the empire gave to the Jewish religion (and contrariwise they would receive the brunt of persecution when the Jews rebelled against Rome). It was only when they separated from the Jews that the Christians were open to all sorts of accusations which may sound strange to our ears. They were accused of "atheism." This is understandable if we remember that to the Christians the old state gods meant nothing and therefore their denial of them was official atheism. This atheism charge also included the subversion of the state since the state looked upon its official religion (no matter what people and leaders thought unofficially) as a strong cohesive force in the empire. To attack this force was to attack the strength of the state.

Another source of irritation was that the Christians kept aloof from many aspects of public life and people could not help but notice their absence from some public activities. They would not buy meats at the public market which had been offered to idols. A Christian jeweler would not decorate a pagan statue. Christian patients rejected the hospitals where pagan priests wandered through with their incantations. They would not attend the gladiatorial combats nor serve in the army since they were pacifists—although this would change in a few centuries. They shunned luxuries, not as the stoics of old, but for deeper reasons: as wanting to follow Christ more fully. The Christians, then, were "different" and as Justin tells us, the very name "Christian" became associated with suspicions of every kind. Because of their eucharistic meal in which they ate the Body and Blood of Christ they were even accused of cannibalism. Then there were those just waiting around for the Second Coming and so did not work, conveying to their neighbors a picture of indolence under the guise of religion. Even Paul felt the necessity of getting after such Christians by issuing his famous statement, "If anyone will not work, let him not eat" (Thessalonians 3:10). Others responded to the expected Second Coming by indifference. In their lifetimes phrases like "strangers and pilgrims" were common enough. Their attitude was expressed well in a line from the *Epistles to Diognetus*. Speaking of the Christians it says: "They live in their own countries, but as aliens; they share all duties like citizens and suffer all disabilities like foreigners; every foreign land is their country, and every country is foreign to them." Such a description of alienation prepared some for martyrdom. Finally, some Christians did not help matters. They often failed to communicate properly their beliefs. Some in their desire for martyrdom went out of their way to be antagonistic. For all these reasons, the Christians were hated, the cause of many public uprisings and left the civil officials no choice but to persecute them.

We mentioned in passing above that the early Christians were pacifists and would not serve in the army. In the light of modern thoughts about warfare and conscientious objection as a result of the Vietnam war, it is worth looking at the development of Christianity from such pacifism to militarism. There is no clear evidence of Christians serving in the army during the first century and a half; or, if they were in the army, they left after baptism. A partial reason for this abstinence was that the Christians might be forced to engage in idol or emperor worship, but the fear of spilling blood was predominant. Tertullian noted that a Christian would rather be killed than to kill; and Minucius Felix said it was not right to see or hear about a man being killed and commented that in fact the Christians "did not even eat meat rare" such was their horror of blood. Cyprian, Arnobius, the canons of Hyppolitis all said that a soldier must refuse to kill. Later, concerning killing in war, St. Basil the Great said those who did so should abstain from Holy Communion for a three year period. Origen added his thoughts, "Christians should beware lest for warfare . . . we should take out the sword, for no such occasion is allowed by this evangelical teaching." Lactantius said that killing is forbidden in such a way that no exception is to be made.

Pacifism was such a characteristic of the early Church that a pagan adversary, the Roman Celsus, warned that if everyone became Christian it would spell disaster for Rome for the Eternal City would be without military defense. It must be noted, however, that with the barbarians pressing near and spilling over the boarders some Christians began to fight. But it was really from the time of Constantine on (early fourth century) that a whole change was made in the Christian's attitude towards war and peace.

Constantine, as we shall see, was willing to try out any god who would grant him victory. He tried Christ who, he felt, came through. Christians, of course, were elated to have the persecution over and become a preferred class. Suddenly, in the logic of things, the sword had become a friend and theology lost no time underpinning Constantine's victory by the sword and from there, the spread of the faith by the same means. Jesus, in short, became a kind of god of war. The irony went full circle when by the year 416 one *had* to be a Christian to serve in the Roman army! Before long several theories (notably Augustine's) appeared about the "just war." When the barbarians came into the Church they brought with them a taste for violence (indicated by their choice of warriors for saints: St. Michael, St. Peter, St. Gerald the soldier, etc). Christians and their leaders,—clerics, bishops and archbishops—freely went into battle to the extent that the Church found it could not control Christian violence (even with "Peace of God" truces). It wound up diverting it into the Crusades of the twelfth century. The Kingdom of the Prince of Peace was to be established over the Moslems by the sword. It is no wonder that, later on, perplexed Buddhists would remark that wherever Christianity has spread blood has flowed—a remark far removed from that of Celsus!

This development was yet in the future. Meanwhile, getting back to the first persecutions of the Christians we observe that in July of 64 A.D. a terrible fire broke out in Rome. The Christians were blamed although it is said that Nero really caused the fire. This was the first persecution and it gave to the Church it first martyrs whose names and deeds would fill the devotional books of the early Christian communities. Sts. Peter and Paul lost their lives in this persecution probably having been denounced by the Jewish Christians. Afterwards, there was a relative time of calm which the Church used to grow and organize. During this time converts were made even at high levels. In evidence of this one of the oldest Christian cemeteries is located on the Via Salaria, the property of a Roman aristocrat. Other persecutions broke out under the emperors Domitian and Trajan (claiming the great St. Ignatius of Antioch), Hadrian, Antonius (claiming St. Polycarp of Smyrna) and around the year 162 Marcus Aurelius (claiming Sts. Felicitas and Perpetua and St. Cecelia). Under the emperor Commodus the first known African martyrs were made. Ironically, the better emperors unleased the fiercest persecutions. The reason was that the more seriously they took the state religion and its cohesion for the empire the more seriously they persecuted dissent. Decius was the first emperor to make the Christian persecution worldwide and deliberately sought to kill off the leaders in the hopes of killing off the movement. All the way up to 303 the emperor Diocletian was issuing decrees against the Christians. Finally with the emperor Galerius in 311 the first toleration was given to the Christians. This toleration may have come through the emperor's mistress who was a Christian or it may have been the result of the influence of the Neoplatonist school under Plotinus whose tolerance may have had an effect. In any case the ebb and flow of the persecutions was at an end. Under Constantine Christianity would be given freedom of worship and under one of his successors Theodosius it would become the state religion. There were to be no more persecutions except for a brief revival of paganism under Julian whom Christian history has dubbed revengefully "the Apostate" (361-363).

EARLY HERESIES

Along with the external persecutions early Christianity had to endure a more severe stress: internal disunity of doctrine. There was, to begin with, some similarity between Christianity and the Mystery religions and this alone helped to blur the difference for some people. Not only that, but there were, of course, different traditions among the church-communities themselves. The Aramaean churches, the Asiatic churches, the Syrian and Roman churches, each had their own traditions and that further helped confuse the doctrinal issues. Thus clashes took place not only between the heretics and the Christians, but between the various Christian communities. Yet the truth was important to the Church and doctrinal orthodoxy was a constant concern in the struggles of the first centuries. It was only later forms of Christianity that tended to denigrate doctrine.

Contrary to the monotonously recurrent opinion that orthodoxy was not a factor in primitive Christianity, the Church from the start, through the time of Paul to that of John and beyond, had an acute sense of the confessional or dogmatic principle. Concretely, this was a matter of thanksgiving for the boon of salvation. It found a first expression in the hymns and confessional formulas conserved by the New Testament writers, notably Paul. These were followed in the second century by hymns and creeds. As christological lyric proved to gnostic interpretation, the Old Testament Psalms, christologically interpreted, were adopted in their place. The concern for orthodoxy under the new conditions of the antignostic struggle and of persecution in diverse provinces of the Empire, lay at the root not only of the creeds but of the accent on the allegiance to the bishop. Indeed, all developments from the late first century to the age of Constantine seem to have taken contour and direction from the commitment to orthodoxy as a positive and indispensable religious value.[3]

Still, some degree of doctrinal distortion was to be expected for Christianity could only be explained in terms and in the language then current and in those days there was not a section of the empire that did not have its infinite variety of religious sects and interpretations of life. In the process of attracting converts Christianity tried to present its case in the only language they understood, that is, an adaptation of the terminology of their own present beliefs. Obviously there was much room for misunderstanding and at its early stage the Church had no precedents, no ready-made definitions to guide it. No one put the problem better than the great nineteenth century Cardinal Newman:

> . . . Every Catholic holds that the Christian dogmas were in the Church from the time of the Apostles; that they were ever in their substance what they are now; that they existed before the formulas were publicly adopted, in which, as time went on, they were defined and recorded, and that such formulas, when sanctioned by the due ecclesiastical acts, are binding on the faith of Catholics, and have a dogmatic authority. . . .

> Even before we take into account the effect which would naturally be produced on the first Christians by the novelty and mysteriousness of doctrines which depend for their reception simply upon Revelation, we have reason to anticipate that there would be difficulties and mistakes in expressing them, when they first came to be set forth by unauthoritative writers. Even in secular sciences, inaccuracy of thought and language is but gradually corrected; that is, in proportion as their subject-matter is thoroughly scrutinized and mastered by the cooperation of many independent intellects, successively engaged upon it. . . .

> Language then requires to be refashioned even for sciences which are based on the senses and the reason; but much more will this be the case, when we are concerned with subject-matters, of which, in our present state, we cannot pos-

sibly form any complete or consistent conception, such as the Catholic doctrines of the Trinity and Incarnation. Since they are from the nature of the case above our intellectual reach, and were unknown till the preaching of Christianity, they required on their first promulgation new words, or words used in new senses, for their due enunciation; and, since these were not definitely supplied by Scripture or by tradition, nor for centuries by ecclesiastical authority, variety in the use, and confusion in the apprehension of them, were unavoidable in the interval. . . . Not only had the words to be adjusted and explained which were peculiar to different schools or traditional in different places, but there was the formidable necessity of creating a common measure between two, or rather three languages—Latin, Greek, and Syriac.[4]

Again, the point is that at the beginning there were no special doctrinal requirements beyond the simple affirmation that "Jesus is Lord." The Christians of course believed in the resurrection and such, but there was no formulated doctrine. Rather the creeds and special formulas became a necessity as heretical opinions arose and struck at the heart of the Christian faith. From these conflicts came the early creeds and the formulated dogmas of Church history. But it is important to remember that they arose out of the need to keep the faith intact and that they would run into the difficulties as described by Cardinal Newman.

There would be other great heresies later as we shall see, but during the times we are considering—the first two centuries—three main ones were prevalent: Gnosticism, Marcionism and Montanism. Gnosticism was the most pervasive and troublesome and had a great reactive effect even as it appeared in apostolic times. An amalgam of popular Near Eastern beliefs and philosophies it was really an attempt to reorientalize the faith.[5] Gnosticism claimed to be the private knowledge of a select few and its basic teaching was the antagonism between the world of matter and the world of spirit, the former being evil and the latter good. If this is so, the world and its creation were evil things and obviously the work of a lesser evil "god." Necessarily God would not take a body and become man so Christ's body was but a phantom and his death merely a piece of play-acting. Having appropriated just enough of the language and symbols of the Christian faith Gnosticism managed to deceive many and was a special distress to the early Church. In *Acts* 8:9-24 we find St. Peter clashing with the Gnostic spokesman (and some say, founder) Simon Magus. From a library of the Gnostics uncovered in 1945 in Egypt we know now that much of the early church's theology was in reaction to Gnosticism. St. Paul, for example, was greatly influenced and much of what he wrote, especially his epistles to the church-community at Corinth, was intended mainly to refute Gnostic ideas.

This refutation went further. As we have indicated it triggered the definite formulations of what actually was believed and held to be Orthodox. Reaction as a matter of fact produced the three stable Christian sources of orthodoxy (1) the canon of Scripture (2) early creedal statements and (3) the episcopacy, as authenticating the oral traditions. Early creedal formulas like those used at baptism, the earliest creeds, the epistles and the Fourth Gospel all show definite signs of reactions to Gnostic teachings.

Marcionism, appearing about 120, tried to go further than Paul in setting aside the Law; it held there were two gods, one the creator of the material (evil) world and the other master of the spiritual realm. About forty years later the third heresy appeared, Montanism. It held that the Second Coming of Christ was imminent and so it undertook to form a group of elites and prophets who placed themselves solely under the guidance of the Holy Spirit. Such were these heresies and several other "schools" of heretics. The founders of such schools were individuals with highly personal views and who tended to lead their adherents away from the main body of the Church. There is a noticeable difference between them and the Christian bishops. Irenaeus described the difference when he wrote: "The heretics are all later than the bishops, to whom the Apostles have transmitted the churches, and the manifestations of their doctrine are different and produce a veritable cacophony. But the path of those who belong to the Church, dwelling throughout the world and holding firm to the tradition of the Apostles, shows that all have one faith and one kind of organization."

EARLY WRITERS

There were not lacking those Christians who in the face of constant persecution tried to uphold the faith and encourage the faithful. Such would be those who replaced the Apostles after their death. These were the "Apostolic Fathers" who in no way presumed to fill in for the Apostles and who were quite conscious of their inferior position; but they wrote to pass on the Apostolic teachings and form an important link to the ages that immediately followed them. Such Apostolic Fathers would include the famous names of St. Clement of Rome who wrote his letter around the year 90, a letter which was an attempt to settle the schism that arose in Corinth. There was St. Ignatius of Antioch who was the first to use the term "Catholic" of the Church and who wrote seven letters on his way to being martyred in Rome under the emperor Trajan. There was St. Polycarp who died a martyr in 155; the man who wrote the *Epistle of Barnabas* and the writings known as *The Shepherd of Hermas* with its interesting dream episodes, the *Didache* or *Teaching of the Twelve Apostles* giving us valuable information about early liturgy and practice in the Church. These last two documents go back to the end of the first century or the beginning of the second. They were largely inter-community writings which presumed familiarity with Christian life and teachings and were written to instruct and encourage the faithful.

But more was needed. The force of the early heresies and persecutions based on misunderstanding and prejudice called for an out and out defense of the Christian teachings and so the Church produced its defenders or "apologists" as they are known. These are the writers who went out to meet the intellectual enemy. They sought to answer the objections of the pagan philosophers and the Jewish detractors. They strove to "prove" the doctrines of Christianity in the systematized manner of the various philosophical schools. In fact, they went even further. They sought to demonstrate that as a matter of fact the present Christians were the authentic heirs to the Graeco-Roman civilization; that therefore Christians do not reject the world in which they are living, but accept it wholeheartedly. They, in fact, are the empire's best citizens and have made the Empire greater. In Christianity, Hellenism had found its true meaning. So ran their defense of the Church. Names among the apologists would include Tatian, Athenagoras and particularly the better known Justin Martyr and St. Irenaeus. The latter was active around the year 177 and was the first in a long line of theologians and biblical scholars which would include Hippolytus, the great Origen, the Gregorys and Basil in the East and Ambrose, Jerome and the towering St. Augustine in the West. It was Irenaeus who began the theology of the Atonement and Redemption and who offered the first theory on how Jesus' death and resurrection saved mankind. Tertullian (150-230) was the first to transfer the Greek intellectual word-containers to Jewish Christianity and who coined words like "Trinity" and "consubstantial"; Clement of Alexandria openly wanted to recast Greek philosophy into Christian terms. These scholars were trying to meet the critics on their own ground. Once the early heresies like Gnosticism were subdued and there was no doubt that Jesus was truly the Son of God then the speculations began. If Jesus was man and God—how could such two opposites be reconciled? These Apologists and Church Fathers and later on the famous Church Councils would try to come to terms with such questions about Christ, His nature and the correlative questions of the Trinity.

It is interesting to note that all this defensive and speculative activity was taking place in the East, the origin of Christianity. In the Latin West theological conflicts were less. Gnosticism was relatively impotent there and dogmatic speculation was not strong. In fact, the Latin Church (which meant largely, Rome) had a reputation for being conservative as is evident in its much more subdued liturgy and songs. It tended to be more legalistic and philosophic. Significantly Westerners like Tertullian, Minucius Felix and Cyprian of Carthage were all lawyers (though Tertullian was really speculative in many ways) and they represented a more legal approach to Christianity. They and their Latin Church tended to retain a greater respect for the traditional poets and Roman writers and were more influenced by the Stoic foundations of a Western Cicero than the theological foundations of an Eastern St. Paul.

CHURCH AND PAGANISM

It is equally significant also that the early apologists and Fathers tried to come to terms with paganism because it soon became obvious that paganism also could boast of the good, the true and the beautiful. How to explain this? How to make a case for the difference of Christianity, if there was a difference? Various explanations were given. Tertullian used the idea of natural law; some maintained that good paganism came from the Old Testament which meant in effect that the pagans plagiarized the Scriptures. In time Christianity would claim that anything good in paganism was inspired by the preexisting Son of God, the "Word" of St. John's Gospel but when this "Word became flesh" then he naturally superceded not only Moses (Old Testament) but Socrates (classical paganism and philosophy). In fact, whether they knew it or not, the pagans should have realized the "Christian" influence in their own writings. Just as in the Jewish Scriptures the "suffering servant" of Isaiah 53 was Christ, so in the ancient pagan writings evidence could be found of Christian revelation. Virgil above all came to be considered as a forerunner of Christianity and later on in medieval times legends would abound about Virgil's supernatural knowledge of Christianity. It is no accident that the greatest medieval poet, Dante, called Virgil "my master and my author" and it is Virgil who leads the poet through the Inferno. The famous Greek prophetess, Sybil, was pressed into Christian service the same way. Catholics may still remember in the lovely hymn *Dies Irae* which used to be (and still is in some places) sung at funerals that the first verse tells of the coming day of wrath on the testimony and dual authority of King David and the Sybil.

> That day of wrath, that dreadful day,
> Shall heaven and earth in ashes lay,
> As David and the Sybil say.

Actually the Christians were doing what the Jews had done when confronted with paganism: they were adapting and synthesizing. As we mentioned before it was in this process that the Christian religion was shaking off its Jewish forms and donning the thought patterns of the pagan Hellenistic world. It was Clement of Alexandria (again, that great city of Hellenistic culture) who set the pace by declaring that the revelation of Christ takes many forms appropriate to the various cultures. If the eternal "Word" were manifest in the ancient philosophies and then in the Jewish Scripture, so it must make a new manifestation to the current Greek world. It must now doff its Semitic form and put on the Hellenist form. Christianity must now speak the language of Plato and Homer. It must transfer to the Greek culture. Gradually, classical paganism became to the Christians what Judaism had become: irrelevant. Philosophy teachers were considered as harmless and theology (it was felt—wrongly) had effectively replaced philosophy. Philosophy would become simply a tool to "prove" doctrine and to that extent it died.

From such an attitude major results would arise in later centuries to plague the Church. When the whole framework of society changed and it was no longer Christian; when the political and cultural underpinnings of Christianity began to erode, the Church would not have the philosophical tools with which to work out a new image. Neglecting and despising philosophy, the Church would be unprepared for the fifteenth century Renaissance and its heir the eighteenth century Enlightenment which would find in philosophy different principles which supposedly were hostile to the Church. The Church would be ridiculed for holding on to a theological system no longer viable in the modern world. The secular and profane would take over with revenge and the Church would have to wear the mantle of being anti-intellectual and antiscientific, the price of her early put-down of philosophy. The historian Gibbon waxing indignant would proclaim that Christian theologies have superceded the exercise of reason, resolved every question by an article of faith, and condemned the infidel or sceptic to eternal flames. In many a volume of laborious controversy they exposed the weakness of the understanding and the corruption of the heart, insulted human nature in the sages of antiquity, and proscribed the spirit of philosophical inquiry, so repugnant to doctrine, or at least to the temper, of a humble believer.[6]

THE MESSAGE: JEWISH OR GREEK?

It was at this period—the period of Christian apologists and the Fathers of the Church—that the basis was laid for a charge that would find expression in the twentieth century. The charge was that the original, simon-pure Christianity was so penetrated and so over-layed with Greek philosophy and language, so "hellenized," that much of Christianity's pristine Judaic richness had been lost; initial truths were frozen into Greek-thinking categories and the spirit of Christ was stratified into rigid Greek formulas. In other words, the charge would be made that the truth of divine revelation had been subordinated to the philosophy of the Greeks, that Alexandria was too successful. Tertullian and Origen were thought to be especially guilty. Later, the medieval Catholic theologians would be accused of the same crime: hellenizing Christ. The point (for example, to groups like the Protestant Reformers of the sixteenth century) would be that we have inherited a perverted form of Christianity. We must eschew all dogmatic formulas as useless, especially those of the first four Church Councils, in order to find the truth. This criticism, which still persists, is being put to rest. Scholars like Pelikan have shown that this is not true; that in fact, the technical words used by the medieval theologians predated the rediscovery of the Greek philosophers like Aristotle and the terminology used by early Church Councils "did not canonize Aristotelian philosophy as indespensible to Christian doctrine. . . ." Pelikan says:

> Taken as it stands, "hellenization" is too simplistic and unqualified a term for the process that issued in orthodox Christian doctrine. . . . Although theologians quoted Scripture in support of ideas originally derived from philosophy, they often modified these ideas on the basis of Scripture. . . . Indeed, in some ways it is more accurate to speak of dogma as the "dehellenization" of the theology that had preceded it and to argue that "by its dogma the church threw up a wall against an alien metaphysic.[7]

Or, as another modern writer puts it,

> Indeed, like the councils that followed, Nicaea attacked autonomous wisdom in the name of tradition. Far from being a triumph of the hellenization of Christianity, it repudiated the substance of hellenic and specifically neo-Plantonic thought about God. It did not, however, repudiate hellenic techniques of thought. . . .[8]

MONASTICISM

Before we close this chapter we must make reference to another kind of expansion in the third century development in the history of the early Church. This is monasticism. There were many direct and indirect causes for its appearance. First of all for many Christians in the middle of the third century there was the dilemma of how to handle the Roman requirement that they carry a certificate testifying that they had sacrificed to the gods. Many like Bishop Cyprian of Carthage simply avoided the problem by fleeing to the hills as others fled to the caves and oases of the Nile. Actually, the Nile Valley was the haven for all sorts of people who were duck-

ing the law: criminals, tax delinquents and even pious asce-
tics would hide in the vast expanses. Some Christians who
initially escaped there to avoid Roman persecution settled
there and led holy lives. The Jewish ascetical Essene group
may have had its influence on the early Christians.

Around the year 270 men began to go into the desert for
more noble reasons. For one thing, Christianity was becoming popular, mediocre people were joining and initial rigor
was being relaxed. People like Tertullian, for example, were
being scandalized that Pope Callistus (d. 222) accepted repentant sinners back into the Church. Cyprian of Carthage
who coined the famous saying "outside the Church, no salvation" took his own words seriously and pleaded the case for
readmission to the Church of backsliders who had aposta-
tized by pretending to sacrifice to the gods during persecution time. But not all were happy with this "laxity" and such
uptight Christians tended to seek out the desert for a more
rigorous and perfect Christian life. Origen, the greatest theologian until Augustine, gave a strong impetus to such asceticism when (if we can believe Eusebius the first Church
historian) he had himself castrated in order to avoid temptation. The rigor of his life was a powerful stimulus towards
increasing asceticism. Then there were those who simply felt
that the mainstream of Christian piety left something to be
desired and they too went into the desert to find God.

The first historical figure we can identify is the famous St.
Anthony whose life was written by St. Athanasius. This *Life
of Anthony* had a tremendous influence and before long people were joining Anthony in the desert and centers were
springing up throughout Italy, Gaul, England and Ireland.
St. Pachomius, unlike Anthony who lived alone, was the first
to form a communal group. After Christianity was permitted

in the empire the monastic movement really grew and great foundations were made under St. Basil and Gregory of Nyssa in the East and Cassiodorus, Jerome, Augustine and the great founder of monasticism in the West, St. Benedict.

The monastic movement would in the future of the Church have enormous contributions to make—and a few disservices. On the plus side, the monks would preserve learning and culture during the so-called "Dark Ages." They would frequently set the pace for holiness, piety and reform in the Church. They would be the "Nation's Innkeeper" during the Middle Ages. They would be a continued discomfort to the established hierarchy in the capitals and cities throughout the empire and they would figure most prominently in Church councils and heretical in-fighting.

On the minus side were two items. The early desert-type of monasticism came to be associated with almost pathological asceticism and rigorism. (We see traces of a rigorist attitude in the Church's early refusal to forgive adultery, idolatry and murder more than once.) There were incidents of self torture, people living on top of pillars for years, squatting in boxes or perpetually standing in an upright position. Others loaded themselves with heavy chains, engaged in total abstinence from food during Lent, etc. The roots of such practices cannot be found in Greek culture or paganism and certainly not in the Gospels, but somehow a strong fanatical rigorism got into the Church. It was expelled at a later date but not altogether and to this day it lingers here and there.

The second minus of the rise of monasticism was that the monks inadvertently fogged the question of the Christian vocation. They helped create the image of the "evil" world as the scene of ambition and war and pride and greed and lust and left the distinct impression that salvation in such a world was nigh impossible. Those who did not opt to go into the desert were compromised. If one were not a monk or nun, would salvation be possible? If one had to withdraw from the "world" in order to be saved, what hope was there for the vast majority of ordinary men? The net result—as can be seen in the long, long litany of the Church's saints, most of whom are in religious life—was that there never developed an invigorating lay spirituality until some beginnings were made in the twelfth century with the foundation of the basically bourgeois religious orders of Dominicans and Franciscans and their Third Orders. Later in the seventeenth century, St. Francis de Sales would especially write on behalf of the laymen's spiritual life. Finally, the division between the lay and clerical state became unduly pronounced and all charisma became clerical property.

Thus we have seen the struggles of the early Church. The terrible persecutions whose martyr's blood, as Tertullian said, became the seed of faith and did much to win the admiration and applause of the Church's enemies. There was the fantastic spread of Christianity and with this gain, the debit of early heresies which were active in the time of Peter and Paul. To offset this the Church raised up the apologists and the Church Fathers. They would meet the charges, hand on orthodox teaching and bring to the fore the canon of Scripture and the early creeds. Finally, the monastic life would catch on and spread and the monks would become the great bearers of reform throughout the centuries. There only remains now one more point which we shall take up in the next chapter before we move to the Church in its new found freedom days; that is, the structural organization of the early Church.

NOTES

1. Danielou and Marrow, *op. cit.*, p. 128.
2. E. R. Dodds, *Pagan and Christian in An Age of Anxiety*, p. 136-138. Cambridge at the University Press. 1965.
3. Ben F. Meyer, *The Church in Three Tenses*, p. 84. Doubleday and Co., Inc., Garden City, New York. 1971.
4. Quoted in Philip Hughes, *The Church in Crisis: A History of the General Councils, 325-1870*, p. 20. Hanover House, Garden City, New York, 1961.
5. There is a ten volume publication in process from Claremont Graduate School in California on Gnosticism. It will be a translation of the original Coptic documents discovered in 1946 and should throw much light on the origins of early Christianity.
6. Quoted in Pelikan, *op. cit.*, p. 41.
7. *Ibid.*, p. 55.
8. Ben F. Meyer, *op. cit.*, p. 111.

III

The Structure of the Early Church

PRIESTS AND LAITY

To the average Catholic the structure of the early Church poses no problem: it was the same as it is today; it is identical. If he were to put his understanding into diagram form, that diagram would go something like this:

From the beginning

1. CHRIST .... directly appointed His
2. TWELVE APOSTLES .... including, over them, Peter as
3. THE POPE .... Peter and the other eleven Apostles personally ordained their successors, namely,
4. THE BISHOPS .... who ordained as their successors the
5. OTHER BISHOPS .... and so on until the present time. Thus is seen a series of links in the continuous chain of

6. APOSTOLIC SUCCESSION

Somewhere within this diagram the Apostles passed on the priesthood as well, and somewhere in the course of time the cardinals came to replace the bishops as the rulers of the Church under the leadership of the pope (the "president and his cabinet"). This is the picture. Yet the evidence in the New Testament points out quite clearly that we have to modify this diagram. The testimony indicates that in the early Church there were many forms of ministries and structures that defy any rigid diagraming. It is true we do not have much detailed information about them. The years, say, from 30 to 90 A.D. are hazy although after that we possess a fairly accurate picture. In any case, realizing that we will not arrive at a full answer concerning the organization of the primitive Church we can at least correct our former knowledge and give some reasonable probabilities which are more in keeping with the evidence.

First of all we must remember that the Church began in Jerusalem, the scene of Jesus' passion, death and resurrection and the great drama of Pentecost. Church-communities were formed which, as we have seen, did not separate themselves immediately from the Temple and Judaism in general. The organization must have been loose as the new Jewish Christians struggled with their identity. When persecution broke out the Greek-speaking Jews who had become Christians had to flee. We saw that they fled to the scattered Jewish communities throughout the world including such Greek-speaking cities as Antioch, Ephesus, Corinth and others in Africa and Asia. They even fled to Rome itself, the imperial city of the still reigning emperors, around the year 40 (so that when Peter finally did go to Rome he found there an already existing church-community; he did not start it). Thus in each city there appeared these church-communities. Although not all of them had the same kind of structure, as we shall see below, we know one certainty common to them all: they contained clergy and laity.

This is obvious to Catholics, to many Protestants and to members of the Orthodox churches. It is worth mentioning, however, since it was one of Luther's contentions that *all* Christians in the early Church were looked on as priests and so there was no need for a special priesthood and consequently no distinction between clergy and laity. Scholars, however, including the recent work of Lutheran J. H. Elliott[1] reject this. On the contrary there is general agreement with the statement of Yves Congar that "nowhere in the New Testament is there any reference to the worship and priesthood of the faithful in the Eucharist or even in the sacraments . . . or in the Church's public worship." Even twenty centuries later the rather imprecise comments of Vatican II that "the faithful join in the offering of the Eucharist by virtue of their royal priesthood" do not overrule the fact that the New Testament itself did not make the association between the general "royal priesthood" of the faithful and the liturgical worship of the Eucharist.

We should anticipate here the comment that nowhere in the New Testament is there mention of priests as we know them. True, but there is no doubt that they existed. Scripture scholar Father Raymond Brown suggests that because the infant Church did not at first disassociate itself from Judaism, priests were simply taken for granted (for Judaism had them). No special mention needed to appear. As a matter of fact, the special and specific mention of priests in the early Church is not evident until the Church *does* separate itself from Judaism. It does this because the notion of the Eucharist as a sacrifice only gradually becomes apparent to the Church. Side by side with this new self-understanding of sacrifice the correlative notion of priests to offer this sacrifice comes to the forefront. Thus Father Brown, in an observation that may startle some Catholics, says:

Such a picture of the development of the Christian priest-hood must of necessity modify our understanding of the claim that historically Jesus instituted the priesthood at the Last Supper. This statement is true to the same real but nuanced extent as the statement that the historical Jesus instituted the Church. By selecting followers to take part in the proclamation of God's kingdom. Jesus formed the nucleus of what would develop into a community and ultimately into the Church. By giving special significance to the elements of the (Passover) meal that he ate with his disciples on the night before he died, Jesus supplied his followers with a community rite that would ultimately be seen as a sacrifice and whose celebrants would hence be understood as priests.[2]

Once more, such a comment points up the fact that our notions of the ministries and structures of the early Church are uneven because the Church itself was uneven at that time; it had not fully unfolded. It would have to reflect on itself for a long time before the implications of everything that Jesus said and did became apparent. It would be the work of the early Church Fathers and Councils to bring into ultimate formula many of the realizations. Again the slow dawning of the Last Supper as a sacrifice and its concomitant priesthood is a case in point.

THE TWELVE

In our search for answers about the structures of the early Church we can add another factor. There were the Twelve Apostles and they did have a unique place. They had seen the Lord, witnessed His risen state, been His companions and knew His mind. Clearly they were important and held in high esteem. We modern Catholics like to think of them as traveling all over the world and founding churches. Actually, according to the New Testament, this was not so. Most of them stayed put. They were not primarily missionary apostles. Rather they were like "Founding Fathers." They were the Resource of the faith *par excellence*. They were the pillars of the Church with all of the stability and permanence that that phrase implies. They were the collective witness to the event and to the message of Jesus. They were the living depository of what He said, did and taught. To this extent they did not have to travel. On the contrary, there were apostles besides the Twelve who did travel. They were not among the unique Twelve but they were apostles nevertheless. They had seen the risen Lord (Paul in his epistle speaks of Jesus appearing to some five hundred brethren after His resurrection) and, most determining of all, they were sent to preach the Gospel, the sign of a genuine apostle. The original Twelve or the church-community (or perhaps Christ Himself) appointed them in order to ease their own job of preaching the Good News. Thus they became the traveling apostles, the missionaries and founders of various church-communities. The most famous among these was, of course, St. Paul, and he is considered a true apostle though not numbered among the Twelve. These "secondary" apostles (if you will) did not stay at one particular church-community. They moved on, keeping in touch by letters and delegates (for example, the epistles of St. Paul; his delegates, Timothy and Titus).

PRESBYTER-BISHOPS

In addition to the "secondary" apostles we have during the very lifetime of Paul and the Twelve several more elements of structure. There are for example the deacons about whom we shall speak in the next chapter and there are the presbyters. There is evidence that these presbyters actually ruled the church-communities. As Founding Fathers the Twelve themselves were free of administration and rule. The itinerant apostles were just that: they founded church-communities and then moved on. The stable ruling power left were the presbyters. We do not know exactly when they came on the scene but it was during the lifetime of the Twelve. We are not certain of the exact nature of their office although most scholars hold that it was identical with that of bishops. In any case, we find in the *Acts of the Apostles* many references to the presbyter-bishops. In chapter fifteen, for example, we find that the Christians at Antioch charge Paul and Barnabas to go to Jerusalem "to the apostles and presbyters." When they arrive they are received "by the church, and by the apostles and presbyters". After their report "the apostles and presbyters assembled to consider the matter." Then "it pleased the apostles and presbyters, with the whole church, to send to Antioch" two messengers who took a letter which read: "The apostles and presbyters to the brethren at Jerusalem." In addition to this and other such explicit reference to the existence of presbyters, Paul and Barnabas themselves appointed them in their own church-community foundations.

The interesting thing is that the presbyters were a committee. They formed a group, the presbyterate, and as such ruled over the various church-communities. But there was one further development. It is not clear how it started but the results are indisputable. Somewhere along the way there was either a chief presbyter or bishop from the very beginning or else a chief presbyter-bishop emerged later:

> Very soon, however, the word "bishop" appears in the singular, implying that in a community there would be one bishop among many elders. Paul, for example, outlines the duties of various offices and writes about "a bishop . . . the office of a bishop" in the singular, then about "deacons" and

"elders" in the plural. We can only suppose that the title of bishop was gradually given to the senior elder (or perhaps to the elder celebrating the Eucharist at the time), who then became the chairman of the elders.[3]

In any case, recent scholarship has shown that by the end of the first century (not the second or third as formerly thought) the single "monarchial" presbyter-bishop was the general rule everywhere. In short, the single bishop had replaced the presbyterate committee. Certainly by the time of the martyr St. Ignatius of Antioch who died around the year 110 the single monarchial bishop was prevalent if not universal (Rome seems to remain an exception being still ruled by the presbyterate).

FUNCTION VERSUS OFFICE

The next step in structural development is this: when the original Twelve Apostles died and when the "secondary" founding apostles died, then these presbyter-bishops took their place. Significantly, they did this, not necessarily by being appointed by the Twelve or by the "secondary" apostles themselves (though this could be in some cases), but by being appointed *by the church-community*. There were two reasons for this. First of all, the Church as a whole succeeded the Twelve. The witness of the Twelve was passed on to the living Church. It was the living Church that was to give evidence to the event of Christ, to ordain and to consecrate. The whole Church called a man to his office. Notice the reference in the *Acts* just quoted above: Paul and Barnabas were received "*by the church,* and by the Apostles, etc. . . ."; then "it pleased the Apostles, presbyters, *with the whole church.* . . ." Secondly, what was therefore important to the Church was not that there be some kind of lineal descent, some physical connection, from one of the Apostles. What was important was that the men in question—the new presbyter-bishops—faithfully reflect the apostolic witness and tradition. In his epistle to Titus Paul says, "The bishop as God's steward must be blameless. . . . In his teaching he must hold fast to the authentic message . . ." (Titus 1:7ff). In short, the *function* was more important than the office. In and with the Church they were to preserve the Church in its apostolic foundation. The bishops were to be the permanent resident authorities and to re-present and reinterpret the living Good News of the Gospel to all ages. They were to be authentic purveyors, with and for the Church, of the Christ-event and the Christ message. If there was to be any idea of "apostolic succession" at all from the original Twelve, it was to be a succession of message as obtained from them; a totally faithful witness to exactly what was handed down by and through them. Perhaps modern Presbyterian theologian John Macquarrie puts it best when he says (and his words, very rewarding, bear careful reading):

> . . . Let me simply draw attention to the parallel between the episcopate and other "embodiments" (the canon of Scripture, the sacraments, the creeds) which we met when considering the first three notes of the Church. The episcopate, like the others, protects by an outward institution the inner life of the Church. In all the threats of heresy and perversion to which it has been exposed, not only in the early centuries but later, the Church has held to its apostolic heritage. . . . The episcopate cannot be treated as if it were on a different footing with the other embodied forms associated with the fundamental notes of the Church.

> [Professor John Knox] shows how the various features of the early Catholic Church were intended to establish its unity and integrity, and . . . developments of the New Testament understanding of the Church. In particular, he draws an

analogy among the canon, the creeds, and the episcopate. All came to be regarded as "apostolic," which means that the early Catholic Church which in reality established these forms (or in whose experience they were first established), thought of itself as doing no more than recognizing what had been established by the apostles themselves. It is not a question of whether, as a matter of historical fact, the apostles wrote the books ascribed to them in the New Testament; or whether the Apostles' Creed was actually composed by the apostles; or whether the apostolic ministry in the form of the historic episcopate was plainly and universally present from the beginning. We are to think of these rather in the context of the Church as "a visible, historical community," possessing an identity and yet developing in response to new demands and opportunities. The point about the various forms is that although they required time before they developed to the point where they clearly emerge in history, they express the mind and character of the Church as it had been since the apostles.[4]

Again, a bishop was authentic, not by necessarily being "ordained" by one of the Apostles, but by being appointed by the Church (which afterwards imposed hands on him) to lead it in witnessing to the apostolic tradition. Any bishop has "Apostolic succession" who can trace his lineage to this function.

There is every indication, we repeat, that the church-community appointed the bishops or, in the words of Macquarrie, "established these forms." The power of ordination was given to the Church at large. The Church could confer the powers on those whom it chose. This whole idea will be new and perhaps startling to the average Catholic. Yet he should recall a parallel. It is constant Catholic tradition that, even though in the Gospels the commission to baptize was given *only* to the Eleven Apostles, *any* person, even an unbeliever, can baptize. How to explain this unless the baptizing power of the Twelve was passed on *to the Church* rather than to individuals? It appears not too far-fetched to suggest that the power of ordination was handed down the same way. It is the Church as a whole which is the recipient of the Apostolic power and tradition and it seems evident that it was the Church which called men to the office of bishop. As we shall see in the next chapter, this also explains the long tradition of the people electing their own bishops. It is of further interest to note that this very point was brought up at the Bishops' Synod meeting in October, 1971. The official report on priestly ministry contains these excerpts:

> As scholars reflect on the data of scripture and the earliest tradition of the church, they realize that the older popular understanding of apostolic succession has been too mechanical and oversimplified. It has perhaps been too quickly assumed that the twelve apostles appointed immediate successors, from whom in turn further successors were commissioned in an unbroken historical chain down to the present day.
>
> Actually scripture and early church life point rather to the view that bishops succeed to the mission of the apostles, and then only by way of partial assumption of their function, namely caring for the churches founded by earlier missionary apostles.
>
> Theological reflection suggests that in a sense it is the entire church which succeeds the apostolic college, a succession realized in a dramatic but by no means exclusive way by the episcopal college of the Catholic church. For this reason the episcopate must be more clearly linked to the Christian community, precisely to manifest its apostolic credentials.[5]

Thus the episcopacy, as Father Brown reminds us, like the priesthood, was established by Christ Himself only in the same nuanced sense that it emerged, under the guidance of the Holy Spirit, from an implicit principle demanded by the nature of the Church that Christ founded. "The fundamental 'apostolic succession' is therefore that of the Church itself and of each individual Christian. . . . What is required is the perduring agreement with the apostolic testimony. . . . Apostolic succession is thus primarily succession in the Apostolic faith and personal confession, as well as in the apostolic ministry and life. . . ."[6]

THE COLLEGE

Another important aspect of early church structure in regards to the episcopacy must be mentioned. A man was appointed bishop, not merely as the ruler and head of this or that particular church-community, but also as a member of the larger Church. He was brought into the "college" which had the whole Church as a concern even though he was rooted in one locale. To show a bishop's essential unity with all other bishops therefore in forming this college there arose the custom (and later the law from the Council of Nicaea) that at least three bishops must co-consecrate another bishop. This explains that even to this day in the various canons of our Mass liturgy we find phrases such as:

> We offer them for N, our pope,
> for N, our bishop
> and for all who hold and teach the Catholic faith
> that comes to us from the Apostles (Canon I)

> Lord, remember your Church throughout the world;
> make us grow in love
> together with N, our pope,
> N, our bishop, and all the clergy (Canon II)

> Strengthen in faith and love your pilgrim
> Church on earth;

your servant, Pope N, our bishop N,
and all the bishops
with the clergy and the entire people your Son
has gained for you (Canon III)

These prayers reflect the most ancient realization that a bishop must be sensitive to the needs of the entire Church and is in relationship to the whole Church as well as to the members of his church-community. We must hasten to mention here briefly that there would be one person who would be the outward sign of this unity among bishops. There would be one person who would be the visible expression of the college, an external sign of the whole Church: this would be Peter and his successors. Not that the unity of the whole college proceeds from Peter; "rather, he amalgamates it into an effective unity."[7]

To move beyond our time of inquiry, we should state that since the bishops were an essential unity, a college, then they quickly learned to confer with one another. They began very early to meet in local councils to consider mutual questions. Inevitably, as would be anticipated, bishops of the more prominent cities became quite important and they and their cities were noted focal points of church life. Such men became Patriarchs and could be found in such ancient dominant cities as Alexandria, Constantinople, Antioch and Rome. At times the local councils of bishops were not sufficient so throughout history all the bishops of the entire Church would meet. These meetings are the great General Ecumenical Councils of the Church. There would be twenty such gatherings beginning with the Council of Nicaea in 325 to Vatican II in 1963.

Later on, as we shall see, when Christianity became the

religion of the Roman empire the political importance of bishops who wielded such spiritual power and leadership over the multitudinous Christian people became apparent to the Roman emperors. Emperors like Constantine quickly tried to utilize these men as cohesive forces in the empire. The bishops in many ways replaced the civil governors in regulating the people and keeping the peace. There would be no difficulty in seeing that more unscrupulous emperors and kings of the future would use the bishopric as a political tool. In any case, the actions of such emperors and kings would be a testimony to the power and dominance of the episcopal position. But over and above such abuses that would later creep in, the episcopacy was and would continue to be a most powerful force for stability in the Church.

OTHER MINISTRIES

We are not finished yet. We have spoken about the Twelve, apostolic succession and the presbyter-bishops and their functions. To add to the confusion and to our uncertainty as to exactly what the organizational set up was for the primitive Church we have indications of other jobs. Strange ministries are mentioned in the New Testament and we simply do not know what they all mean. Here, for example, is St. Paul's first epistle to the church-community at Corinth (12: 28): "You, then, are the body of Christ. Every one of you is a member of it. Furthermore, God has set up in the church first apostles, second prophets, third teachers, then miracle workers, healers, assistants, administrators, and those who speak in tongues." Elsewhere the New Testament mentions other ministries such as deacons and widows. Who they were and exactly what they did we do not know. Again, the obvious point is that there were a variety of ministries, that the Church was not obviously confined to one particular structure, that it need not be now.

It is possible, of course, that the structure as we Catholics know it—pope, bishop, priest, laity—has its origins from Christ Himself. We are not confined to the New Testament. Not everything was written down there as John reminds us (John 21:21-24) and Paul himself quotes from the sayings of Jesus which we know nothing about. But the point is not what is *not* written down in the New Testament, but what is. And what is written down tells of a variety of church structure and ministry, that other variations besides the episcopal system are possible. As John McKenzie puts it:

> First of all, it is obvious that pluriform structure is general in the New Testament. Nothing suggests a uniform structure imposed from above. This does not imply that development beyond the New Testament is impossible or undesireable; it does imply that such a development, when it occurred, was based on other than biblical reasons. To the degree to which these reasons were historical other structures can be suggested by other historical reasons. Pluriformity is not contrary to the New Testament, whatever else it may be contrary to.[8]

CONCLUSIONS

From all that we have seen it is evident that our original diagram at the beginning of this chapter will have to be altered. Probably it should go something like this:

1. CHRIST .... gathered the unique
2. TWELVE APOSTLES ..... as the foundation of His Church. These Twelve appointed to service
3. THE DEACONS .... and also what we might call

4. THE "SECONDARY
   APOSTLES" .... these "secondary" apostles
   were mainly itinerant,
   founding church-communities and moving on. They
   left the ruling of such places
   to

5. THE PRESBYTERATE .... which was a committee appointed by the Church. In
   this presbyterate there were
   contained, or there emerged
   the

6. SINGLE "MONARCHIAL
   BISHOP" .... who with all other bishops
   formed a "college." This
   college both guided and reflected the community and
   presupposed a close rapport
   with it. The visible image of
   the Church and hallmark of
   episcopal unity was

7. THE POPE .... who did not have to be at
   Rome to be pope since
   Peter was pope when he re-
   sided in Jerusalem and in
   Antioch. (When he went to
   Rome, the Roman see and
   the papacy were joined.)
   Besides, there were

8. OTHER MINISTRIES ..... such as "healers," teachers,
   prophets, widows, elders,
   etc.

Again, we must remember that in the first decades of the
Church the scheme of this diagram developed unevenly in
the various church-communities. Rome and Corinth, for example, seemed to have held on longer to the presbyterate.

Yet, as remarked earlier, by the year 100 or shortly thereafter the monarchial bishop was the general rule and would remain so. It is interesting to compare the two diagrams. In the second given here the "apostolic succession" is implied in the way explained previously. The succession is a succession of the function to witness to the apostolic tradition. Also, the role of the Church itself is more prominent as is the collegial aspect of the episcopacy. But there are some practical conclusions for the modern Catholic looking back at this development of the Church.

First of all, from the beginning the Church seems to be hierarchical, at least in the sense that there are clergy or officers and laity. Indeed there seems to be an implied desire from Christ that this should be so for the right ordering of his Church. The sheer sociological need for ordering among human beings would require a hierarchy of some kind—perhaps not the hierarchy of sacred orders as the Catholic Church would claim, but certainly a hierarchy of function. Even such a Catholic critic as the Reformer Calvin declared the need for ministers and said that "the Church cannot be kept safe, unless supported by those guards to which the Lord has been pleased to commit its safety." Calvin further proclaimed, "For neither are the light and heat of the sun, nor meat and drink, so necessary to sustain and cherish the present life, as is the apostolic and pastoral office to preserve a church on the earth." Thus, although the entire church-community must be concerned about matters that pertain to itself yet it needs guidance. It must have someone to interpret the mind of Christ to it. In a word the Church is not an egalitarian society; it is hierarchical. "There are limits to democracy in any Church which can claim the name of Christian. The authentic Christian gospel is not established by a majority vote; it comes down from two thousand years of Christian experience and testimony, which has overwhelming weight and authority."[9]

Secondly, since the Church is a hierarchical structure any free-floating ministries and any "underground" churches so popular in recent history must not only have some structure; they must have some contact with the larger community-church in order to maintain themselves in authentic tradition. Also, wholly "spiritual" churches contradict Christian origins:

> . . . The idea of a pneumatic Church is an attractive one and always has been. A handful of dedicated Christians working in a community in almost invisible fashion, exuding good will and love, and unconcerned about mundane things such as finance, administration, and communication, sounds terribly appealing. But even if it were possible for a community of humans to exist without a formal structure (and it is quite impossible), those who would object to a structured Church and would prefer a pneumatic one should take the matter up with the Founder who wanted His Church to be a thoroughly human organization and seemed prepared to accept the fact that in this human organization there would be all kinds of human imperfections. . . .[10]

ECUMENICAL DIMENSIONS

Finally, the fact that the episcopate was a structure that gradually developed in the early Church rather than having been a firm blueprint handed down by Jesus Himself (at least as determined from a critical reading of the New Testament) raises some interesting ecumenical speculations. The first and most obvious speculation is the question, "Is the episcopate *essential* to the Church?" The episcopate, as we have seen, is historical and it authentically points to apostolic foundations and tradition. Still, there were some community-churches in St. Paul's lifetime that had no bishops but lived in close harmony with neighboring community-churches that did. It was not even necessary that bishops be present to ordain. The Catholic is surprised to learn that priests may indeed ordain and that there is a constant tradition which holds that there is no distinction between bishop and priest. Gratin's *Decree* sums up centuries of theological opinion when it says, "A priest is the same as a bishop and it is only by custom that bishops preside over priests." As theologian, Harry McSorley puts it:

> Is it any wonder, in the face of strong doctrinal, canonical and historical tradition, that the Council of Trent refused to accept the proposal that the difference between presbyter and bishop was of divine institution? Such a definition would not only have condemned the continental reformers, but a great number of Catholic theologians and canonists as well, including at least two Fathers of the Church. . . . Even after the Second Vatican Council a Catholic theologian is free to hold that, under certain circumstances, an ordinary priest may ordain another priest.[11]

The point is that even within the Church there is a wide latitude concerning a variety of functions, offices and ministries. The point is that if the Catholic Church will permit valid ordinations without a bishop (under certain circumstances), why not allow the same for the non-Catholic denominations? In fact, the Catholic Church declares them to be more than "denominations" but recognizes them as having membership in the Church of Christ. The Decree on Ecumenism says, "Nevertheless, all those justified by faith through baptism are incorporated into Christ. They therefore have a right to be honored by the title of Christian, and are properly regarded as brothers in the Lord by the sons of the Catholic Church" (No. 3). If basic membership in the Church requires faith and baptism, is there any cause (provided that there is agreement on doctrine) why other ministries cannot be valid?

The ecumenical question is that with such variations might it not be possible for the Church of today to also recognize and even legitimatize other forms of church-community rule other than that of a bishop? Could not the Church which made the original clergy, appoint others? Could not the presbyterate be revived? Not that it should be, but in theory it could be. More to the point, might not the Roman Catholic Church recognize another church's clergy? This would presume, of course, that this other church would agree on all doctrinal essentials with the Roman Catholic Church. But, for the sake of argument, if it did, could not the Church simply recognize the other church's clergy and by this simple recognition and appointment "ordain" them? Father Raymond Brown, who raises these questions adds these wise words:

> It may be objected that entry into union with a non-episcopal church without insisting on episcopal ordination is tantamount to admitting that one form of church government is as good as another. This is not necessarily true: such a union does not deny our belief that episcopacy evolved in the Church under the guidance of the Holy Spirit, but recognizes that through unfortunate historical circumstances some Christians have not been able to appreciate how the episcopacy serves as an effective sign of unity and apostolicity. In particular, we may think of the medieval period when bishops became lords or princes and when the absentee bishop was not exceptional. The lack of pastoral concern in this reaction led some of the reformed churches to consider the episcopacy as a corruption of the Gospel rather than as an effective means of perpetuating it. We cannot expect such churches, which in the meantime have developed an alternative struc-

ture suddenly to regain an appreciation of the episcopate, especially if our insistence on it prolongs the divisions of Christianity or if they are asked to accept a ceremony of episcopal ordination in which they have no real faith.[12]

In the light of these words, then, a further flexibility in community-church structure is possible and the Catholic may expect some developments along these lines in the future.

That the history of the structures of the early Church is quite complicated has been evident throughout this chapter. The Catholic thought that his present knowledge of the pyramid structure of pope down to parish priest was the only true one. It turns out that there is much more variety than formerly thought. The high level theologians are investigating these points and ecumenists are working hard to reconcile Catholic-Protestant structures.[13] The point for the reader is that he at least should be aware of the basis for the discussion. He should realize that a very open alive issue of his modern Church is once more rooted in the history of early Christianity.

NOTES

1. Raymond E. Brown, S.S. *Priest and Bishop: Biblical Reflections,* p. 14. Paulist Press, Paramus, N.J. 1970.
2. *Ibid.,* p. 19. We must remember, of course, that for Catholics "the ordained ministry is not simply a function within the Church but an essential aspect of the ecclesiastical mystery itself." Richard McBrien, *Who Is A Catholic?,* p. 111.
3. Michael Rogness, *The Church Nobody Knows,* pp. 84, 85. Augsburg Publishing House, Minneapolis, Minnesota. 1971.
4. John Macquarrie, *Principles of Christian Theology,* pp. 368, 369. Charles Scribner's Sons. New York, New York. 1966.
5. National Catholic Reporter, October 8, 1971. Documentation Report.
6. Hans Kung, *Why Priests?,* p. 44. Doubleday and Co., Garden City, New York. 1972.

7. *Sacramentum Mundi*, Volume I, p. 89. Herder and Herder, New York. 1968.
8. *Concilium*, volume 74, p. 21. Herder and Herder, New York. 1972.
9. Quoted in Macquarrie, *op. cit.*, p. 378.
10. Andrew Greeley, *The Hesitant Pilgrim*, pp. xiv, xv. Sheed and Ward, New York. 1966. Note also Richard McBrien's words in his book *Who Is A Catholic?*, p. 112. "There is a tendency, too, among some Catholics to minimize or even reject the place of ministry in the Church. Occasionally the rhetoric of the so-called 'underground Church' reflects this spirit. The charismatic is exalted at the expense of the structural; the tyranny of the old legalism is supplanted by a new tyranny of the spirit (with a small 's')."
11. Concilium, *op. cit.*, pp. 29, 30.
12. *Op. cit.*, p. 84.
13. As a matter of fact the Roman Catholic and the Lutheran theologians have met to discuss the Eucharist and the Ministry and both have concluded that each Church is able to recognize the clergy of the others as valid and that their Eucharist is valid. See the very interesting series called *Lutherans and Catholics in Dialogue* (volume IV) published jointly by the U.S.A. National Committee of the Lutheran World Federation and the Bishops' Committee for Ecumenical and Interreligious Affairs, 1970. Copies obtainable from the United States Catholic Conference, 1312 Massachusetts Ave. N.W., Washington, D.C. 20005.

IV

Ministries, Worship and Practices

DEACONS

In the variety of ministries and structures of the early Church a prominent place is given to the deacon. The diaconate or office of deacon developed gradually in the primitive Church but it was there from the very beginning. In fact, it was an imitation of the Jewish levite. Such levites were connected especially with Temple religious ritual and service and aid to the needy. The Jewish levites served as door-keepers to the Temple, administrators, chanters and keepers of the sacred vessels. They worked full time and were supported by the people. The Christian deacon simply appropriated all these functions for the new Church.

At the start the office of deacon was loosely structured and only gradually precise guidelines were established for them. A step towards this was taken in the famous episode in the sixth chapter of the *Acts of the Apostles* (6: 1-6). Here is the story of the Apostles appointing the seven deacons to wait on tables so that they themselves would not "neglect the Word of God." Later Christian writers would take this particular incident as the inauguration of the diaconate but this would be inaccurate since deacons were present before the account in the *Acts*. Interestingly, what prompted the move was the complaint that only the Jewish Orthodox widows were being taken care of. The Greek-speaking Jewish widows were being neglected (the old rivalry again). To serve these, the seven deacons were chosen and they were chosen as full time leaders and administrators in the Church. They were not part time or minor officers.

The deacons' task generally fell into three main categories. First and foremost, they assisted in the liturgy. In the second century Justin Martyr describes this diaconate function:

> At the end of these prayers and thanksgiving, all present express their approval by saying "Amen." This Hebrew word "Amen" means "so be it." And when he who presides has celebrated the eucharist they whom we call deacons permit each one present to partake of the Eucharistic bread, and wine and water; and they convey it also to the absentees.

Tertullian informs us that the deacons also assisted at the marriage liturgy and that they baptized. During persecution time the deacons on occasion were the ordinary ministers of confession and reconciliation as we learn from the African Bishop Cyprian:

> They who have received certificates from the martyrs, and may be assisted by their privilege with God, if they should be seized with any misfortune and peril of sickness, should, without waiting for my presence, before any presbyter who might be present, or if a presbyter should not be found and death becomes imminent, before even a deacon, be able to make confession of their sins, that, with the imposition of hands upon them for repentance, they should come to the Lord with the peace which the martyrs have desired, by their letter to us, be granted to them.

In this connection it is interesting to observe that as late as the time of St. Ignatius of Loyola, the founder of the Jesuits (sixteenth century) he and others believed that in an emergency one could confess even to a layman. This may have some origin in Cyprian's third century deacons who could hear confessions.

Secondly, the deacons took care of the sick and the needy. There is also some evidence in the church-communities of Egypt that the deacons even had the power of administering the sacrament of the sick. Service to the community was their watchword. They dispensed the charity and distributed the community funds. For this reason a most frequent admonition to the deacons was that they be honest men.

Thirdly, the deacons helped to administer the Church. They were thus very closely associated with the bishop. They often traveled with him and became his eyes and ears. Bishop Ignatius of Antioch could write, "I send you greetings in the Blood of Jesus Christ, wherein is joy eternal and unfailing; all the more so when men are at one with their bishop—and with their clergy and deacons too." Many deacons followed their bishops to death. When Cyprian himself was finally martyred at Carthage in 258 his deacons stayed beside him and were killed with him. When in that same year the pope was arrested four of his deacons stayed with him also and died with him. One of these was the famous St. Lawrence, the deacon with the gallows' humor; he told the torturers who were burning him to death to turn him over as he was done on one side. At Rome Pope Fabian (d. 250) divided the city into seven administrative offices each under the authority of a deacon and their assistants, the subdeacons. (Later these deacons would become very powerful.) Deacons had the function of bringing the sacred gifts to the altar at episcopal consecrations. Thus the deacons, from the beginning, assisted at the liturgy, aided the sick and needy and administered the Church under the bishop. Yet, even in early times tensions were beginning to show themselves which would eventually undermine the whole diaconate office.

DECLINE OF THE DEACONS

Signs of tension were slight but real between deacons and bishops and priests. Basically, the problem was one of power. The bishops and priests on occasion felt that the deacons were becoming too powerful. After all, they did handle the money and they did run much of the Church's administration. It is quite clear, for example, in the Church's first General Council of Nicaea that the permanent diaconate is taken for granted but it is also clear that the deacons are being put in their places:

> It has come to the attention of the synod that in some regions deacons give the eucharist to presbyters. This is in accord neither with canon nor custom, that those who do not have the power of offering give the body of Christ to those who offer. Moreover, it is known that some deacons attain the eucharist before the bishop. Let those things cease and let deacons remain within their proper place, knowing that they are ministers of the bishop and less than presbyters. . . . Nor may a deacon sit in the midst of the presbyters. This is done contrary to canon and order. If anyone does not wish to obey after these constitutions, let him desist from the diaconate. (Canon 18)

What added to further friction was the growing power of the priests. As they took over more and more functions their roles became confused with that of the deacons and the two suffered what we call an identity crisis. The deacons lost out. Ironically in our times the problem has reasserted itself as lay people take over more and more of the priests' former functions.

> During the long and eventful centuries from Nicaea to the reformation the permanent diaconate at first flourished and then declined. The seeds of diaconal decline were already

planted with the rise of sacerdotalism (growing power and
office-functioning of the priests) in the third century and
the restrictive legislation of the early fourth century. A confusion of roles between deacons and "priests" and a struggle
for identity continued into the Middle Ages. Gradually the
diaconate receded in importance until the diaconal order
became merely a preliminary and ceremonial step to the
sacralized priesthood.[1]

Still, although the trend of diaconate decline had begun,
deacons remained very much on the scene through the ages.
For example, the Irish are reminded that St. Patrick was the
son of a married deacon and the grandson of a priest. St.
Ambrose, St. Jerome, St. Augustine and St. Athanasius (a
former deacon) all mention deacons as being quite active. As
a matter of fact crotchety Jerome complained of them being
too powerful especially those at Rome. Such deacons in fact
became so proficient in assisting Pope Leo the Great (d.
461) in the management of Rome that they were known as
the "bishop's deacons." The Middle Ages would continue to
look upon the deacon as the bishop's vicar general. But friction was growing and the diaconate was being less a full
time permanent job and more a temporary office, perhaps for
a maximum of five to seven years.

Around the eighth century a theme which had been lurking around for a while began to emerge more strongly; that
is, the diaconate was but a preliminary step to the priesthood.
By the eighth century a favorite comparison was that the deacon was likened to Christ washing his disciples' feet, the
priest to Christ consecrating the bread and wine at the Last
Supper, and the bishop to Christ solemnly blessing the apostles. By the tenth century the diaconate had become almost
totally a temporary and ceremonial order although deacons
still functioned in the capacity as assistants and aides to the

bishops and some still had great administrative powers. By the thirteenth century St. Thomas Aquinas was stating that deacons were clearly inferior to the bishops and priests. They could not baptize by power of their office but only as necessity demands and they could not administer the sacrament of the sick even in necessity (both functions we have seen the deacons did as part of their job). By the time of the Reformation in the sixteenth century the temporary diaconate had been reduced to merely liturgical functions. With the coming of the city life even the deacons' traditional role of charity was taken over by new urban secular organizations.

RESTORATION

At the Council of Trent there was a realization that the primitive diaconate should be restored in view of the great needs of the Church. However, lurking in the back of many council fathers' minds was a fear of a too powerful diaconate which distressed Jerome in the fourth century. In addition there was the worry that the role of the priesthood, already attacked by the reformers, would be further confused or lessened by a restored diaconate. Nevertheless Trent did restore it although it did not function. Trent saw the diaconate as a part of the order to the priesthood and although its service aspect was stressed this never became implemented until after Vatican II.

Impetus for implementation came later from Germany. There the restoration for the diaconate was underway especially as a result of the wars experience and the horrors of the prison camps of Hitler: a group who served was clearly needed. In 1951 the diaconate was reestablished and in 1957 Pius XII was sympathetic to a universal restoration but felt the time was not yet ripe. Actually, what was worrying many prelates was another related issue: celibacy. If the Church once more admitted married deacons, would this not erode the discipline of a celibate clergy? Would not married deacons undermine the unmarried priesthood? No one wanted to open such a Pandora's box. Still, the need was urgent especially in large cities where a sense of community was lacking. Deacons on full time could do wonders in comforting the sick, baptizing babies, helping to administer parishes, etc. Finally, on September 29, 1965 the fathers at Vatican II voted overwhelmingly in favor of the restoration of the permanent diaconate to serve as ministers of the word (preaching, reading lessons), liturgy (baptisms, distributing communion and such) and charity. Guidelines were issued: a deacon may be ordained if he is twenty-five or older but the young men must remain celibate. Married men of thirty-five or over may also be ordained (with, of course, the consent of their wives). The deacons will be incorporated into a diocese just as the priest is and paid as full time workers by the diocese. What will be his duties? The Vatican decree states that, with his bishop's approval, the deacon may administer baptism, give communion and benediction; he may assist at marriages if no priest is available, preside at funerals, preach, administer charities and assist the laity. In the United States several centers have been set up for the training of deacons.

The return of the full time deacon will obviously have many benefits for the community. Nevertheless, as we have mentioned above, his return may have an unsettling effect on the life of the priest:

> Since the third century priests have often preempted functions appropriate to deacons and laity. In America the parish priest sometimes became all things to all men. When America urbanized, specialized, and went to college the priest found his functions siphoned off one at a time by a progressively

better educated laity. No longer was he the best equipped social worker, teacher, counselor, administrator, coach, lector, or even preacher in an area. Yet his familiar role as an activist among activists was so deeply ingrained that the priest of the secular age eventually found himself in a confused and, until people got over the shock, disedifying identity crisis.[2]

The point is, if the deacon returns he will bring the identity crisis to a head. Then, too, for the 1970's, by admitting and reestablishing the permanent diaconate, the question of marriage and the ministry does come to the fore once more, the very question which troubled the fathers of Trent and Vatican II. A married diaconate—will it be the step to a married clergy? The 1971 Bishops' Synod meeting in Rome, acknowledging the question of priestly celibacy which such issues have raised has come out in favor once more of a celibate clergy. But as the married diaconate really becomes quite prominent, will they be able to hold the line?

DEACONESSES

There is one more issue concerning our investigation of the diaconate which we have not treated: women deacons. In the early Church there was a group called "widows" who seemed to have some official status. Paul mentions them several times and again seems to mention them as a recognized group. However, by the third century the deaconesses had replaced the widows. It was only natural that women should serve thus in the Church for there were many functions and ministrations that women could do best. The only restriction seems to be that of not allowing women to read the word of God and preach. St. Paul, no lover of women, said succinctly, "During instructions a woman should be quiet and respectful. I am not giving permission for a woman to teach or tell a man what to do." Male chauvinism goes way back. Yet women did minister to the early Church with great success. Tertullian wrote of the women deacons who did various jobs. Significantly, however, women were "chosen" not ordained. They were never admitted to the ministry, to sacred orders.[3] They served but never within the male concept of being ordained to do so. Nor did women get far in the liturgical ministry. Tertullian, Cyprian and Hippolytus were opposed to such and former liturgical functions which women did perform in the primitive Church became exclusive male property. The Council of Nicaea would state clearly that deaconesses were *not* to receive the imposition of hands because they were considered as numbered "among the laity."

In the East the women fared a little better and deaconesses were still active there for a long time. They frequently collaborated with the deacons especially in ministrations to female patients. Still, the prevailing attitude was that, although the deaconesses' work was important, it was not a sharing "in orders." In fact, the scholastic theologians in the late Middle Ages declared that women were inferior to men and incapable of receiving orders. St. Thomas Aquinas was only reflecting the prevailing opinion when he wrote, "Since therefore in the feminine sex there cannot be signified some eminence of grade, because woman has the state of subjection, so she is unable to receive the sacrament of order." Vatican II in resurrecting the office of the permanent diaconate left unmentioned the role of women. There is no question that orders of deaconesses existed in the early Church as we have shown. But by the eighth century this order had declined in the West and finally even in the East and the former work of the deaconesses has been taken over by religious women. There is no theological reason why women cannot be ordained to the diaconate and in reality there are many diaconal functions that could best be done by them.

THE ELECTION OF BISHOPS

We have seen in the last chapter that there is no evidence that indicates that the Apostles themselves appointed individual men to succeed them with all of their prerogatives. Equally certain, however, was that there was leadership. There was no such thing in the early Church as purely unstructured, democratic communities. There was a ministry, an order, an office, a hierarchy.[4] By the second and third centuries the bishop was the important man in the Church but still one beholden and dependent on the entire Church and *elected by the people.* Cyprian made the famous statement, "I decided to do nothing of my own opinion privately without your advice and the consent of the people".[5] After Nicaea in 325 there was a measurable decline of this interdependency between community and bishop in the East, though the West still held to it. The Eastern metropolitan became more autocratic, more closely allied with the state and a powerful church-civil figure especially in the large cities. Only 150 years after St. Paul the great Origen could complain about the eastern bishops of the large cities being absorbed in their own power, associating with the influential and cutting themselves off from the poor and needy. Commenting on such a situation Father O'Meara, in a powerful sentence, says, "He (the bishop) was the judge of a past tradition now extensively separated from its intrinsic note of promise about man's future. He became a powerful prince and a potent piece in political chess."[6] But this should not have been for ideally the bishop was (and is) intimately related to the community as servant, leader and presider.

Interaction was the keynote. Yet, as time went on, instead of leading the community he simply became an archivist: he preserved the past without relating that past to the present and future growth of the community. He was no longer the leader of the eschatological community; he became a distant figure of the status quo separated charismatically and physically from his flock.

In the West the close interaction between community and bishop continued a while longer. The people still chose their bishops for almost a thousand years and it was only in the late 900's that the pope began to figure at all in the election of bishops. Thus Pope Celestine I said, "No bishop is to be imposed on unwilling subjects, but the consent and wishes of clergy and people are to be consulted." Pope Leo said, "On no account is anyone to be a bishop who has not been chosen by the clergy, desired by the people, and consecrated by the bishops of the province with the authority of the metropolitan." A sixth century council repeated the same idea, "No one is to be consecrated as a bishop unless the clergy and people of the diocese have been called together and have given their consent." The real threat to popular election came from the princes and the great struggle ensued between the rights of the community to elect the bishop and the right of the prince or emperor to confirm or veto the choice. But in the terrible confusion and chaos of the times the bishopric became, as in the East, a political prize. By the ninth century in the West the election of a bishop was confined to the clergy. By the time of Pope Nicholas I (d. 867) the papacy began to intervene. By the tenth century the laity and local clergy had no real say. Their vote, as it were, was taken over by the nobles and the aristocracy. In the eleventh century the papacy and the monks worked together to free the elections and wrest them away from the princes and nobility.

With social conditions not permitting safe and orderly local elections anyway the papacy gave more and more guidance as more and more appeals to settle election contests went to the pope. Gradually the bishop ceased to be elected at all and was chosen by cathedral chapters. By the twelfth century only the elite were in on the bishop's election: chapters, kings, princes or pope. The people no longer had any say. Later the field dwindled even more as king and pope chose the bishop in an arrangement whereby the king continued to nominate and the pope confirm his choice. (This lasted till the time of Napoleon in 1801 when the government gave up all rights of nomination.) For the past century or more the appointment of a bishop has been the pope's exclusive prerogative free of state interest (except where Concordats with certain governments made it otherwise). This was not ambition or papal greed; rather this was brought about simply by the emergencies of history. The Church was fighting for survival and the papacy was leading the fight; a grateful church would back the papacy in everything.

Thus was the evolution of the choice of bishops from popular election to papal appointment. With the great masses of people coming into the Church, the turmoil of the barbarian invasions, the dark ages, the Church as a community of mature people in constant intercommunication inevitably got lost. The role of the bishop *had* to diminish from charismatic leader to preserver of law and order, civil servant and guardian of orthodoxy. It was inevitable that both chaotic times and large impersonal numbers should have allowed the election of a bishop over a community to be decided thousands of miles away by someone outside that community (a centralized papacy). In recent times there has been a distinct movement to restore the popular election of bishops and so make the words of Cyprian, Celestine and Leo real once again. Several dioceses in the United States, for example, permit their clergy to propose nominees for the bishopric. On May 12, 1972 Pope Paul VI issued a document assigning priests and *laymen* parts in the process leading to the nomination of candidates for bishop. The final choice would rest with the Holy See, but now each bishop must make private consultations with his clergy and certain qualified laymen about the choice of a new bishop. This is still not a complete open and democratic kind of choosing, but it represents a growing trend towards a more democratic Church and a return to the practices of the early Church. Finally, there is growing insistence in today's church that the bishop who unwittingly became a kind of "president of the corporation" must change his image. The agitation in the 1970's is that the bishop should return to his role as a man for the community; that he live among the people, be chosen from among them and dialogue with them. The bureaucratic bishop is on the way out as the people clamor for a pastoral type, one of their number and sensitive to their needs.

EARLY WORSHIP

There were several distinctive features about early Christian worship even when it was deciding about its relation to the Temple. Its liturgy included a baptismal rite and primitive formulas. There were also early creedal affirmations that arose in connection with baptism. The sayings and deeds of Jesus were hardening into routine patterns which would emerge in the written New Testament scriptures. Over and above the Temple association the Christians met privately. St. Paul tells us though, that not all Christian meetings were harmonious. He speaks of drunkenness at the Christian open-house get-together. He informs us of people shouting and competing to be heard. He mentions that their worship was held in private homes (Philemon 2) as it continued to be for several centuries so that at the end of the second century the apologist Minucius Felix could write, "We have no temples and no altars."[7] Indeed the "Church" was the community of the faithful who gathered for worship at the homes of hospitable Christians. But this was the key. Above all the moments of friction, in addition to the catechism, almsgiving, works of mercy and prayer mentioned in the *Acts of the Apostles* the central act of unity and worship was the eucharistic meal.

The Mass or eucharistic meal liturgy followed the general lines of the old synagogue service. There was the chanting of the scriptures, the recitation of psalms, prayers, instruction and hymns. After this instruction service (liturgy of the word as we call it) there was the great prayer of "thanksgiving" or "eucharistic" prayer. This great prayer was called the anaphora or canon. It was a narrative telling of the wonderful works of God and thanking Him for them. (This narrative aspect is most evident in our modern Fourth canon.) The earliest eucharistic prayers that we possess are found in the *Didache* written about 125 A.D. Some twenty-five years later we have this description of the whole procedure from the pen of Justin Martyr:

> On the day called after the sun (Sunday), all gather for a communal celebration. The memories of the apostles are read as long as time permits. Then the one presiding admonished his hearers to practice these beautiful teachings. We say prayers in common for ourselves, for the newly baptized, and for all others throughout the world. Then bread and wine are brought to him who presides over the brethren. He gives praise and glory to the Father in the name of the Son and of the Holy Spirit, and gives thanks at length for the

gifts we have received from Him. The whole crowd standing up cries out in agreement, "Amen". Amen is a Hebrew word and means "so may it be." Then the bread and wine over which the thanks have been offered are distributed among all those present. This food is known among us as the Eucharist. The deacon brings a portion to those who are absent.

The celebrant was free to make up his own eucharistic prayer. About the year 215 the priest Hippolytus gave this model,

The Lord be with you . . . and with your spirit; Lift up your hearts . . . we have lifted them up to the Lord; Let us give thanks to the Lord our God. . . . it is right and just. We give You thanks, O God, through your beloved Servant, Jesus Christ, whom You did send us in recent times as Savior, Redeemer, and messenger of your will . . . who, in order to acquire for You a holy people, stretched forth his hands in suffering that he might release from suffering those who believe in You. And when he was delivered up that he might abolish death and show forth the resurrection, he took bread and giving thanks to You said, "This is my Body which is broken for you." And likewise taking the cup, he said, "This is my Blood which is shed for you. When you do this, make memory of me." Making memory therefore of his death and resurrection, we offer to You this bread and chalice, giving thanks unto You for finding us worthy to stand before You. We beseech You to send Your Holy Spirit upon the oblation of the Church, to gather into one all Your holy ones who partake of it, that we may glorify You through Your servant, Jesus Christ, now and forever.

We can sense the similarity to our second and third canons of today.

This certainly was not *the* Roman Mass of the third century for at this time there was still no fixed formula but only a fixed framework. As a matter of fact, variations in the eucharistic liturgy were present from the beginning, even concerning what we call today the words of consecration:

> As all of us know, the accounts presented by the three evangelists Matthew, Mark and Luke, and St. Paul differ widely in many particulars. Not even the words which our Lord pronounced over the bread and wine are reproduced in the same form. And, besides, the oldest extant texts of the Mass present the account in still different forms. What can be the reason for this diversity? It seems that this diversity can best be explained by supposing that the varying biblical texts represent, not so many hazy recollections of what our Lord said at the Last Supper, but the actual liturgical usages of the primitive Christian communities, each shaping and developing its own redaction of the tradition. If this is true, as we believe it is, then the New Testament accounts of the Last Supper disclose the first glimmerings of the liturgical life of the Christian communities of the first century.[8]

Thus Hippolytus presents his example only as a model, a suggestion. Still, the formats presented here were kept substantially throughout the ages for nothing in the Church was more conservative than the eucharistic rituals. That is why right up to the present day every Mass contains elements already present in the second century formulas. We might note that because the biblical psalms and canticles were so pervasive, hymn singing did not develop very far in the first centuries. Only in the fourth century men like Paulinus of Nola and the great St. Ambrose would give poems and hymns to the Church. Both East and West shared pretty much the same developments. It was only later in the general separation of East and West that the liturgies became separated. The East generally retained more of the ancient rites and formulas. The West became Latinized, less effusive and open more to Western cultural influences so that to this day there are various rites in the Church among East and West.

As we know many changes in style, ceremony and even vestments have occurred throughout the centuries within the rites. Vestments, for example, gradually became standardized and the clergy began to wear distinctive dress. For the first five centuries the clergy's dress did not differ from that of the laity. St. Augustine dressed like everyone else and his contemporary, St. Ambrose (fifth century) remarked that it was by his charity that people were to recognize a bishop, not by his clothes. Actually the change came in the fifth and sixth centuries. After the barbarian invasions the laity abandoned the long traditional Roman and Oriental dress in favor of the invaders' short clothes. However as this fashion changed the members of the clergy continued to wear the long robes (cassock). Special vestments existed for liturgical ceremonies but our modern church vestments are modeled from the dress of polite Roman society of the fourth and fifth centuries.

There is a certain fascination in seeing how throughout the ages in the West many additions to the Mass have obscured its meaning and purpose. Court and medieval ceremony, especially from France, intruded as is evidenced in the ermine wrap of the bishop, the princely throne, the ring, the kissing, etc. Gradually the priest began to turn his back to the people, the altar was pushed against the wall, the language became unknown (Latin) and physical separations such as the altar rail were erected. Obviously the people's role was effectively reduced to one of spectator. Undoubtedly out of concern for such passive spectators, in the Middle Ages a man named Amalar of Metz worked out in elaborate detail how every movement in the Mass was a presentation of Christ's passion and death. The washing of the fingers was Pilate, the cord around the priest's waist was the cords that bound Christ, the fore-Mass was the Old Testament, the last blessing was Jesus blessing his disciples before his ascension into heaven, etc. All this was well meant but it was erroneous. Such "passion-play" interpretations were a far cry from the intimate meal-sharing of the Last Supper. It would be only a matter of time when the insufficiency of this sort of allegorizing would become apparent. The pristine meaning of the Mass would have to be restored and liturgical renewal become a reality. In our own day when such renewal has been accomplished (though by no means completed) Pope Paul VI in his Apostolic Constitution of April 3, 1969 felt obliged to appeal to the past:

> No one should think, however, that this revision of the Roman Missal has been suddenly accomplished. The progress of liturgical science in the last four centuries has prepared the way. After the Council of Trent, the study of ancient manuscripts in the Vatican library and elsewhere, as Saint Pius X indicated in the apostolic constitution *Quo primum*, helped greatly in the correction of the Roman missal. Since then, however, other ancient sources have been discovered and published, and liturgical formulas of the Eastern Church have been studied. . . ."

POPULAR DEVOTIONS

Besides the official liturgical worship such as baptism and its catechesis and the Eucharist, there were popular devotions as well among the Christians of the early centuries. It was during the fourth century that Lent came into being. Sunday became an official holiday in 325. Christmas began to be celebrated in Rome around the year 336. Other private devotions took their cue from the monks; prayer, fasting, and almsgiving. Perhaps the most prevalent popular devotion was the cult of the martyrs, those who paid the final price of commitment (the word martyr is Greek for "wit-

ness"). Mass was often celebrated near and finally on the
tombs of Christian martyrs. A great deal of the lives-of-the-
saints type of literature grew up. Relics grew in importance
and from the earliest times the pilgrimage became a fixture
of the Christian life, right through the late medieval ages.
The modern mind finds it difficult to appreciate the medieval
pilgrimage to the gravesite or relic of a popular saint. We
cannot fathom that the sincere pilgrim in gazing at the relic
was doing so, not as a tourist, but as a worshiper deeply convinced of the supernatural, the after-life and the intercession
of God's friends. There was a spiritual involvement. Since
the home of Christianity was in Jerusalem this explains the
desire of the Christian to go there, to visit the very spots trod
by Christ himself. This will be a factor in the first Crusades
which had all the earmarks of a great pilgrimage.

THE FERVENT CHURCH

It was inevitable that in its fervor the early Church should
tend to strictness in many ways. A balance always emerged
but not before some Christians went too far, fell into heresy
and split off from the main body of the Church. We shall
see some of these people in the next chapter. But even for
those who did not spin off from the Church a certain strictness was evident in many ways. For example, we have seen
how the monastic movement (the one perfect Eastern contribution taken over by the West) was partly inspired by the
desire to live a more perfect life, free from the cares and distractions of this world. There was a desire to take the Gospels seriously and the fear that this could not be done "in
the world." There were the Donatists in Africa (whom we
shall mention in the next chapter) who felt that any Christian
who lapsed in time of persecution should not be readmitted

to the faith. Tertullian (who became so rigorist that he fell into heresy) was angry with the pope for being lenient with sinners. Some Christians were so scandalized at the story in St. John's Gospel where Jesus forgave the woman caught in adultery that they deleted it from the Scriptures. Yes, fervor to the point of rigorism was an element. There are two areas in particular where rigorism shows up in the Church: confession and celibacy. Let us look at them.

CONFESSION

The early Church was ever conscious not only of sin but that Jesus came to redeem the sinner. Jesus had said, "I have come to call sinners not the just" and even his death-bed legacy was a body "given for you" and blood "shed for the remission of sins." St. Paul said that Jesus' death reconciles man with God. Baptism, of course, was *the* place for repentance and forgiveness. Baptism for the early Christian signified his putting on of the "new man," his total and unanswering dedication to the perfect life as enjoined by the Gospel. The question naturally came up of sins committed after such a definite step as baptism. Penance took care of this. In fact penance was often called the "second baptism" as a graphic description of its role. Usually this penance or "second baptism" was an official community affair involving formal procedures and routine; it was, as we would say today, a canonical procedure. Tertullian and Cyprian mention a period of mortification and prayer before reconciliation to the Church and to the Eucharist.

Yet, the rigor of the early Church was soon apparent. Three sins were held to be capable of being forgiven only once. Actually, in theory any sin could be forgiven "seventy times seven," but this "unicity" (one time only) was a disciplinary thing. The three sins were murder, adultery and idol-atry (apostacy). For the first few centuries these sins could be confessed and forgiven only once as befits (according to the ideals of the times) the fervent Christian. Any Christian who would commit such sins a second time was obviously unfit for the kingdom of God or at least incapable of meeting the demands of the Gospel. Even when St. John Chrysostom and Pope Innocent I in the fourth century tried to be more lenient they were criticized for so doing. Let us here carry the story ahead of our time. The fifth and sixth centuries saw a slight increase in the private confession (as distinct from the canonical public confession) though the Third Synod of Toledo in 589 condemned private confession as an abuse. We owe the private confession to the Irish monks of the seventh and eighth centuries who introduced it to the mainland. By the beginning of the ninth century frequent confession was urged (for example, by the great St. Boniface) and by the end of the ninth century the confession of devotion was added. Needless to say with the introduction of the private confession the strictures on those three sins were lifted, but the existence of such a discipline shows once more the fervor of the early Church. The rigorist attitude showed up also in the very severe penances given, some of which took years or a lifetime to complete. It is no wonder that with the three sins being forgiven only once plus the harsh penances that confession became a death-bed sacrament, something put off to the very end.

CELIBACY

Celibacy has been an issue through the centuries and per-haps never more than in modern times. Yet most people do not realize that the ideal of celibacy is definitely to be found in the Gospels and that the *law* of celibacy (which is another matter) is based squarely on this ideal and the ideals of primitive Christianity. Celibacy therefore is not a medieval addition, but is rooted in Scripture and in the rigorism of the early Church which we are examining here. The ideal came from Jesus himself. It was he who pointed out that his followers who have discovered the hidden treasure of the kingdom of God could not really do otherwise than to leave all things, including marriage, and follow Him. Once the disciple had discovered that kingdom he could not think of going back to married life (Luke 14:26) or bother with mere possessions (Mk 10:21 and Matt 19:21). There are, Jesus said, eunuchs for the sake of the kingdom of God. Not everyone can accept this but for those who can, celibacy is a Gospel imperative. No one summarizes this attitude better than the modern theologian Edward Schillebeeckx:

> Thus the meaning is to love God above everything. The suggestion that whoever belongs to Jesus' group in a special way cannot do other than leave everything and give up married life is an authentic biblical fact, in its essence independent of ancient ideas about man and the world. It can only be explained on the basis of the incalculable inner logic of a total surrender to the kingdom of God, next to which everything else pales by comparison. In the synoptic gospels, "celibacy" is not presented as an abstract idea, not as a requirement imposed from without, not even as a desideratum. Jesus approvingly states a fact of religious psychology: in view of their joy on finding the "hidden pearl" (Mk 4:11) some people cannot do otherwise than live unmarried. This religious experience itself makes them unmarriageable, actually incapable of marriage; their heart is where their treasure is. Paul already thematizes this experience; he sees its inner logic as an ideal towards which all Christians are invited (1 Cor 7:7–8; 28–35).[9]

So far there is no suggestion that there is a legal necessity that all Christians be unmarried. But there is something in the Gospels more basic than any legal statement, namely, that a religious experience of great force becomes, for some people, a condition that makes marriage impossible, not because they despise marriage but because they are so caught up with the Kingdom of God that it demands their undivided allegiance. Again Schillebeeckx reminds us that "the law of celibacy in the Western church is, with all its advantages and disadvantages, only a juridical formulation of the inner logic of a particular religious experience."

EARLY CONFUSION

The early Christians then often practiced continence and those who were married lived as brother and sister. St. Paul himself exclaimed that "given my preference, I should like you to be (unmarried) as I am. . . . I should like you to be free of all worries. The unmarried man is busy with the Lord's affairs, concerned with pleasing the Lord, but the married man is busy with this world's demands and occupied with pleasing his wife. This means he is divided . . ." (1 Cor 7:7 and 28ff). The point is that remaining continent and/or celibate was found in the Gospels and the early Christians took it to heart. One of the less happy by products, however, was that another thought, foreign to the Gospels, entered the picture. It was the old pagan "matter-is-evil" theme which made not only celibacy attractive but marriage evil. All the Church Fathers resisted this interpretation vigorously. In so doing, however, they never quite got rid of the ambivalence they handed on to posterity. Their theme in effect said that marriage indeed was very good (and the world owes them a lot in this regard since they were bucking the pagan trends of the times)—but virginity is better. In fact, the argument arose (again based unmistakably on the Gospels) that baptism itself with its open commitment to Christ implied celibacy. Celibacy was not a question for the cleric, but the ideal for *every* Christian. Again the Fathers tried to keep the balance between upholding marriage and celibacy. Again the point to be emphasized is that all discussions of celibacy, both in the early Church, the medieval Church and the modern Church must begin with the Gospel and the first Christians' awareness of what it meant to surrender all for the sake of the kingdom. Let us quote Scripture scholar Raymond Brown:

> As I have said, I am not going to enter the debate of whether this is *wise* regulation; but I would certainly defend the Church's right to make such a regulation for its own ministry, precisely because the priesthood is heir to an institutional antecedent (presbyter-bishop) as well as to more charismatic antecedents (disciple and apostle). Celibacy is not unrelated to discipleship (it is for the sake of the kingdom of heaven that the challenge to celibacy is issued, Matt 19:12); nor is it unrelated to the apostleship (Paul wishes that the other missionary apostles were unmarried as he is—1 Cor 9:5 with 7:7–8). We find already in the Pastoral Epistles the tendency to introduce regulations about the married status of presbyter-bishops. The regulation of 1 Tim 3:2 that a widow who has remarried cannot be a presbyter-bishop is not really different *in kind* from the later church law that a married man cannot serve as a priest.[10]

FIRST LEGISLATIONS

The rationale behind the requirement of celibacy for clerics is not hard to discover. If the ordinary Christian in virtue of his baptism should have such total commitment as to leave all things (marriage) for the sake of the kingdom, how much more he who by profession as it were is ruler, minister and church official? The Council of Nicaea (to move ahead through the centuries) wanted to make some pronouncement about mandatory celibacy for clerics but hesitated to do so for fear of encouraging the rigorists we mentioned above who were downgrading marriage as evil. What this Council did do in 325 was to forbid marriage *after* one had received an important office in the Church. (Both East and West still follow this prescription.)

EAST AND WEST

Two traditions appeared after this. The Eastern part of the Church held that a man may get married before ordination, but not afterwards. For their higher clergy, the bishops, they still preferred a celibate and to this day for the most part pick their bishops from the celibate monks. The West at first made a law saying that a priest cannot marry after ordination and if he does that marriage is considered invalid. Later the West in the twelfth century made it a law that *in order to be ordained* a man must be celibate. Before this twelfth century law requiring celibacy in order to be ordained the West had unrealistically tried to urge continence on the clergy who were married. That is, after ordination a priest or bishop was urged to live as brother and sister with his wife. This was hardly workable especially during some of the bad periods of the feudal Middle Ages when unworthy men aspired and obtained the episcopacy. It was after that failure that the Second Lateran Council made it obligatory that celibacy was a requirement in order to be ordained. This law in the West has been repeatedly upheld by the Council of Trent in the sixteenth century and the popes of the twentieth century. It has been mentioned at times that the medieval Church wanted a celibate clergy so that clergymen's sons would not inherit Church property. This was certainly one motive given the feudal arrangement of medieval society (as we shall see) but a minor one and definitely not determining. "Anyone who interprets the law of celibacy as an ecclesiastical abuse of power for the benefit of the hierarchical organization, although this did occur in certain areas, makes a caricature of history."[11]

In modern times there have been two developments on the issue of celibacy. One is that Vatican II has been cautious not to offend marriage and the dignity of the married laity. Thus the phrasing concerning celibacy simply says that celibacy makes it "more easy" to give oneself totally to God. In a word, celibacy is not essentially bound up with the priesthood but has a close connection with it. The second is the real issue which is *not,* "Is there any connection between Jesus and celibacy?" for we have seen that there is. The real issue is one of law. Can the Church, should the Church, oblige celibacy by law? Can a freely given charism be legislated? Some would contend that there has not been due emphasis given to the other words of Christ, "Not everyone can accept this"—and what about those who cannot? Must they be denied the priesthood? At the same time celibacy still has a real evangelical meaning and has been rediscovered in modern day Protestantism. Celibacy, no matter how it fares in the future, can never be dismissed as meaningless and still leave the Gospel intact. Again, Father Brown puts the matter well:

> The fact that the Western Catholic Church has demanded celibacy of its priests may also be seen as an application of the principle of discipleship. Of course, the Church knows that in the New Testament celibacy was not *demanded* of

all who followed Jesus or even of the Twelve, but it was held up as an ideal to those who were able to bear it (Matt 19:12, 1 Cor 7:7–9). Since this ideal was held up precisely for the sake of the kingdom of heaven, from a very early period the Church has not deemed it illogical to seek candidates willing to live by the ideal of celibacy among those who want to devote themselves in a special way to promoting the kingdom of heaven. By the law that allows only a celibate clergy the Western Catholic Church has ensured a large scale, public witness of the celibate life. I do not wish to enter here into the complicated and heated debate of whether the law should be continued; but I would contend that, precisely because the witness of celibacy is conspicuously lacking in many other Christian churches, the Roman Catholic Church has an ecumenical duty to the Gospel to continue to bear an *effective* witness on this score. Perhaps this would be possible without a law, but one must admit that it is the law of priestly celibacy that makes it clear that those who accept it are doing so for the sake of Christ and not simply because they prefer to be bachelors. *Some* of the forms of optional celibacy being proposed would soon lead to obscuring the vocational character of celibacy and would reduce it to a personal idiosyncrasy.[12]

In other words, no matter how celibacy is decided on as a mandatory *law* for the clergyman, it still retains its pristine origins in the Gospel and is an important *ideal* in witnessing to Christianity.[13]

THE IDEAL OF THE PRIMITIVE CHURCH

One of the most enduring aspects of fervor in the early Church is the splinter group. This is the group, whether it remains within the Church or breaks off from it, which seeks a firmer, more basic Christianity. Some of these groups have remained within the Church, such as the monks and religious orders; others have broken off, such as the early heretics, the

Montanists and Donatists. The noteworthy thing, however, is that there exists almost a "tradition" of radical groups (in the sense of "root" Christianity) up to the present day. And mostly the radicalism is some aspect of a rigorous fervor, an imitation of the demands of the early Church. As a matter of fact there is a loose term called the "Believers Church" which maintains that it was really the heretics who have maintained Christianity in its pristine purity throughout the centuries; that especially after Constantine (whom we shall meet in the next chapter), when the Roman Empire and the Christian religion joined, Christianity got off course. It was the small groups, considered heretical by the larger (political-religious) body which kept the candle of the primitive Church lit. In fact as we shall see in the chapter on the Reformation the main thrust of such "heretics" was to look backward, to restore what they considered the virtues of the primitive Church. Especially in the centuries preceding the sixteenth century Reformation there was a plethora of sects with strange sounding names: Albigenses, Waldenses, Manicheans, Cathars, Humiliati, the Poor Men of Lyons, Publicans, Henricians, Leonists, Varini, Brethren of the Free Spirit, Lollards, Picards, Fraticelli, Anabaptists, Quakers, Moravians, Hutterites, the Plymouth Brethren, Mennonites, Disciples of Christ, Methodists, etc. to name a few. All would claim (along with the major Reform bodies) that Roman Catholicism and even Protestantism had obscured the basic primitive Church as founded by Christ and that their particular denomination represented a return to that ideal or at least a survival of the original fervent church of apostolic times.

Actually there is a certain myth about the primitive Church in that the Reformers of the sixteenth century and the Believers Church groups tended to idealize the picture.

For example, one has only to read Paul's first epistle to the Corinthians alone to find that the early Christian church-communities contained factions, jealousies, hatred, backbiting, uncharity, etc. Paul scolds the Corinthians for being divided into factions over him and a man named Appolos, for putting up with one of their congregation who entered an incestuous marriage, for relapsing into impurity and so on. He gives many practical and disciplinary directives all indicating that the pristine Church was made up of human beings still in need of redemption.

A CHURCH OF CHARISMS

It is also worth noting that in time of stress one or other charismatic aspect of the primitive Church would be picked up once more. As we shall see in this book, for example, when certain Protestants got tired of all the sterile theological wrangling and fighting with the Catholics and other Protestants, they retreated into pietism, a movement centering on the emotions and feelings. The Quakers were one of those movements with their emphasis on the "inner spirit" and prophesying. The Moravians represented a group which wanted to go back to the communistic type of communal Christian living as described in the *Acts of the Apostles.* The Amish in our country are a group of Moravians who live in New Testament simplicity and represent a return to primitivism. The cry for many such groups was for the simplicity, common living, sharing and the charisma they found in the New Testament.

In the early 1970s one of the growing phenomenon of a return to some of the charisms of the early Church is the Pentecostal movement among Roman Catholics. In fact, it is called a Charismatic Renewal and puts the emphasis on a deep experience of the Holy Spirit in the lives of its members. There is a tendency to emotionalism, the practice of prophesying and the speaking in tongues—charisma of the New Testament. Pentecostalism in the United States started in the spring of 1967 and later that spring about sixty persons gathered at Notre Dame for a meeting. In 1968 their number grew to 150; in 1969 to 450; in 1970 to 1,400 and at the meeting at Notre Dame, Indiana in 1972 there were some 11,500 participants. The important point for us in these opening chapters of the book is to note how sensitive the leaders of the Pentecostal Movement of the 1970s are to the dangers that lurked in similar movements in the early Church. Three main problems which bedeviled the groups then are precisely the very problems that the leadership warns against in modern times: emotionalism, anti-intellectualism and elitism (which implies splintering off). The affinity to the early Church and particularly to the gifts of prophesying and speaking in tongues among Pentecostals is unmistakable. The simple point we wish to make here is that no one can appreciate and assess the various "Believers Churches" or religious movements within the Church without knowing something of the early Church and its experiences.

We must leave the early Church, its structures, ministries and practices. The Apostles are dead, the church-communities are spread all over Asia and Europe and the persecutions are reviving in full vigor. Still, organization has been improved and the Church has moved ahead and gained in strength and numbers. In fact, very shortly a new age is approaching for the Church: a day of liberty, freedom and theological refinement. The age of Constantine is at hand and to this we must turn in the next chapter.

NOTES

1. Edward P. Echlin, S.J. *The Deacon in the Church*, p. 16. Alba House, Staten Island, N.Y. 1971. I am indebted for most of this section to this small but excellent book.
2. *Ibid.*, p. 131.
3. The Anglican Church has ordained two women as deaconesses. Their Board of Bishops, however, has (so far) turned down the proposal to ordain them to the priesthood. The Jewish faith has its first woman rabbi.
4. Notice that the process in selecting the deacons was democratic, the work of the entire community. Yet after the election of the deacons they were "appointed" and consecrated into their office by the disciples. Thus there is evidence "of an apostolic office (or bishop) who somehow confirms or ratifies the action of the people. The whole episode indicates how impossible it is to categorize the early Church into any single pattern or structure." Rogness, *op. cit.* p. 83.
5. We might mention here, perhaps to the surprise of some Catholics, that government in the Church need not necessarily be centered in the bishops. They were given the spiritual mission to teach and sanctify (Matt 28:18), not to govern. Many early bishops like Augustine and Cyprian did not govern. That was done by some other body. It could be today—or could come about—that decisions about schools, parish boundaries, finances, etc. be made by people other than bishops (as in some places parish councils or pastoral councils do). The centralization of Church government in the hands of the episcopacy is neither scriptural nor necessary. It just turned out that way.
6. Thomas F. O'Meara, "Emergence and Decline of Popular Voice in the Selection of Bishops", p. 27 in the book *The Choosing of Bishops*, editor, William W. Bassett. The Canon Law Society of America. 1971.
7. However, by the beginning of the third century a milestone was reached: buildings are specifically set aside for Christian worship. One such church (built during a relatively peaceful time between persecutions) has been found. It is called the Dura Europos and was built before 256. It is an ordinary house transformed into a church.
8. Joseph A. Jungman, S.J. *The Early Liturgy*, p. 37. Notre Dame Press, Notre Dame, Indiana, 1959.

9. E. Schillebeeckx, *Celibacy*, pp. 24, 25. Sheed and Ward, New York. 1968.
10. Raymond E. Brown, S.S. *op. cit.*, p. 37.
11. E. Schillebeeckx, *op. cit.*, p. 61.
12. Brown, *op. cit.*, p. 25, 26.
13. Celibacy is not the main problem of the modern clergy in spite of considerable publicity. The recent National Research Center study on the American priesthood ranked celibacy way down on the list of serious problems. Cf. Andrew Greeley, "After the Synod" in *America*, Nov. 20, 1971. p. 424.

We have not touched on arguments on how celibacy has been abused. Garry Wills says, "Priests are not more accessible than other men, but less—at both the literal and the symbolic level. Most Catholics have easier access to their (married) doctor than to their (unmarried) pastor. I can more easily talk to my Senator than to my bishop. Many things explain this remoteness, but the most obvious explanation takes the form of a vicious circle: The priest (it is said) should remain celibate to be less remote; and then a remote life style is built around him to keep him celibate. . . . Where priests are concerned, we were told that having no family would make a man more open and caring. If that were true, then we should require celibacy from the President. . . . The married person is allowed sex . . . the better way is that of the priest, who is 'above all that'. . . . Religious celibacy, to be justified at all, must be a radical, exceptional, exceedingly private choice related to crisis. To make of it a taming institutional device is to mock the spirit of freedom for which it should stand. . . ."

His article ("Sex and the Single Priest" *Playboy*, July, 1972, p. 99 ff.) is provocative and summarizes well the liberal questioning of celibacy in the 1970s, though it misses some of the basic theological focus presented in this chapter.

V

The Fight for Orthodoxy

CONSTANTINE

Politically, during the third and fourth centuries the Roman Empire was going through severe crisis. There were civil wars as men vied for the imperial power. It became so that the army wound up making and breaking emperors. From 217 to 253 there were twelve emperors and not one of them died a natural death. After 253 it is difficult to count the emperors enthroned and deposed. This internal power problem was certainly a great source of weakness. There was, however, another source of weakness, an external problem which we shall talk about in the next chapter: the constant pressure on the empire's borders. Applying this pressure were the great German barbarian hordes. We might mention also the chronic financial chaos of the empire and problems of inflation and famine.

Finally, in the year 303 the emperor Diocletian decided on a plan to help stabilize the empire. He divided the vast empire into two sections, the East and the West. Each section was to be administered by a senior emperor assisted by a junior emperor who had the right of succession. This, Diocletian hoped, would prevent the frightful and enervating infighting over the throne. To further assist this plan, Diocletian voluntarily resigned and four men took his place: the senior emperor, Constantius Chlorus and his junior partner, Serverus, in the West and Galerius and his junior partner, Maximinus, in the East. Unfortunately upon the death of Constantius Chlorus the plan broke down. His son Constantine, usurped the power and Serverus, the rightful successor, was killed.

In the midst of all this political maneuvering Constantine startled the whole world by becoming a member of the minority sect of Christianity. Now a Christian (though as was the custom he remained unbaptized till his deathbed[1]) he reputedly saw a vision over the Milvian bridge where he was to meet his rival. The vision, according to Eusebius who was writing some twenty-five years later, was a cross in the sky with the words around it saying, "In this sign you will conquer." Constantine had this sign painted on his shields and he defeated his rival thus becoming sole emperor of the West. One of his first acts was to give Christianity freedom by putting it on an equal footing with paganism. Galerius did the same in the East. Finally in 324 Constantine became the sole emperor of both East and West.

Constantine, as we said, gave to Christianity the equal status enjoyed by the pagan cults. Now Christians could worship publicly and their priests were also exempt from civic duties. Constantine could and would go no further than this for the vast majority of his subjects were still pagan and he had no intention of alienating them. To Christians this was enough. Now they were free. Persecution would be no more (except for a brief one under Julian). The emperor himself was one of them. Soon, under the emperor Theodosius I, Christianity would become the state religion and paganism would be outlawed.

CHURCH AND STATE

We must take time here to point out the implications of what it meant for Christianity to be free and later to become the state religion. It meant that from the beginning of its full freedom Christianity was allied with the empire. It meant that a tradition was started which held that Christianity best flourished under the protection of the empire; that, indeed, the empire and the emperor were really divinely appointed to rule and to render that protection. The thousand year union of the Christian State and Christian Church had its origin here. The beginnings of the state-church theory were laid at this time. The Church needed the empire and the empire needed the Church. They were partners divinely ordered to run the world. At least this became the predominant theory in the West. The partnership was not like the East where the emperor ran the Church. In the West any attempts to do this were met with resistance. In fact the struggle to keep the state in its place would form a long, long conflict in the church of the Middle Ages. No, the partnership was one of separate entities, the Church being primary in the spiritual realm and to that extent superior to the state; the state having charge of the political realm but always within the strictures of Christian morality as interpreted by the Church.

We cannot fault the early Christians who looked upon the church-state union this way. Having just emerged from some two hundred and fifty years of persecution and semi-terror it would be quite understandable that they would look upon Constantine and the empire as their saviors. It was a very easy step to feel in the afterglow of release and freedom that the empire and the Church were made for each other. We can sympathize with the bishop who later attended the Council of Nicaea. As he walked down the long aisle in between scores of Roman soldiers to take his place beside the emperor himself, he rightfully wondered if the millennium had arrived. The scars of persecution were still on his body. Could he be blamed for his thoughts? Later on could even the great Augustine be blamed if he said that the empire was divinely ordained for the Church? Indeed, the alliance from the start was a "natural" one.[2]

It was to turn out not to be always the best alliance, but that is another chapter. Meanwhile in the years ahead another very logical result occurred from the empire's liberation of the Church. The Church took over the Roman organization genius and can be called from this point on the Roman Catholic Church. It acquired all of the trappings: the large buildings, the court ceremonial, the discipline. The Church, too, would have an absolute ruler, the pope, and a group of bishops elected by the people. Since these bishops were officially celibate they could not make an issue of hereditary power so that that evil was averted. Yet they had to be constantly renewed by election by the people in a most democratic process. On the other hand the bishops exercised their power, not in the name of the people, but in the name of God. The point is that the Church was thus enabled to combine the absolutism of a divine right monarch built upon a foundation of democracy and representative government.

Later, as the emperors abandoned the West for the new capital at Constantinople, a vacuum was left at the ancient capital of Rome. More and more it was filled by the pope thus enabling ancient Rome to become the religious capital of the new religion. Bishops freely ruled over their subjects and indeed the emperor freely allowed this. The bishops thereby became a kind of privileged class. In fact the bishops in the chief towns of the empire came to be known as archbishops and those in the big cities, such as Antioch, Alexandria, Constantinople, Rome, were known as patriarchs. The Roman patriarch was preeminent for he could claim descent from Peter who died in Rome. By the fourth century several councils gave the Church the right to legislate in its own affairs and run and own its own property. This was accepted by the emperor and the Church's rights became a part of the public law of the empire. We see here also the beginnings of two separate jurisdictions and systems of penalties. In the future, emperor and pope would clash over clerical immunities. Nevertheless, having its own laws, the Church was truly becoming a separate power, co-equal in its spiritual realm to the empire in its political realm. The theory of the two swords, that is, the spiritual and temporal powers, working closely together, was formed.

> Christianity thus became the official, and gradually also the normal, religion of the Roman Empire. The effect on the Church was mainly bad. As converts came in no longer by conviction, but for interested motives or merely by inertia, the spiritual and moral fervor of the Church inevitably waned. To the empire the official change of religion made little difference: the old corruption and oppression of the masses by officials and landlords went on unabated, and the last remnants of public spirit faded away. Nor is this surprising for the object of the Church was not to reform the empire but to save souls. To contemporary Christian thought the things of this world were of little moment, and the best Christian minds preferred not to touch the pitch of public life lest they be defiled. Men of high conviction and character became bishops or hermits, and government was left in the main to careerists.

> Nevertheless, to the future of Christianity its official adoption by the empire was momentous, for Christianity thus acquired the prestige and glamor of the Roman name; it

became synonymous with that ancient civilization whose grandiose buildings, stately ceremonial, luxurious life and ordered discipline fascinated the uncouth barbarians of the north. . . .[3]

COUNCIL OF NICAEA

All that we have just said was to develop in the near future. For the time being we return to Constantine. It is likely that in Christianity he perceived the cement of unity for his vast empire. In this he was to be disappointed. Christianity, he discovered, was often divided within itself. The first infighting he ran into was the Donatist heresy. It arose this way. In previous persecutions some Christians had lapsed from the faith. Some even handed over the Scriptures to be burned. There were those who were willing to readmit the former to the faith but not the latter. The bishop of Carthage opposed such rigorists led by a certain Donatus. This controversy plus the chronic political rivalries among the Africans aggravated the situation. The matter was brought to Constantine and he in turn referred it to the pope who decided against the Donatists. They refused to submit, so Constantine called the local council of Arles which in 314 also condemned the Donatists. They still rejected the condemnation. Violence broke out and the Donatists stayed on to plague the Church in Africa for a long time.

Right after this the most disastrous heresy in the early Church broke out: Arianism. It too began in Africa, in Alexandria. Arius held that Christ was merely a creature. His opponent, Athanasius (a deacon at the time) held that Christ was more. He was the Son of God and existed as such from all eternity. Constantine, fresh from the intrigues of the Donatist controversy, was horrified at the prospect of another schism within the Christianity he had hoped would bind the empire. At last, he took a step which would become a precedent for many ages: he decided to settle the matter by consensus. He would call a world-wide council. Thus he sent a circular letter to all of the bishops:

> That there is nothing more precious in my eyes than religion is, I think, clear to all. Whereas it was previously settled that the congress of bishops should be at Ancyra or Galatia, it has now been decided for many reasons that it should meet in the city of Nicaea in Bithynia . . . in order that I may be near to watch and take part in the proceedings. I therefore inform you, beloved brethren, that I wish you all to meet as soon as possible in the above-mentioned city of Nicaea. . . .

There was not an overwhelming response to the emperor's letter. The pope excused himself on the grounds of poor health and old age but sent two deacons to represent him. Bishops from both East and West did come, however, and so in 325 the first ecumenical Council of the Church, the Council of Nicaea, was held. Constantine took an active part in the proceedings and no doubt his royal presence stifled some freedom of discussion. Nevertheless, the Council of Nicaea pronounced against Arius and adopted the word "consubstantial" to denote the two Persons of Father and Son sharing the one divine nature of the Godhead. It was as a matter of fact the word proposed by Constantine himself (prompted by his Spanish bishop-advisor) and the formula of the Trinity was on its way to being fixed. The Nicene creed containing the controverted word pleased neither the Orthodox party nor the Arian party but no one dared to tamper with it until after the emperor's death. Arius was banished by Constantine from the empire. Here for the first time we have the state inflicting a civil punishment on a

Church condemned heretic. This was the foreshadowing of the various inquisitions of the Middle Ages.

Other pertinent matters were settled at Nicaea. For example, the Council decreed that bishops must be co-consecrated by at least three bishops (as we have seen in the last chapter). Bishops and clergy were not to wander around the continents but to stay in their own sees. The practice of kneeling at prayer on Sundays and during the time between Easter and Pentecost was condemned. This makes the modern Catholic wonder, but he should recall that the Eastern position of prayer is standing. Kneeling was condemned, then tolerated and then, in the West, became the normal praying position. Bishops, priests and deacons were not to have female companions to keep house for them unless they were relatives. Here we see another indication of the early celibacy stance the Church adopted. However, as we have seen, another motion at the Council provided that if a man were already a married priest he did not have to separate from his wife (a motion to the contrary was voted down). Instead, an old rule was kept; a man could marry before ordination but he could not marry after ordination. Also, at this Council the date of Easter was fixed for there had been much controversy over it. Once more, Constantine set the tone for antisemitism by declaring, "It seems unworthy to calculate this most holy feast (Easter) according to the customs of the Jews who, having stained their hands with lawless crime, are naturally, in their foulness, blind in soul."

CHRISTIAN INTOLERANCE

In the year 330 Constantine made a momentous political decision. He transferred his capital from Rome to the old town of Byzantium in the East. He renamed it Constantinople and rebuilt it. It took five and a half years to complete. He filled it with grand buildings. Monasteries and convents were founded here and art, music and architecture flourished. In a word, a whole new civilization emerged from Constantinople, the Byzantine Empire, a combination of the West and the Orient. The vacancy at Rome was quickly filled by its bishop, the pope, to whom the people turned for leadership and assistance. Constantine died in 337, having been baptized by an Arian bishop on his deathbed. His empire was divided between his two sons one of whom supported the Orthodox creed and another the Arian creed. Generally, it turned out that the West was Orthodox and the East Arian, a fact worth mentioning as one more facet in a rivalry which one day would split them. In any case, the situation at this time was similar to the situation in Germany at the time of the Reformation. Whoever was the prince, the people had to accept his religion. Thus, depending on who was predominant, Orthodox and Arian leaders were banished and restored according to the views of the prevailing emperor.

This sort of religious rivalry was settled in a way that startled both sides. In 361 the emperor Julian succeeded to the throne. He was a mystical type, favorable to religion but disenchanted with Christianity for its harrassment of the pagans. He therefore restored paganism, persecuted the Christians and only his death in 363 brought relief. He was succeeded by Theodosius I, the emperor who not only restored Christianity but made it the official religion of the empire. The Church naturally began to grow stronger under such auspices. The clergy were gathering privileges, monasticism was growing. Ancient philosophers were being bent to the service of the Church and intolerance of the pagan was growing. We have already taken note how pagan temples were sacked and how being a pagan or denying the Trinity were punishable by death. Not all Christians were pleased with this of course. Men like St. Hilary refused to use force against the pagan but preferred reason. His approach to the pagan in his writings was to foreshadow the great medieval scholastic tomes. Hilary, however, was the exception. More common was the attitude of the great St. Augustine who appealed to the political arm to suppress heresy. In fact, Augustine would refine the church-state relations by proclaiming in his famous *City of God* the superiority of the Church over the state. (By stressing the Church's spiritual foundation he did the Church a great service: when the barbarian invasions which occurred in his lifetime shook the old Roman Empire to its foundations, the Church did not topple with it.)

FOUR MORE COUNCILS

Since the Arian controversy was still raging, Theodosius called another council, the second ecumenical Council of Constantinople in 381. (We notice that the first eight ecumenical councils were called by the Byzantine emperors who would often treat the pope like a court official.) Nicaea's creed was reaffirmed. If this Council hopefully settled the Arian question it raised others. One which was to prove mischievous over the ages concerned the see of Constantinople. The Council gave to the bishop of that see a new prestige based on the fact that it was now also the imperial city. After the bishop of Rome, the Council said, the bishop of Constantinople was to rank next. This was a dangerous step in a growing web of ecclesiastical rivalries. Already, for example, there were hard feelings between the centers of Antioch and Alexandria which represented different schools of theology. Arius was an Alexandrian and it was an embarrassment for that city to have him condemned by two Councils. When the see of Constantinople was vacant twice an

Alexandrian candidate was set aside in favor of the recent incumbent, St. John Chrysostom, who was deposed by a series of intrigues. This sort of jealousy among the cities gives the clue to the future problem caused by the Council's nomination of Constantinople as the second see of importance. It would not be long before that city sought a primacy over all the Eastern sees. It would not be long before there was a rivalry with Rome itself and eventually a split with it.

More major heresies and more councils were in the offing. The issues were as confusing as they were often symptomatic of factional rivalries mentioned above. Still, on the benefit side was a growing unfolding of the meaning of what Christ said and did and who he was. These great Councils performed a great negative service. They did not exhaust all the meanings of the Christian religion nor did they set Christian belief into one final, everlasting formula. They did not pretend that they said all there was to say about Christ. They only said that whatever he is and whoever he is and whatever he did and whatever his life meant, it is *not* what the heretics claim. What Christ meant would have to be unfolded for ages to come and every age would have its insight. The Councils' definitions were negative guides to what Christ did not mean, whatever else he meant. Some later churchmen would try to use the formulas of a council like that of Chalcedon as positive statements; that is, that the statements contained the last accurate word on revelation concerning Christ: that all things must reflect such statements. They failed to understand them, as we said, as negative guides in the search for fuller truth. Scripture scholar John McKenzie expresses the idea:

> In these early heresies, the church acted as teacher rather than proclaimer. . . . Had heretics not introduced the language of Greek philosophy to define the content of their belief, the church would not have had to employ the same lan-

guage to define Catholic belief. . . . The church then became aware that, if this belief is to be safeguarded, other propositions not directly belonging to belief must also be safeguarded. . . . Thus in the Christological and Trinitarian controversies of the fourth and fifth centuries, the simple statement of belief that Jesus is the Son of God was not enough; the church also arrived at fairly precise definitions of nature, substance, and person, which permitted it to formulate its Christological and Trinitarian beliefs as belief that God is three persons subsisting in one nature. Was it necessary that belief be formulated in these terms? Absolutely speaking, it would seem that it was not, but one can rarely speak absolutely in history and cover all the facts. So many erroneous ways of stating belief appeared that the church settled on a single formula which would remove the errors which it knew. The formula would not necessarily protect it against errors which it did not know.[4]

The issue which provoked the Church's third ecumenical Council of Ephesus centered around the bishop of Constantinople, Nestorius. This man wanted to know *how* Jesus was at once human and divine. His answer to this question was that there were two persons in Christ (as against the Orthodox teaching that there was only one). A logical conclusion was that therefore Mary was not the Mother of God, only the human person. Bishop Cyril of Alexandria was ready to take up the fight. We must notice that he was bishop of Alexandria and as such a rival to the Antiochene school of thought represented at Constantinople. Cyril sent protests to the pope who condemned Nestorius and who asked Cyril to receive his submission. Cyril went beyond the papal instruction. Instead he drew up a series of twelve propositions which Nestorius must sign. This would hardly be likely since the propositions were written in distinct Alexandrian terminology which no bishop of Constantinople could sign. It would be like General Motors signing a safety promise couched in the slogans of Ford. So Nestorius appealed to the emperor while the twelve propositions made the rounds stirring up all kinds of controversy.

In due time the Council of Ephesus was called in 431 and it was a network of intrigues and complications. The pope's delegates were late in coming and Cyril opened the Council anyway. The members of the Antioch school were delayed, and so forth. Anyway, the Council condemned and deposed Nestorius. Then when the people from Antioch arrived they denounced the Council. The emperor arrested Cyril and Nestorius both and wound up restoring Cyril and banishing Nestorius. The hard feelings between Alexandria and Antioch were aggravated.

COUNCIL OF CHALCEDON

If Nestorious claimed that Christ had two persons since he had two natures another heresy appeared, that of Monophysitism, which taught that Christ had but one nature (not two, human and divine, as the Church taught). Again, the issues involved were argued from opposite sides by the two schools of Alexandria and Antioch. It was an involved situation with much conflict of personalities, intrigue, deposition, imprisonment and the interference of the emperor. Finally in 451 the fourth ecumenical Council of Chalcedon was called and the heresy condemned with a definition of faith footnoted by the pope.

At the Council of Chalcedon other matters were discussed. One was a protest of imperial interference in Church affairs—a kind of first official sally in the general warfare between Church and state that lay in the future. Another decision was the reaffirmation of the primacy of honor for the see of Constantinople after Rome. This brought protests from the pope,

Leo the Great.[5] One of the more far reaching results from Chalcedon was not any doctrinal pronouncement but an emotional reaction. Once more the school of Alexandria met defeat at the hands of a Council. The clergy and the monks were so upset that they rallied to the side of their bishops and wound up denouncing the whole Council of Chalcedon. They elected heretical Monophysite bishops to their sees who were only expelled by imperial troops.

The East was thus more divided than ever along religious lines. (The West, as we shall see in the next chapter was too busy with the barbarian invasions.) As usual every emperor was desirous of healing such divisions which were so politically enervating. As usual that faction which had its own emperor dominated (and persecuted) all others thus adding to religious chaos. Thus, for example, in 477 a pro-Monophysite emperor came to the throne. In his two year reign every bishop had to sign a new formula of faith and condemn Chalcedon. So it would go. Every new emperor had his own once-and-for-all formula designed to bring harmony but which succeeded only in promoting division.

The fifth ecumenical Council of the Church (the second Council of Constantinople) met in 553 as another attempt to heal the split caused by the Monophysite heresy. It was called by the great emperor Justinian, the last of the Latin-speaking rulers. This was a strange council. It decided that, to clear the air once and for all, a solemn condemnation should be made against all those theologians who were friendly to Nestorius and his teachings. Of course, all such theologians and Nestorius himself were dead but this was to be a posthumous condemnation. The only problem was that certain theologians were involved who also upheld the decisions of Chalcedon. It is not difficult to understand the uproar, street-fighting and revolt caused by this approach.

Even the dissenting pope at this point was kidnapped by Justinian (who kept him prisoner for ten years) and only later would this old man, past his eighties, yield to the plan of posthumous condemnations.

After Justinian's death the empire went into political decline. Some fifty years later a new emperor regained some of the prestige, but in striving for unity he ran once more into deep religious divisions—divisions more intolerable than ever in the light of the new Moslem power on the horizon. Once more a new plan was put forth to reconcile religious differences. Once more the plan involved another formula which not only contained the old Monophysite heresy but gave birth to a new one, Monothelism, which held that there was one will (a "unity of wills") in Christ. The emperor accepted the formula and so did the Monophysites. Unfortunately, when this formula was presented to Pope Honorius I (d. 638) he missed the point and in essence agreed with the heretical statement. Naturally his approval helped spread the new heresy of Monothelism. Later the mistake became apparent and then Rome fought the heresy vigorously. Subsequent popes would explain that Honorius had really given approval only to the orthodox parts of the formula and that, besides (as later apologists would say), he gave his approval only as a private person, not as pope for all the Church. A new emperor gave his formula that said let all divisions stand as they were. For this he was condemned by Pope Martin I. The emperor's reaction was to have the pope arrested and imprisoned. Martin finally died in exile.

The sixth ecumenical Council (the third Council of Constantinople) was held in 680. This Council once more gave full affirmation to Chalcedon and condemned all the heretics against orthodoxy. It went even further. It condemned Pope Honorius himself for his failure to understand the formula he approved which spread the heresy of Monothelism. This whole incident of Pope Honorius and the council's condemnation would provide much grist for the Reformers' mill in the sixteenth century. It would be used by opponents against papal infallibility at Vatican I and would be cited by Catholic theologian, Hans Kung, in modern times in his book, *Infallibility? An Inquiry*. However, it is important to know that "The reply of Honorius provided matter for controversy both then and thereafter, but now there is a measure of agreement that he failed to recognize the theological significance of the proposal. . . ."[6]

EAST AND WEST

Before we close this chapter with its maze of councils, intrigues and divisions we must take note of a few points mentioned briefly before. First of all, there was Justinian (d. 565). He would not be noteworthy for his ecclesiastical dealings. His fame would rest on his great restoration of the Roman Empire. Barbarians had overrun much of it in the West and he pushed them back (for the time being) to their original boundaries. His representative ruled in the West at Ravenna in Italy which to this day gives evidence of the great churches and Oriental style with which these Western representatives embellished it. He was also the one who authored the famous Justinian Code of laws which both Church and state would imitate for a long time. With Justinian the East, already associated with the emperor, would become tied to him. Church and state were closely joined. The emperor controlled the election of the patriarch of Constantinople. He sanctioned Church councils. It was characteristic both of Justinian's genius and his union with the

Church that he rebuilt the magnificent church of Santa Sophia in 538.[7] Justinian meted out penalties to heretics, fostered missionary activity and nominated all the bishops, excepting Rome's. Still, he did not scruple, as we have seen, to use the pope for his own ends even while he admitted his primacy.

With such activities as Justinian's plus the fact that the capital of the empire was now in the East, there grew up a natural anti-Roman feeling. Roman territory had been abandoned by the emperors and was being overrun by the barbarians. In a short time there was an obvious difference between the barbarized Rome and the splendid cosmopolitan city of Constantinople. It is no wonder that the East was showing signs of independence from the West and that the see of Constantinople was declared by several councils to come immediately after that of Rome. The Eastern Church even used as the official tongue the Greek language rather than the Latin which was as indicative as anything of its independence from Rome and the West.

We must also repeat that after Justinian the empire went into decay. The barbarians repossessed many of the territories wrested from them by Justinian. Then the greatest of all blows to Europe occurred: the rise of Moslem power and the Moslem invasions. The Moslems quickly overran Syria, Palestine, Egypt, Spain and Armenia. Even southern Italy and Sicily would fall into their hands. In 718 they would unsuccessfully attack Constantinople itself and this city would withstand them for six centuries. Ironically, the reduced eastern Byzantine empire would transfer its ancient Greek culture to the Moslems and they in turn some day would transmit it to the West by way of their conquests in Spain. That culture would be the basis for the re-birth of the West after centuries of isolation caused by the iron grip of the Moslems. Meanwhile, we must return to the end of Constantine's era, to the great invasion poised on the border of the empire.

NOTES

1. It was usual to defer baptism. On the other hand, Constantine had other reasons to defer his official commitment. His crimes included putting to death his father-in-law, three brothers-in-law, his eldest son and his wife.
2. We mentioned in the last chapter that the "Believers' Church" or Free Church people would proclaim that a "fall of the Church" occurred when Constantine established Christianity as the religion of the Roman Empire. Their movement represents a return to the pristine, apostolic, pre-Constantine Church of Christ.
3. A. M. M. Jones, *op. cit.*, p. 206, 207.
4. John L. McKenzie, S.J., *The Roman Catholic Church*, pp. 201, 202. Holt, Rinehart, Winston, New York. 1969.
5. We point out here that Leo did not have the exclusive title of pope (*papa*, father), for it was a title applied to other bishops and even priests. It took several centuries for it to be reserved only for the Holy Father. Nevertheless, it was through Leo that the basis of papal supremacy became explicit and succeeding popes would look to Leo to bolster their claims.
6. Knowles and Obolensky, *The Christian Centuries: the Middle Ages*, Vol. II, p. 106.
7. This great church remains the high point of the Byzantine style. It took ten thousand men five years to build it and it cost, in modern terms, some 134 million dollars to erect.

VI

Chaos and Consolidation

THE CHURCH IN THE WEST

The period of the early Church is over. We now come to the interesting evolution of the Church from its original loosely-knit church-communities into a strong, centralized organization. In the next three chapters we shall trace how this happened, how the strands of Church and state became so interwoven that it formed one cloth called Christendom. Since this process took place in the West we must begin there.

We have seen that with the emperors Constantine and Theodosius Christianity moved from repression to toleration to privilege. It was now the official religion of the empire. The faithful no longer met in secret assembly but now took possession of the old pagan temples and built new ones of their own. During the reign of Pope Sylvester I the great basilicas of St. John Latern, Santa Croce and St. Peter's were begun. St. John Latern's Church, really an enlargement of one of the huge halls of the palace of the Laterani family, was presented to the pope by Constantine in 311. It thus became Christianity's first church and to this day it carries these words inscribed on its front, "The Mother and Head of all the churches in the city of Rome and in all the world."

Privileges were given to the clergy. They were excused from certain civic duties and church officials were to be tried in church rather than civil courts. As we noted previously the Church was enabled to receive grants of money and land and in time many noblemen and kings would give great grants of land making the Church Europe's greatest landowner. The bishops already established in many towns became in effect representatives of the emperor also.

The bishop of Rome already claimed a primacy of honor and privilege as successor to the seat of Peter, but there were other bishops, the patriarchs, who claimed prestige as well though in second place to Rome. The emperor was at the East with a subordinate emperor in the West residing at Ravenna. Several councils had been held. The worship of the Church continued to center around the Eucharistic Meal. Further, we should notice that most Church activity was taking place in the East. The reasons for this are obvious. First of all the Christian religion started in the East. Secondly the East was the seat of the emperor. Thirdly, Christianity was simply not that entrenched in the West. Gaul, Spain, Italy and Africa could be considered as having Christian settlements in the big cities but the rest of Europe and beyond was pagan.

Even at that one of the two areas, Africa, was being racked by controversy. The Donatist heresy was taking place there. This was the heresy which said the validity of the sacraments depended on the state of the soul of the person who administered them. Some bishops and priests had concealed or even come close to denying their faith during some of the Roman persecutions. It was held by the Donatists that if such men administered the sacraments, these sacraments were invalid.[1] The orthodox Catholic view was (and is) that the sacraments do not depend on the sanctity of the minister who gives them. In any case, in Africa rival Donatist bishops were in every city causing confusion and inciting division in the Church. The one opponent against this heresy was the great St. Augustine. He was to be the greatest single influence in the Church for a thousand years. By his defense of the Catholic faith he gave a decided Latin thrust to Christianity (as opposed to the so far predominant Greek thought and writings) and put Latin or Western Christianity on a footing of respectability.

We might mention that Augustine also waged successful war against another troublesome heresy of the time, Pelagianism, which held that man could attain salvation by his own unaided efforts. It was Augustine's contemporary and the one who baptized him, St. Ambrose, bishop of Milan, Italy, who gave another tone to Western Christianity. He was the one who put the emperor in his place (at one time, the emperors resided in Milan) and taught that the emperors were not above the Church. The emperor, Theodosius I had killed seven thousand people in revenge for an uprising. When he went to Ambrose's church for Mass Ambrose refused to celebrate in his presence. The emperor had to do penance and Ambrose set the tone, as it were, for future Western defenses against the encroachments of the state. Another contemporary was St. Jerome the irascible and learned man who translated the Bible into Latin for the West.

Such was the West. Mostly pagan, yet honeycombed with Christian communities, harassed with some heresies, yet producing some men of genius who would give prestige and foundation to Christianity when it was ready to spread there. All the others, what about them? All those who were not Christian in the populous and prestigious East or in the insignificant West were considered to be rude and crude rustics (Latin: *paganus*) or pagans. They were not members of the

Church and therefore they were considered not to be members of society since the Church and the Roman Empire by this time were coterminous. But it was precisely some of these foreign "rustics" who were about to overthrow the Roman Empire in the West and almost the Church itself.

BARBARIAN INVASIONS

On the outskirts of the old Roman Empire the rustic barbarians had been hovering for centuries. As long as the empire remained strong and the Roman armies patrolled the borders and great fortifications were erected the barbarians were deterred from too much activity. However, as the centuries went on and the power of the empire waned the Germanic barbarians increased their contacts. An emperor like Julian, in 358 had even allowed some of them to settle within the empire in return for military service. Some were taken on as mercenaries into the Roman army and this helped to keep the others out since in effect such troops were only one stage less barbarous than their opponents. The last two great imperial warriors of antiquity, the generals Stilicho and Aetius, were Germans. There were other contacts. For one thing some of the barbarians had already been converted to Christianity. St. Justin Martyr speaks of Christianity among the barbarians as early as 165. The only trouble was that these barbarians were converted to the heretical Arian Christianity and this was to prove an enormous difficulty to the Church.

In the fifth century, new and strenuous pressures were being put on these border barbarians. The pressures took many forms. There was the need for land for one thing. There was no way that they could expand eastward since they had been repulsed by the strong Chinese emperors and particularly by the Great Wall of China built precisely in 200 B.C. to keep them out. Westward was the only avenue. Forcing this westward push were the terrible Huns. They swept all before them leaving the other barbarian tribes nowhere to flee except into the Roman empire. Thus, in the year 406 these tribes crossed the Rhine River and invaded the Roman provinces of Gaul (roughly today's France). Wives, children, livestock came in an unending stream. The barbarian invasions had begun and would last some 250 years until the sixth century. Europe would only catch its breath when the Moslems would bring their warring crusade. Finally, in the tenth century the last series of invasions, that of the Vikings, would take place. It is easy to see why with three major body blows in 500 years these ages are called "dark" (although unjustifiably in many ways as we shall see).

It was not only the pressure for land and the fear of the Huns that enabled the barbarians to pour into the Roman Empire. There was the simple fact that already the empire was in decline and internally weak. Military strength was low and, more significantly, the simple will to be great was gone among the Romans. The softness of life, the decay of morals were factors. Then, too, the capital was now at Constantinople, leaving Rome in second place and in fact vacant. The emperor's representative resided in Ravenna, but the strength and the power were in the East. In fact, it was later discovered that the Eastern emperor at Constantinople had made secret treaties with the barbarians, namely, that if they spared the eastern section of the empire, the imperial troops would not hinder their invasion of Italy.

Thus it was that in 407 a Vandal leader, Alaric, invaded Rome and in 410 sacked the city. For the first time in seven hundred years Rome had been invaded! The Eternal City, the heartbeat of the ancient empire, had been desecrated although no emperor had lived there for 140 years. No wonder that many thought that civilization itself had come to an end. Fifty years later the "scourge of God" Attila the Hun led his warriors into northern Italy and it was Pope Leo I who went out with his clergy to talk with him and get him to spare the city for the payment of an annual tribute. The barbarians continued to overrun Gaul, Britain and Africa. The great St. Augustine mercifully died before the barbarians overran his town of Hippo in Africa. The Ostrogoths were the last of the barbarians to invade (with the exception of the Lombards later). A certain Odoacer had made himself the king of Italy and deposed the last subordinate Western emperor in 476. This usually marks the date of the fall of the Western Roman Empire. The Eastern emperor still ruled of course at Constantinople and his authority was still respected, but he was far away and powerless in the West. By the time of Pope Gregory the Great (d. 604) the Eastern imperial rule over the West was restricted to Ravenna, Rome, Naples and Sicily.

This was the pattern all over. Little tribal kingdoms had replaced the unity of the Roman Empire. Still, there is one overriding historical reality that we must remember if we are to understand the Church's role: the barbarians did not wish to destroy Roman civilization. They wanted desperately to adopt and imitate it. So powerful was the Roman Empire, so prestigious its name, so regarded as the depository of a superior civilization that the Germanic barbarians submitted eagerly to the Roman way and tried to follow Roman political institutions. They had no hatred for the Roman life. They wanted nothing more than to become Romanized as soon as possible. Each local barbarian king went out of his way to be recognized by the Eastern emperor. Each barbarian king (sometimes to the point of ridiculousness) sought to wear the clothes, hold the court and affect the titles of imperial Rome.

We can imagine the upheaval Europe was in. The utter despair and confusion were apparent. The West was saturated with German barbarians. But there was one moment of recovery. The great emperor of the East, Justinian, having successfully rejuvenated his Eastern empire, turned to the West. He wanted to restore the whole empire to its former glory and unity. He attacked the barbarians and with great skill defeated them all except the Franks. For a brief moment the empire was united once more and Justinian was celebrating his victories by building the famed Santa Sophia in Constantinople. However, before Justinian could return to conquer the Franks he was diverted by the Persian and Lombard threats on his own eastern borders. The Lombards were finally rerouted to Italy and were the last invaders into Europe. Justinian could have still dealt with both Franks and Lombards but for a new menace at his own doorstep: the Moslem holy wars.

MOSLEM INVASIONS

In the seventh century the Moslems bound together with a new religion set out to conquer the world. Armed with fanaticism and the sword they swept Asia before them and penetrated deep into Europe. The very lands of Syria, Palestine and Egypt which had witnessed the great events of Christianity and which had produced the Church's greatest scholars and martyrs, were now lost to the infidel. (The ill-fated Crusades of a later century would attempt to win these places back.) Christianity in these regions withered away and from this point on the great patriarchates of Alexandria, Antioch and Jerusalem would have no influence in the workings of the Church. The Church in the West would tend to forget these areas of its former glory and origins. Next the

Moslems invaded Africa and crossed into Europe via Spain in 711. On the other end of the empire they assaulted Constantinople itself but were unable to take it. What really saved Christendom from complete conquest were the divisions within the Moslem world itself which caused the thrust of aggression to dry up. As a matter of fact, the Moslem world finally polarized into three distinct political centers—Baghdad, Cairo and Cordova (in Spain). Thus divided it was no longer a united danger but it continued to harass Christianity in many ways and for a long time.

The important thing to remember is that from the seventh century on the Moslems effectively separated Europe from the East. They locked in its economy, made the Mediterranean a Moslem sea, and prevented commercial expansion and development. As we shall see, no wonder feudalism arose. No wonder that capitalism did not arise. No wonder that Europe was landlocked and isolationist and outside stimulation was absent. Only about five hundred years later would there be some headway against the Moslems. Then Europe would break out once again into the waterways; cities could begin to revive, commerce thrive and the Renaissance become possible. But for the time being, Europe was perpetually threatened by the Moslems, hedged in, thrown back on its own resources. The Eastern half spent the rest of its days trying to withstand the Moslem pressure, losing contact with the West—except for Venice—having its moments of glory and still maintaining its influence until its fall in 1453.

CHURCH AND BARBARIAN

Thus from the fifth to the seventh centuries Europe was racked with invasion and assault by German barbarians, Lombards and Moslems. (One more assault remained: the

Vikings.) The Western Roman empire fell. But our interest is the Church. How did it fare? What was its relation to the barbarian? On the intellectual front pagans and Christians had their answers to the invasions. For the pagans, the invasions were a punishment from the gods for abandoning them. For the Christians the invasions were a punishment from God for the immoral lives of the people. St. Augustine's *City of God* was an answer to those who blamed Christianity for the invasions. A fifth century monk gave his answer:

> Events prove what God judges about us and about the Goths and Vandals. They increase daily; we decrease daily. They prosper; we are humbled. . . . You, O Roman people, be ashamed; be ashamed of your lives. Almost no cities are free of evil dens. . . . It is not the natural vigor of their bodies that enables them to conquer us, nor is it our natural weakness that has caused our conquest. Let nobody persuade himself otherwise. Let nobody think otherwise. The vices of our bad lives have alone conquered us.[2]

Be that as it may, the Church provided the one point of stability in the general upheaval of the times. Although many of its clergy were killed, its property dispossessed, yet the Church not only ultimately survived, but grew. One by one the pagan barbarians who had wrecked the old order embraced the Church. Why was this? We must recall that the Church was set to stand the strain of the invasions. It had successfully copied, as we have seen, the Roman organization. There were dioceses, bishops in every large city, with his priests and deacons. In short, it was well organized.

Secondly, we must remember that there was a vacuum left by the emperor's moving his capital to Constantinople. The subordinate emperor left by him in the West was weak. There was no other power left to fill the vacuum but the Church. "The continuity and the authority of the Church of Rome stood out in marked contrast against not only the turbulent heresies and imperial control of the Church in the East, but also against the short-lived kingdoms which rose and fell in the West."[3] Moreover, the Church was conscious of its mission to convert the world. It therefore had to take the lead and so, "it brought the West under the great civilizing influence of Christian doctrine."[4] The barbarians had no common center, no unified tradition of spiritual culture. The northern barbarians had no written literature, no cities, no architecture. Christianity, on the other hand, had all this and more and was able to transmit to them unity and form. Thirdly, the Church had the only trained personnel in existence. Since the barbarians were anxious to become Romanized they naturally turned to these churchmen to help them administer their local kingdoms in the Roman tradition. The pope was generally accepted as the arbiter of doctrine and authority and in the West he became the center of gravity. In a word, what was happening in those early times, was that the barbarian kings needed the Church, its organization and its personnel. The Church needed the protection of the kings. A mutual but uneasy alliance was beginning.

> The new barbarian kingdoms had taken over the military and political functions of the empire—they held the sword, they levied the taxes, they administered justice—of a sort—but everything else belonged to the Church—moral authority, learning and culture, the prestige of the Roman name and the care of the people. A man's real citizenship was not to be found in his subjection to the barbarian state, but in his membership of the Christian Church, and it was to the bishop rather than to the king that he looked as the leader of Christian society.[5]

This is not to say that the Church survived intact. During those hectic times the Church itself could not help but become somewhat barbarized. It was persecuted by the barbarians, its churches destroyed and property confiscated. Its famous Latin literature went into decline. There were no more Augustines. The writings of the Fathers came to an end. Still, the bishops performed their essential administrative duties and so made the Church the one stabilizing influence left. Its schools and books were the only ones in existence. It perpetuated the Roman traditions in its thoughts, administration, laws and language. "In short, it was not because it was Christian, but because it was Roman that the Church acquired and maintained for centuries its control over society; or, if you will, it exercised a preponderant influence over modern society for so long merely because it was a depository of a more ancient and more advanced civilization."[6] The barbarians needed the Church if they were to advance and could not afford to destroy it completely.

THE MONKS

There were other factors which made the Church the preserver of Western civilization when the civil government fell. One most vital one was the monks. In 529 St. Benedict, a contemporary of the Emperor Justinian, had founded his famous monastery at Monte Casino in Italy. From this monastery monasticism was to spread in the West. Before long hundreds of Benedictine communities had sprung up. These monks, above all, would preserve the old Roman heritage and transmit useful arts of agriculture and weaving and the crafts to the countryside around them. We must realize that many of the cities were destroyed by the barbarian invasions, cities in which the Church was most populous. It was the monks and famous bishops like St. Martin of Tours who brought the religion to the countryside. It was the monks who provided in their monasteries the inns and hospitals of the times. It was the monks who by heroic labor turned the tide of barbarism in Western Europe and slowly brought back into cultivation the lands devastated and depopulated by the invaders. The Benedictine monasteries which held the monopoly until the religious orders of the twelfth century, were the real havens of peace and security in a world of upheaval and war. In time, from the Benedictines the Church would draw several thousands of its bishops and twenty-four of its popes. We might add that the monasteries were not founded as houses of learning. This just naturally happened. The monks had to instruct their barbarian converts not only in doctrine but also in the Latin tongue in order to read the Scriptures and partake in the liturgy. Thus it naturally came about that the monasteries were the places of reading and writing, and, in due time, of the arts and sciences.

In addition to all these things, the greatest gift of the monks to the Church was that they provided missionaries to convert the barbarians. They would found monasteries in Gaul and Germany. They would boast of great names like St. Gall and St. Columban. The monks would be the leaders in the spread of the faith. This in contrast to most bishops for we have seen that the emperors had a great tendency to use the bishops as their civil representatives. The bishops became almost appointees of the kings and as such they were often crude, unlettered and immoral. The monks had the spirit and the freedom to be missionaries. Because of the holiness of their lives they were admired. Because they were independent, not bound to a local bishop, they could act freely.

ARIANISM

There was one major problem, however, in the conversion of the barbarians. Many of them had already been converted to the heretical form of Arianism. (Even this embracing of the empire's religion shows how the barbarians were anxious to imitate Roman civilization for they submitted to the Church and adopted its Latin tongue. This can be noticed even today. Whereas all the barbarians were Germanic the Germanic languages have very little foothold in Europe today. Rather the Latin tongues prevail.) These Arian Christians continuously persecuted the Roman Catholic majority and gave the Church many of its martyrs. The Arian king, Theodoric, even went so far as to imprison the pope, much to the scandal of the faithful, for appealing to the Eastern emperor for aid against the Arian Germans.

In any case, the Church needed an ally among the barbarians themselves. They found one among the relatively small tribe of the Franks. Clovis was their king. He was courted by the Church. Later he married a Catholic princess and soon was baptized a Catholic by Bishop Remi of Rheims in 496. Soon his whole tribe followed. Now the Church had a champion and the bishops threw their weight and prestige behind Clovis. In the name of the new faith Clovis broke the Arian Visigoth power and he forced them to accept Catholic baptism. Even after Clovis' death as the Frankish kingdom spread so did the power of the Catholic Church. Since the Franks alone ultimately survived among all of the various tribes they and the Church were therefore to have a permanent influence on Europe. In any case, Arianism would soon disappear. The conversion of Clovis, the fact that the Roman clergy was better educated than the isolated ignorant Arian clergy, intermarriage between conquerors and conquered—all these factors bridged the religious gap. Added to this, of course, was the need on the part of kings to consolidate their newly seized lands and conforming to the faith they found in the empire was a wise move. Besides, since the barbarians were so anxious to adopt Roman civilization whose religion was Catholic Christianity, then what would be more natural than for the Arians to switch sides? Arianism for all these reasons, gave way before Catholicism.

But it was a two way street, the conversion of the Franks. Their kings felt the obligation not only to protect the Church but to interfere as well. By a local council, for example, the king of the Franks got permission to nominate bishops. It was easy to see what would happen. The king would nominate only those whom he could trust and who would be more civil servant than ecclesiastic. It was the beginning of that deadly combination, the prince-bishop who would plague the Church for centuries and who frequently enough would be more civil and ambitious prince than servant bishop—to the great scandal in the Church. It is no wonder that bishops would seldom figure in the great reform movements of the Church, but rather the monks would: the bishops were often the *objects* of reform.

GREGORY THE GREAT

All of the activity of the Church on behalf of the barbarians during the centuries can be summed up in one person, Gregory the Great. Gregory was a monk and this was significant. This means that when he was elected pope in 590 he brought a monk's discipline, missionary instinct and sense of order and rule to the Church. He is often called the founder of the modern papacy in that he began the centralization process towards Rome. He was the first pope to use the title which is still used today, "Servant of the servants of God." He has been called the Father of Europe. By the end of the third century the bishop of Rome was already being called "pope" in a special sense (the term was used generally of bishops beforehand). From the beginning of the Church the popes had exercised and claimed a certain primacy (Clement, Victor, Leo, etc.) and even the rival Constantinople had grudgingly taken second place to Rome. But circumstances forced the papacy to exercise more than a primacy of honor. It had to assume a primacy of jurisdiction and even supremacy. We have seen some reasons already. Rome had been vacated and the vacancy of leadership was filled by the pope. We have observed how it was Pope Leo who went out on behalf of the city to meet Attila the Hun. The pope became the chief magistrate in Rome. He fed the populace when the emperor's representative at Ravenna could no longer do so. By the gifts of land made to him the pope became a political power as well.

If the pope's power of jurisdiction and supremacy had been ill defined previously, it was Gregory who sharpened the definition. He was an able leader and one of only three popes to earn the title "great" after his name. He was fifty years old when he became pope, frail but energetic. Before he became a Benedictine monk he was the highest civil official in the government of Rome. But he had other things going for him as well as filling the void left by the emperor. He had his own personal prestige. He was the first one since the Church Fathers of long ago to write about and interpret religious thought. His homilies and commentaries are still read today and his book *The Pastoral Care of Souls* along with Boethius' *The Consolation of Philosophy* were the two most widely read books in the Middle Ages. He had organizational ability. He reorganized and consolidated church finances so that he made the papacy financially independent and thus enabled to experiment. Finally, he had a sense of priority and knew what the pressing problems were. The most immediate was the invading Lombards whom he temporarily placated by an annual tribute. His other problem was one of support. He was shrewd enough to know that he could no longer count on the Eastern emperor for help. He would therefore have to strengthen his own position and to do this he must have the backing of the barbarians. To have the backing of the barbarians he must convert them all (not just the Franks). Thus Gregory made the papacy an international office. He took every interest in the Germanic tribes wherever they were. He took an interest in the small band of converts among the Lombards. He was concerned about the newly baptized barbarians in Spain. More than any other individual he was responsible for ending Arianism in Spain and Italy and gathering the Irish Church to Rome. But above all, he was interested enough to send forth missionaries. In this endeavor he was the first pope to bring monasticism into active service on behalf of the Church. The combination of papacy and monasticism was to conquer Europe for the Church.

EVANGELIZING THE BARBARIANS

Gregory's great achievement was to send St. Augustine to England. Actually there was Christianity already in England having been brought there by some Roman soldiers in the fourth century, but it was not active. And Britain, of course produced St. Patrick, the apostle of Ireland. No one really knows how Christianity got to Ireland; it was there before Patrick but there is no doubt that he completed its conversion in the middle of the fifth century. Unlike every place else, however, Christianity came to Ireland wrapped in monasticism and has remained that way ever since. There was no city life in Ireland so that the city episcopate was nonexistent. In a word the Irish Church found its natural home in the monasteries, not in dioceses and bishops, etc. Since this was so, the monks, as elsewhere, became the preservers of culture and learning. Since therefore Ireland was a vast monastery it is no wonder that it became "the land of saints and scholars."

Getting back to St. Augustine, this monk converted the king in Britain and then established his see at Canterbury (later to be taken over by the Anglican church) and was the first Catholic bishop of England. Actually there were other monks on the northern side of the island, the Irish monks (such as Aiden and Columba). The two groups—the Irish and Italian monks—soon found themselves in a kind of holy rivalry. A council meeting at Whitby in 664 settled the matter in favor of Augustine's party. The great importance of this act was to bind England to Rome and the pope. English Christianity adopted the forms and administration and policies of Rome and Rome's influence would be felt right up to the sixteenth century when the Catholic king, Henry VIII, would provide the occasion for a break which had been seething some time before him. England later was to return the compliment to Gregory in sending missionaries to them. In time they would send their missionaries back to the continent to evangelize the barbarians there. Their contribution was the greatest apostle of his time, St. Boniface, who is known as the "Apostle of the Germans" (716). Again, the significance for Germany as for England was that they were directly beholden to the pope. Their bishops were subject not to the king but to Rome. These countries would look to Rome for leadership. This meant that while in Rome the popes were still technically under the Eastern emperor who ratified their election either directly or through their representatives at Ravenna, the new Christians knew only the pope as their leader and they revered him as the Vicar of Christ. This meant that the pope had an independent base of wealth and the allegiance of whole nations who looked directly to him. No longer would the papacy have to be in the position of subordination to the emperor, especially those Eastern emperors who had abandoned the West to face the barbarians alone and who on different occasions antagonized the papacy.

> When Boniface embarked on his mission, religion and culture in the Frankish kingdom were at a low ebb, and the victorious tide of Moslem invasions was sweeping over the Christian lands of the western Mediterranean and northern Africa. By 720 the Saracens had penetrated as far as Narbonne; and in the following years all the old centers of monastic culture in southern Gaul, such as Lerins, were sacked. . . . But the creation by St. Boniface and his Anglo-Saxon companions of a new province of Christian culture on the northern flank of Christendom had an importance that far exceeded its material results. . . . It involved a triple alliance between the Anglo-Saxon missionaries, the Papacy, and the family of Charles Martel, the *de facto* rulers of the Frankish kingdom, out of which the Carolingian Empire and the Carolingian culture ultimately emerged.[7]

And antagonism there was. Fifty years after Gregory this antagonism from the Eastern emperor flared up again. The Eastern Emperor Constans II had sent Pope Martin into exile. In 692 the grand Emperor Justinian almost did the same to Pope Sergius over a theological quarrel. But there were signs that this sort of subordination would not last long. In 725 when the Emperor Leo II tried to force the iconoclast heresy on the West the pope hedged. The emperor had expected to find him as docile as the other patriarchs but the pope distinctly showed his defiance. He was not ready yet for an open break for the emperor, even far away, was still too powerful. The papacy would have to wait for a more opportune time. More precisely, it would have to be assured of a powerful protector to defend it against the emperor if need be. As a matter of fact there was such an ally in the background. He belonged to the church-related Frankish tribe. He was a local mayor in the palace of the Frankish Merovingian kings and he was fast supplanting that decadent line. His name was Pepin and under his great grandson, Charlemagne, the great marriage between the Church and the Western empire would take place and the Eastern emperor would become a mere figurehead to the West.

NOTES

1. Pope Gregory VII would almost resort to the Donatist heresy in trying to reform the clergy in the eleventh century.
2. *Barbarian Europe, Great Ages of Man Series,* by Gerald Simons and the Editors of TIME-LIFE Books, New York, 1968, p. 15.
3. Denys Hay, *The Medieval Centuries,* p. 22, Harper Torchbooks, Harper and Row, New York, 1964.
4. *Barbarian Europe, op. cit.,* p. 57.
5. Dawson, Christopher, *Religion and the Rise of Western Culture,* pp. 31, 32, Image Books, a division of Doubleday and Company, Garden City, New York, 1958.
6. Henri Pirenne, *A History of Europe,* p. 59, University Books, New Hyde Park, New York, 1936.
7. Dawson, *op. cit.,* pp. 61, 62.

VII

The Carolingian Era

THE HOLY ROMAN EMPIRE

Clovis, the founder of the Merovingian dynasty was king of the barbarian tribe of the Franks. We had noted in the last chapter that he had become a Catholic and that his whole tribe followed him. In enlarging his kingdom he also spread the faith. What happened to him and his descendants afterwards? His kingdom under his descendants became weaker. There was no real central government and so in time the many local princes grew in strength and wealth at the expense of the Merovingian rulers. Besides, with the feudal arrangement whereby local princes took over the protection, land and care of the peasants they often became more wealthy and more powerful than the king himself. Moreover, the king, in order to purchase the loyalty of such princes would give them some of his land and thus in due time reduce his own power. As a result, in place of one united Frankish kingdom under Clovis many minor municipalities arose which were practically independent of the king. It only remained a matter of time before some strong figure, some local prince, would arise and substitute his clan for the old Merovingian clan of Clovis.

The man who was destined to make this replacement was

Pepin. By gathering land through intrigue and warfare his Carolingian clan became quite prestigious. This prestige was considerably enhanced by Pepin's son, Charles Martel (the Hammer). He was the one who defeated the Moslems at Poiters (in France) thus confining the Moslems to Spain and saving the rest of Europe from their invasion. People almost forgot that Charles despoiled Church property and buildings to finance his army and the newly invented institution of having knights on horseback as a kind of standing army. In any case the Church had more reason to remember his son, Pepin the Short. This was the man who felt that the only way to soften and eventually annex his troublesome pagan neighbors was to convert them to Catholic Christianity. Thus Pepin lost no time in giving every cooperation to the great St. Boniface. We must remember, however, that Boniface was an English Benedictine and loyal to the pope. To this degree Boniface unconsciously became an intermediary between Pepin and the pope. It was a quickly growing mutual relationship. Pepin decided to take advantage of it.

Pepin had a legal problem. He was actual ruler of the Franks but technically the old Merovingian line was the royal family. He asked Pope Zachary whether it was right that the old impotent family should rule when in effect he was doing all the work. The pope, wisely following Gregory the Great's assessment that no longer could the West look to the Eastern emperor for assistance, gave the answer that it was not right. The ruler in practice should be the ruler in theory. Accordingly Pepin was crowned king and the Carolingian line replaced the Merovingian line. The high significance of the event lay in the fact that Pepin was now in effect king by the approval of the pope. Pepin was beholden to the papacy. The papacy in turn henceforth associated itself with the Frankish empire and turned its back forever on the Eastern emperor. The papacy had its protector now. It did not need the East.

In 750 simultaneously with the arrangements to make Pepin king the Lombards in northern Italy again went on a rampage and were invading further south. In fact they captured Ravenna where the Eastern emperor's representative resided and from which he fled. Rome itself was now in peril. Since arrangements with Pepin were not complete the pope appealed to the Eastern emperor for assistance. Help did not come and Pope Stephen III arranged a forty year truce with the Lombards, which they promptly violated. Then the pope decided to make the long hard journey over the Alps to entreat Pepin's aid. Pepin agreed and took his army over the Alps and defeated the Lombards. It was at this time that another significant event took place. Pepin gave some of the conquered land to the pope. This was known as the "Donation of Pepin" and the lands formed the basis for the papal states. This was the property which in centuries to come would make the pope not only a spiritual leader but a sovereign power as well. This was the property which in time would be a source of conflict with kings and governments. This was the nucleus of the property which stood in the way of Italian unification in the nineteenth century and which at that time Victor Emmanuel I would seize causing Pius XI to flee to the Vatican as its voluntary prisoner. Finally a concordat between Pius XI and Mussolini in 1929 would cede the papal states to the Italian government leaving only the 108 acres forming today's Vatican City; but that is another drama we shall investigate later.

For a moment we must pause to note that Pepin's action in giving lands to the pope was based on the *Donation of Constantine.* This was one of the great forgeries of the Middle Ages (and forgeries were common ways of shoring up a point or claim in those days). It was supposed to be a document written by Constantine to Pope Sylvester in 315 (really written in the eighth century). It tells how Constantine gave to the pope and his successors the supreme temporal power in the West, the universal rule in both spiritual and temporal realms and the lands of the Roman Empire. Pepin believed in that document, as many others did, and so he felt that he was only restoring to the pope lands taken by the Lombards, lands rightfully the pope's. Pepin's Donation, in other words, was based on Constantine's: he was only giving back the pope his property. It was also in virtue of the *Donation* document that the pope felt he had the power to transfer the imperial lands which belonged to the emperor in the East to the Franks.

We must again point out another novelty in these goings on. For the first time the pope was also formally a prince, a sovereign king in charge of states. He and his clerics would run these states but obviously they would be subject to the jealousies and intrigues of the old time Roman nobles and military leaders who formerly (before the Lombards) ran these lands, and who would ever aspire to seize these lands once more. The implication of this would bode ill for the papacy some day. It would mean that since such states were protected militarily by papal troops the only way such Roman barons and nobles would ever again be able to control the papal states would be to manage somehow to control the papacy. Unfortunately, this came about. In other words, since the pope was now an earthly ruler what would be more natural than that unscrupulous men should covet the papacy? To be pope was not to be spiritual leader alone. To be pope was to be a temporal power.

For the present, however, the picture was ideal. Empire and Church were interrelated. Rome, the capital of the old

Roman Empire became the capital of Christendom. Now there existed a true religious empire with a king of the Franks who was so "by the grace of God." The groundwork laid by Pope Gregory the Great in the sixth century was fulfilled in the eighth. This church-state ideal would reach its height under Charlemagne. The origins of the *Holy* Roman Empire were at hand.

CHARLEMAGNE

Charlemagne (literally "Charles the Great": 768-814) was the son of Pepin the Short. He is one of those figures in history who completely captured the popular imagination. His name was to remain the most honored for the rest of the Middle Ages, and deservedly so for his achievements were many. He was a first class warrior (and lusty barbarian of five wives and many mistresses). He waged war against the pagan Saxons, those who had not migrated to England. This was the first religious war on the part of the Christian state for the Saxons must accept baptism or die. He next defeated the Avars, the Slavs and fought well against the Moslems. One of his battles against the Moslems occasioned the first epic poem of the late Middle Ages, *The Song of Roland.* Finally at the pope's request he defeated the ever troublesome Lombards and thereby he annexed Italy to his kingdom as well. All in all Charlemagne's empire included almost all of Europe.

By the very fact of his conquest of Italy he became its ruler and indeed was given the title "Patriarch of Rome." He had no choice but to have an intense interest in the Church and indeed he came to consider the Church as a kind of partner. There were dangers in this paternalism (for example, an overlordship such as the Eastern emperors had

over the Eastern Church), but the Church was not unhappy.
In fact when Charlemagne was attending Christmas Mass in
the year 800 Pope Leo III craftily surprised him by placing
a crown on his head and bowing before him as one only does
to the emperor. Charlemagne according to his biographer was
annoyed. Not that he minded being dubbed as emperor but
he minded being beholden to the pope. In any case the result was clear for his times and ever after. Charlemagne was
not merely king as his great grandfather Pepin had become
when he replaced the old Merovingian line; no, he was a
genuine emperor of the West in the old Roman tradition. The
sole and real emperor of the East was hardly pleased with
this usurpation but what could he do? He did the only thing
left. Since the Roman Empire had always tolerated kings
along with the emperor (remember that in Christ's time
Herod was king while the emperor Tiberius was reigning),
he pretended to recognize Charlemagne as such. Grudgingly,
some fourteen years later the Eastern emperor finally bowed
to reality and accepted Charlemagne as a "brother" emperor.

Thus far, under the impulse of the *Donation of Constantine* supposedly giving the pope full spiritual and temporal
power the pope had transferred in effect part of the Eastern
empire to the Franks and had just given the imperial crown
to an outsider (Charlemagne). The pope indeed was a kind
of super emperor himself now. He lost no time in taking on
the trappings of such a title. The papal palace, for example,
was changed to the Sacred Palace in 813. The pope for the
first time put on the imperial scarlet and officious imperial
titles were conferred on papal officials. Once more, there
were those who felt that this was a far cry from the Church
started in a stable in Bethlehem; a far cry from the fraternity
of the little church-communities of the *Acts of the Apostles.*
No wonder that groups in succeeding ages would claim that

the *Donation* had seduced the Church and the reformers would see a vast difference between Apostolic and imperial Christian Rome.

In any case, Charlemagne's coronation was one of the most significant events of the Middle Ages. It signified the rebirth of the old Roman Empire but a Christian one (The Holy Roman Empire as it would be termed in the twelfth century). As a matter of fact Charlemagne wanted to restore the old Roman Empire and except for Moslem Spain and England he did. There was another significance. The serious beginning of emperor versus pope was implanted here. That is why Charlemagne was annoyed in being crowned by the pope. If the pope could give the crown he could take it away. In a showdown it would be the pope who would have the final say. That is why from the start he refused to return to the pope many of the lands seized anew by the Lombards. Even then he was wary of papal ascendancy. But the die was cast and ever afterward (until the title did not really matter anymore) every emperor would feel the compulsion to be crowned as "Holy Roman Emperor" by the pope. The two powers were now officially united and the mosaic in St. John Lateran's would hold true for centuries. There is depicted Pope Leo III and Charlemagne kneeling in front of St. Peter and receiving from him, one the keys of heaven and the other the pallium, the symbol of civil power. Both are thus equals in the running of men's lives but significantly both receive their mandate from the Church (Peter). Still, historian R. W. Southern has a shrewd observation:

> It seems very likely that the papal coronation of Charle-magne as emperor was intended to show that the pope could delegate imperial authority in the West to whom he would, in accordance with the terms of Constantine's gift. But it is certain that Charlemagne did not acquiesce in this view of his position.

Indeed it is evident that the idea of a Western empire as a means of extending papal authority was a mistake from beginning to end. It was a mistake primarily because in creating an emperor the pope created not a deputy, but a rival or even a master. The theoretical supremacy implied in the act of creation could never be translated into practical obedience to orders given and received. Hence the pope's practical supremacy over his emperor came to an end at the moment of coronation. It is not surprising that the popes of the later Middle Ages sought to exercise their supreme temporal lordship through other channels than the empire, which Pope Leo III had rashly created for this purpose on Christmas Day 800. This action was the greatest mistake the medieval popes ever made in their efforts to translate theory into practice.[1]

DECLINE OF THE EMPIRE

There were many reasons why Charlemagne's empire began to decline. For one thing it was too big and it could not endure that size for long. Secondly, there was always the tension between king and his princes many of whom were more powerful than Charlemagne. They were rich in land, had absorbed many people into their feudal domains and were powerful enough to be almost independent of the royal will. In short, they were very effective in undermining the kingship as a central power. Finally, under Charlemagne's sons and grandsons who took to warring against one another the empire dissolved into fragments. The once proud empire broke up into some fifty smaller municipalities and some five major divisions. Eventually by the Treaty of Verdun in 843 two large sections remained, the future France and Germany, with a vague buffer area in between: the future Netherlands, Belgium, Luxemburg, Switzerland and northern Italy. There were several other external forces to hasten the disintegration of the empire. New invaders were harrying Europe: the

Magyars, the Slavs, the renewed Moslem attacks which penetrated as far as Italy sacking Rome in 844, and, above all, the Vikings.

From the Scandinavian north in the ninth century the Vikings descended. They included the Swedes, the Norwegians and the Danes. They had been active of course before. For some two hundred years the Norwegians had been assaulting Ireland and other places. These Vikings were hatefully anti-Christian and destroyed Christian foundations wherever they went. They usually made straight for a monastery because there there was portable wealth. They besieged the towns all along the Mediterranean, sailed up the rivers in Italy and France (attacking Paris in 886). Some places were spared only by the age-old practice of buying off the marauders. It was at this time that medieval Europe took on its appearance of being dotted with castles for protection against the Vikings.

Charles the Simple, one of the last of the Carolingian line in France (before the Capets took over) decided to allay the Viking terror by offering one of their leaders, Rollo, some land in France. Charles hoped that the Vikings would thus settle down and also defend their land (and the rest of the country) from fellow Vikings. Rollo accepted and in time his Viking descendants accepted Christianity and intermingled with the native population. They became known as the Normans (a shortening of Norseman or North-men) and their territory is still known as Normandy, an area made famous in World War II by the Normandy invasions of the Allied Forces. Five generations after Rollo, one of his descendants would be the famous William the Conqueror who in 1145 would leave his Norman France, cross the channel and conquer England. As we shall see by this event he began the deadly and senseless rivalry between France and England and helped usher in the modern age of nation states. In any case, the Viking raids left Europe in a state of almost total waste and chaos. Civilization suffered a great setback. Learning declined, disorder reigned everywhere and the effect was immense both on society and on the Church as a contemporary lamented: "The Northmen cease not to slay and carry into captivity the Christian people, to destroy the churches and to burn the towns. Everywhere there is nothing but dead bodies—clergy, laymen, nobles and common people, women and children. There is no road or place where the ground is not covered with corpses. We live in distress and anguish before this spectacle of the destruction of the Christian people."

FEUDALISM

The breakup of the Carolingian empire left the field open to the local lords and nobles. Power became localized in these nobles. They were the real rulers and so feudalism was born. Feudalism rests on the fact of a decentralized government. Small counties or areas pulled in as so many self-contained islands. Primarily such feudal areas were created for war: war against another's feudal domains, protection from the terrible Vikings, robbers and outlaws. Since the feudal enclave was primarily military then obviously the relationship of the master or lord of the area to his subjects or vassals was that of allegiance. The lord swore to protect his subjects, they swore to give him soldiers, service and loyalty in return. Many of these little islands became quite powerful (ruled over by the famous counts and lords of history and literature) and they did provide a stabilizing influence. They became in effect like the Greek city-states of old. Feudalism certainly answered a need in troubled and fitful times but it eventually worked havoc with the Church.

Several factors converged to make this true. With the

feudal system the building of monasteries and churches was done by the local lord. He even staffed them so that the priest or abbot could be hired or fired at will. By the eighth century churches created in this manner, beholden to their lay masters, far outnumbered those churches under the authority of the local bishop. In short, the parish churches had fallen into the hands of the laymen as disposable property. We can see the consequences of this. A priest or abbot or bishop who was a hireling of the local lords, his vassals, must have a double allegiance: to the spiritual needs of the people and to the master. As vassals they had to supply soldiers and give military service. They had to do homage to their lord and attend the feudal courts. It is not difficult to see how the lord would naturally tend to appoint his own men as priests or abbots or bishops within his little "city-state"; how such clergymen would often be more warrior than cleric; that priestly functions would be subordinated to the military functions. The clergy thus became closely allied with the secular order of the day. We shall see how in another hundred years, under the German emperor, Otto I, the bishops became in effect national servants in a German state Church. The German bishops would gain a reputation as mighty warriors and it became a common saying that one thing was certain: a German bishop could not be pious. They were in effect, soldiers with miters.

There was one other problem connected with feudalism. The local lord (or emperor) began not only to appoint bishops and priests, but also to "invest" the bishop. That is, he gave his appointee the symbols of his office, the crozier and the bishop's ring. The lord might permit the traditional election of the bishop by the people or the abbot by the monks, but if he did not like the candidate he simply withheld the land on which the monastery or diocese lay. Obviously this whole system undermined the authority of the Church. This problem of "lay investiture," that is, a layman investing a bishop with the signs of his office, would have to stop. Equally obviously, this system would not be stopped without a great struggle between Church and state.

More scandals followed from the general chaos of the times. Lay investiture produced its counterpart evil: simony, the buying or selling of church offices. It worked both ways. An unscrupulous lord might sell a diocese or abbey. An unscrupulous churchman might buy it for his cousin or nephew or bastard son. Naturally if the new bishop or abbot had to pay a high price for his office he in turn would tax his peasants and clergy to regain his money. Such cynical practices were certainly demoralizing in other ways. In time clerical celibacy became an empty word. By the ninth century some monasteries had resident prostitutes and priests and deacons openly took wives and mistresses. In short, a vicious circle had begun in the clerical ranks. Unworthy men were putting themselves into church offices and church offices were being filled by unworthy men. No wonder that some bishops were little more than barbaric and coarse warriors wearing the miter; that many never saw their dioceses; that the practice of charging fees to dispense the sacraments arose. The one salvation for all of the mess was a strong papacy. Unfortunately the general deterioration of the times reached the highest office as well.

THE PAPACY

The basic problem for the papacy was certainly hidden when Pope Leo crowned Charlemagne as emperor in 800. The Holy Roman Empire had been effected, but there were some unanswered questions. How, for example, would either side prevent the other from encroaching on the other? The emperor still appointed the bishops. But if the emperor appointed the bishops and the pope conferred the imperial title could not one blackmail the other if the need arose? With Charlemagne in general there was no problem, but this was not to be the case with his successors. True, Pope Gregory IV came out on the side of Lothair, Charlemagne's grandson, in the contest for power with his father, Louis. The very fact of the pope's intervention and his bestowal of the crown on Lothair was significant. In fact, the papal power ascended as the fortunes of the empire descended. Several strong popes took advantage of this. Pope Nicholas I (858-867) was a forceful pope who not only preached the equality of papal and imperial power but preached the superiority of papal power. Nicholas stated flatly—and acted accordingly—that the pope could intervene in imperial affairs.

Papal power continued to grow. There were at this time the famous "false decretals," another forged document circulated in the ninth century in northern France claiming that the pope had power over all of the episcopacy (not primacy of honor which all admitted, but primacy of jurisdiction and power); that therefore Rome was the prime see (in the sense of ruling superiority) and the pope the prime ruler over all his fellow bishops. It is doubtful that such a strong pope as Nicholas would need those forged documents to prove his position nor that he used them, but they did exist and were used by some to bolster papal power. In fact, Nicholas went so far as to try to compel the Eastern Church to reconfirm his primacy and, as we shall see later, felt free to excommunicate its patriarch, Photius. Nicholas' successor, Pope John VIII (872-882) felt sure enough of his position as to crown as emperor not Carloman, personally chosen by the previous emperor, but Charles the Bald. The point was that in the decline of the Carolingian empire the popes were able to become strong and to make and break emperors. Ironically they could do this only as long as they had the protection of the very emperors they were domineering since the pope and his small papal states would never have any real power to resist aggression.

This logic however worked both ways. If the pope could make or break the imperial crown would it not be possible, if the emperor's protection were withdrawn or enfeebled, to obtain from the pope the crown by force, violence or intrigue? The answer was a shameful affirmative. When Charles the Bald died and the empire really broke apart and the feudal lords were coming into their own, the papacy was left exposed. For the next years the papacy was at the mercy of the current strong man. Charles the Fat, for example, forced Pope John VIII to crown him emperor in 881. A certain Gui, a local feudal strongman from Spoleto, forced Pope Stephen VI to crown him as emperor. He forced Pope Formosus to crown his son, Lambert, the same way. Later when this Pope Formosus intrigued to oust Lambert whom he had unwillingly crowned, Lambert stormed into Rome, had the now dead pope's body exhumed, conducted a trial over the cadaver and handed the dead body over to the populace who threw it into the Tiber River. This sordid incident as much as any reveals the distress of the times and the low level of civil and ecclesiastical life.

Louis, King of Burgandy, had himself crowned by Pope Benedict IV in 900. Another local feudal lord forced the same honor from Pope John X. With no strong central power since the decline of the Carolingian empire these unscrupulous men and their wicked families used the papacy for their own ends. Nor did they and others hesitate in the barbarity of the times to use every treachery to get their men on the papal throne. Family rivalries in fact revolved around the papal prize. As indicative as anything is the fact that from the end of the ninth century to the end of the tenth there were thirty-seven popes, some of them murdered, many of whom were, as a matter of fact, good men who died at the hands of their opponents. Roman families like the Theophylact, Crescenti and Tusculoni got their hands on the papacy and for the next seventy years rotated their proteges on the papal throne even while local reform councils were being held to rescue the papacy. These men were the personifications of the bad popes of history. Pope Adrian II (d. 872) was married and his wife and daughter lived at the Lateran palace. Pope Stephen VI was imprisoned and strangled in 896. John VIII was hammered to death. John X was murdered. The Theophylact family had two daughters, the notorious Theodora and Marouzia. Pope Sergius III had a son by one of them and this son later became John XI. This was the pope who would witness the marriage of his mother to her brother-in-law. (These women had the grand idea of being empresses of Rome.) Pope John XII was not yet twenty years old when he became pope. He lived the life of a layman and gave great scandal. He died while visiting his mistress. Leo VIII was a layman; yet he was elected pope to the horror of both East and West. Benedict VI was strangled in 974 and Pope John XIX was assassinated in 984. John XIX was a layman who in one day received all of the ecclesiastical orders in order to ascend the papal throne. Pope Gregory V was poisoned in 999. Sylvester III sold his papal title to Gregory VI. In all, the average reign of the popes in those disastrous times was about three years. In between the intrigues of the Italian families the emperor Otto I (the greatest emperor since Charlemagne) and his successors Otto II and Otto III were trying to force their choices on the papal throne, generally good men at that. But every time they returned to their native Germany one of the local families would depose their choice and insert their own. It was during this period, by the way, that the legend of a woman pope, Pope Joan, came into being. This "fact" was discovered, the story goes, when the "pope" gave birth during a solemn procession. The origin of this legend most likely is based on a misreading of the common abbreviation of *Joan.* for *Joannus* (John) in early medieval manuscripts. Whatever the origin of this popular legend it must have received some reinforcement from the times when the shady ladies mentioned above ran the papacy and provided some of its mistresses.[2]

To appreciate how such a sad state of affairs could exist at the very highest level of the Church we must recall once more the general chaos of the times.[3] The Vikings had just left Europe exhausted. The East and West were fighting at the moment over the Photin schism (which we shall see again). The Moslems were renewing their attacks on Europe and Italy. They sacked the great monastery of Monte Casino (Benedict's first foundation we may recall) in Italy and Rome itself was threatened. There was no strong emperor around to protect Rome or the papacy. All kinds of rivals were seeking to be emperor and therefore seeking to control the papacy which crowned the emperor. Italy was in a state of seige and the local Italian families were vying for control both political and spiritual. Without any real central political strength (such as Otto would provide) and strong popes, the disgraces listed above were inevitable. But there was hope. Underneath all this evil, all this deterioration of the Church, a spirit of reform was inexorably moving. The papacy simply had to be rescued from outside manipulation. The monasteries needed reform. The secular clergy needed rescue from the lay investiture problem. Celibacy was honored more in the breach than in the reality. Simony was rampant and the times are filled with examples. For instance, the count of Toulouse went into "partnership" with another noble in 1016 to charge 100,000 shillings as the price for the privilege of nominating the archbishop of Narbonne. The emperor Conrad II in 1025 appointed bishops to Loege and Basle for a high price. There is the oft quoted comment of an archbishop of Rheims who said in 1069 that his office would have been more enjoyable if he did not have to say Mass now and then. In brief, the needs were so great that an answer had to come. And it did. And it came, not unexpectedly, from the monasteries for we must always remember that most bishops were in reality princes beholden to their feudal lords. As objects of reform themselves and with their vested interests in their lord's service reform could hardly be expected from them. No, it must come and did come most gloriously from the monks.

CLUNIAC REFORM

We must keep in mind that in spite of the corruption at high places, the manipulation of bishops and popes by unscrupulous kings or noblemen, the essential structure of the Church remained intact. Indeed, no other structure was available for, as we have said so often, the Church was the ghost of the old Roman Empire.[4] There was the papacy, the bishops, their see cities and surrounding dioceses. There were the parish churches which in the tenth century had multiplied all over the countryside. And there were the monasteries. In spite of princely patronage and interference they remained the centers of piety, the idealized refuge in troubled and turbulent times where a man could flee from the world and find peace and holiness. In fact the monasteries increasingly drew men into their walls particularly if a monastery could boast of a holy man, a saint. Even some of the knights, repenting their ways, became monks. As such the monasteries continued to draw those sincerely interested in holiness and so as time went on the demand grew for a better and stricter discipline. Such were the beginnings, here and there, of what would erupt into the great monastic reform of the eleventh century, the Cluniac reform—a reform movement that would last the next three centuries until it petered out.

The monastery at Cluny had one big advantage since its founding in the tenth century. Each monastery was not autonomous but under the great Abbot of Cluny. Therefore each monastery was not subject to its local abbot who might be a nobleman's kin or protege, but to the one over-all abbot at Cluny. He in fact ruled over some 3,000 priories and he in turn was loyal to the pope. Moreover, the Cluniac order was egalitarian. The smallest peasant could advance as far as his talents would lead him. Thus the Cluniacs were for the most part men of talent, ability and high moral standards. Many a bishop came from the Cluniac monasteries and from this sort of infiltration gradual reform was brought about. However not only were the monasteries working for reform, but also, outside of them there were many outstanding bishops mightily concerned:

> Another approach to the problem lay in the many attempts which were made by individual reforming bishops. In Italy there were outstanding bishops like Atto of Vercilli (d. 964) and Rathier (d. 968) at Verona; in Germany we may mention Wolfgang at Ratisbon (d. 994), and his two successors in the same see, Bernard (d. 1022) and Gothard (d. 1039); while in France and most notable were Gerard at Toul (d. 994) and Fulbert at Chartres (d. 1029). These men were indefatigable in visiting their dioceses, in checking abuse, in raising the

very low standard of clerical literacy and in fighting to secure an incorrupt and chaste clergy. Yet a good bishop might be followed by a bad one—some rich man's son or a relation of the prince—and all the good work might be undone. . . .[5]

Such men were convinced that the dependency of the Church on the imperial and princely power was immoral. The Church could never flourish and fulfill its mission until it became absolutely independent of all temporal powers and interests. Bishops belonged to the Church, not to the prince. Priests belonged to the Church and not to the world or their wives and family (for the marriage of priests was tolerated in practice). The reformers therefore had a program. No ecclesiastical appointments should ever be made by a layman. Priestly celibacy must be restored in all its vigor so that the sons of the clergy should not continue to inherit church property. The Church must be wholly spiritual and canon law must be completely observed. Since the Church must be free of temporal interests and free of king and emperor, it must of necessity gather round its spiritual head, the pope. Such was the essence of the Cluniac reform.

It began to get hold in the tenth century and spread everywhere by the eleventh. A whole new spirit, a whole new piety was the result. Monasteries were founded in vast numbers. Religious enthusiasm ran high. Piety and processions and ceremonies were everywhere. There was now no monastery that did not boast of its saints and of its miracles. Rioting among the laity broke out protesting the marriage of priests. The "peace of God" was introduced which interrupted wars on feast days. It is no wonder that the eleventh century became the age of great church building and great donations to the monasteries and to the Church. There was regeneration abroad. The big question was: would it reach up to the high places? Would and could the Cluniac reform rescue the papacy? It could and it did. As we shall now see in the following chapter two great forces were joined: monasticism and the papacy and together they would lead the Church to a renewal and a period of fruitful reform.

NOTES

1. R. W. Southern, *Western Society and the Church in the Middle Ages*, p. 99. Penguin Books, Baltimore, Maryland. 1970.
2. A movie has been made about "Pope Joan" which will obviously have to be judged on its artistic merits rather than its historical ones.
3. We should also note that the scandals just listed come to us from not always reliable sources.
4. Hobbes said this disparagingly of the Church but his remark was more accurate than he thought.
5. Denys Hay, *op. cit.*, p. 68.

VIII

Rise of Papal Power

THE GERMAN EMPERORS

It was not only the whole spirit of Cluny that eventually led to a reform in the papacy but also, with no little irony, the efforts of the German emperors. The irony, as we shall see, was that the emperors' success in placing good men on the papal throne was the very cause of the future conflict between emperor and pope. Let us backtrack a minute. In 919 Otto I became king of Germany. This was not the Germany we know today. Rather this was what was left when Charlemagne's grandsons divided his empire into three parts with three Carolingian kings over each, one of them being emperor. The middle section (the northern Italy, central Germany, Holland, Belgium and Switzerland of today) soon fell into disarray with the result that the remaining two sections divided the middle between themselves. The upshot was that there were now two kingdoms comprising what we may roughly call the future France and Germany (parts of the middle section would remain for centuries bones of contention as they swung from one kingdom to the other until, very late in history, they gained independence). As we shall see, the last Carolingian in "France" died out and was replaced by a new line, the Capet line. In "Germany" the last Carolingian, Louis the Child, died and in 911 the local princes and magnates elected the new Saxon line of Henry the Fowler. Henry was a hard-working king and bequeathed a rather strong kingdom to his son, Otto I. Otto is rightfully called the "great" and may be regarded as the first German monarch. When he became emperor the Holy Roman Empire of Charlemagne was revived—minus France—and the axis had swung from France to Germany. In fact his kingdom is considered by the Germans to be the first kingdom or "reich." (Later Hitler would call his infamous "kingdom" or rule the Third Reich, the second being the Hollenzollern rule under Chancellor Bismarck.)

Otto was quite conscious of the power of the princes for as we shall have occasion to mention again there was really no such thing as a centralized government in the Middle Ages. Often princes and lords were more powerful than the king who might be merely a desired figurehead. Local lords were the real rulers of their terrain and frequently had policies at variance with those of the kings. Otto therefore decided to offset the power of the princes by wooing the Catholic bishops. He made them his secular princes and rulers, his vassals. He gave them lands and made *them* lords on a par with the princes; or in effect, Otto secularized the Church in Germany. The possession of the diocese or see became the possession of the empire. It was inevitable that such bishops would be beholden to the king. We have already seen in the last chapter how the German bishops were more noted for their military service to the king than their piety. Of course, the investiture problem was most pronounced in such a situation.

> This alliance of Church and king became the cornerstone of the new political order established by Otto the Great—an order which was consummated by Otto's coronation at Rome in 963 and the restoration of the Western Empire. The new Empire was thoroughly Carolingian in tradition and ideals.

Indeed, Otto I went even further than Charlemagne in his reliance on the Church in the practical administration of the Empire, so that the bishops acquired the functions of government. This conversion of the episcopate into a territorial and political power was to some extent common to all the lands that had formed part of the Carolingian Empire. . . . But nowhere did the process go so far, or have such serious political and religious consequences, as in the lands of the Empire in Germany and Lorraine, where it was destined to condition the relation of Church and state for six hundred years. Even the Reformation did not exhaust the consequences of this anomalous situation, and the German episcopate remained inextricably entangled with the political order until the ecclesiastical principalities were finally liquidated in the age of Napoleon.[1]

The whole situation can be compared to the President of the United States (if he had the power to do so) making the Catholic bishops governors of the fifty states and members of his cabinet. In due time it would not be difficult to see that a strong president would not only pick such governors but see to it that the proper men became bishops in the first place. He might even go so far as to give the bishop his insignia of episcopal office as well as swear him in as governor of his state. It would not be difficult to see either that soon such a bishop would be more politician than cleric, more loyal to state than Church. This is roughly something of the situation that prevailed under Otto the Great. The pope could hardly be happy about this state of affairs but at this particular time he was being besieged and Italy was being threatened. The pope not only could not protest against Otto but actually had to beg him for aid. The price of this aid was that the pope crowned Otto as emperor. Otto was now Holy Roman Emperor although his empire was restricted to Germany and northern Italy (not France) and this would have momentous effects on both Church and state.

Italy, for one thing, as part of the empire, was now tied to Germany. This naturally meant that the Church was also similarly tied. Indeed the emperor felt quite responsible for the Church and for the papacy. As an aside we might mention that this over-concern with Italy and the papacy distracted Otto and his successors from Germany proper. The result was that while France and England would soon emerge as great nations Germany would not for many centuries and all because its emperors were constantly being wooed by the largely unrealistic concept of a Holy Roman Emperor in charge of Italy and the Church. In any case Otto continued his dominance of the Church. He appointed bishops and the popes. Otto I, Otto II and Otto III all had their choices on the papal throne one time or another. In fact, Otto III had even decided to move to Rome with a dream that he would sit at the pope's side as the two of them jointly ruled Christendom.

It must be admitted that the German emperors were also bent on reforming the papacy in picking good popes and deposing bad ones, although for their own ultimate designs. They could not but be dissatisfied to see the papacy the plaything of the local Italian families. Thus, when a new German emperor Henry III went to Rome for his coronation as emperor he went full of zeal determined to rescue the papacy from the contending families. He deposed the current rival popes (there were three put forth by different families at this time) and put in his choice, Clement II (1046). Clement II was a good pope as were his successors Damasus II, Leo IX and Victor III. (We shall see more of Leo IX later.) They were Germans and were filled with the spirit of Cluny and free of Italian connections but precisely as such they were bound to have conflict with the emperor for now the scattered reform movement became centralized in the papacy. We must remember that one of Cluny's programs was that the Church should be free in order to function. The emperor's interference was clearly contrary to that freedom. What place, these better popes argued, could the temporal power of the emperor have in such a total spiritual reality as the Church? It was not right that the popes should be beholden to the emperor—even a well meaning emperor—who appointed them. Besides in the last analysis the popes knew that it was they who must make the Cluniac reform workable. If the key figures were the bishops (and they were) then the popes must control the bishops, not the laity such as local princes, kings or emperors. The latter should not be the ones investing the bishops with their office. No, the bishops must be free men, not beholden to emperor, king or local lord. In other words, lay investiture must cease.

The first really able and spiritual pope in two centuries and one filled with the spirit of reform and who was to influence the power of the papacy for centuries to come was Leo IX. He begins the real growth of papal power. He made alliances with the Normans, he was the one who dealt with the Eastern Church, sent delegates and began the vast amount of centralizing correspondence. We shall see Leo IX later in talking about the East-West schism. However, the man who was to bring the crisis to a head was Pope Nicholas. Even his name was significant for the first Nicholas was an ardent opponent of imperial power. This Nicholas would no longer openly tolerate the protection and the appointment by the emperor. He threw down the challenge when he decreed in 1059 that hereafter the pope was to be chosen only by the college of cardinal bishops and that the papal election did not even have to take place in Rome if conditions were unsettled (as they often were) but in any safe place. Nicholas, in true Cluniac spirit went further and condemned simony and forbade a married clergy.

GREGORY VII

Nicholas' policies were successful as was apparent in the choice of his successor, for the College of Cardinals in their first election elected an avowed anti-imperial as next pope. Finally, open warfare broke out with the election of the next pontiff, the long-time mentor to previous popes, Tuscan Hildebrand who became Gregory VII in 1073. Gregory is often called the founder of the papal monarchy. He was a Cluniac reformer and as such he did not and could not believe that reform should come from the civil power, however well meaning. No layman, Gregory was convinced, not even an emperor should run the Church. What this meant, of course, was that Gregory decided that the old concept of the divine right of kings had to go. It was different with a Charlemagne who was truly a universal ruler, but now the empire had shrunk into the several feudal municipalities. Christianity and a single empire were no longer coextensive, but Christendom was "larger" now than the territory of the empire. In other words, the pope who represented a religion that transcended the boundaries of the empire should now assume universal power and full political and spiritual supremacy. That is why Gregory encouraged remote territories such as Spain, Denmark and Hungary to accept the protection of the Holy See implying that he, the pope, was the real universal center of things rather than any emperor. To achieve this end Gregory lost no time in aligning the proper roles of civil and ecclesiastical power. A whole series of propaganda tracts on each side of the question began to flood the countryside. Gregory drew up the famous *Dictatus papae* (Rescripts of the pope) and by his letters left no doubt of the position of Church and state. Among the many things he insisted on were: the pope could be judged by none, the pope alone could depose and restore bishops; he alone could make new laws, move bishops, depose emperors and absolve subjects from their allegiance to their rulers etc. Certainly this was a large and bold extension of papal power. Gregory would soon have the opportunity to put his notions to the test.

Two years after his election Gregory acted. He forbade clergymen to marry and the people were not to receive the sacraments from them (a position which could be interpreted in the old Donatist heretical sense). He condemned and forbade the lay investiture to any ecclesiastical office under pain of excommunication. No emperor, king or local lord was to henceforth bestow the ring and crozier to any man and make him bishop. We can see the urgent crisis this provided for the emperor if we recall that the German kings and emperors had made the bishops their feudal princes. If the emperor could not continue to control such bishops the very ground of his control system was cut out from under him. His own men, as it were, were suddenly removed from his employ. The emperor, Henry IV could not but respond with resistance. His first tactic was the usual one of trying to get Gregory declared as unworthy of the papacy and thus deposed. Henry miscalculated badly. He failed to take into account the effects of the Cluniac reform nor could he get enough support from his own followers. Gregory on his part had powerful allies such as the other non-German bishops, Henry's own Saxon political enemies, the Normans and the powerful Countess Miltilda of Tuscany. Gregory responded to Henry's maneuvers by excommunicating him thus freeing his subjects from allegiance. Henry, seeing his weak position had no choice but to submit for the time being. Thus we have the famous and often romanticized scene at Canossa on January 28, 1077. Gregory was on his way to a council meeting and stopped at the castle of Canossa (one of Miltilda's).

Henry sought him out there in the snow and piercing winds and for three days waited outside for an audience. Gregory had no illusions about Henry's sincerity, but what could he do, especially for one seeking spiritual forgiveness? Gregory absolved him and the matter was over.

Henry quickly regrouped his forces, attacked the name of Gregory and set up an anti-pope. Gregory re-excommunicated Henry who in turn marched on Rome to enforce his will. Gregory shut himself up in the impregnable Castle Sant'Angelo. Henry was forced to flee Rome before an advancing Norman army which freed Gregory who died outside Rome in their company. The sequel to this story was that Henry's anti-pope was simply not received even though he took up his residence in the Lateran palace. Gregory was acknowledged as the true pope and even venerated for his courage; and later Henry was forced to abdicate before his enemies. Finally, the whole struggle between emperor and pope really ended in a compromise which, under the circumstances, was a victory for the papacy. In 1122 a Concordat of Worms was signed which allowed the bishops to be appointed solely and only by the Church but, after their installation, they must swear loyalty to the emperor who had the right of veto. Actually, the power struggle between pope and emperor would see-saw back and forth for centuries to come and in reality the only thing that solved the problem, as we shall see, was no solution at all: the whole struggle simply became meaningless as both the notions of king and pope fell into disrepute and Europe found out that it could do without both.

However, more immediate far reaching results were to occur beyond the vision of the antagonists. One interesting side effect was that, with the imperial power in Church affairs definitely and officially broken, the princes filled the vacuum and were greatly influential in the appointment of the bishops since, we recall, the bishops were still secular princes holding fiefs from the prince landowner. Pope Pascal II interestingly enough wanted the bishops to solve this problem by the simple solution of abandoning their fiefs but to this the emperor would not give his consent for he knew that should this happen the vast territorial wealth of the bishops, conceded to them by successive German kings, must fall into the hands of the lay princes. It is worth remarking therefore that in this instance the vast wealth of the Church was a policy of the crown for its own political purposes.

CONSEQUENCES

Much would be made of Gregory's outlandish pretensions in later centuries—nor were his the last words: there were the pretensions of Innocent III and Boniface VIII which went even further. Outrageous as such claims may seem to be to modern eyes (and we shall examine them in another chapter) we must not read modern concepts into medieval situations. Gregory was basically trying to reestablish the Church's right to rule itself and to free the Church of state control:

> At first Gregory seems to have hoped for imperial cooperation in implementing further reforms. But Henry IV's resistance to his decree banning lay investiture prompted the pope to excommunicate the emperor in 1075 and again in 1080 and to justify his action on the basis of the superior character before God of the ecclesiastical power. It must be emphasized, however, that although a profoundly significant and potentially revolutionary confrontation with lay authorities did in fact take place throughout Europe, this was not the purpose of the papal action. To Gregory and his succes-

sors this confrontation seemed necessary to the achievement of their aims. Its ultimate consequence, a papal interference in lay affairs rather than the opposite, was scarcely foreseen at the time.[2]

Gregory indeed started the great centralizing trend which his successors would continue to the point of absurdity and which would collapse by the middle of the seventeenth century but this trend did not substantially compromise the essential Petrine office. Rather the seventeenth century collapse to come was an end to an era, a policy, a style—not the end of the papal office itself. We must remember that the legal concentration of all civil and Church authority in the papacy was a product of human decisions and can be traced to specific dates in history such as Gregory's time. This whole process did not touch the essential office of the pope whatever that might be.

Another fact worth attending to. Pope Gregory VII has been at different times accused of being a visionary who attempted to ruin the state, a calculating cleric who wanted to subordinate the state to the Church. Historian Henri Pirenne makes this comment:

> For these reasons, Gregory has been regarded as a sort of mystical revolutionary, an Ultramontane endeavoring to ruin the State. But this is to introduce modern ideas into a conflict where they are entirely out of place. To begin with, in the case of Gregory there was no trace of Ultramontanism. Ecclesiastical discipline was still very far from being dependent on Rome. He made no claim whatever to nominate the bishops. What he wanted was to ensure that the Church should no longer be defiled by secular meddling. As for his conflict with the State, what does the accusation mean? The Empire was not a State. It was actually governed not by the Emperor but by the princes. As we have seen, there was no

administration; nothing in the shape of what we must call, for the want of a better term, a central power, giving it a hold over its inhabitants. If the Emperor's power was diminished what injury was inflicted on society? None, since it regarded him with indifference; since it was not he who defended and protected it. No catastrophe could follow from the victory of the Pope, and the Church was bound to benefit by it. If we are to understand the situation we must regard it from this point of view. We must forget that this was the heart of the feudal period, and that social and political evolution were on the side of these princes, who, as we have seen, were the real organizers of society. And they were on the side of the Pope. The feudality was working for him, just as he, without intending to do so, was working for it. A little while ago it was the rising bourgeoise that was taking the part of Rome; now it was the feudal magnates. Here what we call the State is not secular society, but the royal power, subjecting the Church and diverting it from its mission in order to support itself.[3]

Pirenne's description of the emperor as simply a royal person without capital, court or power is accurate as we shall have occasion to show elsewhere. Thus Gregory was not defying the (fictional) state; he was fighting against a specific royal personage who wanted the papacy for his own ends.

A final unforeseen and unintended irony from the whole lay investiture victory was that Gregory was unconsciously but actually inaugurating the complete secularization of the state. This would come many centuries later but seeds had been planted. The close cooperation of kingdom and church which was the ideal of the Carolingian empire gave way as that empire waned and disappeared. From now on there existed the possibility that if the Church could do without royal interference, the state could do without the Church. Where national states would grow up in the future this nascent novelty would become a reality.

VICAR OF ST. PETER

Having seen the inauguration of the centralized papacy under Gregory VII let us take time for the rest of this chapter to see how far this power went. The contrast to what the papacy was to what it became will be more apparent if we return to a very old phrase of the pope as the "Vicar of St. Peter." This strikes us modern Catholics as an awkward title for we know another. Yet there is no doubt whatever that the most significant root of papal prestige in the centuries prior to Gregory VII was the fact that St. Peter lived and died in Rome.[4] Peter's tomb was for centuries the touchstone of Christianity, the observable, physical, material link to Christ himself. Peter was in every sense the "rock" on which the Church was built. Thus early and medieval men swore on the tomb of St. Peter and documents incessantly called on Peter as witness to this or that. Because of the centrality of Peter the pope's position was unique for he, the pope, was considered nothing more or less than Peter personified. St. Peter, as it were, was still active—but through the pope. More than once there was the spontaneous acclamation that Peter has spoken through such and such a pope. Devoted Christians, missionary monks, bishops, all were conscious that Peter was involved and that they were claiming converts, not for pope so and so, but for Peter. From the eighth to the eleventh centuries the most active force in Rome was Peter and his "presence" was the main source of Western unity during these centuries.

It must be especially noted that this unity, centered on the presence of Peter, did not necessarily have anything to do with administration. As R. W. Southern puts it:

> It was a unity compatible with the very slightest exercise of administrative authority. The affairs of the church received

little direction from Rome. Monasteries and bishoprics were founded, and bishops and abbots were appointed by lay rulers without hindrance or objection; councils were summoned by kings; kings and bishops legislated for their local churches about tithes, ordeals, Sunday observance, penance; saints were raised to the altars—all without reference to Rome. Each bishop acted as an independent repository of faith and discipline. They sought whatever advice was available from scholars and neighboring bishops, but in the last resort they had to act on their own initiative.[5]

After the eleventh century, as we have seen with Gregory VII and shall see with Innocent III, the era of centralized administration came in, an era which has lasted down to modern times. Yet such a trend in centralization ironically started out almost by accident and for the highest motives:

In essence it [the papal reform under Gregory] was to be a thorough overhauling of the body ecclesiastic, a purging of its major abuses, notably simony, clerical marriage, immortality, and over-much involvement with things secular. This was to be done by means of various improvements in the machinery of ecclesiastical government, in particular its more effective centralization in Rome. As a consequence, the papal office gradually assumed a new character. Under the influence of contemporary canonists, Rome came to be regarded as something more than the see of the Apostle Peter and the place of his tomb, a holy object of pilgrimage, and possessing a spiritual predominance over all other churches. It became in fact the center of an effective system of jurisdiction, sometimes referred to as the papal monarchy.[6]

VICAR OF CHRIST

From the eighth century on we have already noted the beginnings of the growth of papal centralization. We saw the *Donation of Constantine* set the tone by claiming that the pope was to be an active and, above all, an independent ruler. The *Donation* document, we recall, was a forgery[7] telling how Constantine gave the pope and his successors the supreme temporal power in the West, the universal rule in both the temporal and spiritual realms, the role as the only and genuine heir to the old Roman Empire. Circumstances did not permit strong popes to fulfill this ideal. They had to content themselves with ruling the universal church through their archbishops. However, it seems in the seventeenth century for some reason that among the English the notion arose that no archbishop could exercise his functions unless he received a pallium or sign of his office from Rome. In any case this soon became the universal practice in the Western world. This was a major step in making the pope more central and the arbiter of orthodoxy since in many cases he would have to judge the orthodoxy and worth among rivals for the job. Still, communication was poor, papal legates were not numerous and there were no ecumenical councils. The circumstances were not ripe for any immediate spread of papal power. This is why, as we have noted before, Pope Leo III crowned Charlemagne in 800. He had hoped to state as fact what the *Donation* had said, that he was ruler of the West. By crowning Charlemagne the pope was in effect saying that he did control the West by controlling the emperor. Also, as we noted, in this he made a momentous mistake for he wound up creating not a puppet, but a rival and sometimes a master.

The *Donation of Constantine*, it must be noted, was the work of someone else other than the pope. It was the work of some men who were filled with a romantic concept of the past, who wished to restore what they considered the power and grandeur of the pope before the German emperors took over. This forged document therefore had great appeal. Soon, under Gregory VII whole sections of the *Donation* were included into new collections of Church law. Still, the *Donation* fell short in some respects since, for one thing it depicted the pope on the receiving end of the emperor Constantine's authority. This intermediary of the emperor was disturbing and soon for this reason the *Donation* document became out of date as papal support sought another basis. Other texts took its place, texts which were unrelenting in their affirmation that the pope, from God and by divine decree, was the supreme ruler in all Christendom both in spiritual and temporal matters. If in the eighth century the popes had turned from the Eastern emperor to tie their fate to the Carolingian empire, now in the eleventh century, under Gregory VII, they even turned from the Carolingian successors to stand alone.

Perhaps as significant as anything is the noticeable shift in terminology in the old phrase we saw above, the "Vicar of St. Peter." Now the phrase (which is still with us) took its place: the "Vicar of Christ." The idea was that the papacy was now determined to rest its prestige not only on the past (Peter) but to the present and future as innovators and universal rulers (Christ). Thus Innocent III could claim, "We are the successor of the Prince of the Apostles, but we are not his vicar, nor the vicar of any man or Apostle, but the vicar of Jesus Christ himself."

EVIDENCES OF PAPAL CENTRALIZATION

In the next hundred years after Gregory VII and thereafter, the centralization process reached its peak. The whole picture can be seen by reference to the vast amount of business and the consequent administrative machinery needed to handle it. From all over the Western world came letters to Rome. Even granting the fact of a rapidly expanding society from the eleventh to the fourteenth centuries, the amount of letters written by the popes at his time reveal the extent of centralization. For example, under Pope Sylvester II who died in 1003 there are about ten papal letters a year. Under Leo IX who died in 1054 there are some thirty-five papal letters. Under Pope John XXII who died in 1324 there are some 3,646 letters a year. Again, the need for a growing bureaucracy is obvious for the correspondence covered a multitude of matters from the granting of benefices to the settling of major and minor jurisdictional quarrels. By the twelfth century the papal court was handling thousands of litigation cases. It is no wonder that canon law received its greatest impetus during these centuries. By the thirteenth century the whole papal bureaucracy was highly complex and highly efficient. Thus the foundation was laid for the charge of later centuries of the Church as a pyramid with its ruling monarch, the pope, at the top and his total control of men's minds and spirits.

As indicative as anything else of the growing Roman activity are the Church councils themselves. From the seventh to the twelfth centuries there were only three of them, all held in Byzantine territory with no Westerners attending except the papal delegates. On the other hand, from the twelfth century to the fourteenth there were seven ecumenical councils all held in the West, all called and presided over by the pope and almost exclusively Western in attendance.

Further testimony to the rapidly growing centralizing machinery at Rome is the fact that from 1159 to 1303 every pope was what history has termed a "jurist pope"; that is, every one of them was a lawyer. The preoccupation with law and order is evident. What is also evident is that as much as such popes did bring stability to medieval society and laid the foundation for modern society, much of this achievement was done at the expense of their primary pastoral tasks. Interested in keeping the wheels of papal government going they could not give the time and energy to the spiritual leadership that was needed. In short, such popes were hardly distinguishable from any other able secular leader.

Also significant is the fact that because the papacy had become such a center for immense daily business the world was disturbed but not let down when the papacy moved for seventy years from Rome to Avignon. Since the papal set-up was where business was conducted then it really made no difference as to place. Indeed, the whole business machinery had moved into fantastic elaboration. It must always be remembered, however, that papal power grew largely because it satisfied the needs of the great mass of clerics and even, as it turned out, the needs of the secular princes. When these needs were rerouted as they were in the fourteenth and fifteenth centuries then all of the seeds of disaster inherent in the papal system sprung up and choked it to death. Meanwhile, the system continued to grow and it included three main categories: indulgences, arbitration and appointments to church offices.

INDULGENCES

The really first large scale granting of indulgences goes back to the Crusades when the participants were granted by the pope complete remission of the punishment due to their sins. Note that this was granted by the pope; it was his personal gift. Later indulgences were granted to anyone who performed a service for the Church and still later were really granted for anything at the discretion of the pope. Afterwards the pope granted to others the privilege of granting indulgences; people like confessors, priests, royalty, etc. Even to this day anyone who has made a retreat will hear the retreat master end with the words "By the power given to me by the Holy Father . . ." and usually there are prayers for the intention of the pope. Indulgences were also at first granted for large fees, then for smaller fees and then simply for a good work done, such as going on a pilgrimage. Thus Pope Boniface VIII in 1300 granted a plenary indulgence for those who visited Rome during the Jubilee year which occurred once every hundred years. Gradually the time was reduced until such jubilee years were every twenty five years. It was Clement VI in 1343 who put the granting of indulgences on its theoretical basis. He said:

> One drop of Christ's blood would have sufficed for the redemption of the whole human race. Out of the abundant superfluity of Christ's sacrifice there has come a treasure which is not to be hidden in a napkin or buried in a field but to be used. This treasure has been committed by God to his vicars on earth, to St. Peter and his successors, to be used for the full or partial remission of the temporal punishments of the sins of the faithful who have repented and confessed.

The average Catholic reader will recognize this teaching as substantially the same as he learned in grammar school. Finally, local churches besides those in Rome were given the same privileges and from then on the whole indulgence business flourished and went into all kinds of degrees and subdivisions. By the time of the fifteenth century the ways and means of giving and granting indulgences were beyond counting; and since the "spiritual treasury" was inexhaustible there could be no theoretical end to it. We will remember, however, that it was on this precise occasion of selling indulgences that Luther took his departure from the Church in the sixteenth century. We may also remark that with the proliferation of indulgences and with the ease with which they were obtained they were eventually debased from overkill. Still, the whole indulgence matter was evidence of papal control and papal power.

INTERNATIONAL POLITICS

By the thirteenth century the assumption was that the pope possessed all political power as well as supreme spiritual power. The emperor was his delegate *par excellence* and depended on papal coronation for his existence. Since the emperor was the chief "delegate" it was most necessary to dominate him to keep the lesser lords in line; hence much of the in-fighting and rivalry between emperor and pope. Obviously, with this set-up the pope had to enter politics full time and only direct papal jurisdiction over all civil and religious matters could assure the papacy of supremacy. This accounts for the constant preoccupation of the popes in international politics and why a man like Innocent III had his hand in every country of Christendom. This explains why the papacy became the seat of all arbitrations among the secular princes. In Italy of course, where the pope was a fellow land-holding prince he could not play the role of neutral Grand Arbiter; he had to enter into the very military activity and defenses of his territories. Those readers who saw the movie *The Agony and the Ecstasy* saw that Michelangelo's mentor (and tormentor) Pope Julian II (played by Rex Harrison) was not adverse to leading his soldiers in battle and was as much at home in soldier's armor as in papal robes.

GRANTING BENEFICES

As we have seen in the first chapters of this book the Church from the beginning had a more democratic process of choosing its leaders. The community was involved whether by popular acclamation or through its representatives—and this included the election of the bishop of Rome or the pope. Oddly enough because of the strength of tradition and habit no rules were ever laid down for a papal election before the year 1059 and then only sketchily. Until the eleventh century the one who claimed to represent the people in the papal elections was the emperor. Since he was a kind of spokesman for the Western Church he felt deputized also to speak for them in the choice of the pope. The only trouble, as we have seen in the cases of the German emperors, was that they were too far removed from the scene at Rome leaving any papal vacancy to be filled by the men on the spot. The "men on the spot" were the clergy and people of Rome or, more precisely, the ruling noble families. We have seen the disgraceful machinations of the Theophyact and Crescenti and Tusculoni families. So other powerful families were able to get their men on the papal throne. Innocent III, Gregory IX and Alexander IV were of the Conti family. Celestine III and Nicholas III were of the Orsini family. Honorius III and IV from the Savelli family and so on. Moreover there was rivalry not only among the local Italian families but later among the French families. Even when Nicholas II, in order to be freed of outside control, made the election of the pope dependent on the cardinals, matters were not cured. In fact, for the nobles they were simplified for now all that they had to do was to influence just the electing cardinals and not a lot of other extraneous people.

Besides, there were no rules among the college of cardinals itself for there were cardinal bishops and cardinal deacons and cardinal priests. Did they all have an equal vote? The confusion is evidenced by the fact that in the one hundred and twenty years after Nicholas' decree most of the anti-popes of the Middle Ages were produced thus reflecting the uncertainties listed. The situation was not brought under control until the Lateran Council in 1179 when the requirement was given that two-thirds majority secured a valid election. In 1945 was added a two-thirds majority plus one. Still, an unforeseen problem came when the nation states arose and the cardinals began to divide seriously along the lines of national interests. Such divided interests caused the Great Western Schism whereby three popes were elected and the uncertainty as to the real one remained in doubt.

EPISCOPAL ELECTIONS

We have already spoken of the election of bishops in a previous chapter. Here we may merely recall the general trend. From the eighth to the eleventh century the theory that a bishop was chosen by the people was in practice translated through the local lay ruler. Kings, after all, were responsible for the temporal and religious well being in their domains and so they could claim to represent both clergy and people. However, by the twelfth century the clergy had taken over in the persons of the canons of the local cathedral. However, since it was inevitable that there would be factions, squabblings and rivalries an arbitrator was needed. Who else could this be but the pope? This opened the way for more direct papal control which was not long in coming, especially as the theory to support it was being formed by the twelfth century. The current phrase was the "plentitude of power." The pope had it and the other bishops shared in it. It was not a true "college" of equals but a board of junior partners to a senior partner. In any case, by the fourteenth century all episcopal confirmations were in the hands of the pope. Pope Benedict XII summed it all up in 1335:

> We reserve to our own ordination, disposition and provision all patriarchal, archepiscopal and episcopal churches, all monasteries, priories, parsonages, and offices, all canonries, prebends, churches, and other ecclesiastical benefices, with or without the cure of souls, whether secular or regular, of whatever kind, vacant or in the future to be vacant, even if they have been brought to be filled by election or in some other way. . . .

We must not think that therefore the lay rulers were now completely out of the picture. On the contrary things were only made more simple. The lay ruler, instead of dealing with a network of clerics and canons, etc., had to deal with only one man now, the pope, and by force, bribery or compromise secure the confirmation of his loyal friends to episcopal sees.

Finally, we must mention that papal centralized control extended beyond the bishops all the way down to the most humble ecclesiastical office. Obviously this naturally led to literally thousands of petitioners at the papal court to fill the multitudinous clerical offices. The sheer volume of taking care of all of this was stupendous and was a challenge to the enlarging papal curial machinery to handle it. However, even here the whole system eventually backfired for obviously those with power and money behind them were to get the better offices: the ones, in other words, with the greatest amount of secular support—which meant the kings and local nobles. Thus the system once more merely simplified the access of the mighty to the affairs of the Church and reinforced the very undue influences it was designed to suppress.

SIGNIFICANCE

There is one final overview in our look at the rise of papal power and centralization. We saw that with all of the business flooding into Rome it was necessary to have many laws. Eventually these laws, some old, others innovative, if their sheer volume were not to collapse the whole system, had to be codified. Thus in the middle of the twelfth century a man named Gratian assembled all of the existing material and laws into one vast code. For this achievement he is regarded as the founder of canon law. Under the lawyer popes Gratian's codification was expanded. This code along with other decretals were collected into the *Liber Extra* of Pope Gregory IX. What is significant about all this was the quite measurable change in Church order and structure. This was evident in its internal life as well as its external organization:

> . . . The decretals rather than the Gospel became the basis for moral judgments. Even the sacraments came to assume a legal complexion, and a sacramental jurisprudence developed. Baptism was now considered as a legal act through which in law the newly baptized became a member of the Christian body, itself a juristically constructed entity. Matrimony was considered as a legal contract whose validity depended on avoidance of canonical impediments drawn up by the Holy See. Ordination to the priesthood was determined by legal enactments which placed jurisdictional rights above holiness of life as qualifications. A knowledge of canon law became requisite for ecclesiastical preferment. Throughout the remainder of the Middle Ages, canon lawyers rather than theologians dominated the papacy. The role of the papacy in medieval theological matters is incredibly unimpressive.[8]

Furthermore with all of the laws centered in the person of the pope then the old structures tended to disappear or become empty forms. This would mean that the old metropolitans, archbishops and bishops who controlled and commanded their local areas or sections were superceded by the centralizing power of the pope. One more thing—and this is very important—it meant that collegiality and collaboration of any sort was on its way out. If the "fullness of power" rested with the Holy Father, what need was there for consultation, local councils and area synods? In short, the community was suppressed and corporative rights were re-routed into papal channels. The papal General Ecumenical Councils now took over and only the popes could summon them. The rights of canonization passed from the bishops to the popes who act freely on their own. The cathedral chapters right to elect its own bishop, as we have seen, was undermined by papal restrictions and reservations. A whole one sided development was taking place: the absolute papal monarch. There was only one culminating power left and that was given at Vatican I in the 1870's: the pope was declared infallible and he alone.

From all that we have said, we can see that it has been a long, complicated road from the original church-communities of the first centuries to Byzantine and Frankish imperialism to Roman centralization. The Church has changed its "look." Gone are the old varieties of ministries and simple terms such as presbyter and deacon and widow. They have been replaced with the terms of officialdom: chancellor, cardinal and pope. Gone is the circle concept of community. It has been replaced with the pyramid concept of ascending hierarchical power and control. We shall have occasion to mention later how the modern Church is deescalating the pyramidal structure. The internationalization of the curia, the formation of a Synod of bishops, the establishment of local parish councils and so forth are all reactions in the modern Church to a medieval pyramidal Church that had grown too top heavy.

NOTES

1. Dawson, *op. cit.*, p. 91, 92.
2. Dolan, *Catholicism*, pp. 165, 166. Barron's Educational Series, Inc., Woodbury, N.Y. 1968.

3. Pirenne, Henri, *op. cit.*, p. 184.
4. "Archaeological discoveries provide additional information about the Roman Church at this period. The excavations carried out under St. Peter's on the Vatican Hill show that in about the year 120 the memory of the apostle Peter was already venerated there. It is even possible that it may be Peter's tomb which has been discovered, but in any case it is certain that his memory is preserved there by a monument. The priest Gaius, at the end of the century, says he saw the trophies of the apostles Peter and Paul on the Vatican Hill and on the road to Ostia. The fact that this monument is in a cemetery seems to confirm that it is indeed a memorial of Peter at Rome. The *graffitti* on the wall around the monument are also evidence that he was venerated there." Danielou and Marrou, *op. cit.*, p. 53.
5. R. W. Southern, *op. cit.*, p. 96. The following pages in this chapter rely on ideas from this book.
6. Marshall W. Baldwin, *Christianity Through the Thirteenth Century*, p. 165. Walker and Company, N.Y. 1970.
7. For an interesting essay on medieval forgeries, see "Approaches to Medieval Forgery" in the book *Medieval Church and Society* by Christopher Brooke, New York University Press, N.Y. 1971, p. 100.
8. Dolan, *op cit.*, p. 74.

IX

A Time of Greatness

PAPACY AND REFORM

In the last chapter we have seen how the papacy reached the height of its power. At no other time in history were Church and society so interpenetrated. Everything else in fact seemed to reach its peak at this time earning for the thirteenth the epithet, "the greatest of the centuries." This may indeed be an exaggeration for there were many flaws, but there were enough events and developments to give some substance to the title. What had happened was that the reform movement had unleashed new spiritual forces. The creative elements which we associate with the achievements of the late Middle Ages came from the dynamic fusion of this reform movement with the papacy. A central unity had been created joining most of the active elements in Christian society in a common program. There was a common cause, a supra-territorial spirit, a whole European brotherhood that brought out the best in everyone. Look at what happened: the first universities were founded. Scholasticism hit its stride. Chivalry flourished and the new romantic notion of love was introduced. Towns were revived, a merchant class was starting, civic life was growing and hospitals were being built. The Gothic cathedral came into being and learning flourished producing some of the greatest scholars of any age. New religious orders were founded. The list is impressive. So in this chapter we must examine the greatness of the age before the shadows fell. We can do no better than to start with an event that reflected the whole spirit of papal reform. It formed a constant background to the late Middle Ages for two centuries and was in no small way responsible for the revival of commerce and all that went with it. We refer to the Crusades.

THE CRUSADES

The Crusades lasted from the eleventh to the thirteenth centuries. Although they ended up in dismal failure they started out with genuine idealism and religious fervor. We must recall some background. First of all the Moslems had surrounded Europe and in some areas penetrated into it. For centuries they were to remain a chronic source of fear, conflict and confinement. However, by the tenth century they were beginning to lose some ground in Europe and the Christians were having some military successes here and there. By the eleventh century the Christians were taking the offensive against the Moslems. It was partly in the spirit of these local successes and actually as a continuation of them that the first official Crusade got started.

Secondly, we have already made reference to the pilgrimage as an act of popular piety in the Middle Ages. We saw that even more than the two other great centers, Rome and Compostela, Jerusalem was the object of special veneration. Pilgrimages increased and many references were used with the image of the Holy City such as the "new Jerusalem" as referring to the Church. Many a person wanted to see the land blessed by the sufferings and the death of the Savior. Particularly around the year 1000 the usual hopes or fears that the world would end gave special urgency to the desire to see Jerusalem before it all happened. Many reasons underlay the First Crusade, but there can be no doubt that the majority of people joined it in the spirit of a pilgrimage.

Finally, the thought of a Crusade was not entirely unprepared for. The Byzantine empire of the East was being constantly beseiged by the Moslems and often asked aid of the West. This petition was a mark of its desperation since East and West had recently split over emotional and doctrinal differences. Another factor was that although the Moslems had been quite tolerant of the Christians, allowing them to visit the holy places in Palestine, a new group of Moslems began to crack down. In any case, an appeal from the emperor of the East was made once more to the pope. It is worth noting that the appeal went to the pope, not to any emperor or king, a fact which was a commentary both on the weakness of the kings and the growing universal power of the pope. The pope who answered the appeal was Pope Urban II. He was the successor of Gregory VII whom we recall had recently died in exile at odds with the emperor. This was Henry IV who, after Canossa, had revived his desire to rule the papacy. Henry was still on the warpath having installed an anti-pope in Rome. This explains why Urban was at the little French town of Clermont. There in 1095 in a masterful speech to a large mob who had originally come to look into the investiture quarrel with Henry IV Urban called for the First Crusade. The speech skillfully combined an appeal from the highest spiritual and practical motives. The honor of God demanded that sacred Christian shrines should be in the hands of Christians, not infidels. Besides, a Crusade might provide more land and food. This last appeal was not lost on the majority of Frenchmen there who were suffering from famine at the time.

We must recall that the spirit of Cluny was alive and so

the response to Urban's appeal was instantaneous and al-most fanatical. Immediately the crowd picked up as the Crusading slogan Urban's impassioned "God Wills It!" They painted red crosses on their shirts and shields so that no more red paint or cloth could be found in Clermont that day. There was no doubt that in this excited response genuine religious motives played a powerful part. After all, there was a prom-ise of a full indulgence for the sins of ones life for all Cru-saders. Men were truly incensed at the thought of Christ's tomb in infidel hands. They felt true religious response. In such a large undertaking there had to be other motives in the background of course. Perhaps in the back of the pope's mind he felt that the Western Church could extend its in-fluence at the expense of the East. For some feudal nobles the prospect of a Crusade gave a legitimate outlet for their warlike and landless sons. For others the appeal may have been in the postponement of their financial debts, or the simple thrill of adventure and the enticement of new lands and new wealth.

There were the usual fanatics like the rabble-rouser, Peter the Hermit, who prematurely led a group of naive enthusiasts to the East and to their easy deaths. The first real Crusade finally got started which interestingly included no kings or emperor (still a papal enemy) but mostly French knights and nobles. They were on their way, full of fervor. Unfortu-nately the fervor to kill the infidel spilled over to the Jews many of whom were killed by the Crusaders on their way to the Holy Land. The archbishop of Cologne gave thousands of Jews sanctuary in his palace but the Crusaders massacred them anyway.

> . . . When the Crusaders cried out "God exalt Christianity," it seemed often to be a mandate to abuse Judaism. When Pope Urban II, the disciple of Gregory VII, addressed the

Crusaders as "the children of Israel," his words may well have carried for his excited listeners a reminder that the Jews were children of the devil, Jesus' murderers, and God's enemies. What point was there in redeeming the Holy Land, asked popular preachers of Crusading like Peter the Hermit and Walter the Penniless, if they left behind them the worst offenders of all? Hence as great masses of humanity began to tumble together preparatory to setting out for the Levant, they began to swoop down upon one Jewish community after another . . . In almost every instance local officials—ecclesiastical and feudal—sought to quell the rioters, with some success in a few places.

Thereafter, however, the inevitable accompaniment to every Crusade was a preliminary bloodbath . . . St. Bernard of Clairvaux, the chief preacher of the Crusade, vainly sought to persuade Christians "to leave the Jews in peace. . . ."[1]

Finally the Crusaders reached Constantinople. On their part they were literally overawed. There was no village in the West to compare with Constantinople. It had paved streets, night lights, shops, parks, theaters, a magnificent imperial palace, a hippodrome whose doors later on would wind up as the doors of St. Mark's Cathedral in Venice and the splendid basilica of Justinian, Holy Wisdom. The Easterners, on their part, were aghast at the crude "Franks" (which was the name for barbarian) who did not wash, fought among themselves and whose clergy were actually in armor along with the common people. Enamoured and hesitating at the wealth of the city the Crusaders had to be prodded by the pope to get to the business at hand. Finally they made it to the walls of Jerusalem and in 1099 the city fell in a massacre so severe that the blood literally flowed like a river through the streets. Even the Crusaders themselves were later ashamed for the fierceness of the conquest.

After this the Crusaders began to settle down and proceed to carve out for themselves four kingdoms along the Mediterranean. They should have known that so far away from home and in the middle of hostile people it would be impossible to maintain them. Still, these outposts lasted for some two hundred years. Meanwhile, to care for their sick and to protect their kingdoms in the Holy Land unique military religious orders were founded, the Knights Hospitalers and the Knights Templars. Ironically as badly as the Crusaders got along with their fellow Eastern Christians they got along much better with their infidel enemies with whom they lived side by side for these two hundred years. In fact the Crusaders got to cherish luxuries they never knew about such as Persian carpets, brocaded walls, inlaid furniture, wide windows and running water. It was this romance with the East that would produce the revival of trade.

There were other Crusades, eight in all, but none of them ever matched the fervor and piety of the first one. The great St. Bernard preached the second Crusade but it failed to achieve anything. This was partly due to the lackadaisical response of the comfortable Crusaders already in the East. Besides, cynicism was setting in as is shown by the fact that some took the cross of the Crusades but paid someone else to go in their places. The third Crusade was notable in that three of Europe's great kings took part: the emperor, Frederick Barbarossa (he drowned while on the Crusade); King Philip of France who deserted the venture and Richard the Lion-Hearted of England who worked out a compromise with the Moslems. A fourth Crusade was preached by Pope Innocent III himself but was shamefully turned by Venice toward commercial ends. Venice forced the Crusaders to sack a rival Christian city and even Constantinople itself in 1204 thus forever confirming the breach between East and West.

As time went on it got harder and harder to get people to go on the Crusades outside of adventurers and the riff-raff. The Holy places were lost, regained and forever lost again to the Moslems. The Crusades still had some glorious moments but they lost their appeal and their spirit as men's interests turned to other matters. But there were long-range results both good and bad. East and West were now more personally hostile to each other than ever before. Commerce was reopened. Luxuries and new foods and materials were imported from the East giving great stimulus to trade, navigation and the rise of the Italian maritime cities. An unhappier result was the introduction of the holy wars. Back in the ninth century Charlemagne had at least offered the Saxons baptism or death. Now it was simply death to the unbeliever. Extermination not conversion was the forerunner of punishment for the heretic. The inquisition was just around the corner. For the moment, however, the Crusaders represented an ideal of a war for Christ out of the highest motives and they would produce many a hero and saint along side of the scoundrel and self-seeking villain.

REVIVAL IN LEARNING

Literacy was almost completely restricted to the Church whose clerics wrote and spoke the official Latin. The Church ran such local and monastery schools as there were. By the twelfth century, however, several schools were emerging in the newly expanding towns which would grow into the great universities. The first medieval universities, unlike those of today, had no fixed quarters: any place where the small corporation (*universitas*) of pupils and masters could meet would do. In time rooms were rented still making the whole small university quite portable. As in modern times there was often hostility between the small university people and the town. Riots in which several were killed were not unknown. It was the pope who ruled that the university had the right to rule its own affairs and could pull out of a town, something which no town, anxious for prestige and wealth, wanted.

Actually what stimulated it all was the introduction to the West of the ancient Latin and Greek authors in translations made by the Moslems and Jews. The Greek pagan, Aristotle, who was to have such a tremendous influence on the Church was the chief import of study. Furthermore new types of schoolmasters arose, men who forced their pupils not just to memorize but to think. Perhaps the most famous of the time was Abelard (d. 1142) known more today for his romance with his pupil than his intellect. Yet he had the keenest mind of the day and asked probing questions about faith and reason. He asked so many and so deeply that he was condemned by churchmen and evoked the fulminations of the great St. Bernard himself. He was the real forerunner of the scholastic scholar and he anticipated the work of the great St. Thomas Aquinas a hundred years later. When Abelard was about forty years old he became tutor of the eighteen-year-old Heloise. At first it was all business and afterwards romantic love. Heloise became pregnant and they went off to her sister's home where the baby was born. Abelard wanted to marry her but Heloise was at first unwilling to ruin his teaching career. They finally married and the girl's uncle had Abelard castrated. He became a monk and Heloise a nun. Abelard continued to come under attack for his theological opinions and in the end he submitted to authority. It is not surprising that he has become the epitome of the star-crossed lover and the liberal intellectual persecuted by the establishment.[2]

A contemporary of Abelard, and the man who really started the revival of theological speculation was St. Anselm of Canterbury. His line of thinking was shaped by the views of the time which had revived a deep sense of sin and thoughts of the suffering and death of Christ. He wrote a book *Why Did God Become Man?* in which he outlined the common theory of Redemption held today. In Anselm's society where rank was important it was easy for men to understand that insult is measured, not by the deed, but by the dignity of the person offended. As far as God goes Adam's insult was most grave because of the infinite dignity involved. No mere man could repair the harm. Adequate apology demanded an equally infinite person; in a word, God himself. Thus Christ, the God-become-man alone could offer satisfaction. This in essence is what the modern Catholic holds. Because of its severe legal approach this theory has come in for much criticism today.

In any case, the universities received stimulus from thinkers like Abelard and Anselm. By the twelfth century there were founded the universities of Paris, Bologna, Padua, Oxford, Cambridge, Vienna, Prague, Heidelburg,[3] Basel, Salamanca,[4] Louvain, etc. By the thirteenth century Aristotle was really coming into his own. Pagan Aristotle's teaching met great opposition, was condemned, yet refused to go away. Men like St. Albert the Great, St. Bonaventure and, most of all, St. Thomas Aquinas "baptized" Aristotle. St. Thomas himself did not escape the censure of the theological faculty at the University of Paris where he taught. His old teacher, St. Albert the Great, now eighty-four years old, had to come to his defense. Fifty years after his death in 1274 Thomas became quite acceptable and under Pope Leo XIII in the twentieth century Thomas' system of thought became the Church's official line. We must not neglect to mention

Thomas as saint and poet and it is to him that we owe the venerable Benediction hymns sung by many generations of Catholics, the *O Salutaris* and the *Tantum Ergo*.

From this general revival of learning came not only the wandering scholars but also the first wandering troubadours who sang their love songs in the vernacular and poked fun at the fashions of the times and the foibles of the Church. They are responsible for introducing the new concept of romantic love and the cult of courtesy. This was a concept which formed a reaction to the loveless marriages arranged strictly for property and power consolidation purposes. Now real love was extolled and the love between those not married to each other for "Medieval marriages were entirely a matter of property, and, as everybody knows, marriage without love means love without marriage."[5] These songs and poetry of the troubadours in time turned to other themes besides love. Noble and spiritual themes appeared later on and refinement and courtly culture came into play as against a brutal and rough society. The great epic, the *Song of Roland* was composed at this time. Other stories became the forerunners of the modern novel such as the tales of the legendary King Arthur and his knights of the Round Table. In the next century, the English would come into their own with Chaucer's *Canterbury Tales*. When the troubadours went to Italy the Italian dialects took over and within a hundred years produced the language in which Dante's *Divine Comedy* was written. Courtly culture and troubadour love would find its best expression in that wandering troubadour, St. Francis of Assisi.

We must pause from these achievements to point out here seeds which would sprout in a later age to choke off the Church. One obvious difficulty was that by their very nature universities would be hard to control. New ideas and theories would arise which would severely challenge the faith. St. Thomas and his followers by extolling reason so highly as capable of reaching truth in its own right would provide ammunition for those theorists of a later time who reasoned that political institutions could therefore rest on logic and reason. In effect, this was saying that the state did not have to base itself in churchy foundations for its validity. The state would be free of the Church to the degree that it has its own rationale.

There were other famous notions arising in the universities which were to have profound theoretical effects. One rather refined one worth mentioning was the controversy whether abstract universal concepts really represented reality or were just convenient terms to describe essentially a collection of individual terms. This schoolman's argument was to have great practical results in the future. If abstract concepts were only nominal catch-all words then there are no universal ideas such as truth or, more ominously, government or Church. There are only individual citizens and individual Christians. In short, there is no such entity as "Church," no need for a universal papacy. Esoteric thoughts like these would do much to underpin Church dissenters and reformers of a later time.

CATHEDRALS

Medieval art had one purpose: to make the people feel inspired and awed. Way back to the time of Constantine emperors had encouraged church building. We recall the splendid Holy Wisdom basilica of Justinian. When the barbarians came they brought their talent for metalworking and woodcarving and ubiquitous animal motifs. The Irish Book of Kells and other manuscripts demonstrate the exquisite miniature drawings and paintings. Gregory the Great gave impetus to Church music in the chant named after him. In the eleventh century there was a spasm of church and monastery building as a result of the Cluniac reform which developed and matured the Romanesque style with its arches and splashes of interior color tapestries.

In the twelfth century appeared the first Gothic cathedral built by the famous Abbot Sugar. Others soon followed his example and shortly magnificent cathedrals sprang up all over Europe. Notre Dame was begun in 1163 (though it took ninety years to complete), Chartres, the queen of all cathedrals, was started in 1194 and completed in 1260. Then came Rheims, Amiens and others. They were feats of designs and architecture. Using the ribbed vault and flying buttresses they gave a graceful, airy and spacious effect filled with soft light coming in from literally walls of stained glass. A Gothic cathedral was often the work of the town in every sense. Chartres was built by the men, women, children and lifelong enemies carrying stones on their backs. For the cathedral was more than a church. It was a source of civic pride, the center of town. Plays were performed on its steps. Preachers spoke their sermons there. Business was conducted inside. Town meetings which literally meant the towns people were fitted into the cathedral. Finally, the cathedral was the place of worship and a living stone catechism. There were hundreds of pictures and images portraying man's journey to God, beset by devils and aided by angels. Later on the snobs of the Renaissance would look down on such masterpieces calling them barbaric or "Gothic" (the name of one of the barbarian tribes). Ages since the Renaissance, however, have continued to look upon the great Gothic cathedrals as magnificent works of art. Lord Clark of Saltwood catches the spirit when he writes:

We know from the old chronicles something about the men whose state of mind these faces reveal. In the year 1144, they say, when the towers seemed to be rising as if by magic, the faithful harnessed themselves to the carts which were bringing stone, and dragged them from the quarry to the cathedral. The enthusiasm spread throughout France. Men and women came from far away carrying heavy burdens of provisions for the workmen—wine, oil, corn. Amongst them were lords and ladies, pulling carts with the rest. There was perfect discipline, and a most profound silence. All hearts were united and each man forgave his enemies.

. . . Chartres is the epitome of the first great awakening in European civilization. It is also the bridge between Romanesque and Gothic, between the world of Abelard and the world of St. Thomas Aquinas, the world of restless curiosity and the world of system and order. Great things were to be done in the next centuries of high Gothic, great feats of construction, both in architecture and thought. That was the age which gave European civilization its impetus. Our intellectual energy, our contact with the great minds of Greece, our ability to move and change, our belief that God may be approached through beauty, our feeling of compassion, our sense of the unity of Christendom—all this, and much more, appeared in those hundred marvelous years between the consecration of Cluny and the rebuilding of Chartres.[6]

THE TOWNS

There had always been a few European towns around, but they were small fortress places or residences of the bishop. Perhaps they had a cathedral or a monastery. But the towns never grew. The barbarian invasions, the Slavic invasions, the Viking maraudings, the whole land-locked economy imposed by the Moslems left no need nor any role for towns. However, as we have seen, it was the Crusades that reopened on a large scale trade between East and West. Certain maritime towns like Venice began to flourish. Eventually, with Moslem powerlessness, even the Baltic Sea became accessible. The great Fairs of the Middle Ages began to grow into great enterprising centers where men from all over the world brought their goods. It was no accident that, with its extraordinary coastline and Venice's predominance, the Italian towns should first grow into large centers. It was therefore no further accident that with commerce, the means of exchange should arise in Italy. There arose the first banks (from the word *banc* or bench at which they transacted business), credit and, above all, the revival of money. In due time in the face of so much commercial pressure and the new stimulation of capital the Church was forced to change its attitude on usury. In a previous land economy taking interest on loans was considered exploitation. In the new money economy this could not be the case anymore and so the Church modified its stand.

Along with this revival of trade, commerce, money came a new merchant class of people. For the first time large groups were not attached to the soil but were wanderers, carriers of new merchandise and new wealth. Eventually when commerce became more a way of life it became practical to have fixed towns of trade. The town began to grow (it was crowded, wretched, narrow and unsanitary—but *free*) and for that reason it drew serfs and artisans into a growing middle class dedicated to keep the common peace, their common liberties and prepared to obey their common officers. It would only be a matter of time before these people took a hand in the running of their towns and started civil administration on its road. In due time also, a few prominent merchant families ruled the towns. Merchant guilds appeared to prevent competition among the artisans and civic pride was born. The medieval town of the eleventh and twelfth centuries became thus a real conglomeration of free people engaged in trade, craft and industry with a free civil government. If at one time a man would travel in Europe from monastery to monastery, it was soon becoming a case of traveling from town to town and like the monastery, the town became an oasis of security and peace in a world of insecurity and war.

It should be obvious from this condensed description of the rise of the town that drastic changes in Church and society were in the offing. They were imperceptible at first but they would be quite telling. For example, the town, as its administration grew, began to employ secular personnel. This secular personnel began to use in its transactions, not the traditional churchy Latin, but the vernacular. This was a sign of the growing reality that Church was not as important as before. The people in towns indeed were religious—witness the many religious guilds founded at the time—but the feeling grew that the Church should keep out of business matters. The towns would do even more to weaken the Church's hold on society. For one thing it would give rising monarchs an independent source of wealth and therefore of power. Towns had a natural tendency towards a fierce independence and life styles. They would create a class of business-minded people who one day would attack Church legal procedures, clerical financial exemptions and educational monopoly. In short, the towns, although allied with the papacy against the empire, would be the pivot for a whole new secular orientation of life.

NEW RELIGIOUS ORDERS

To demonstrate how rapidly and basically society was changing we may note that for almost seven hundred years there was practically only one religious order in the Church: that of the Benedictines.[7] Then, in the twelfth century about eight major types of religious communities appeared on the scene with many derivative branches. No longer was the Benedictine Order held to be the only safe road to heaven. No longer, as in the past, did kings and nobles seek the spiritual aid of the monks in the unwavering belief that the spiritual weapons of the monasteries were as necessary to the safety of the kingdom as armed knights. No longer would all manner of men turn to the monks asking them to do penance for them since all feared hell as the end of those who left repentance incomplete. (This was before the medieval doctrine of purgatory was formed.) No longer would the Benedictines be the only outlet for the landless children of the noble families. Now rivals would appear on the scene.

Not that for these seven hundred years the Benedictines did not perform great service to Church and state and give countless missionaries. But by the twelfth century a certain decline had set in. Life was becoming more complex. Some monasteries had become rather socially exclusive, their sources of revenue were drying up, and they had fossilized into great symbols of stability from which no innovations could be expected. As society expanded, new ways were looked for and into this vacuum came the new orders. First, there were the Augustinians (Luther's order), an informal group compared to the structured Benedictines, dedicated to practical service to others (in contrast to self perfection of the former monks) and to survival in a world of change.

The new order of the Cistercians, on the other hand, wanted to flee change, flux and the world and to return to pristine Benedictine rigor and purity. Thus the Cistercians fled the world and pushed far into the uninhabited lands of Europe. They grew rapidly but soon, like all other noble projects, they succumbed to success. They were so successful in clearing the land, improving agriculture and livestock breeding that, in spite of themselves, they became wealthy frontiersmen with the frontier virtues of work, aggressiveness and organization. Nor should it be forgotten that they were practically the first order to offer frontier sanctity; that is, holiness was open to the illiterate who were welcomed into the monasteries.

FRANCISCANS AND DOMINICANS

As a sign of the changing times, it is significant that the new towns brought into existence the two most influential orders of the times, the Franciscans and Dominicans. The older orders like the Benedictines and Cistercians were rooted in the soil, but these new orders represented a decided shift away from the country to the city. They were bourgeois middle class orders founded by middle class men (Francis was the son of a merchant). These orders, as Henri Pirenne reminds us, "lived on the alms of the bourgeoisie; they recruited their ranks from the bourgeoisie; and it was for the sake of the bourgeoisie that they exercised their apostolate, and the success of this was sufficiently proven by the multitude of brothers of the tertiary order, among both the merchants and the artisans, who were associated with the Franciscans".[8] Thus, there was something new. An order of brothers (*fratello* in Italian), or friars. They were not, as of old, to withdraw from the world, but to penetrate it. They gave to the age the common spectacle of the traveling friar and itinerant preacher.

The Franciscans, of course, were founded by the universal saint, John Bernadoni, nicknamed the Frenchman or Francis for his preference for French fashions. He made his decisive conversion to Christ the day he forced himself to kiss the sores of a leper. From then on, with his high taste for romance, he chose to live the simplicity of the Gospel or, as he would say, to court Lady Poverty. Unlike others Francis did not hate material things and his was not a stoical attitude embracing poverty for its own sake. Francis sought poverty as a means of liberation: the freedom to be, to grow and to rejoice in the beauty of the world. It was no sour-faced mystic who composed the *Canticle of the Sun* or who saw delight in all the creatures on earth. It is not without reason that the modern age has chosen Francis as the patron saint of ecology. It was no spiritual Scrooge who invented the Christmas crib and sang happy songs. He loved the towns and dedicated himself to preaching to the lukewarm.

Francis' followers soon grew in numbers and in spite of local jealousies from the monks and secular clergy he obtained from Innocent III approval for his new order. Inevitably with rapid growth dissension took place and with heavy heart Francis resigned his leadership. He died in 1226 and was canonized two years later. Much of the difficulty was over style and order. Was it practical to beg one's food from day to day? For five men this was no problem but for five hundred? How strict should the order be in following poverty? In due time many interpretations of the Franciscan ideal arose which splintered off into many Franciscan groups we know today.

> . . . of course, St. Francis' cult of poverty could not survive him—it did not even last his lifetime. It was officially rejected by the Church; for the Church had already become part of the international banking system that originated in thirteenth-century Italy. Those of Francis' disciples, called Fraticelli, who clung to his doctrine of poverty were denounced as heretics and burnt at the stake. And for seven hundred years capitalism has continued to grow to its present monstrous

proportions. It may seem that St. Francis has had no influence at all, because even those humane reformers of the nineteenth century who sometimes invoked him did not wish to exalt or sanctify poverty but to abolish it.

And yet his belief that in order to free the spirit we must shed all our earthly goods is the belief that all great religious teachers have had in common—eastern and western, without exception. It is an ideal to which, however impossible it may be to practice, the finest spirits always return. By enacting that truth with such simplicity and grace, St. Francis made it part of the European consciousness. . . . It was only because he possessed nothing that St. Francis could feel sincerely a brotherhood with all created things, not only living creatures, but brother fire and sister wind."[9]

In spite of severe internal problems, Francis' spirit continued in his friars, in the related woman's order founded by his friend, St. Clare, and in the Third Order of associated laymen which were the forerunners of the many lay confraternities that exist today.

Dominic Guzman (d. 1221) was a Spaniard. He had joined the Canons Regular of St. Augustine and had been sent along with a papal delegation on a mission to convert heretics. Dominic soon perceived that the official pomp and high living of the papal delegates were going to win back no one. Rather, poverty, simplicity and learning were necessary. He therefore gathered like-minded men around himself to be an order of preachers who lived a life of poverty. From this emerged the Dominicans. They soon spread all over Europe, like their new contemporaries, the Franciscans, and drew into their ranks some of the West's greatest scholars. By the way, St. Dominic is said to have received the rosary from Our Lady and given it to the world. Actually, this is a legend propagated by the Dominican Allen de Rupe in the fifteenth century. The rosary, at least in a primitive form, had been around as early as the ninth and tenth centuries and rosary-makers were common. In England there was a street called the Paternoster Row named after the craftsmen who produced such strings of prayer beads.

It was not long before both Dominicans and Franciscans entered fully into academic life and the new universities which so far had been little more than training grounds for civil administrators. But the friars wanted to convert the world and had to delve into every branch of learning. They brought a new dimension and excitement to study and expanded theology. It is not surprising therefore that the greatest names in medieval theology belong to the friars: Albert the Great, Aquinas, Eckhart, Bonaventure, Duns Scotus and William of Ockham.

As far as the people went both orders were a welcome reaction to the formalized attitudes of the regular clergy. The friars proved to be an effective antidote to the pervasive anticlericalism of the times which looked askance on the low morals, conduct and learning of the regular clergy. Both Franciscans and Dominicans soon developed into a corps of professional clergy, preachers, university teachers and confessors and their work on behalf of the Church at this period can hardly be over-estimated. They became the personal agents and emissaries of the reformed papacy. Later on, however, this prophetic and evangelizing vocation of the first friars became subordinated to the demands of ecclesiastical power politics. This produced a split in the reforming movement from which medieval Christendom never quite recovered.

ALBIGENSIAN HERESY

There were no heresies in the Church for eight or nine hundred years. It seems strange that heresy should reappear in the Church at the height of her power. Perhaps heresy did not have a chance to get a foothold before through the sheer preoccupation of the Church with other matters such as the various invasions over the centuries and consequent adjustments. Now the Church was consolidated and with consolidation came a certain rigidity and intolerance. In any case, in the height of her glory, the rift of heresies appeared. There was one heretical group called the Waldenses started in the twelfth century under Peter Waldo who called for reform and a return to primitive Christianity. He had ample reason to call for reform. The Crusades had fallen into disgrace and failure. Some of the Crusaders had even been excommunicated for looting a Christian town. Clerical celibacy was still a dead issue and the religious orders were ineffectual. His group started out, like the Franciscans, as a preaching sect. They led austere lives and began to teach heretical matters. They were forbidden to preach and finally excommunicated. They became more extreme and incurred the hostility of the community. They were forced to flee into the towns of northern Italy where they hung on until obtaining religious and political freedom in 1848.

There was a more dangerous and more widespread heresy at this time which the historian Gibbon has called the fourth great crisis in the Catholic Church. This was the Albigensian heresy named for the town of Albi. This sect revived the old Manicheism and Gnostic heresies that matter was evil and there were two principles at work. They rejected a visible church and all authority. They denied that Christ had a human body and therefore they had to reject the Eucharist and the Mass. They allowed no images. Sex was evil and, like the Gnostics of old, they had their society of the "perfect."

Everything was done to root them out. St. Bernard preached against them but to no avail. They grew stronger, drove Catholics from their churches and in general posed a serious threat. The Count of Toulouse asked the pope to send legates to repress the heresy but this met with only minor success. Impatiently Innocent III excommunicated the Count and in retaliation one of the count's men killed the monk who carried out the excommunication. Next, a crusade was launched against the Albigensians and carried on with great cruelty on both sides. The campaign went on for twenty years complicated by political overtones as rivals sought to possess the lands lost by the above mentioned excommunicated Count (as we shall see his lands were finally appropriated by the growing kingship). The crusade ended with the heresy still intact. One more tactic was left.

In 1233 Pope Gregory IX inaugurated the Inquisition (not to be confused with the later Spanish Inquisition). Influenced by the new emphasis of Roman law the death penalty and use of torture were introduced for heresy and the Fourth Lateran Council gave the Inquisition its final form and approval. It was a newly founded tribunal—a kind of ecclesiastical Interpol—to seek out and punish heresy. The Franciscans and Dominicans figured prominently in this new office. Heresy was to be punished not only for the good of the Church and state but for the good of the individual himself. The mentality of the times went like this:

> Heresy was considered the greatest of all sins because it was an affront to the greatest of all persons, God; it was worse than treason against a king because it was directly against the heavenly sovereign. It was worse than counterfeiting money because it counterfeited the truth of salvation, worse than patricide and matricide, which destroy only the body. Whatever penalties were appropriate for these crimes were all the more fitting for the greatest crime. To burn the heretic was an act of love toward the community, deterring by fear others who were inclined to the same sin. It was an act

of love toward the heretic, for he might be recalled by fear of the fire and save his soul.[10]

Men of all ages have rationalized torture and death as necessary for the preservation of the "truth." During Reformation times Luther would condone the killing of the peasant uprisers. Calvin would burn Servetus at the stake. Cromwell would kill in the name of the Lord. The Puritans would seek out and burn "witches." Queen Mary would kill Protestants and Queen Elizabeth would kill Catholics. Every government would have its purges of political purification. Still, the Inquisition and its use of torture to elicit confessions was a distinct backsliding of churchmen; it lent itself to abuses and harmed the innocent. Here the Church slid back into barbarity and no excuse need be given the Inquisition except, as Father James Broderick remarks, that of defending the exaggerations or blatant efforts to turn the whole issue into controversial advantage.

SUMMARY

The twelfth and thirteenth centuries in many ways were indeed glorious and represent something of a Golden Age. There were the rise of the new religious orders, the building of the churches, monasteries and glorious cathedrals. This was the age of the start of the great universities. It was the age when theology reached its perfection in the system of St. Thomas Aquinas. It was the age of great saints: Robert, Anselm, Bruno, Bernard, Albert the Great, Bonaventure. It was the age of great teachers: Abelard, Aquinas, Peter Lombard, Ockham. It was the age of the Franciscans, the Dominicans, St. Louis and Dante. It was the age of the town and the growing merchant class. It was the age of novelty in many ways. Commerce was being renewed and the economy was undergoing rapid expansion. Capitalism was on the scene: capital, money, credit and banking were started at this time. New notions of romantic love were being purveyed by the troubadours and vernacular literature was beginning.

It was the age of perfect papal power firmly based on the two strong pillars of law and wealth. Pope Innocent III who died in 1216 is considered to be the greatest of the medieval popes, a man genuinely dedicated to the cause of reform. Professor Knowles gives us a true assessment of this great man:

> Innocent III's pontificate is the brief summer of papal world-government. Before him the greatest of his predecessors were fighting to attain a position of control; after him, successors used the weapons of power with an increasing lack of spiritual wisdom and political insight. Innocent alone was able to make himself obeyed when acting in the interests of those whom he commanded. We may think, with the hindsight of centuries, that the conception of the papacy which he inherited and developed was fatal, in that it aimed at what was not unattainable and undesirable, the subordination of secular policy to the control of a spiritual power, but this conception was as acceptable and desirable to his age as has been to our own the conception of an harmonious and peaceful direction of the world by a league or union of nations.
> . . . It is impossible to dismiss the whole of Innocent's government of the Church as an exhibition of power politics to the exercise of an ambitious and egotistical man or even as an achievement of mere clearsighted efficiency. He appears rather as one who was indeed concerned to use and extend all the powers of his office to forward the welfare of something greater, the Church of Christ throughout Europe, and the eternal welfare of her children . . . the judgment which sees in him no more than a mitred statesman, a papal Richelieu, a loveless hierocrat, does not square with the evidence. The man who, in the midst of business, could recognize and

bless the unknown and apparently resourceless, radical Francis was not only farsighted but spiritually clearsighted. He died when the world still needed him, when he might have saved the papacy, as he saved the Church, from imminent disaster. He died at Perugia; his court left him, and his robes and goods and very body were pillaged by his servants. Yet he did not die alone, for it is all but certain that Francis had been present at his side.[11]

Nothing was foreign to Innocent's interests. He put all of France under interdict at one time. He intervened in England, fought for the rights of the clergy in Norway, interferred in the politics of Denmark, Hungary and Poland and protected the Jews from violence. There were six ecumenical councils between 1123 and 1274. Innocent called the great Fourth Lateran Council, the "first in the Middle Ages which really attempted to grapple with the problem of the parish priest and his people."[12]

This last point was important because now with the ministrations of the friars the ordinary people could receive instruction and spiritual help more than ever before. Preaching to the people became so important that many cathedrals were specifically designed to center around the pulpit. Still, people did not receive the sacraments much as is evidenced by one of the canons of the Fourth Lateran Council commanding the faithful to receive Communion at least once a year. There was some irreverence in Church and it was to promote a more reverent attitude towards the Blessed Sacrament that the feast of Corpus Christi was introduced in 1264 (the feast for which St. Thomas wrote the Benediction hymns).

It was the age of great devotion to the Blessed Mother to whom most cathedrals were dedicated. It was the age of increasing devotion to the passion of Christ. The old Latin hymns were written at this time: *Salve Regina* and *Jesu Dulcis Memoria.* No less a person than Innocent III is supposed to have written the beautiful *Stabat Mater.* It was an age of the flowering of many arts. In Germany the people were pioneering in mining and the use of the water mill. The Franciscan Roger Bacon was filled with a new scientific spirit. Medicine moved ahead, given impulse by what was learned by the Crusaders in the East. In many ways it was a time with many contradictions, but greatness was there. But it was not going to last. Already there were shadows cast over the "greatest of the centuries."

NOTES

1. Schweitzer, *op. cit.,* p. 87.
2. There are reputable scholars, however, who maintain that the whole story of Abelard and Heloise is a hoax.
3. People over thirty-five will remember this university as the setting for the operetta, *The Student Prince.*
4. This famous university inspired the medieval quip, *"Quod Deus non dat, Salamanca non praestat"*, which roughly translates as "If you haven't got it, Harvard won't help".
5. Kenneth Clark, *Civilization,* p. 64, Harper and Row, New York, 1969.
6. *Ibid.,* p. 56 and 60.
7. For this reason the time between St. Benedict (6th century) and St. Bernard (12th century) is known as the "monastic age" or the "Benedictine centuries."
8. Henri Pirenne, *op. cit.,* p. 240.
9. Kenneth Clark, *op. cit.,* pp. 77, 78.
10. Roland H. Bainton, *The Horizon History of Christianity,* p. 211. Avon Books, New York, N.Y. 1966.
11. Knowles and Obolensky, *op. cit.,* pp. 290, 291.
12. Marshall W. Baldwin, *op. cit.,* p. 281.

X

East and West

THE MYSTERIOUS EAST

It is a major tribute to the effective tragedy of the split between East and West that few Europeans or Americans know anything about the East. The East for the average Western man, for the average Western Catholic is "mysterious." One pictures Persian carpets and exotic customs and all the other images inherited by a movie-going public. This ignorance need not have been and only a great deal of insensitivity and misunderstanding has brought it about. For the Christian this ignorance is a double tragedy because the East is the origin of the Christian religion. All the first great ecumenical councils were held in the East and some of the greatest saints and theologians have their origin there. So, we must insert this brief chapter in order to examine what happened. We must survey the causes and the events that have led to the schism within the Christian Church—the first long and lasting shadow over Christendom.

We have taken note in the early chapters concerning the first Church councils how elements of friction were present early between East and West (which always translates as between the sees of Constantinople and Rome). Many of the heretics were from the East but that is only because Christianity was strong there and very weak in the West. More to the point: in the effort to settle heresies which were rending the empire asunder, emperors tried every which way to bring about reconciliation. And here we have one of the crucial inherent problems contributing to the final split. The emperors beginning with Constantine himself felt obliged to have a kind of protectorate over the Church. They felt the compulsion to establish religious unity and doctrinal purity. In short, they thought it a part of their imperial mandate to regulate the Church in the interest of the state. Thus it was that the emperors, in their efforts to suppress heresy, were the authors of many formulas of doctrine. It was they who called all the first councils. It would be they who would continue to be a constant third party to disturb Christian harmony between East and West.

The emperor moved the capital of the empire to Constantinople. This had the effect of raising that city to a special prominence. Obviously its patriarch had to be an important personage and equally obviously, in the logic of the emperors, they must favor, choose and control their patriarchs. This imperial interference might not have been so effective except for the fact of the Moslem invasions. By taking over much of the East they suppressed the old patriarchates of Antioch, Jerusalem, Alexandria and the like, leaving only Rome and Constantinople to share the Christian world between them. From the very start Constantinople knew it was a late-comer on the Christian scene and easily gave the nod of respect and primacy to Rome. Still, at one of the early councils Constantinople could not resist declaring itself to be at least *second* most important see after Rome. This brought protests from Pope Leo for the declaration was ominous. But in general there was harmony and interaction for the first seven hundred years. There continued to be a united empire of both East and West with its universal ruler, the emperor, residing at Constantinople. His Eastern deputies were very much in evidence at Rome and at Ravenna (the Western co-capital). Particularly after the Moslem onslaught the West was full of Eastern clerics and no one minded. In fact of the seventeen popes between the years 654 and 752 all but five were of Eastern origin. Emperor visited Rome and pope visited Constantinople in the seventh century.

Still, there were differences of no importance to the mind but only to the emotions. East and West did things differently. The West, for example, reconciled penitents in front of the church while the Greeks did not. They received communion differently, the Easterners used leavened bread at Mass, their clergy could marry and could confirm while the West did none of these things. Such nonessential differences would be blown up all out of proportion when other more serious events would inflate them. Such as? Such as the insistence of some Eastern emperors to impose Eastern ideas on the West. Such as the emperor who imprisoned Pope Martin I in 649 for disagreeing with him on doctrine and formula. Such as another emperor trying to arrest Pope Sergius for the same reason. These instances left bitter memories (and fear) in the West. One of the most disastrous cases of imperial interference came with the iconoclast heresy. We might recall how the Eastern emperor forbade the use of images and in 729 tried to force this position on the West. The pope reacted to this and the quarrel was long and bitter and many lost their lives. The emperor punished the pope for his resistance by raising taxes and confiscating papal property. The important result to note is that not only was this one more serious friction but it had the effect of shying the popes away from the overbearing East. The search was on for a protector in the West. The feeling was born that only continued dominance could come from the East and perhaps the Western Church should cut its moorings.

POLITICAL SEPARATION

The idea of cutting politically loose from the Eastern emperor was not without some support. With the loss of much of the Eastern areas to the Moslems the balance in numbers was tilted in Western favor. There were more Christians there now. Then there were the efforts of the great Western missionaries. They were bringing into direct papal influence whole countries and whole tribes. Soon there would be practical support for Western independence. Moreover, when the barbarians did come into the Western Church they added a certain discontent. They did not like the idea of those Greek popes who did not speak Latin. They were upset by the Eastern styles at the papal court. In brief, the feeling grew that Rome ought to be the exclusive property of the West. Such was the feeling when the opportunity for a political break with the empire presented itself. We might recall that the Lombards were the last of the barbarian invaders to ravage northern Italy in the eighth century. They succeeded in breaking the hold of the Eastern power there. The pope was not sorry, in the light of all that we have said, to see the imperial power broken but he was not ready to be dominated by the Lombards either. He needed an ally to fill the vacuum. This was the occasion when he turned to Pepin who drove out the Lombards and donated their land to the pope. The net result was that Italy was now divided between the papacy and the new upstart Carolingian empire. With the crowning of Charlemagne in the year 800 the political break from the East was complete. We have already taken note that the pope crowned Charlemagne by surprise as an overt notice to the East that he now had his own man. Even though the Eastern emperor technically was still the universal ruler in both East and West, in practice there were now two co-emperors. Emotionally and spiritually there was still unity and Christendom was one; politically there was division.

CHARLEMAGNE

In the year 787 the pope sent his delegates to the last commonly acknowledged general council of the Church, the Council of Nicaea. The pope sent only delegates in the realistic appraisal that the West had no men of learning, no theologians to compare with the sophisticated East. Charlemagne disagreed. He felt slighted at Western smallness and wound up ridiculing the whole council and letting go of a lot of invective against the "stupid" Greek Church. In effect he was telling the Greek world that it should not be so theologically high-hat and he was indirectly warning the pope that he should not be so influenced by the East. He should stick to his Western allies. The Greeks of course laughed at the fulminations of a man who could neither read nor write and the pope had no intention of replacing the sophisticated Greek theologians with Western barbarians.

Charlemagne's interference and denigrating of the East did not stop there. He decided to play theologian himself. The background was this: at the very first Church Council in Nicaea in 325 the Fathers had come up with the Nicene Creed which declared that the Holy Spirit proceeds from the Father. However, somewhere in the seventh century someone or some group in the West had unofficially added the phrase "and the Son" which in Latin is *filioque*. Charlemagne adopted this addition and, true to all rulers of the times, he insisted that everyone else in his kingdom make the addition too. The pope was unhappy about this and in Rome he alone did not make the addition but everywhere else it was made without papal authority. After all, the popes were reluctant to tamper with a version of the creed which had been accepted by all of Christendom these many centuries. However, by the eleventh century the subtle pressure on Rome caused it too to quietly add the word. Now for the first time there was a clear-cut case of an actual theological difference between East and West. Naturally the Easterners strenuously objected for, as they reminded all, any alteration to the creed was expressly forbidden by the councils of the Church. This whole incident illustrates just how far apart East and West had traveled in two centuries. Rome had in effect adopted a Western point of view almost by osmosis for it had lost theological contact with the East. In fact, to show how much distance was really traveled we may remark here that from the middle of the eighth century there is not another Greek pope until another seven hundred years! In any case, the whole creed issue opened the door to the disaster of the Photian affair.

PHOTIUS

The Photian affair started out in the usual maze of intrigue. A certain Ignatius was appointed patriarch of Constantinople. When the empress who appointed him was forced out of power Ignatius was deposed and in 858 Photius took his place. Obviously there was here a question of who was the legitimate patriarch. Pope Nicholas I declared in favor of Ignatius. The pope's decision was ignored. What was not ignored was the deep resentment that the Roman pope was interfering in the internal affairs of the East. An open schism broke out. This was not all. To add to the tension another event took place at this time. A certain ruler in Bulgaria (an Eastern area) was baptized by the Byzantine missionaries but, for political reasons, he requested the pope to send him a Western hierarchy. Roman missionaries were quickly dispatched. The point was that certain areas of Bulgaria had never at any time belonged to the Western Church. This was blatant poaching and the East feared a total takeover by the West. As if this were not enough the West insisted in adding the fateful *filioque* to the creed there.

Photius, no friend of Rome, quickly denounced the *filioque* addition as heresy and had a local council depose and excommunicate Pope Nicholas who had used some strong language in making papal claims. A sudden change of government forced Photius to resign. Union with Rome was restored. Ignatius too was restored only to be finally replaced by Photius when he died. This time both Photius and pope were more moderate in their approach and full communion was restored. But the damage had been done. This was the first out-in-the-open clash between the East and West over the Roman primacy.

We may comment here that there was never any question that the pope had a certain primacy. The real question was what was its extent and did it include jurisdiction? Was Pope Nicholas justified in poking into Eastern ecclesiastical affairs? Did the pope have the final word? or, to put it another way, was he infallible? Actually, there was ground for discussion on such issues. After all, we must recall that the Council of Constantinople in 680 saw the condemnation of Pope Honorius. That was most significant. It meant that Rome concurred in the condemnation of one of its popes and therefore there really was common ground between the errors of the East and those of the West. In other words, whatever papal claims meant concerning infallibility it was not absolute. It left room as the case of Honorius showed. The Council of Constantinople gave hope therefore that the issue of infallibility need not be an insurmountable problem. The whole attitude in these matters can be summed up in the following words (which could be written today) written in 1136 by an Eastern bishop to a bishop in the West:

> My dearest brother . . . we do not deny to the Roman church the primacy amongst the sister (patriarchates); and we recognize her right to the most honorable seat at an Ecumenical Council. But she has separated herself from us through her pride when she usurped a monarch which does not belong to her office. . . . How shall we accept from her decrees that have been issued without consulting us and even without our knowledge? If the Roman pontiff, seated on the lofty throne of his glory, wishes to thunder at us, and, so to speak, hurl his mandates at us from on high, and if he wishes to judge us and even to rule us and our churches, not by taking counsel with us but at his own arbitrary pleasure, what kind of brotherhood, or even what kind of parenthood can this be? . . . We should be the slaves, not the sons, of such a church, and the Roman see would be not the pious mother of sons but a hard and an imperious mistress of slaves. . . . I ask your pardon when I say this about the Roman church, for I venerate her along with you. But I cannot follow her along with you through everything; nor do I think that she should necessarily be followed through everything.[1]

We can see in the quotation not only the Eastern complaint against the West but the source of dissatisfaction in the West itself. It was this sort of understanding of Rome and the papacy that would lead Luther to revolt for at first Luther did not repudiate the papacy as such: only its pretensions. Interestingly, it is words like these that are the foundation for much of the agitation after Vatican II about papal infallibility, the drive towards an internationalization of the Roman curia and the drive towards decentralization still taking place at this writing. The modern trend toward national hierarchical meetings is based on the belief of the fundamental equality of all bishops including the bishop of Rome. As far back as the second century Ignatius of Antioch said that the Church is fully manifested wherever the bishop who represents the eternal priesthood of Christ celebrated the Eucharist in the presence of the faithful. Of course, part of the problem between East and West over the exact nature of papal primacy was that the East was not always consistent in their grounds for rejection. They did not have a firm theoretical basis to refute papal claims. On the other hand, the West had by now a fully developed theory which was consistent and complete. This situation naturally aggravated the tension between the two.

MICHAEL CERULARIUS

As background to the case of Michael Cerularius we must make mention of a growing "nationalism" in both East and West. The Greek or Byzantine empire had regained some of its lost territories with the result that it achieved a new sense of solidarity and identity. The West was now wedded to the Frankish kingdom; it had its protector. The net effect was that the mentality of both sides changed considerably. The East felt itself now politically equal to the West and superior culturally. The West looked on the East as heretical and decadent. It was from this mental set that the principles in the Cerularius affair would speak.

Ironically, at the beginning, the time was ripe for reunion for both East and West were facing a common enemy in the eleventh century. The Normans had invaded southern Italy, an area which belonged politically to the East but ecclesiastically to the West, at least up to the eighth century when an emperor had transferred the territory even ecclesiastically to the East. The common interest was therefore that the emperor wanted to regain political control from the Normans but he needed the West's aid to do this; and the West wanted to regain ecclesiastical control. Cooperation in this venture against the Normans might go a long way towards unity. Unfortunately, the bishops in southern Italy were quite unwilling to have Latin ways imposed on their Greek churches and harsh comments were made. Pope Leo IX wrote letters on the West's position. He was very strong on papal claims. He lavished praise on the emperor but distain and chastisement on the patriarch. In turn the patriarch of Constantinople, the ambitious and immoderate Michael Cerularius, imposed Greek customs on the Latin churches there. The pope's spokesman at Constantinople, Cardinal Humbert (who also, it is felt, authored Leo's letters), retorted with equal incivility leaving the impression that reunion meant the total acceptance by the East of the Roman claims and customs. The ultimate result was that on July 16, 1054 the Cardinal excommunicated Cerularius and in turn a synod excommunicated the Cardinal and his associates. This mutual excommunication of East and West was something of a point of no return.

Pope John XXIII of our era, who had been nuncio to the East—Bulgaria, Turkey and Venice (as the latter's patriarch)—and thus in sympathy with the East has concluded that both sides were responsible for this sad event. Still, all relationships were not completely broken and at least the lines were very definitely drawn up: reunion would mean a package deal: the pope would always politically support the Greek emperor in return for Greek ecclesiastical obedience. This package remained by far the most attractive consideration for many centuries. We close the Cerularius affair by mentioning that the mutual excommunications rendered in 1054 were lifted on December 1, 1965 by Pope Paul VI and the Patriarch, Athenagoras I.

THE CRUSADES

We have observed in another place how, contrary to the directions of Innocent III the Crusaders rerouted themselves to Constantinople and in 1203 captured that city. The following year they sacked and looted it. This was a terrible blow and increased the hatred of the East for the West beyond measure. Moreover, in the political turmoil of the times the pretender that the Crusaders ostensibly helped to the throne was murdered. They then proceeded to put a Latin on the Greek throne thus inaugurating a Latin empire in the heart of the East. They divided the European sectors of the Eastern empire among the Franks and the Venetians. The Greek emperor and his Greek patriarch were forced to stay in exile at Nicaea. The pope accepted the already accomplished fact and tried to bind the empire and its churches to the West. Naturally the pope harbored a hostile attitude to the Greek emperor and patriarch at Nicaea. It was finally in 1261 that a new emperor recaptured Constantinople and restored the right Eastern emperor and patriarch. Emotionally this whole episode could hardly endear the Easterners to the Westerners, even though political urgency compelled the search for reunion to go on.

THE COUNCILS OF LYONS AND FLORENCE

There was a brief moment of possible reunion. It took place at the Council of Lyons in 1274. Actually negotiations were opened for political motives. The Eastern emperor wanted the pope to put pressure on the king of Naples who was threatening to invade the Byzantine empire. To achieve this he was willing to talk over reunion between the churches. Terms were agreed on and the East accepted substantially Western demands; but the high level agreement came to nothing. The common people were a factor. On both sides they simply refused to accept agreements made by their leaders so deep was the mutual antipathy.

There was one final try. Prior to the fourteenth century a new attitude was emerging on the part of the Easterners. They were coming to see the West in a new light. This was largely due to the writings of Thomas Aquinas. To the Greeks here was a Westerner who "baptized" one of their ancient philosophers. Here was a cultured and worthy mind. Clearly the West was emerging from its barbarian state and was now worth listening to. It was unfortunate that the West never arrived at a similar respect for the East. Still, the West had grown somewhat. A new spirit of self-criticism had set in and the West was ready to admit its sins in bringing about division. The stumbling block was still papal claims. However, by the fifteenth century time was running out for the Easterners. The Moslems were at their doors. They needed Western aid. So the East came to the West, to the Council of Florence. The emperor himself came and many of his Greek bishops. Actually there were long and fruitful theological discussions. The East in a poor bargaining position because it needed Western military aid submitted to the demands of the West to accept its teachings. The Greeks agreed to the Nicene creed's addition of the *filioque,* the primacy of the pope and all the rest. In one sense it was moral blackmail although in another sense genuine theological advancement and agreement had been made. But it all made no difference. Once more centuries-old mutual distrust and hatred would not permit the common people to accept what was agreed to at the Council of Florence. The bull of reunion which was drawn up at Florence on July 6, 1439 and proclaimed in 1452 at Constantinople came to naught. It came to naught except for some Eastern churches in the Ukraine area which accepted union with Rome to become known as the Uniate churches to this day. The Greek church, however, refused to accept the bull. There was not time for persuasion or anything else. In six months time the Moslems captured Constantinople. It and the Greek empire fell in 1453 and the union of Florence fell with it. Rome now had the field to itself. A strong, unyielding, centralized papacy had indeed saved Western unity and gave it political stability during its own tumultuous times. It was just too bad that the price of this was division within Christendom itself.

RETROSPECT

It may be well to end this sad story of Christendom's division with the summary of the historians Knowles and Obolensky (the latter an expert on Eastern Church History):

> . . . The Greeks could not but feel that Rome had chosen to be alien. These forces of division were aided by the conquests of Islam, which eliminated the balancing weight of the other eastern patriarchs . . . It is true that, regarding things solely on the level of history, the tradition of Christian unity was strong, and the tradition of the primacy of some kind of the apostolic see of Peter was primitive and widespread. Events, however, were to show that human weakness and unwisdom were too strong for higher considerations of the common good to prevail. On the closed world of the ninth or eleventh century—closed to the minds of the age, whatever might be the movements of Muslim, Hungarian or Northman— when all thought was Christian and when intercourse be-

tween East and West was rare and very slow, legal distinctions, ritual differences, and alleged heretical opinions seemed far more dangerous and abominable than the bitterness and hostility aroused by acts of violence, mutual excommunications, and the extravagant manifestoes. No doubt the errors and faults of individuals and groups were many and grave. The irresponsible and brutal acts of power on the part of emperors, with regard both to Rome and their own hierarchy, the accidental but serious shock of the Iconoclast campaign, the weakness and debasement of the papacy, the factions of Rome and Italy, the intolerant, unspiritual jousting of Anastasius the Librarian or Humbert. . . . the almost complete lack of wide and charitable vision on the part of both popes and patriarchs of Constantinople after the pontificate of Gregory I—all these had their share in making the calamity fatal. . . .[2]

NOTES

1. Quoted in Knowles and Obolensky, p. 101, *op. cit.*
2. *Ibid.*, pp. 114, 115.

XI

Half-Way Reflections

WHAT HISTORY TEACHES

This brief chapter may be skipped for it is an interruption of our narrative. For those who are interested, however, it represents a pause to weigh the ramifications of what we have learned so far halfway through our book. The interruption is in the nature of a reflection on what the Church of post-Vatican II is up to; for what the modern Church *is* up to is ultimately based on some of the history we have seen so far—and that history is the means of understanding the Church better is the whole point of this book.

Look at what we have learned so far. We have learned, for example, that the pope need not be Italian for we have come across Greek and German popes. We now know that the pope does not necessarily have to reside in Rome for we have seen that Peter in fact resided first in Jerusalem and then in Antioch, and the Church was still the Church. We have seen that the pope does not have to appoint the bishops to their dioceses, that in fact the people or the rulers used to do this task. We have seen that the clergy need not wear special clothes since they did not do so for five hundred years; nor do the clergy need special titles for we have seen that even the term "pope" was applied to any bishop or cleric for several centuries. We have seen that the clergy need not be unmarried for celibacy is an ideal only "for those who can take it." Indeed we have learned that the clergy need not even be men for women had offices and functions in the primitive Church. We have learned that the liturgy need not be celebrated in the same way, in the same language, in every region of the globe. We have seen that there were many ministries in the early Church, that not every church-community had a bishop, that a committee rule is possible; that indeed other denominations may have valid ministries. The list is rather impressive and supplies us with some foundation for many of the changes in the modern Church.

WHO IS THE CHURCH?

But we must go deeper and raise some other issues that show distinct but subtle change throughout the ages. For example, Vatican II says that the Church is the whole People of God. This may, at first glance, not sound like much, but in the light of the past few chapters this definition is obviously an attempt to settle old scores. We have seen how the Church practically became identified solely with the pope and hierarchy. Even today perhaps seven out of ten Catholics, if asked what they mean by the Church, would respond in terms of the clergy. They would be unconsciously echoing the framework laid in the Middle Ages and (as we shall see) prompted and expanded in the Council of Trent and Vatican I. They would be picking up a late tradition from the time of Gregory VII when the real cleavage between clergy and laity became apparent.[1] Not long after Gregory the Lateran Council began to talk of "clergy, religious and laity." The liturgy cemented the division when it clung to the Latin which only the clergy understood, when the priest turned his back to the people, when the altar rail was introduced as both a physical and symbolic barrier between clergy and laity.

Vatican II (and many scholars and theologians before that) went back, as it were, to the first chapters of this book. They saw, not a division, not the old pyramid with the laity on the lowest strata and the pope on top. They saw rather a community, a whole people interacting with their various gifts and ministries, each having his own function in the Christian family. Vatican II, again tutored by many theologians and scholars, saw that the clergy and laity were not distinct (except for function) in dress, language or life style. The Council saw a community of all the people. Then the Council looked at what the Church had come to be, a kind of super corporation with the hierarchy as chairmen of the board and the people left with the threefold duty of "praying, obeying and paying". So the Council said that we should get back to the way it was, that the Church, as a matter of gospel-fact, is all the people and that the whole Church's mission applies "equally to the laity, religious and clergy" (Dogmatic Constitution on the Church, n. 30) and that indeed independently "the lay apostolate is a participation in the saving mission of the Church itself" (n. 33) not merely a subordinate arm of the hierarchy. In a short while after Vatican II some of the practical applications of this historically renewed vision became obvious. Parish councils were established in many places, the Synod of bishops was evoked to work with the pope, the laity began to participate in the liturgy as lectors, cantors, etc. The altar rails were removed, churches were being built "community-style," the laity were given a voice in the appointment of their bishops, in the election of the pope and were put on papal and diocesan commissions. And all because two points of history were compared.

THE POPE

From what we have said above it is also obvious that the pope's role has to be seen in a different light today. As we shall see in a later chapter when Vatican I defined papal infallibility some saw in this the crowning and perfection of absolute, monarchial papal power started by Gregory VII. Some people felt that infallibility meant that in practice the pope alone was the entire Church wrapped up in himself, that he would never need to consult anyone and that councils would be obsolete. Vatican II corrected all that. In the early Church, we saw, every church-community was independent under its own leader (bishop) and yet in communion with every other church-community. Bishops conferred with one another and consecrated each other to demonstrate their unity in diversity. Each bishop was bishop *in his own right* not in dependence on or through designation by the pope. The episcopal college and the pope together form the hierarchical structure, neither one being able to do without the other, neither being independent of the other and both being the recipients of a divine commission from Christ. The pope and the bishops are the symbols of unity, the practical spokesmen for the authentic tradition of the Church. We might recall some of the words of St. Irenaeus quoted in chapter II: "The heretics are all later than the bishops to whom the Apostles have transmitted the churches. . . ."

To be sure, the pope is the head of the college of bishops but he is nothing without the college and vice versa. His primacy does not mean, as it developed after the time of Gregory VII until the definition of infallibility, that the pope has all jurisdiction all over the world of himself, that he can act independently of his fellow bishops. On the contrary, it must be historically maintained "that the pope and the bishops *cannot* exercise their respective functions one *against* the other, and should not whatever the circumstances do so one *without* the other. Certainly the pope will fulfill his functions as necessary and irreplaceable *leader* of the College, and the bishops will fulfill their functions as necessary and irreplaceable directing *members* of the same College. . . ."[2] This concept explains why, for example, Pope Paul VI has acted differently from, say, Pope Innocent III or Pius IX. Unlike those two pontiffs he knows he is not the whole show. He knows that he and the college of bishops are inseparable. For this reason he has convened the Synod of his fellow bishops to work with him. At this writing he has a commission working on the revision of the proceedings for the election of the pope, a procedure which would permit as voters representatives of national and regional bishops' conferences and some priests and laymen. The role of the pope is thus seen, not in the role of an absolute medieval sovereign, but in the light of the early church-communities. Thus, "modern theology portrays the pope for what he is: the leading moral authority in the Church, who, nevertheless, shares our human condition in all things, including sin and error. His authority, though supreme, is never divorced from that of the rest of the college of bishops, nor indeed can it be independent of the Spirit that has been given to the whole Church."[3] And, again, all this because two points of history have been compared.

THE KINGDOM OF GOD

Boniface VIII we shall meet in the following chapter. He is the pope who, pressed by the rising nations and failing to read the "signs of the times," resorted to the most extreme form of papal authority to bolster his position as the temporal and spiritual leader of the whole world. In his famous bull, *Unam Sanctam* he wrote these words:

> We are compelled by the true faith to believe and hold that there is one, holy, Catholic and Apostolic Church. This we firmly believe and simply confess. And outside of this Church there is neither salvation nor remission of sins. . . . We are taught by the evangelical works that there are two swords, the spiritual and the temporal, in the control of the Church. . . . Therefore both the spiritual and material swords are under the control of the Church, but the latter is used for the Church and the former by the Church. . . . Therefore if the temporal power errs, it will be judged by the spiritual power. But if the spiritual power errs, the minor will be judged by the superior—the supreme spiritual power can by judged by God alone, not by man. . . . We therefore declare, say, affirm, and announce that for every human creature to be submissive to the Roman pontiff is absolutely necessary for salvation.

Needless to say, Vatican II has reversed this extreme position. The Church now officially recognized that others can and will be saved, even those who are not baptized. "The Catholic Church rejects nothing which is true in these religions," says the council in its Declaration on Non-Catholic Religions (n. 2). Of those who *are* baptized the same council says, ". . . all those who have been justified by faith through baptism are incorporated into Christ. They therefore have a right to be honored by the title of Christian and are properly regarded as brothers in the Lord by the sons of the Catholic Church" (Declaration on Ecumenism).

Such words display a better sense of history and theology, a better understanding that the Kingdom of God and the Roman Catholic Church, as Boniface implied, are not one and the same thing. Anyone who is united to God by charity is in the Kingdom. The Catholic Church is penetrated into that Kingdom but not identical with it. The good Moslem, for example, may be a member of the Kingdom of God. The evil Catholic may not be. The Church exists to bring men into the Kingdom, here on earth and hereafter (for the Church is always eschatological). The Christian Church (of any denomination) is that body of baptized members who believes in the Lordship of Jesus and the mission of the community which professes his name. The Catholic Christian Church is the same plus the additional conviction that the college of bishops with the pope at its center and head is an indispensable factor (given by Christ) in the formulation and the proclamation of the gospel of Christ. Thus Protestant and Catholic alike belong to the Church. The Catholic, however, believes that it has the *fullness* of revelation, the fullness of Jesus' expression for his Church. Thus a convert from Protestantism is not looked upon as one who has left his sinful and erroneous ways. Rather he is looked on as one continuing his Christian tradition and moving into a fuller degree of it. All of this, we realize, sounds terribly esoteric and the reader will have to refer to better books on the subject. Our point is that, whether we understand all this or not, Vatican II has arrived at such conclusions only by seeing what the Church was in history, what it became and what it ought to be. With its emphasis on the Church as the People of God, with its notions of the Kingdom of God the Church is trying to correct an historical process.

DOGMA

We ought to bring up another rather complex subject merely as an indication of the directions in which the modern Church is going. It concerns dogma or Church doctrine. We saw in chapter V that the first councils of the Church produced several formulas on the nature of Christ; but we saw that such formulas or doctrinal statements had more of a negative value: they helped the Church to have a yardstick to measure statements as to what the truth was not: that is, whatever the truth was about God and Christ we would always know through conciliar statements that such and such a statement was not true. Moreover, such statements were made in the language and in the context of the times. We know today more of the history surrounding them. Thus theologians may legitimately challenge such statements as to their language, their style, their thinking-patterns, their conditioning and even their content. For example, theologians may ask *how* Jesus is present in the Eucharist and they may find that the old term of St. Thomas Aquinas' time, transubstantiation, is not adequate anymore and perhaps a fuller term might be better.

Secondly, dogmas are not so immutable that they cannot develop. How they do is a most complex and subtle issue which we are not competent to discuss here. All that we wish to point out is that history has conditioned dogmas and that the Church now realizes that even dogmas are caught up in the process of living history and can move. Says Vatican II, "There is a growth in the understanding of realities and the words which have been handed down. . . . For as the centuries succeed one another, the Church constantly moves forward towards the fullness of divine truth until the words of God reach their fulfillment in her" (Verbum Dei, art. 8). The point is that what God communicates is not so much information as it is Himself. The "information", the dogma, is not nearly as important or as necessarily fixed as we might think. This is why there were a variety of creedal statements in the early Church, even, as we have noted already, in the variety of the words used for the consecration of the Mass.

Catholics, of course, accept Church dogmas as indispensable illuminations and starting points for obtaining a deeper understanding of the meaning of being a Christian. When the entire Church as a matter of fact does teach and accept a statement of faith as true, then the individual Catholic accepts this as a valuable *guide* for the meaning of his Christian life. He knows that the statement has not captured the whole reality and can grow, develop and be modified as God (not the information) becomes more real.

This is why, historically, there have been schools of theology such as the Franciscans, the Dominicans, the Jesuits, etc. They represent different ways of thinking about the same faith. As we shall see in a later chapter, it was only in the time of Pius IX and Pius X that one school of theology was permitted which soon became an ideology. These things remind us once more that the Church is rooted in history and that if the theologians are doing an excessive amount of questioning today (even on the most "untouchable" subjects) this does not necessarily mean that there is doubt; it means trying to see the dogma in a different light, trying to see what the historical conditioning was in the first place, trying to see how much is "content" and how much is culture.

THE MESSAGE OF JESUS

We have yet to see the Reformation of the sixteenth century or the Modernist movement of the late nineteenth century. When we do we shall see how the Church reacted. For example, the Protestants extolled the Bible, so the Church reacted by overemphasizing tradition. The Protestants viewed the Church a little too spiritually so the Church reacted by emphasizing the external, organizational structure. The Protestants attacked the sacraments and the notion of the Mass as a sacrifice, so the Church reacted by giving the sacraments heavy legal overtones and freezing the Mass in layers of rubrics. The Modernists made attempts to break through all this, to put out feelers to the new ideas and the new science of their time, so the Church reacted with infallibility. The point is, once more, that today's Church is seeing the historical process involved, is cutting through it all and asking more ultimate questions, namely, what *is* the message of Jesus? Do our inherited expressions help or hinder that message? Does our language, our idea-wrappings proclaim Christ or the organization? What does the gospel say? Can we say it better? Have we said it worse? What view, for example, does the old Baltimore catechism give of the Church and of Christ? Is that the view we want? How historically conditioned is it? Better still, is that the view of the gospels and the early Church? These are some of the questions and reflections that history has prompted.

THE GREATNESS OF THE CHURCH

We must take advantage of these pages to make a final point. Because by definition history is made up of the large world-moving events and personalities we have no real record of the little people, the vast majority of humanity that lived and died in the Ages of Faith. As a result we tend to dwell, inevitably, on the mass movements, the large passions, the great leaders. These alone do not make history but of them we can write because their records are bold and open. But what about the average people in Western civilization? What did the Church do for them, how did they respond to the Church? They were no more caught up in many of the dramatic events and personalities in their day than the average man is in our day. They lived their own lives quietly.

Life, to be sure, was often difficult in the early and late Middle Ages. Economic conditions were often harsh. People were exploited, as always, by their nobles and lords, by their clergy and bishops, by the Church itself. The times were barbarous. Yet, the Catholic Church did much and inspired much. We have no idea, for example of how many small parishes were served well, how many clergy gave sincere and humble service to the people. As Lutheran historian Martin Marty put it:

> Unfortunately the general illiteracy of the times and the enduring edge of barbarism and violence made the people sometimes superstitiously dependent upon the sacraments and sacramental objects and upon the parish priests who seldom measured up to their calling. Illiterate themselves, products of inadequate training and often warped cloistered environments, grasping and greedy, many used the Church and the fear of the masses to advance their own interests. But these generalizations have never done justice to the countless examples of parish priests who quietly went about their business gaining the respect of their flocks and serving them with the sacraments and with Christian counsel. The conservative Reformation never wished to repudiate this continuity of evangelical counsel in the centuries that preceded it.[4]

We know that the monasteries were havens of refuge and peace for many. We know that the monasteries preserved our cultural heritage. We know that the Church not only preserved and increased social culture, but also the spiritual culture. Men were inspired to do great deeds and they lived with a total conscious awareness of the supernatural which the modern secular world finds it difficult to comprehend. There was greed and lust and all the other vices of the human condition, but for all there was always an ultimate Answer, a Final Judge. Many a rapacious and greedy nobleman wound up his days in a monastery. Many an evil lord expiated his sins in magnificent acts of charity. There was no pope, no matter how political or how bad that did not understand that he too must answer to God.

People had a synthesis to their lives. They might (and often did) ridicule the errant monk or the drunken priest, but they had a most awesome respect for the priesthood and the sacred ministry itself. We have seen how capable people were to suddenly rise to great religious fervor. Saints, mystics, visionaries and plain holy people nurtured by the Church were a part of every age. People were consistently conscious of God and no matter how far into superstition this sometimes went, this consciousness remained a powerful reality. How else to explain the most exquisite stone carving in a cathedral in a position that could not possibly be seen by the public? How else except that the hidden piece of art was done, not for men, but as they were wont to say, "for the greater honor and glory of God"?

The Church not only civilized and educated the barbarian, but sanctified him. In the tenth and eleventh centuries the great peace movements emerged which the Church directed and promoted. From this came the Peace or Truce of God forbidding fighting on certain days and giving immunity for certain categories of persons. The liturgy was a most powerful source of inspiration to the men of the Middle Ages. As Christopher Dawson puts it:

> Meanwhile throughout the West the liturgy was becoming more and more the center of Christian culture. . . . Whatever else might be lost, and however dark might be the prospects of Western society, the sacred order of the liturgy remained intact and in it, the whole Christian world, Roman, Byzan-

tine and barbarian, found an inner principle of unity. . . .
It is almost impossible to convey to the modern mind the
realism and objectivity with which the Christian of those
ages viewed liturgical participation in the mysteries of salvation. . . .[5]

We know that with all of its vast problems the Church as
a whole never lost its sense of mission. We have seen that
individual popes and bishops and priests were sometimes
corrupt, ignorant and worldly, but religion remained very
lively all the while for example in the tenth and eleventh
and twelfth centuries. The founding of monasteries, the
whole reform movement that we wrote about, that of Cluny
and Gregory VII, shows that many were truly concerned
with the Kingdom of God and with restoring the Church to
a better image of Christ. The personal guidance and ministrations given by the friars is beyond measuring. The schools,
orphanages, hospitals are beyond counting. The learning,
theology and synthesizing still compel our admiration. And
beneath all of the growing legalisms the basic centrality of
Christ and the gospel message was preserved. Perhaps the
greatest gift of all in its two thousand year history is the
Church's ability to renew itself, to raise up its prophets, to
withstand the purifying fires, to bend to the times, to reassess its identity constantly, to admit its faults (most spec-
tacularly at the Council of Trent as we shall see) and to be
open to the Spirit.

All of this must be said at this juncture. We are approaching the Reformation in the chapter after next. We have to
be reminded that all of the reformers were Catholics and
mightily concerned about the image of Jesus which had
become quite obscured. The tragedy of loss and division is
still with us but we should recall that even they did not dis-
parage the mighty work of the Church throughout the cen-

turies, nor did they hate the Church. For most it was a question of love and the desire to see the Church once more in its former spiritual glory. Reform of the Church that nurtured them, not revolution, was the original intent.

We must end our reflections here and return to our narrative.[6] Such reflections have been offered to help the average Catholic realize that current probings in the Catholic Church actually have an historical basis; that they do not arise from shallow and light reasons (although inevitably all change produces some shallow and light by-products). Such reflections help us to see the Church as not really fixed to one life style in the broad sense of the old Roman-Frankish appearance that most Catholics were brought up on. Such reflections show us that the Church as a community of believers in the Lordship of Jesus has come a long way; that history is turning out to be a valuable tool in judging what is necessary to that Church, what is cultural and what needs to be reformed. As we said, let us now return to our narrative. We left the Church at the height of its political power, at the crest of the wave. But that wave is about to crash and it all started when all those feudal counties began to conglomerate into what we call today the nation.

NOTES

1. We must remember that what really started out as ecclesiastical reform ended up as political power, but it was not originally meant to be that way.
2. Concilium, volume 64, p. 90, 1971.
3. Richard P. McBrien, *Who Is A Catholic?*, p. 162. Dimension Books, Denville, N.J. 1971.
4. Martin Marty, *op. cit.*, p. 137.
5. Christopher Dawson, *Christian Culture and The Western World*, p. 42.
6. There are several good popular books that take up the issues touched upon in this chapter. See the bibliography.

XII

The New Nations

NATIONALISM

Besides the disaster for Christian unity when East and West went their separate ways, other shadows were beginning to lengthen across Christendom. These shadows would become substance very quickly so that by the end of the fifteenth century we could say that the Middle Ages were over (which largely meant the Church's influence) and the modern secular ages had begun. Nor was this transition without its pain and disillusionment similar to that experienced in the present day as we move from the modern age to the technological age. The first element we might notice in the steady disintegration of the Church's prestige and influence was the rise of nationalism. Up to this time we have spoken of "Christendom," that mystical half-reality which encompassed all the peoples of East and West who were baptized. Territorial boundaries were irrelevant for all men were Christians. Now, however, in the thirteenth and fourteenth centuries, the nation-states began to appear. People became conscious that they were Frenchmen or Englishmen or Spaniards and as this consciousness grew Christians would fight one another for national honor. The rise of such national spirit is attributable to the rise of the kingly monarchy. Formerly, as we have seen so often, kings were not as we have learned to think of them from the movies or story books. They were little more than local mayors, petty magnates, whose own nobles might be more powerful than they. There was no centralized government as we know it today. But it was beginning to grow, and it grew at the expense of the Church. Let us examine briefly the fortunes of England, France, Germany and Spain to see how and why this happened.

ENGLAND

In the year 901 King Alfred the Great temporarily checked the advances of the invading Norsemen. These viking Norsemen were hardy. They renewed their attacks and attached England for a while to Denmark[1] but finally Edward the Confessor recovered the throne. With Edward, however, begins the drama of England's rise. He died without heirs but he had picked the French duke, William of Normandy, across the channel in France, to be his successor. William had to fight for his claim in Anglo-Saxon England and in the famous battle of Hastings in 1066 his invading forces from France won the throne. (We might recall the irony here: William and his Normans were themselves Vikings who had invaded France and settled in "Normandy"; they had by now become so acclimated that they invaded England, not as Scandinavian Normans, but as Frenchmen!) The culturally superior Normans had great difficulty in merging with the inferior Anglo-Saxons. There was much disorder and William decided that the only means of unity was a strong monarchy. He proceeded to keep strict control over his subjects and his properties. In his famous *Doomsday Book* he listed all his properties and chattel in England. The local lords became his vassals for there were no rival princes there to detract from the power of this outsider.

We must remind ourselves of an ever-present reality at this point. This new King of England, William the Conqueror, had come from Normandy in modern France. This meant that he had his properties in France and at the same time was king of England. He was thus the King of France's vassal and at the same time his own independent king. Understandably the kings of France could not be long happy with this arrangement as we shall see. In any case, William was eventually succeeded by Henry II the first Plantagenet. Under this king a written constitutional law was made. A better and more equitable system of trying legal cases based on evidence and a more fair system of legal justice was introduced. In this latter desirable program Henry ran into conflict. What about all those exemptions for Church clerics? They had many traditional exemptions from the civil law that bound the ordinary man. This dilemma was brought to a head by the famous Council of Clarendon whereby the king declared that from now on clerics were bound by the same law as anyone else. To back up his intentions the king forbade appeals to the pope. Naturally there was opposition from the Church, an opposition most personally irritating to the king for his own chancellor and friend whom he had made the archbishop of Canterbury had turned against him. This was St. Thomas a Becket who refused to honor the Council of Clarendon and who excommunicated those bishops who sided with the king. At last, as the well known story goes, Henry exclaimed one day in exasperation, "Who shall rid me of this miserable clerk?" A band of Henry's knights overheard this remark and they ran and murdered Thomas in his cathedral. This incident has been celebrated many times in literature most particularly in T. S. Eliot's famous poem *Murder in the Cathedral* and in the movie, *Becket*.

The incident had a bad reaction. The nobles began to resist Henry's growing power and in fact put a halt to it. Henry backed down on the Council of Clarendon. After Henry's death the monarchial fortunes declined even more. Henry's son, John Lackland had his troubles. Under him taxes rose, English holdings in France dwindled and, most of all, he and his country were handed a crushing defeat by the French in the battle of Bouvines in 1214. The king was in a very weak position. Stephen Langton, the Archbishop of Canterbury, took advantage of this to lead the barons and nobles to demand some of their rights back, rights taken over by the king. They held secret meetings and plotted rebellion. Finally, in 1215 they confronted the hapless king and wrung from him that milestone of human liberty, the Magna Carta. Although this document was a typical nobleman's document—it gave all the rights to the nobles, not the peasants—still it was important in the respect that it said that the law must be observed by all, and this included the king. No longer could he be arbitrary. Moreover, the king could levy no taxes without the consent of Parliament. Parliament, in fact, got its start under John Lackland's son, Henry III. This king, in spite of everything, continued to levy taxes and was faced with a resistance movement led by a Simon de Montfort. Simon, with two knights from every section and two burgesses from every town faced the king with an impressive show of strength. Henry took the hint and when the next time came around that he wanted to levy taxes he summoned the knights and burgesses on his own. Thus began the English Parliament and under the next king it would become a permanent reality.

FRANCE

France's road to a centralized monarchy was quite different from that of England's. In England the nobles finally brought the king under the law. In France the nobles were so jealous, so divided that the king himself emerged as the referee and lawmaker above them. We might remember that the Capet line had taken over the old Carolingian line. This line settled in Paris and ruled so quietly and so long—some two hundred years—that the kingship slipped into a hereditary one. As time went on, Paris, the first permanent capital in Europe, became an important center. The court was there —in contrast to the still wandering courts of the other local kings. By the twelfth century it had attracted an archbishop, a school and in 1163 Notre Dame cathedral was started. Moreover, France had already shown signs of greatness even in her vague formative years. It was in her lands that many religious orders were founded. Most of the Crusaders came from these Franks. Gothic art had its beginning there. France became the center of theology and we have seen how every notable scholar of the times flocked to the new university of Paris. Paris also happened to be an international market place and the tolls collected there enriched a series of kings. Then, too, by putting down banditry and maintaining order the king caused the townspeople to look to him for support and redress rather than the feuding nobles. The French court thus became a center for justice. In brief, a very stable capital of growing prestige, a hereditary kingship, financial stability and an open court of justice all helped to coalesce in the emergence of a strong monarchy.

Just as William the Conqueror might be called the founder of the English monarchy so Philip II might be called the founder of the French monarchy. By marriage he extended his territories and sent out royal judges to try cases all throughout the land. In addition the French victory at Bouvines had given him enormous power and prestige to add to his expansion. Slowly the king began to annex the smaller kingdoms and countries held by the local princes. As we have seen in another chapter this was the time that the king took advantage of the Albigensian heresy to confiscate their territories. St. Louis was the beneficiary of all this growing power when he ascended the throne. He used it well. He founded hospitals, asylums and homes of various kinds. Most of all, he had his good will ambassadors roaming throughout the land redressing grievances in his name and bringing matters to his attention. Soon there was no part of France that did not have some contact with the king. St. Louis' peaceful policy changed abruptly under his successor, Philip the Bold (d. 1285). Under him France began an aggressive policy of external expansion. Taking advantage of the weakness of the German empire France was moving northward and eastward adding to her territories. She even established herself in Naples and in Hungary and had her eye on Spain. France was on the way to becoming a great political power.

It was with Philip the Fair who inherited all this prestige in 1285 that real progress was made towards the monarchy. He was an administrative genius. He surrounded himself with competent civil servants and lawyers whose talent, not position or birth, brought them into his service. He steadily built a legal system carefully on the foundations of the old Roman theories of law which were interpreted to remind all that the king himself was the chief lawgiver. He was the king who inaugurated the French equivalent of the English Parliament, the Estates-General. This was only an advisory body at the time but would play a major role centuries later in the French Revolution. He allied himself with the causes of the new merchant classes of the new towns. All in all slowly but surely the kingship was beginning to rest on its own foundations. It would no longer need the prestige of the Church. Not that there was any hostility—yet. Only that the monarchy was becoming sufficiently independent not to need the Church.

HOSTILITY BETWEEN ENGLAND AND FRANCE

Hostility between France and England was built in from the beginning. One obvious problem to which we have alluded is the fact that the King of England had property in France. Several French kings had made small skirmishes against England to drive them out but they had not sufficient strength to do more than that. It was with the arrival of Philip II that a strong attack was made against England. He found a pretext to confiscate England's properties in France. War ensued and even Germany was brought into the battle. The result was decided by the famous battle of Bouvines giving France a great victory and forcing the King of England, as we have seen, to concede the Magna Carta to his disgruntled subjects. The hatred and rivalry did not end here of course. We may look ahead to a century and a half later when the desires of the English kings to conquer the more populous and wealthy France led to the futile and unproductive Hundred Years' War which not only heavily involved the two principles but also engaged all of Europe at one time or another. But before we see that sad spectacle we must turn to the relations between the Church and these new emerging nation-states.

CONFLICT WITH THE CHURCH

If we would reduce the entire matter of the severe conflict between the emerging states and the Church at this period to one word that word would be: money. We recall that with the growing centralized papacy a whole new machinery was needed to run it. To finance this machinery required vast sums of money. Thus it was in the eleventh century that the Church introduced the Peter's Pence. Next the Church began to tax all local churches throughout Europe and thus unwittingly developed a refined system of international finance through her use of the Italian bankers. In any case, the various rulers resented this one-way flow of money from their kingdoms; money at times often used against them in warfare by the pope! But the real test came with the emerging nations who were just starting their rivalry and their military campaigns against each other. This cost money. Money meant taxes. It is not by coincidence that both France and England hit upon the same source to tax: the Church. In this both countries ran afoul of current Church theory that its revenues were always traditionally exempt from civil assessments. Only the Church could tax her own clergy and her own property. The kings were seeing it another way. A showdown was in the wings.

THE PAPACY

As far as France goes, the contest of power was between the two antagonists, Philip the Fair and Pope Boniface VIII. We have seen how Philip was the possessor of a new and strong emerging nation. Let us take a look at the papacy up to Boniface's time. It was once more the center of intrigue from outside rulers. In spite of Pope Nicholas I's attempt to have the papal election confined only to the cardinals, St. Louis' brother, Charles of Anjou and king of Sicily, had designs on all of Italy. He worked hard and successfully in getting a majority of French and Italian cardinals to elect the kind of pope he wanted, Clement IV. This pontiff made many French cardinals. The very real influence on such cardinals by the French king was offset by Pope Gregory X who in 1271 invented the conclave whereby the cardinals are shut up in a closed room for the papal election. This device did not succeed for a Frenchman, Martin IV, was elected anyway in 1280. He was followed by Nicholas IV who died in 1292. By now the intrigue and maneuvering were quite pronounced. The cardinals settled on that old temporary measure: they would elect a compromise candidate. Thus they went and got an old hermit, almost literally dragged him from his cell and elected him as Celestine V. The old hermit was duly installed in the Lateran palace and proceeded to amuse the sophisticated prelates by building a rude hut amid the splendor. He could put up with the luxurious surroundings this way, but he could not swallow the fact when he learned that he was expected to be the puppet of the French king. His only recourse was to remove himself from the scene. He therefore duly resigned the papacy! He went back to his old hermitage and later took his place in the canon of the saints. In this highly unusual situation the cardinals elected in his place a Roman noble, Boniface VIII.

BONIFACE VIII

Boniface was a man to be reckoned with, one determined to restore the dignity of the papacy in the style of an Innocent III. In the light of the preceding circumstances he lost no opportunity to assert the primacy of the ecclesiastical over the civil power. He added a regal crown to the papal tiara and had his ministers carry two swords before him in procession—a sign of church and state.[2] At another time this would have been impressive, but the sad fact was that Boniface was out of context. He was no longer dealing with Christendom. He was dealing with new independent nation-states.

This was the pope who had to deal with England and France's audacity in taxing church property for their internal exploits of consolidation and external military rivalries. He dealt with the matter by immediately issuing his famous bull, *Clericis laicos* threatening excommunication against any lay ruler who dared to tax the Church. England and France were both unimpressed with this old and over-used penalty. Actually, the papal bull contained nothing new. It was the old traditional doctrine of the two powers of Church and state which previous popes had proclaimed many times before. Long tradition had consecrated the doctrine and so, in perspective, it was the kings of England and France who were violating tradition. The pope was merely reminding them of this.

But, as we have said, the picture was different now. This was a political situation and the question at stake was really the sovereignty of the new national powers. Boniface's failure was not to recognize this, not to sense a new spirit among the people, a new national pride which would defy even the Church. Perhaps Boniface had visions of another solitary Henry IV at Canossa or a humiliated Frederick Barbarossa at Venice. Such visions would never again materialize for whole nations who were willing to admit guidance in the spiritual realm but unwilling to admit any papal prerogatives in the political arena which would limit their new solidarity.

England had a history of bucking church interference. We recall the premature Council of Clarendon which tried to put clerics under the civil law penalties the same as everyone else. In 1279 England forbade land to be donated to the Church. In 1351, some fifty years after the time we are considering, England forbade papal appointees to the bishoprics of England in order to prevent the Italian prelates from coming into their country and taking over lucrative positions. Thus when Boniface issued that bull England retorted by decreeing that any cleric who did not pay the tax was to lose his legal protection and his temporal property.

PHILIP'S REACTION

And France? Philip hit where it hurt. He prohibited monies and letters of credit to leave France for Rome. Thus he dried up at a time when the pope could ill afford it a needed source of papal revenue. Boniface backed down for the time being. He might have stayed backed down except that in the year 1300 the first Jubilee year in the Church was proclaimed. From all over the world people came. Boniface became so intoxicated by this show of numbers that he misread it as backing for his claims. He failed once more to realize that these people were not ready to transfer their spiritual allegiance to the political realm. Immediately he reprimanded King Edward of England for marching against the Scots and his injustice and violence towards that people. Edward turned right around, presented the pope's complaint to his country and the whole nation as one rejected the pope's interference in their affairs.

Next came Philip. He had the boldness to have imprisoned a French bishop. Boniface demanded his release and for good measure once more forbade church taxation. Philip responded to this the same way Edward of England did. He appealed to his people. He called the forerunner of the Estates-General who backed Philip all the way. At this time even the lawyers and theologians got in on the act repudiating papal claims to interfere in political matters. The whole issue became one of public debate—which could not have served Philip's purpose better. Boniface was stunned. His only reaction was to come out with *Unam Sanctam*, the most extreme statement on papal power that has ever been written and which has provided material for anti-papalists—both Catholic and Protestant—ever since. He reasserted that the pope was supreme in all matters on earth, both spiritual and temporal and in an oft-quoted passage of papal extremity he proclaimed that it is necessary for salvation "for every human being to be subject to the Roman Pontiff."

Philip was not one to let the matter end there. He was determined to destroy Boniface. Knowing the unusual circumstances of Boniface's election (remember he had replaced the retired Celestine) Philip pretended to call into question his legitimacy. Later he included the charges of heresy, simony and immorality. The pope must come to France to stand trial. Boniface, now 86, had gone to the town of Anagni for the summer. Some French troops broke into his bedroom and verbally, and perhaps even physically, abused the old man. They kept him prisoner for several days until he was freed by the townspeople. He died three months later at Rome. His successor did not live long enough to resolve the tension. His successor, however, solved the problem in a way as to bring the papacy into total disrepute. In 1305 the cardinals elected a Frenchman, Clement V, who considered himself first and foremost as a vassal of the French king. He filled the college of cardinals with relatives and followers of Philip and, as an ultimate blow, moved the papal court from Rome to the French city of Avignon. There he and his successors were to remain for seventy-two years thus earning from their opponents the biblical epithet "the Babylonian captivity." Philip had won. The prestige of the papacy fell to a new low. Philip's new pope revoked Boniface's bulls and Philip enriched himself by having his pope suppress the great Crusading order of Knights Templars. As we pointed out two chapters ago, people were scandalized but the papal machinery went on in Avignon as easily as in Rome for the site of administration and finances which the papacy had come to represent did not matter. People became cynical. Besides, they had other things to occupy their minds.

GERMANY

Germany was very slow to develop a monarchial government. The reason was the same old one. The emperors, as emperors of the Holy Roman empire, were too busy pursuing the grand illusion of restoring the old Roman Empire of the Caesars; they were too busy fussing about Italy and subduing the pope. As a result Germany was left to disintegrate into a series of small municipalities, a mass of civil and ecclesiastical particles at the mercy of the strongest local lord. Emperor Frederick Barbarossa was a strong man who used his time as emperor pursuing the myth of the empire. Perforce he must turn once more to Italy, to Rome. To do this he had to pass through the now independent Italian towns that had sprung up on the plains of Lombardy. He stomped through with terror and force. Eventually Frederick even got to choosing the pope since there were two contenders for the job at this time but no one would recognize his choice, his anti-pope. To add to this Frederick was badly defeated by the Lombard towns and wound up at Venice kissing the

feet of the legitimate pope, Alexander III, a scene remi-
niscent of Henry IV standing in the cold of Canossa begging forgiveness of Gregory VII. Frederick ended his career,
we may recall, by drowning while on the Crusades.

Frederick's grandson, Frederick II, was an interesting person. A free thinker, skeptic and schemer he was a man of
talent and far ahead of his time in social legislation. His
mother was a Sicilian and so he wished to join Sicily to Germany. This could only mean putting the squeeze on the
pope and his territories. He was excommunicated several
times and finally Innocent IV deposed him as emperor in
1243 and gave Sicily to France. Frederick died with the
same problem he tried to solve: a divided empire and a
neglected Germany. In fact so far did the fortunes of Germany decline, so leaderless was it that sometimes the princes
elected children to be their kings and they sold their votes to
rivals. Eventually so indifferent did the matter become that
the electing of the emperor came down to a mere seven
princes in Germany who sold the crown to the richest clients.
This was the origin of the college of Seven Electors who
henceforth elected the emperor. At one point the electors had
sold the crown to two rival claimants at the same time. When
one rival dropped off the scene the Electors in 1273 gave the
crown to the colorless Rudolph. He was important in the
light of the future. He was the first Hapsburg, a dynastic
family that would dominate the stage of Europe for centuries to come. By and by Germany became united to Bohemia and annexed some of the Slavic areas in the East,
while some of its western territory spun off into the influence of France. But it remained divided, economically backward and far behind the other emerging nations. Even here
the struggle of the popes with these emperors must be seen

in the context of the times. Once more Henri Pirenne puts
it in perspective:

> It must be repeated that the motive which for two and a
> half centuries had determined the hostility of the Emperors
> to the Papacy was by no means their eagerness to defend the
> temporal power against the encroachments of the Church.
> To envisage the question thus is to transport into the heart of
> the Middle Ages ideas and problems which belong only to
> our modern times. Neither the humiliation of Henry IV at
> Canossa, nor that of Frederick Barbarossa at Venice, nor that
> of Otto IV at Bouvines, was the humiliation of the civil power
> before priestly arrogance. In reality, the conflict was not a
> conflict between State and Church; it was an intestine strug-
> gle within the Church itself. What the Emperors wanted was
> to compel the Popes to recognize them as governing the uni-
> versal Church, a right which they claimed was theirs from
> the time of the Carolingian Empire, as the Ottos and Henrys
> had done, or from the time of the Roman Empire, as the
> Hohenstaufens had done. Their pretensions thus imperiled,
> in every country, that temporal independence of which, by
> the strangest of confusions, they had been regarded as the
> defenders. The cause of the Pope was the cause of the na-
> tions, and with the liberty of the Church was bound up the
> liberty of the European States. . . .[3]

SPAIN

Spain was between Germany and France in development.
It did not have much of an identity yet for the chronic reason that it was still occupied by the Moslem invaders since
the seventh century. These Moslems were practically natives. They built beautiful cities and cultivated their civilization. We must remember that it was through them that
the Greek philosophers such as Aristotle found their way to

the West. Normally after six or seven hundred years they would be expected to mingle with the natives and fuse a new culture as had been done so often before in history. One factor prevented this: religion. The Moslems were not Christian. They were the hated infidel. The Spaniards on the other hand were fiercely Christian and no compromise was therefore possible. Only extermination could be the answer. To be a Spaniard was to be Christian and thus national sentiment got inextricably tied up with religion. Thus the relationship between the Moslems and the Spanish was that of a Holy War which prevented cultural fusion of any kind.

It is likely that victory over the Moslems could have been won sooner except that Spain was divided internally. Aragon was at odds with Castile. In 1195 the Moslems seemed on the verge of such a complete conquest that the pope intervened, got the two kingdoms to combine their forces and in 1212 to shatter the Moslem offensive. From this point on the Spanish Christians moved steadily ahead. In 1238 they captured Valencia, in 1226 Cordova and in 1248 Seville. They eventually left the Moslems with a foothold in Granada and only the internal quarrels of the various Spanish kingdoms kept them from expelling the Moslems altogether. The important thing to note is that as these victories were won several Spanish areas tended to gather around the prominent cities of Castile and Aragon. The latter was better situated since it was on the Mediterranean and could reach out to Europe and feel its influence. Barcelona was soon to become an important seaport and in a short time this outlet to Europe was to be involved in the affairs of Sicily and Naples.

Yet it was in the inland Castile that the true Spain was finding itself. The Castilians fought most gloriously against the Moslems and gave rise to their popular local hero, El Cid (the counterpart to the French hero, Roland). It was in Castile that the national language and character were formed. Even so, all of Spain was beginning to find a national identity. Their commerce in wool was increasing and leading them to trade with the Low Countries. They were emerging as a strong sea-going people and a Portuguese prince, Henry the Navigator (1394-1460), was even now outfitting ships that would venture far into the unchartered waters of the Atlantic.

THE HUNDRED YEARS' WAR

We must include in our secular survey of history during the thirteenth to fifteenth centuries a mention of the Hundred Years' War. This was in reality a series of on-again-off-again military campaigns. There were many reasons for the hostilities. English property, as we saw, was in France. France and England were fighting over water rights and trade priorities. Perhaps most of all there was the rivalry of nationalism. People were becoming conscious of their own traditions and language, that they were Englishmen or Frenchmen or Spaniards. The monarchies were becoming the focal point of national consciousness. A whole new spirit was abroad. Rivalry was paramount. In fact the Hundred Years' War was based on the desire of the Kings of England to conquer the French nation for glory. It began with the English King, Edward III. When Philip of France's son died (thus ending the old Capetian line) Edward, a cousin, claimed the throne and promptly invaded France. In 1346 the English, armed with a new and devastating weapon, the longbow, crushed the numerically superior French forces thus inflating English national pride.

All the evils of war followed, threatening to overturn the

new national states. A major problem was money to finance the war. Another was national spirit which ebbed and flowed as battles were won and lost. Many uprisings of the common people occurred in both countries as a result. In 1356 the English again invaded France and captured the French king's son whom they took back to London. The people of France exploded. They mocked the Dauphin, ruling in his father's absence. Peasants rose up against their masters but they were cruelly crushed and hanged. The Estates-General demanded that the king be more responsible to them as taxpayers. Such internal trouble only let England advance further into France and take over more property and this was galling to Frenchmen everywhere.

England, too, was having its internal problems for the same reasons. Taxation was quite burdensome because of the war. In 1381 the peasants revolted there also and were similarly cut to pieces by the nobles. Moreover, when England suffered certain military reversals at French hands Parliament took the crown away from King Richard and gave it to Henry of Lancaster whose son, Henry V renewed the offensive against France. At this point France was about to be taken over completely by the English; only the central and southern parts, entered by way of Orleans, remained to be subdued. But it was at this time that history was altered. There was a maid in Orleans, Joan of Arc, who was convinced that she heard heavenly voices telling her to save her country. She won the approval of the Dauphin who gave her some troops. Dressed in men's armor and riding a white horse she so inspired her soldiers that the English were routed. Eventually Joan was captured and turned over to the English. Under English pressure a Church court found her guilty of heresy and in 1431, abandoned by that same Dauphin whose coronation as king she had witnessed in

Rheims cathedral, she was burned at the stake. Yet her spirit lived on and in 1453 (the same year that Constantinople fell) the English, except for the area of Calais, were expelled from France. The Hundred Years' War was at an end. As for Joan, twenty-five years later after her death the Church reversed her sentence. In 1920, five centuries later, the Church canonized her as a saint.

UPHEAVALS

This chapter has almost been one of pure secular history. Almost, but not quite. Men were still Christians and the Church was still in power. Still, we cannot help but notice the shift of emphasis and the basis of present and future conflict. England was still Christian but signs of strain with Rome were showing. The Council of Clarendon forbidding clerical exemption from civil law was a premature sally in hostilities with the Church, but it was a sign of the direction England would take. The introduction of Parliament and the desire of the people to govern their own national spirit boded no good for the international Church. Forbidding papal episcopal appointees for English sees was another step in England's desire to run her own affairs.

France too showed the Church that she intended to go into the future with or without her. Philip the Fair had bested Boniface VIII and had so captured the papacy that it was actually residing at Avignon, his town, as his puppet. Germany's Frederick had been subdued and Spain was fighting for her identity against the Moslems to pose much of a problem right now. But the world was materially changing. The face of modern Europe was beginning to show. Rivalry between Christian nation-states was now a reality with the Hundred Years' War. Everything was in the process of change. Before long—only forty years plus—a whole New World would be opened up. The West and the Church might have survived all of this were it not for the spiritual change also that was beginning at this time. There were changes in the minds of men. New mystical leanings and movements outside the mainstream of Christianity were starting and forerunners of the Protestant Reformers were making their voices heard in the land. What was coming to a head was what historian Henri-Daniel Rops described as "the crisis of authority, the crisis of unity and conditioning both, the crisis in men's souls, in their consciences and in their minds." To this we must now turn.

NOTES

1. These Vikings absorbed Christianity and transferred it to the north countries.
2. Boniface was the product of a century's long stream of canonical thought which ran in the direction of universal papal dominion. What was learned at Bologna (specializing in canon law) was practiced at Rome. On the other hand there is a tradition of canonical thought which was more conciliar and corporate which was defended even in Boniface's time by a series of canonists.
3. Henri Pirenne, *op. cit.,* p. 292.

XIII

Outside the Mainstream

UNREST

Underneath the external sameness the structures of late medieval society were tottering. New nations had arisen. France and England were at each other's throats. The Germanic empire was disintegrating and Italy, if possible, was more divided than ever. The Moslems were about to seize Constantinople. The towns were having trouble. There riots and strikes accompanied the demand for free competition as men sought to throw off the controls of the guilds. The new towns, heavily taxed to subsidize the warfare of the new nations, were wresting more and more privileges for themselves. Economic depressions were severe. Parliaments and Estates-Generals were signs of the unrest of the people and their desire to have a say in their rule. The nobility was becoming decadent. The knights no longer had any practical loyalty to their lords but sold their military services to the highest bidder. As a matter of fact, the Church was proving a haven for the sons of the nobility and so more and more nobles monopolized her upper ranks. Thus the Church was losing much of her democratic character and considerably undermining her intellectual and moral vigor. More than that: as a result there was beginning in the Church a new period of decadence and worldliness.

The old ideals of Church and society still persisted of course, but they were, as we shall see, being shaken and they lacked any great vigor. And there were no great leaders around: no more Bernards or Gregorys or Innocents. If anything the times were characterized by unrest, rebellion and criticism permeating every strata of society. There was—and we shall meet some—no lack of visionaries, mystics and reformers. All of the unrest thus described would shortly affect the common man who in turn would shake up the Church for we must remember that the real power of the Church lay in the people who supported it. In a deeply religious society men could not but think of the Church as eternal and necessary for salvation. Even a Frederick Barbarossa or a Henry IV would never have denied the Church her spiritual mission. And as long as they and the common people thought the Church was the visible kingdom of God and necessary for salvation so long that Church would continue to dominate. But when men's confidence would wane and new and strange thoughts would appear in public (not just underground), then public support would weaken and with it the Catholic Church. With this in mind we now turn to one major event which shook that confidence in the Church, the Great Schism.

THE GREAT SCHISM

The Great Schism divided Christendom for forty years (1373-1417). Here is how it began. We must recall that the popes were residing, not at Rome, but in Avignon. The popes were all French and all captive to the French king and all unabashedly chauvinistic. For example, of the 134 cardinals made by seven of the French popes in the fourteenth century, 113 were French. All this was as pleasing to the French as it was odious to the rest of the Christian world, especially to Italy and most especially to France's archenemy, England. Sooner or later there had to be attempts to rescue the papacy and restore it to Rome. Finally it happened. Under the prodding of St. Catherine of Siena, Pope Gregory IX returned to Rome in 1377 among great rejoicing. Unfortunately, Gregory died the following year. Then the expected happened. Around the terrified cardinals meeting in Rome for the election an irate mob was howling for an Italian pope. The cardinals, fearing for their lives, complied and elected Urban VI. Had not Urban been so irascible—he alienated even his supporters—no more would have been made of this forced election. As it was its validity was questioned—and, of course, France was largely behind this. So once more the cardinals assembled and elected Clement VII (a French name as opposed to the "Roman" name of Urban). Urban refused to concede to this replacement and such was the uncertainty of the identity of the real pope that all of Christendom soon became divided with even saints taking opposite sides. However, whatever the theological issue, politics soon became involved. Now there were two popes, two headquarters, two sets of cardinals and two curias and two sets of papal successors. To appreciate the situation try to imagine two presidents of the United States, each with his own cabinet and own senate and congressmen, issuing conflicting laws and demanding separate allegiances. So it was then. In each country whole hierarchies of rivals sprung up making the whole situation quite unbearable and endlessly confusing.

France, Scotland, Spain and Naples supported the French pope. Therefore rival England, Germany and Bohemia supported the Roman pope. There could surely be no better indication that the universal concept of Christendom was dead for people were rallying no longer to the Church but to their respective nations. In any case it took no time for sincere men to become disgusted with the whole matter. A solution was needed. The only solution left, since the last traditional resort, the pope, was the problem, was to call a council.

A General Council was opened in Pisa in 1409 with kings and princes attending as well as prelates. Naturally each pope refused to honor it or attend since it was called by the cardinals. The council in turn, feeling that neither pope was really worthy of the office anyway elected a third! (This third pope died quickly and was followed by the infamous anti-Pope John XXIII who so dishonored the name that no pope till modern times would use it: Pope John XXIII who called Vatican II into session.) For five more years this situation dragged on. Finally the Council of Constance was called by the Emperor Sigismund in 1414 and settled the schism. One pope was deposed (John XXIII for his scandalous life), another condemned and another was forced to renounce his claims. On November 11, 1417 the council elected Martin V and the schism was over although recent research has shown that both the Councils of Pisa and Constance really gave up hope of deciding who was the true pope and to this day no one knows for sure. But whatever the truth, the results of the original attempts are still with us.

One result that would agitate the Christian Church for centuries to come was the theory of conciliarism which, simply stated, held that a general council is superior to the pope. After all, it was argued, the councils settled things in the early Church. One of them had even condemned a pope as heretical. Why not replace the monarchial structure of the Church with a council rule? The situation that prevailed in the Great Schism only underscored the need. Not everyone agreed about this of course and much dissension took place within the very council discussing the issue. Men like the famous and respected John Gerson theorized that the real source of papal authority were the priests and indeed all the baptized, that power resides in the Church as a whole and lawful election only communicates it. For the same reason the whole Church could correct, punish and, if necessary, depose a pope. In a general council every person, he held, really had a right to vote, cleric or layman. Elements of this theory are being discussed to this very day. As historian Philip Hughes has observed about the Council of Constance and its discussions which resolved the Great Schism:

> . . . This same council that had brought the schism to an end had sown the seeds of much future dissension. Whatever the niceties of Canon Law that had safeguarded the legitimacy of its liquidation of a complex problem, the fact remained that the Council of Constance had judged two claimants to the papacy and condemned them, and that it had elected a new pope. And it also declared, in explicit terms, that General Councils were superior to popes, and it had provided that every five years this General Council should reassemble and the pope, in some measure, give to it an account of his stewardship. As far as the wishes of the Council of Constance went, a revolution had been achieved, and the Church for the future was to be governed in a parliamentary way, and not by the absolute, divinely given authority of its head. The forty years that followed the council were to see the successive popes—Martin V, Eugene IV, and Nicholas V— wholly taken up with the effort to destroy this new theory and to control the councils which it bred and inspired.[1]

Msgr. Hughes was right. For the next forty years the popes were engaged in various plots to lessen the force of the implications of the Council of Constance and its conciliar theories. We must insert a word of caution however. The Council of Constance has often been taken as instituting novel theories concerning the pope and the general councils. As a matter of fact from the twelfth century onwards there was a steady tradition about the limitation of papal powers so that the Council of Constance "can no longer be seen, as people liked to think, as having taken an unheard-of initiative or having indulged in unseemly excesses stemming from hasty and unconsidered improvisations."[2] The council that really tried to be novel, that of Basle in 1431, was all set to master the pope and settle the matter of council superiority once and for all. The pope unfortunately was a poor diplomat and only strengthened their resolve. He dissolved the council which simply refused to be dissolved and in fact which turned around and suspended the pope. The pope retorted by excommunicating the council. Finally both met in compromise. The council wanted to set up a permanent watchdog committee over the pope and his curia but the pope balked at this. So, the council once more deposed him.

Meanwhile, what was eventually to aid the pope's cause was a brewing tragedy. We have seen how the Moslems were threatening Constantinople and how anxious the Eastern emperor was to get the support of the West. To achieve this end the emperor and his prelates came to the Council of Basle to discuss the East-West theological differences. The pope shrewdly moved the Council of Basle to Ferrara and then to Florence leaving a disgruntled rump council sitting at Basle. We might recall that the anxious Greeks accepted all the terms of the West even the papal primacy. This was the wedge and the support the pope needed. A council, made up of both East and West, had reaffirmed his primacy and that was that as far as he was concerned. The rump council still at Basle fulminated but finally fell apart and disintegrated after weakly re-condemning the pope and electing an anti-pope—the last one in history[3] (if "elect" is not too loose of a word since there was only one cardinal present at this "election"). The papacy, for the time being, had triumphed over conciliarism. Yet, on the other hand, the papal residence at Avignon and the Great Schism dealt an almost mortal blow to the papacy and is a definite mark of its decline.

STRANGE VOICES

The Great Schism had surely shaken men's confidence in the Church. Such a catastrophe could now bring to public notice things that had been only whispered in small circles up to this time: dangerous theories that would find echoes in a later age. Not that there had not been strange and prophetic voices before. There were individuals for example who protested the Church's wealth. Poverty had a popular appeal in the twelfth century but it had no unifying force to achieve anything like reform. Critics (then as now) could not reconcile the poverty of the primitive Church with the pomp and power of the ecclesiastical organization of their day. Actually Pope Pascal II tried to disentangle the Church from its wealth but he did not succeed. Men like Arnold of Brescia who died in 1155 felt that the Church's wealth was a betrayal of Christ's teaching.[4] His voice was muted and his movement ended in failure. Another popular movement was the Poor Men of Lyons (Waldensians) headed by Peter Waldo. He was converted in true medieval style, gave away his wealth and in 1173 gathered followers dedicated to a life of poverty around him. He and his group were met with suspicion and silenced. They were driven into more radical postures and finally into heresy and then they were condemned. It is interesting to note that Peter Waldo's life and conversion paralleled that of another man who just a few years later was to get his poverty movement approved by the Holy Father: Francis of Assisi. Arnold of Brescia and Peter Waldo were but early voices outside the mainstream that would be repeated over and over to become a chorus in the sixteenth century when the Reformation broke. There were three more influential voices that we must mention. One voice belonged to a man who lived some thirty-five years before the Schism, a certain Marsilius of Padua. He wrote a pamphlet accusing the papacy of maintaining a false position and that in fact the papacy was quite incompatible with Scripture (a theme of the Protestant Reformers). The pope was merely another bishop, he said; the Church did not include only clerics but laymen as well. It was not a monolithic structure but a community of believers (a theme of renewed Catholics today). He held that the state alone should own property and wield civil power and the clergy should in effect be in the employ of the state. Finally he held that supreme authority belonged to a general council rather than to the pope. Marsilius is significant for what he anticipated and also because he represents a growing class of church critics.

Another man who lived through the Great Schism in England was to voice similar sentiments, John Wycliffe. We must recall that England at this time was protesting papal interference in its internal affairs. England was especially upset that a French pope should be collecting English monies of taxation. Wycliffe personified the protest against the Church and the papacy. He held that all men were equal and therefore there was no distinction between priest and laity. Each man's salvation would rest on his own faith and in fact neither the Church nor the clergy were needed as intermediaries between God and a man. Man could consult the Bible directly for guidance and to this end Wycliffe translated the Bible into English. Because Wycliffe appeared at a time when the English nation was protesting the policies of the papacy his views gained many supporters. Eventually he slipped into heresy. He came up with a teaching of predestination, denied the transubstantiation of the Eucharist and held that the Bible was the sole arbiter in religious matters. He even founded an order of men called the Lollards who were intended to be a contrast to the friars who were not well respected at this time. It is significant that Wycliffe was enabled to die a peaceful and natural death in 1384. The sympathetic hearing he got from his countrymen and the elements of national feeling in his teaching were enough to insure him of immunity from Church penalties.

Wycliffe's immunity did not endure after his death. A new king of England needed papal support and accordingly had to turn against Lollardism as Wycliffe's movement was called. He condemned these heretics, burned them at the stake and forbade the translation of the Bible. Still Wycliffe's influence persisted and many of his root ideas resurrected themselves in the Protestant Reformation. Even before that, however, his ideas were kept alive by being transplanted to Bohemia.

John Huss of Bohemia was a reformer of morals. He upbraided the luxury and scandalous lives of the clergy. But he took over a lot of Wycliffe's ideas especially those on predestination. One rather interesting point that came to be a symbol of his whole movement was that Christians should be allowed to drink from the chalice at Mass (a point finally won by modern Catholics in the 1970's). A while back the Church had restricted the chalice to the clergy in fear that the clumsy laity might spill it. Huss and his followers pointed out that Jesus had said, "Take and drink, all of you." This whole matter became a symbol of resistance to a Church trying to interfere in the lives of its people. Huss added to the tension by castigating the selling of indulgences to finance the pope's wars. Finally he was called before the Council of Constance (that same council trying to untangle the Great Schism).

Actually Huss was glad for the opportunity to express his views to a council. He felt they would be understood and accepted. He was given the promise of safe conduct by the Emperor Sigismund, the emperor who called the council. However, the anti-pope, Pope John XXIII, had him imprisoned and prevailed on the emperor to remove his protection. Huss was heard at the council, misunderstood and burned at the stake for heresy. Huss' influence remained for a long time and factions sprung up around his name. There were the Utraquists, more moderate, and willing to go back to Rome if the chalice were allowed to the people (hence their name: utraquist means "both", that is, both Host and chalice). Then there were the Taborites, more radical, who would make no such concession. The Utraquists finally joined with the Catholics to defeat the Taborites and Catholicism was reintroduced into Bohemia. The anger and discontent remained.

THE BLACK DEATH

Any age has its religious mass movements and the late Middle Ages were no exception. Usually the twin evils of disease and despair provoke them and again there was no lack of either at this period. The average peasant's lot was hard. His life and his property were constantly at the mercy of the endless soldiers fighting their endless wars. The barbarous treatment of civilians all throughout the Middle Ages is a sad commonplace of history. In the middle of the fourteenth century, right at the start of the Hundred Years' War, however, a great disaster struck. It was called the Black Death. It was a form of the bubonic plague brought from the

East probably carried by rats on the home-bound Italian vessels and has been called the worst invasion from Asia since Attila the Hun. It hit Florence in 1348 and in the next fifteen years the rest of Europe. It is estimated that Europe lost one fourth of her population to the plague. Devastation and chaos were everywhere and life came to a halt. There were simply not enough people to till the fields, work the crafts, sail the ships and teach the schools. Economic depression set in. The pope gave charitably of money and land and clergy aided but in so doing they decimated their own numbers. There was almost a complete break with the past.

It is hard for us to appreciate what it must have meant for Europe to lose one fourth of her population and the utter devastation and despair. People saw the plague as a punishment from God. Others claimed that the pestilence was caused by infected air and water. The Jews were charged with doing this dastardly deed so many Jews were slaughtered by the Christians on this account. Movements of popular despair and religious frenzy were launched. We read of crowds of people, sick and diseased, crowding churches in spasms of prayer begging a miracle from heaven to save them. Only a sign at this point could make their lives tolerable. Others joined the Flagellating Groups who beat themselves unto bloodshed trying to appease God. They ran through the towns of Europe drawing their own blood and singing their Our Fathers and Hail Marys. Traditional outlets and devotions did not suffice in such times of anguish and severe emotional stress. A whole new art and preoccupation about death became immensely popular. The painters of the period produced the art depicting the terrors of the Last Judgment and the tortures of hell. Immensely popular were the Dance of Death woodcuts and murals depicting the immediacy of death and the dread of dying without the sacraments. The Black Death did much to crush the spirit of man and turn men beyond traditional devotions.

WOMEN ON THEIR OWN

Before the women's liberation trends of modern times the unmarried female has posed a problem for society. In the Middle Ages the answer of what to do with her was solved by sending her to a nunnery or female monastery. In time whole communities became the retreats for the well to do ladies of the medieval noble families. Many of these women were quite formidable in several ways and had some great achievements to their credit. Unfortunately the women in religious life did not last long. This was primarily due to male dominance in society. By the twelfth century the female monastic life had declined sharply. Such nunneries as remained were mostly refuges for those girls who did not wish to marry. The medieval ideal of virginity gave support to many such.

Some of these nunneries in time became associated with the male monasteries as a kind of unofficial sub-division. In spite of the genuine efforts of many popes to keep these double monasteries open in order to protect the rights of women the double monastery fell into decline. Again, it was the dominant male chauvinism which was underneath it all. Said one abbot to justify getting rid of the women from his monastery:

> We and our whole community of canons, recognizing that the wickedness of the women is greater than all the other wickedness of the world, and that there is not anger like that of women, and that the poison of asps and dragons is more curable and less dangerous to men than the familiarity

of women, have unanimously decreed for the safety of our souls, no less for that of our bodies and goods, that we will on no account receive any more sisters to the increase of our perdition, but will avoid them like poisonous animals.[5]

Modern women's lib would have a field day with this quotation for it renders a prevalent feeling about women in the Church to this day.

Still, in spite of such male sentiments, the pressure remained to provide for the noble unmarried ladies. Nunneries therefore continued to grow especially those which became associated with the Cistercian monasteries which gave them more a nod of good will rather than the dignity of any formalized official status. In Spain particularly great nunneries flourished to the extent that Pope Innocent III was shocked to learn that some of the nuns were giving Benediction, preaching and even hearing confessions! The power and determination of some of these famous abbesses can be seen from the magnificent novel of H. V. Prescott, *Man on a Donkey*, a novel of the times we are considering. As a matter of fact, during the Middle Ages women had gone far in the Church and these lady abbesses just mentioned ruled over large numbers of male clergy. Some of them were not subordinate to a bishop but as abbesses of exempt orders were directly responsible to the pope. The abbesses even appointed priests to their parishes and gave them the right to preach and hear confessions. On occasion abbesses excommunicated difficult priests. In short, these lady abbesses were actually bishops in that they truly exercised ecclestical authority and jurisdiction and were often upheld in this role by Rome. Many of the abbesses were often referred to as Metropolitans or bishops and for centuries they wore the miter, pectoral cross and ring, carried the crozier and were invested with the pallium—all symbols of the episcopal office. It was under the later influence of the Renaissance, the Protestant Reformation (with its Old Testament emphasis on the male patriarch) and the Catholic counter-reformation that once more reduced women in the Church to a subordinate status; and interestingly enough it was only in the 1870's that Pope Pius IX relieved the last exempt abbess of her episcopal jurisdiction over male clergy. But the point is that women, though never in possession of full social equality with men during the Middle Ages, were nevertheless members of the Catholic hierarchy right up to a hundred years ago.

We leave our lady bishops to turn to other women who were seeking some kind of religious life apart from the standard religious orders and structures and indeed outside the mainstream of the Church's traditions. These women were adopting a religious life style which was an out and out reaction to the new conditions of urban life and the changing times. A group of women called the "beguines" had sprung up and put the Church in a quandry.

The beguines were simply an informal movement of women who wished to live life more religiously. It had no connection with men, no rule of life, no authority, no founder, no authorization—and this precisely was what perplexed Rome. The vows of the beguines, if they can be called that, were simply a statement of intention to live their life. They stayed in the world and did not go off to convents. Obviously there was no fault here. These women were doing nothing wrong but rather doing a great deal of right in desiring to live a holy life. They could be accused of no heresy (although this was tried). They were just there: a source of inspiration to their admirers, irritation to their detractors and an enigma to the established Church which did not know how to handle a Christian movement outside its mainstream of traditional religious patterns. By the middle of the thirteenth century they had doubled their numbers to something like 37,000. We mentioned that they lived in the world at their homes. By 1400 however most beguines lived in convents as an order that was not an order. They continued to engage in good works, tended towards mysticism and were fond of getting their spiritual guidance from the friars. It was a great outlet for the single woman inclined to living the religious life in the world. It was a solution to the problem of either being a total lay person or being a religious.

In due time fervor waned, vested interests continued their attacks, some absurdities crept in and before long the Church was looking into all fringe communities like the beguines. The Council of Lyon in 1274, for example, took a swipe against unauthorized religious orders. Some thirty years later another council mentioned the beguines by name, although it ended up saying good things about them. That was significant—these kind words—because it showed the ambiguity of the official Church's handling of an obviously good living group which did not conform to pre-existing patterns. Deep down, the real problem was the tension (to use modern terms) between freedom and authority. By the middle of the fourteenth century the beguines as a movement had pretty much died out, but the whole experience left the Church wondering about institutional religion.

THE "BRETHREN"

There was another movement afoot in Holland after the Great Schism—and perhaps in reaction to it—which had all the characteristics of a free-lance religion and which would further weaken or question the value of institutional religion. We might call it an off-beat mystical school. Actually it had arisen in the Rhineland before spreading to Holland and the Dominicans figure in the movement as guides and leaders. Some of the famous names connected with this movement are Tauler (d. 1361) and Suso (d. 1366). The beguines were associated with the Rhineland movement. We might characterize this movement, and others like it, as a movement of the individual's interior life. To help us see the meaning of this we should immediately bring up the name of the man who best represents this kind of thrust, Gerhard Groote. He represents the sincere layman, uninterested in the formal religious life as provided by the great religious orders, but highly interested in the interior life of the spirit. More than any other Groote represents the desire of the individual to have a reflective religious life of the interior heart. He had no program, no theories, no visions. He was no revolutionary, just a seeker after God in his own soul.

Around Groote formed a group of similarly pious men thus creating another irregular group like the beguines. Again, there was no rule of life. What is more there was a mingling of clerics and laity. This was an unheard of feature and an upsetting one for few concepts were as imbedded in the medieval mind than that the clergy and the laity were separate in every way. Finally, these people worked out in the world earning their livelihood. Again, the old problem for the institutional church and the hostility of the established religious orders: whoever heard of an order without vows? or the absence of a life-long commitment? Such unusual freedom must pose a threat for after all:

> If people could form associations without authorization, choose a superior in some unknown manner, adopt a monastic type of life without the sanction of a monastic rule, read the Scriptures together in the common tongue, confess their sins to one another and receive counsel and correction from no

one knew whom, there would be an end to all order in the Church.[6]

In any case, Groote's "Brethren of the Common Life" as they were called continued to grow living the ordinary life and strongly insisting on work as a means of religious life. They dropped all the old penances, long rites and complicated rituals and chant of the regular religious orders. They kept away from expertise in theology and any seeking after privilege. Rather they devoted themselves to a simple life of useful work and prayer. Their way became known as the *devotio moderna* (the modern devotion), a kind of spirituality that fell somewhere in-between that of the friars and New England Puritans. Above all the very existence of the Brethren was a symptom that a new age had new needs. Eventually, their problem, as so often happens, was that of success. The industry of the Brethren ran into conflict with the powerful working and craft guilds. The Brethren were finally forced into the single occupation of book binding which they did exceedingly well. The Brethren finally petered out but not without having made a great impact. Groote's most distinguished follower and the man who was to write the most popular book in the world second only to the Bible was Thomas a Kempis. He is the author of the famed *Imitation of Christ*, the perfect example of a deep personal and experiential faith and the retreat into the interior soul.

MEDIEVAL PIETY

The "Brethren" as we suggested were sensible relief from some of the excesses of their age. Late medieval life was so full of the strangest contradictions. Deep and abiding piety often rubbed shoulders with the erratic and unusual as we might expect in a society where the sacred and the profane were so intertwined. A host of special blessings, festivals, religious orders had sprung up. At one moment people would mechanically follow the forms of routine religion and at the next moment, at a word, at a sermon that touched them deeply, they would reach to unparalleled heights of religious emotion. Witness the sudden change of heart of the worldling, Francis of Assisi. Ignatius of Loyola and Martin Luther of the next chapter were true medieval men in their emotional and sudden conversions, the one due to war and the other due to a quick thunderstorm.

Nowhere were the extremes of medieval piety more evident than in the cult of the saints. Popular imagination had a field day. The saints became as real and familiar as the trees and sky. They were invoked on every occasion and assigned to every phase of human life and activity. Saints in charge of sickness, gout, headaches, shoemaking, motherhood, impossible cases, etc., came from medieval piety. Obviously the search for and the possession of relics of the saints turned into a fetish for many bordering on the barbaric.

> It was inevitable that this pious attachment to material things should draw all hagiolatry into a sphere of coarse and primitive ideas, and lead to surprising extremes. In the matter of relics the deep and straightforward faith of the Middle Ages was never afraid of disillusionment or profanation through handling holy things coarsely. The spirit of the fifteenth century did not differ much from that of the Umbrian peasants who, about the year 1000, wished to kill Saint Romuald, the hermit, in order to make sure of his precious bones; or of the monks of Fossanuova, who, after Saint Thomas Aquinas had died in their monastery, in their fear of losing the relic, did not shrink from decapitating, boiling and preserving the body. . . . In 1392, King Charles VI of France, on the occa-

sion of a solemn feast, was seen to distribute ribs of his ancestor, Saint Louis. . . .[7]

Even to associate with a holy person was like having a living relic. In fact St. Francis of Paula was literally purchased by a royal collector to live in his palace. Saints and visionaries were consulted by the high and mighty. This explains why some of the saints were always to be found in the royal entourage or why a St. Bernard or a St. Catherine were at the sides of the popes. Actually, so profuse and so overdone was the cult of the saints that when the Reformation attacked this cult the attack met with little resistance even from Catholics.

The liturgy itself, under the influence of the Franks, had gotten away from its original simplicity. Everything became dramatized and lengthened and, to a congregation that did not understand the Latin, new emphases were added. For example, for many the high point of the Mass was the elevation of the Host and the chalice, not the words of consecration. The laity were no longer permitted to carry Viaticum or Communion for the dying and in fact it was considered sacrilegious for a layman to touch the chalice. Probably the single most important change regarding the Mass in the early Middle Ages was the introduction of the private Mass. With such private Masses going on and the public Masses becoming more unintelligible except where overlaid with counterfeit meanings there was a growing tendency to dwell on the sacred species themselves. An interest took hold concerning Christ reserved in the Blessed Sacrament and all kinds of legends about bleeding hosts arose at this period. The feast of Corpus Christi was invented to honor the Real Presence; a glass was put in the monstrance or the tabernacle so that Jesus could "see" out to the people. The notion of the sacrifice of the Mass began to overshadow the earlier notions of the Mass as *eucharistia,* the community thanksgiving to God for salvation in Christ. In a very real sense, the extremes of the cult of the saints, the rerouting of so much of the liturgy and the new legal approach to the sacraments (whose number was only fixed at seven in the twelfth century: St. Bernard, for example held that there were ten), the introduction of the confessional box at the end of the Middle Ages—all these things were in reality "outside the mainstream." They were indicators, as was the moderate and sensitive spirituality of the independent "Brethren of the Common Life" that the Catholic synthesis was breaking up. As the growing nations were attacking the Church externally as it were, these phenomena were attacking the Church internally.

THE CHURCH

We are seeing in the fourteenth and fifteenth centuries not just the individual prophet and mystic who had always been around but a new prominence and publicity to mysticism itself. Better still, there was a new public prominence to greater individual freedom, a certain rebellion from the traditional way of doing things, a reaction against the hierarchial Church. There was a distinct thrust towards the religious value of purely secular life. The Brethren were an example of this. There were mystics of note around: Tauler, Rysbroek, Eckhart. Eckhart said that God and union with Him was open to all men not just to professional religious. The interior life was what counted. Interestingly, too, all these mystics wrote in the vernacular not the language of the Church which again had the effect of undermining the monopoly in religious matters that the Church had taken to herself.

Not that the Church had not made some recovery after the scandal of the Great Schism. Reform was made to some extent. New congregations were founded. Saints flourished during this period: the three Catherines of Siena, Genoa and Bologna; Saints Bernadine, John Capistrano, Colette and Antoninus. Popes Martin and Eugene went out of their way to pick worthy cardinals. Popular piety increased although much of it, as we have seen, centered around the aspects of the passion of Christ and the sorrows of the Blessed Mother. Again, this was because the Black Death had given to men a certain preoccupation with death, the after-life, salvation and indulgences as affecting the rewards to come. Much of this preoccupation about salvation, as a matter of fact, explains the inner spiritual struggles of such diverse men as Ignatius of Loyola, the founder of the Jesuits, and Martin Luther.

Still, the Church was clearly waning. Too many forces without and within were about to shake it to its very foundations. There were all those items we have already seen: the rise of the nation-states and their conflicts with the Church; the loss of the eastern Church; the humiliation of Boniface VIII; the rising skepticism of the schoolmen; the rising merchant class with its yen for profit and progress and its impatience with the moral confinements of the old order, etc. Then, too, other things arose to disrupt and disturb. For example, it was in the fourteenth century that it was discovered that the *Donation of Constantine* document mentioned in a previous chapter was a forgery. The Apostles Creed was shown not to be the work of the Apostles. Some early critical methods were being applied to the Bible. We have already taken note of the writings and activities of Marsilius, Wycliffe and Huss; the confusion caused by the beguines and the Brethren; the writings of the mystics; the tendency to go outside the mainstream of ecclesiastical life. Many of these things, of course, had only a limited appeal and limited effect for the moment. Most people still adhered to the formulas of the institutional Church. The externals were still too important to the crowd. But the discontent was brewing and, as we shall see below, papal life and morals went into another decline. An era was about to come to an end. Before we see its demise we must look at one more element in the changing scene, the Renaissance, an element which aided the downfall of the Middle Ages and the Church though this was furthest from its intent.

THE RENAISSANCE

The Renaissance was partly built on the decline of the Church's influence which was no longer, as we have seen, corresponding to the needs and realities of the age. It was also an embodiment of all of the physical and intellectual ferment that was going on. Men wanted freedom to experiment. Merchants wanted, as we have noted above, an end of political and moral limitations to their money making and expansion. A New World across the ocean was opening up and the Old World did not have the answers to it. Thus the Renaissance became in the context we have described, a kind of collective thrust into the whole area of human activity.

It is not mysterious as to why the Renaissance found its roots in Italy. Here above all other places, town life had developed with a high degree of sophistication. Italy was not united as were England and France. Its towns were fiercely independent and democratic levelling both nobles and commoners into a community of shared commercial interests. Such towns were quite ready to work out their fortunes free of political or ecclesiastical influence. The wealthy ran the towns and often their wealth was only matched by their unscrupulousness and little regard for the ideas and traditions of old. Since banking had started in Italy many families and merchants became wealthy and had more leisure time and began to dabble in the arts.

The old ascetical ideals of the Church were beginning to break down also. In fact traditional asceticism did not set well with the new competitive commercial spirit especially when it forbade interest on money. St. Peter was quoted as saying that we had not here a lasting city and the wealthy man could hardly be saved. This ideal was simply breaking down although it did not disappear altogether. We have a monk like Savonarola who could preach doom and despair in the middle of wealthy Florence and cause that people to burn their works of art and their frivolous books. But in the end they burned Savonarola.

On the other hand, the Church, it must be admitted, did not do much to foster the old ascetical ideals. Many of the upper clergy were caught up in the wealth and the papal court itself was becoming an open scandal of great luxury. Even the monastic orders were no longer the ideal for men (except for the cloistered orders) because they did not respond to the needs of the moment. Increasingly therefore, the lower classes ignorant and rude, entered their ranks. As the new learning spread the religious orders consequently became the butt of sarcastic comments and shady stories such as Chaucer's *Canterbury Tales* written in the fourteenth century. It was not that the men of the time lost their respect for sanctity—it still impressed them as it does men of every age—but they simply would not tolerate an asceticism intolerant and hostile to their way of life. We must mention that this loss of the ascetic ideal had immediate consequences. A vacuum was created in moral ideals and many of the pages of the history of this time are filled with endless assassinations, poisonings, infidelities and crimes. The dark streets of Florence and many other medieval towns provided cover for the most unspeakable crimes.

We must mention that elsewhere economic and social conditions were nourishing the Renaissance. In fact "the age has been characterized by its greatest historian, Jacob Burckhardt, as urban, commercial, and lay rather than ecclesiastical and feudal."[8] New merchants were in other areas besides Italy. The great money lenders appeared at this time in the Low Countries and England which were embarking on a vast amount of trade especially with the New World whose coffee, tea and tobacco were enriching them. The New World was the result of cautious navigational experiments such as those made by Prince Henry the Navigator. As a matter of fact the original discoveries were primarily adventures on behalf of the faith and in the interest of scientific curiosity. The commercial concern of such discoveries did not at first mean anything although later, it is obvious, the discovery of foreign lands would have a major impact on the economy of Europe. The Azores were discovered in 1431; Diaz reached the Cape of Good Hope in 1486; Columbus discovered America in 1492; Magellan encircled the globe for the first time in 1520. When the economic import of these discoveries began to assert itself the Italian cities would decline somewhat and the great centers of shipping would be Antwerp and places in the Low Countries.

So far we have spoken of the Renaissance without defining it. What actually was it? The Renaissance was a revival of learning and art. It nourished itself on antiquity, the rediscovery of the Greek and Roman ways. The Europeans were always aware of course of antiquity since they lived with it but they saw everything in a different light now. They broke away from seeing the world through ecclesiastical glasses. Now they were donning the glasses of the cultured pagan. Greek and Roman art, language, philosophy became the rage. The cultivated man of the Renaissance spoke and read Greek and Latin. The pagan authors, not the Christian, were his source of education. In short antiquity was not only being imitated it was being assimilated into vernacular languages of the time.

Thus the Renaissance had its intellectual impact. It would in effect replace the Church's dominance in the area of thought. Learning became the property of the layman, not just clerics and theologians. The pages of pagan antiquity would nourish his mind and his spirituality as well. In fact, man and his self perfection would be the focus, not the life hereafter. "The proper study of mankind is man" became more than a line of poetry. It became the abiding concern of men concerned with the human in every aspect: the humanists. Such were men like St. Thomas More and Erasmus, the most famous of them all. According to the humanists man was to be prepared for life, not the monastery. Schools must be designed to import, not salvation, but learning. This is why the humanists attacked church schools, their methods and the old time asceticism. Erasmus in his book, *Praise of Folly,* the most popular work of the time, poked fun at the Church and wanted to get education out of her hands. Thus at this time many colleges unrelated to the Church, were founded. It was towards the end result of universal education that Erasmus made his famous translation of the Bible into Greek and Latin.

To this extent the Renaissance was anticlerical but not antireligious. Art and science were no longer exclusively to serve theology but were to be studied for their own sakes.

The Church, in the eyes of the humanists, should remain on but no longer as having the monopoly of all learning. The Church should do everything in its power to create a truly human world and from the human world men would wend their way to God. The Church, in short, was also to be guided by reason and devoted to the humane. It was this attitude which underlay the horror which Erasmus displayed to Luther and the Reformation. As much as these humanists criticized the clergy they saw a need for the Church and were appalled by the violence which Luther unleashed. They had to resent the substitution of force for reason. In this respect, as we shall see in the next chapter, Luther was more medieval than contemporary. His dogmatism and force were more akin to the wars of religious extermination of the German princes against the Slavs than to the reasoned persuasions of the Renaissance men.

It must be stated again that the Renaissance of itself was not consciously hostile to the Church or organized religion. It just went beyond it. In fact, many of the popes patronized the Renaissance and were Renaissance men. This presented its own problems. The popes became too preoccupied with the new learning and did not give enough time to the spiritual side of the Church. Nicholas V who succeeded Eugene IV after the Great Schism was devoted to the Renaissance and it is to him that we owe the fabulous Vatican Library and other monuments in St. Peter's. But even the Renaissance popes took time out for the chronic game of playing power politics among the nations. Wars in Italy were still commonplace and sapped the energy that the popes wanted to spend elsewhere. Elsewhere still meant fighting the Moslems. The popes wanted to regain Constantinople. In fact, unable to rouse the princes of Europe, Pius II himself planned to set off on a Crusade—the last one in history—and died before it really got underway.

Sixtus IV (d. 1484) the builder of the famous chapel named after him, the Sistine Chapel, began the unsavory practice of handing out the cardinals' hats to his unworthy relatives. This had the net effect of breaking up the college of cardinals into factions each jockeying to get his own man in as pope. After Sixtus IV came the unworthy and scandalous Callistus VIII who frankly bought the papacy. He was the first pope to publicly acknowledge his bastard children and give them a place in the Church's administration. He was succeeded both in title and sin by Alexander VI, another Borgia pope who went even further in providing for his bastard children and evil relatives of cutthroats and murderers. Alexander VI died in 1503 and was succeeded by the vigorous Julius II who was both a diplomat and soldier. He did not hesitate to lead his armies himself into battle. Those readers who saw the movie *The Agony and the Ecstasy* may remember the pope in this role (played by Rex Harrison). He was the one who pressured Michelangelo to paint the Sistine Chapel with his masterpiece. Julius also, unfortunately, continued the practice of nepotism. Yet he did manage to balance off his current enemies who might be a threat to the papal states. Julius II was succeeded by a Medici, Leo X, who had been a cardinal at the age of thirteen and who would sit on the papal throne for the next twenty years. He too never lost an opportunity to further the interests of his family. It was also his misfortune to be the pope when Luther began what he called a mere "monkish squabble."

As we close this section we must emphasize strongly that the Renaissance, for all of its intellectual intoxication and artistic activity, did not go into profound philosophical questions and in fact operated well within the old Christian finalities. This explains why in the midst of all of this enlightenment magic could revive and witchcraft trials be renewed. Another point of strong emphasis is this: the Renaissance was essentially an elitist movement. The wealthy few were its patrons. It was an aristocratic movement for intellectual elite and as such there was a marked disdain for the illiterate or those engaged in mundane mechanical tasks. It was the Renaissance men who coined the pejorative term "Gothic" for the cathedrals of Europe. It was these Renaissance elite who could be rather indifferent to the lower classes.[9] Thus, although all men could be caught up in the spirit and adventuresome times of the Renaissance the time and the wealth to pursue and encourage it belonged to the few. There was no telling how far the Renaissance would have taken the times but it was suddenly checked and restyled by another powerful force that appeared in its midst, the Protestant Reformation. At long last the seeds of Marsilius, Wycliffe and Huss had flowered.

NOTES

1. Philip Hughes, *A Popular History of the Catholic Church,* p. 161. Macmillan paperback. New York, N.Y. 1962.
2. Concilium, volume 64, p. 150. 1971.
3. At least officially. There will always be some strange people around. There is a Michael Collin who claims to be Pope Clement XV. He is a former Catholic priest defrocked in 1951 by Pius XII for founding an unauthorized order called the Apostles of Infinite Love. He has his "cardinals" and "bishops" and "nuns" housed in his "Vatican", two concrete buildings in Clemery, France. cf. *Time* magazine, March 15, 1971.
4. cf. F. J. Sheed, *What Difference Does Jesus Make?,* pp. 77 to 79. Sheed and Ward, New York. 1971. For a view of the modern Church's wealth see James Gollin's book *Worldly Goods,* Random House, N.Y. 1971, especially chapter 17.

5. Quoted in R. W. Southern, *op. cit.*, p. 314.
6. *Ibid.*, p. 342.
7. J. Huizinga, *The Waning of the Middle Ages*, p. 167. Doubleday Anchor Books, Garden City, N.Y. edition 1954.
8. Frederick M. Schweitzer, *op. cit.*, p. 119.
9. We might also recall from this chapter that it was the Renaissance which was indifferent to women's position—an attitude picked up from the classical age of Aristotle and Pericles. Slowly but surely women were relieved of their positions in the Catholic hierarchy. Two interesting books on the whole subject of women in the ministry are *The Lady Was a Bishop* by Joan Morris (Macmillan, N.Y. 1973) and *Women Priests: Yes or No* by Emily C. Hewitt and Suzanne R. Hiatt (Seabury Press, 1973).

XIV

The Reformation

ABUSES

In spite of all that we have seen in the past chapters the Church continued to hold sway over Europe. No one seriously considered its overthrow. To the medieval mind the very idea would be civilly as well as religiously unthinkable for society and Church were as one. Yet in the space of fifty years or so that is precisely what happened: millions of Catholics were wrenched from the Church and new churches were founded radically different from the old one. To understand how this happened we must look at the abuses prevalent and the circumstances that brought men to the forefront who (almost unwittingly) brought about this revolution.

There were, of course, the elements already mentioned: Wycliffe's ideas and his Lollard group; Marsilius of Padua and his pro-royalist teaching that Henry VIII would use; John Huss of Bohemia who had religiously disturbed that land; the Great Schism that weakened papal authority; the theory of conciliarism that placed a General Council superior to the pope. Then there were the daily chronic irritations: too many clerical exemptions from civil law; worldly clergy and absentee bishops; unlettered and uncouth lower clergy; the scandalous inter-rivalry between the Franciscans and Dominicans; impotent and sterile monasteries; the low estate of clerical celibacy and the very use of the term "cleric" or "monk" as an insulting word among the laity. But over and above such chronic scandals we might list five major causes of the Reformation: spirituality, money, the papacy, the power of the kings and the new learning.

SPIRITUALITY

There were indeed many reformers active in the Church. There were new and fervent orders rising up, a wave of idealism and fervor but these elements only aggravated the need for a better spirituality. We must not forget that the experience of the Black Death drove men into a greater preoccupation with salvation and death. We must not forget that groups like the Brethren of the Common Life had whetted spiritual appetites and thereby increased the dissatisfaction with the packaged (and costly) piety of the Church. For many "the crucible was personal experience of dissatisfaction with what was offered by the Roman Church."[1] Basically therefore for some the Protestant Reformation was a religious quest for a new spirituality: a desire to renew and perhaps redirect Christian spirituality from external routine to inner involvement. The Reformation was thus a concern for the entire Church, that it get back to the Gospel. Men were looking critically at the old Constantinian concept of the Church which identified it so much with the political order. Men were asking whether the kind of institutional Church that responded to the needs of the violent barbarian age was fulfilling its basic role at the present as a mediator between Christ and man. In the estimation of many, spiritual needs and evangelical virtues had too long been sacrificed to a preoccupation with rights and privileges. For these reasons much of the reformers' denunciations of the Church was aimed not to destroy it, but to purify it. To the end there was always the vague presumption that the new Gospel could somehow be subsumed into the Catholic Church. Genuine doctrinal differences came later and as the result of misunderstanding, a hardening of positions. Most of the people who thronged to the reformers "did not consider themselves in opposition to the Roman Church. Even if they were against the clergy or ecclesiastical prerogatives, they were not really against the Church. The resolute mood of separation came much later. The Reformation was a filial revolt; in other words, a prodding to get the Church to undertake certain changes. . . ."[2] Not all were so interested in such pure motives but for many the Reformation began with a crisis in their hearts, a holy dissatisfaction with the externalized sanctity offered by the Church, a dilemma between Church authority and the freedom of the Gospel.

MONEY AND THE PAPACY

The burdensome taxations (imposed under penalty of excommunication for failure to pay) fell largely on the backs of the middle class artisans and the peasants. What was particularly galling was the widespread suspicion that such tax monies were underwriting the scandalous and luxurious lives of the Italian prelates. Besides, why should the faithful in Germany pay for the siege of Bologna by Julius II? Why should England pay for the rebuilding of St. Peter's? Why should France finance the wars and politics of the pope? Thus for money reasons alone there was strong antipapal feeling in many countries. Roman expenditures and the upkeep of the papal bureaucracy was so great however, that the quest for money and its attendant corruptions went on. Pope Innocent VII at one point even pawned his tiara. Graft became a way of life. Church positions were bought and sold almost on the open market. Dispensations were costly. In fact, nothing seemed free of a price tag from pardons to candles, from masses to the papal office itself. Nor did the papal office holders themselves help. During Luther's lifetime the popes were Alexander VI who flouted his bastard Borgia children to the public, Julius II, more at home on the battlefield than at the papal court and Leo X more Renaissance prince than pope.

However, the popes could hardly bring reform, not only because they lacked the will to do so but because in fact they had lost the power to do so. The new rising nations had eroded that power considerably. In spite of past victories papal dominance in international affairs had dwindled. Kings and local lords won more and more rights to dispose of many of the highest clerical offices in their territories as they saw fit and so churchmen were more loyal to prince than to pope. When Pope Urban called for the first Crusade all of Christendom had responded. When Pius II also called for a Crusade against the Moslems Europe did not respond even when Pius took the Crusader's cross himself and died in 1453 while embarking on the Holy War. Not only did the papacy lose its power in other lands but it became more and more embroiled, as a sovereign power, in protecting its territories in Italy. Because of this immediate local Italian need all the popes of the fifteenth century, with two exceptions, were Italian and since 1522 to the present day have remained such. The papacy had come to require its incumbents to be Italian princes to protect its interests; the papacy became a home-grown interest and the curia provided high jobs (and pay) for the popes' families.

THE POWER OF THE KINGS

The kings were forging strong centralized nations. It is not difficult to see that the international power of an international Church must necessarily be a threat to them. Never far from their minds therefore were plans to dominate the Church, to nationalize it and make it a department of state. Already, as we have noted, they had secured rights to appoint the higher clergy. As the popes became weaker as the kings became stronger they had to resort to the new invention of having papal ambassadors at the various courts (nuncios). Such ambassadors, like any other diplomat, must now cajole, flatter and bargain with the kings. The day of the direct papal thunderbolt was over even though the pope retained considerable prestige and power yet. Because he did the kings were not entirely displeased with Italians possessing their dioceses for such an arrangement also gave the king his man at the papal court, his ambassador, to press his interests. In this way the kings who wanted to reward their loyal followers could secure papal approval of their appointees. Of course such papally approved royal appointees were really the kings' men in church robes and when crisis came they were loyal to the king and not to the pope. In short, because of the weakening of the papacy and the growing power of the monarchs the Reformation, when it came, would succeed only where the king wished it to succeed and fail where he decreed it would fail. At no time was the Reformation apart from the political power:

> The relation between this [the king's forging of strong nations] and the success of a Protestant revolt is undoubted

but not easy to define. It might be said broadly that in England and in Denmark, the Reformation was necessary because limitation of the power of the Church was necessary to the future development of efficient government. Efficient government demanded restraint upon papal intervention, upon ecclesiastical privilege and exemptions, upon the legal right of an authority outside the country to levy taxes.[3]

When the time came, the reality of the king's strength and the pope's weakness would lead the reformers to look to the king for redress and support.

THE NEW LEARNING

This was the time when a new spirit of learning was abroad. Sophisticated scholars like the great Erasmus (d. 1536), pained at seeing the great civilizer of Europe stranded on forms and vested interests, and distressed at seeing the discrepancies in Church and society, set out by his writings to provoke reform. Erasmus in particular used ridicule and perhaps more than anyone else in Europe he lowered the reputation of the popes and the clergy, the monks and the friars, and especially the nit-picking theologians who had become too rationalistic and too little updated with critical scholarship. In his efforts to spread learning Erasmus translated the Bible into Greek so that more might read it. Along with new scholarship was the cry for simplicity in contrast to the convulsions of the Church devotions, relics, cults, madonnas, bleeding hosts, indulgences, etc. In fact, there was a looking back to the "Golden Age" of the Apostles when people thought that all was harmony and peace (in spite of ample evidence to the contrary as we have noted before in St. Paul's epistles). All accretions of the present Church must be stripped away. This thought explains why the reformers were always looking backwards not forward. This desire to discover and reproduce the supposed purity of the early Church was not new. It was behind the Waldensians and Wycliffe and others. The trouble was that up to this time there were really no texts or documents to work with to find out what that Church was really like. Now, however, there were many more discoveries of early Christian literature. There was an increased knowledge of Greek and New Testament studies and new critical methods were being applied to Scripture. For the first time men were able to look directly at the Scriptures and not merely through official Church documents or the liturgy. The new scholarship in other words turned men more than ever to the Bible, especially to St. Paul and his moral teachings. The early Church became more of a reality. The current Church provided more of a contrast. In any case all this was a part of the humanists' attack and that is why a popular saying of the day said, "Erasmus laid the egg and Luther hatched it." To all of this must be added other factors such as the adventuresome spirit engendered by the Renaissance and the invention of printing which could quickly spread ideas. In a word, everything so far mentioned coalesced into what we might call the "ripeness of time." Luther would succeed where other reformers had failed because due to many circumstances the time was ripe for reform and revolution.[4]

LUTHER

Luther was of peasant stock, subject to strong emotions, impulsive actions and speech. At twenty-two he left the pursuit of law to enter an Augustinian monastery. No one knows why he made this sudden decision. There were always present in him emotional anxieties. There was the death of a close friend, an almost fatal injury. Most of all he was caught in a severe thunderstorm wherein, true medievalist that he was, he cried out to St. Anne for help and vowed to enter a monastery if he were saved. In 1506 he made his profession as a monk and remained so for the next twenty years. Yet all during this time he was subject to great scruples about his worthiness, his guilt, the pressure of his sins and the fear of God's punishment. Modern psychoanalyst Eric Ericson in his book *Young Man Luther* had suggested that Luther's stern father was the prototype of his stern and demanding God. In any case Luther could not rid himself of guilt. He would confess his sins for hours on end ". . . yet for all this my conscience could never be fully certified, but was always in doubt and said: this or that thou hast not done rightly: thou wast not contrite and sorrowful enough; this sin thou didst omit in thy confessions, etc."[5]

Finally through his Bible studies Luther came upon his theory of justification by faith alone. He felt St. Paul said it all in Romans 1:17, "The righteous shall live by faith." Man is not made holy then by works or ritual but by faith in God. Man must simply believe that God forgives him. Man is saved only if he ceases to rely upon himself and totally accepts God's goodness. This reliance, this trust, this total confidence is the faith that makes man holy, justifies him. Luther felt a weight lifted with these thoughts which implied little merit to good works, relics, statues, and all the other rituals and superstitions of the Church. However, Luther had no thought of going further, no intent of breaking with the Church. He went on to become a teacher and lecturer at the University of Wittenberg in 1512. Then an incident occurred which sparked his appearance into the public limelight. It was the selling of indulgences. The background was this: Albert of Brandenburg, a twenty-four year old cleric who already held several Church offices aspired to become the Archbishop of Mainz (and thereby one of the electors of the emperor). To obtain yet another office he needed a papal dispensation which, according to the corruption of the times, he had to pay for. Albert borrowed the money from the Fugger banking family and in turn the pope allowed him to sell indulgences, part of the profit going to repay the Fuggers and the other part going towards the rebuilding of St. Peter's. The Dominican Tetzel was chosen to hawk these indulgences near (not in) Wittenberg. Luther was incensed and showed the traditional German hostility to money going from Germany to Rome. On October 31, 1517 he posted his ninety-five theses on the town bulletin board (as was customary) and sent copies to Tetzel's superiors, Albert himself and others. Albert forwarded his copy to the pope. Luther's ninety-five theses were rather mild and quite Catholic, calling for a reinterpretation of the teaching on indulgences on matters not yet defined by the Church.

What should have been a minor irritant became a hornet's nest for Luther had simply nudged too many vested interests at the moment: the whole elaborate money-indulgence system, big names, a banking family, the rebuilding of St. Peter's. Clearly this was not the time to raise moral scruples. Actually Luther seemed to be under the impression that if only the pope knew what was going on he would be shocked enough to put a stop to it. Instead Luther received a reprimand from the pope's censor and Tetzel himself replied vigorously. The controversy was beginning to spread in very small circles. By the next year however his ninety-five theses were more widely publicized and by this time the German nationalists, always ready to needle Rome, were applauding Luther's stand. The Church now proceeded to its biggest mistake: it did not take Luther seriously nor give him a decent hearing, but in 1518 opened proceedings against him and ordered him to appear in Rome. Luther was not sure that he would return alive from Rome and so, in one of the most symbolic acts of the Reformation, he appealed to his political superior, the Elector Frederick of Saxony.

ELECTOR FREDERICK OF SAXONY

Luther's appeal was that he should be heard in his native Germany and Frederick supported this request. Why he did so is a moot question since he did not know Luther and did not share his religious views. Perhaps it was because Albert of Brandenburg was his rival. Perhaps it was because Tetzel was cutting in on his own revenue producing relics, for his church at Wittenberg had cases containing some 17,433 fragments of holy bones including (it was claimed) the corpse of one of the Holy Innocents. Perhaps it was just that like any good German he wanted to show the Roman Curia that it could not proceed the way it wanted to. For whatever reason, Frederick intervened and this in effect saved the Lutheran Reformation from extinction. The pope granted Frederick's request because the old emperor lay dying and the pope did not want any of the contenders to get the imperial crown: not Charles V of Spain nor Francis I of France for both would then surround Italy. The pope in fact favored Frederick himself. Thus the meeting took place at Augsburg in 1518 where Luther held to his rejection of indulgences before the famous Cardinal Cajetan. The following year he met with John Eck at Leipzig. Leipzig lay near the Bohemian border, the land of the burned heretic, John Huss. Eck goaded Luther on, forcing him to admit that sometimes Huss was right and that the General Council which had condemned him was wrong; that, in fact, the pope himself was not infallible. That was the turning point. Luther had actually gone so far as to identify himself with a man whom the Church had condemned.

Still matters were not irreparable for the Church had tolerated many who disagreed with her (like Erasmus). There was as yet no official teaching on justification and the infallibility of the pope had not been defined. In fact a papal commission in 1520 rendered a rather mild verdict on Luther's writings but, with John Eck's instigation, a papal bull of June 15, 1520 condemned forty-one of Luther's propositions. Luther, meanwhile was not idle. He wrote three of his most famous political pamphlets appealing to the nobles to bring about reform and attacking the sacramental system, reducing the sacraments to three and then to two. On December 10, 1520 Luther burned the papal bull before some students who took it as a lark. He also burned a copy of Canon Law thus symbolically rejecting Church authority and replacing it with Scripture alone. Finally on January 3, 1521 he was excommunicated. Four months later he was banned in the empire by the Emperor, Charles V. For safe keeping he was "kidnapped" by the Elector Frederick and spirited off to the castle of Wartburg where he stayed for a year. "It was a time of physical depression and mental temptation. He felt the demons about him. He imagined that he heard a devil taking walnuts from the table and cracking them on the ceiling all night."[6] At this time he translated the Bible into colloquial German. He was not the first to do so for there were some eighteen other translations. Nor was his work accurate or literate. He was not above correcting St. Paul or St. John nor criticizing the epistle of St. James with its heavy emphasis on good works: "You see then that a man is justified by deeds and not by faith in itself." (James 2:24) His translation, however, was an immediate success. With his pamphlets he became the most popular writer in Germany.

THE MOVEMENT SPREADS

The man was becoming a movement. Nothing was formed yet: no creed, no church, but power and politics were gathering their forces to keep the man's position alive. Many, for various reasons, were gathering around his cause. Some joined for noble, religious reasons. In other instances "it is surely noteworthy that at some place the demand for the discontinuation of payments to the Church and for 'evangelical' ministers was made in the same breath as that for greater popular participation in governmental affairs."[7] Some, however, did not join his cause or left it. The humanists, for example, were on his side at the beginning and Luther and Erasmus because of their criticisms of the Church were identified though neither admired the other. In any case Erasmus broke with Luther over what he considered Luther's violence and wildness. In 1523 Erasmus even took up the pen against Luther. The universities and theologians and higher clergy were cool to Luther but the lower clergy eagerly joined him.

THE PEASANTS' REVOLT

Simultaneous with Luther's message the ever restless peasants were stirring against their cruel local lords. (We must remember that there was no central government in Germany.) In 1524 the peasants revolted and some hundred thousand of them were most cruelly crushed. Luther figured in the incident indirectly because some peasants felt that his insistence on Christian freedom and egalitarian priesthood was a clarion call to political freedom and equality. Luther, a political conservative, deplored violence and deplored the peasants using the gospel to justify it. He therefore urged the princes in a famous pamphlet "to slay, stab and kill" the peasants. "These times," Luther exclaimed in a typical over-statement, "are so extraordinary that a prince can win heaven more easily by bloodshed than by prayer." Feeling betrayed the common people, especially in southern Germany, abandoned Luther. Two other results came after the Peasants' Revolt. One was that Lutheranism thereby tended to become more tied to the state since the state (read: princes) had gained more power by the revolt's failure. The second result was the politicalization of Lutheranism. That is, Catholic princes rallied together to prevent another peasant uprising since it was popularly thought that Luther had inspired the Peasants' Revolt. On the other hand the Lutheran princes banded together for mutual protection. From 1525 on then Luther's movement was largely out of his hands and into the hands of the power play between the Catholic and Lutheran princes.

THE COMMUNION CONTROVERSY

Other matters began to go badly for Luther. One was his distress from his fellow Protestants. He could more easily handle the Catholics than his Protestant adversaries. One early controversy concerned the eucharist. Luther taught that the Catholic notion of transubstantiation was inadequate and that the Mass was not a sacrifice for it could not be so verified in Scripture. However, in words that echoed St. Thomas Aquinas Luther believed in the Real Presence, but others disagreed. Carlstadt, an old professor colleague, took a different point of view. Most of all the great Swiss reformer Zwingli disagreed. Before long everyone was debating the matter concerning the eucharist. Finally the two major protagonists, Luther and Zwingli met in October 1529 at Marburg to settle the matter. They left their encounter still in basic disagreement—which had far-reaching results:

The Marburg colloquy was a failure. Theologically, it had confirmed that Protestantism was a divided house. This fact, bitter though it was, gave lie to the exuberant Protestant assertion that men everywhere would agree to the meaning of Scripture if they were only of good will. Now it turned out that evidently such good will was absent among some Protestants or that Scripture did not quite lend itself to the easy interpretation that had been assumed. And which of these two options to favor was surely a painful decision.

The failure to attain agreement meant that both sides clung to their respective theological positions with unwavering determination. The consequences were both far-reaching and disastrous. Protestantism remained a divided house, a fact that influenced the Reformation era no less than subsequent centuries.[8]

THE FAILURE OF REUNION

We must remember that Luther was still under the emperor's ban. Yet, because Charles V was mostly out of Germany, the ban was ineffective. As a matter of fact the emperor was away so long and therefore any Lutheran-Catholic settlement was so deferred, that the truce which merely tolerated the Lutherans became a way of life. Germany was in reality already split. When Charles V did meet with his princes in 1529 he was still not ready to enforce any uniform solution for the simple reason that he was still pressed by many enemies, particularly the everlasting Moslems who were invading the eastern parts of his empire. The point is that Charles needed all the allies he could get and this included the Lutheran princes. All that Charles asked for in 1529 at the Meeting of Speyer was for help against the Moslems, and that everything should return religiously to the old all-Catholic way until a General Church Council should be called. (Charles was continuously calling for a Church council but for reasons we shall see it was not forthcoming; and when it did come Charles did not want it at that inopportune moment.) The minority Lutheran princes *protested* against such an arrangement thus earning their name ever after: Protestants. The real problem, as we mentioned above, was that too much time had elapsed for a reversal of religious positions.

Another meeting was held at Augsburg in 1530 during which both sides were to be heard. The problem was that there was no one Protestant side since there was no one Protestant Church but already several divisions. Philip Melancthon drafted the famous creedal statement which has become the classic statement of Lutheranism, the Augsburg Confession (though his purpose was to stress agreement with Catholicism). The Catholics denounced the Confession with another statement which the emperor asked the Protestants to consider (he still needed their aid against the Moslems). But some of the Protestants could not even accept the Augsburg Confession and some of the Catholics were definitely disinclined to be conciliatory and so nothing came of the 1530 meeting.

There was one tangible result: fear on the part of the Lutherans that the time had come for the emperor to use force against them. They quickly banded into the League of Schmalkald in a defensive alliance but the emperor had need of this very alliance against the Moslems. Still meetings continued to be held even though the reality of a divided Germany was evident. At one point the emperor was able to weaken the League through the indiscretion of one of the Protestant princes, Philip of Hesse. Unfaithful Philip, caught in an unhappy marriage, sought another wife. Luther and others, asked for their opinion, came up with a distinction that would have done credit to the Catholic casuists of old.

They said that while the general law of the gospel forbade divorce it was permitted in the Old Testament. Since Philip was burdened with so heavy a conscience he might divorce his wife though his second marriage was to be kept secret. Rumor forced Philip to reveal what had happened but Luther refused to let Philip make public his (Luther's) advice on the matter; rather he cautioned a "strong Christian lie." There was no doubt that this was a sellout on the part of Luther and his associates and that Philip's position was paramount in getting for him what an ordinary citizen would never have received. In any case, Philip's bigamy should have incurred banishment by the emperor but the emperor used the incident to neutralize Philip from the Protestant League.

Meetings of reconciliation were still going on in 1546 ending in failure; war was declared and ultimately the emperor defeated the League in 1547. The emperor, still trying for a middle course, did not restore Catholicism and political considerations still kept Lutheranism alive. Another meeting was held in Augsburg in 1555 whereby the famous agreement was reached that all subjects must adopt the religion of their princes whatever that might be up to the year 1552. Dissenters might leave the territory. Only Lutheranism and Catholicism were established (the others were not tolerated) and Germany was now officially a divided country. Meanwhile at one of the meetings in 1546 news arrived that on February 18, Luther had died.

SPREAD OF LUTHERANISM

We have seen that by 1555 Lutheranism was a reality and had official status, but it soon fell into subdivisions. A leader like the gentle Philip Melancthon was so agreeable to the restoration of some Catholic ways that he offended the more rigid adherents. Thus Lutheranism split into a moderate party (known as the Philipists) and the strict party. Soon each side was verbally attacking the other. This inter-warfare left the way open for the growth of the Reformed (Calvinistic) churches in Germany. Meanwhile Lutheranism moved into other sections mainly by seeing that a Protestant got elected as bishop for then, according to the Augsburg agreement, his territory would have to follow suit. Thus we read of the inevitable jockeying that led to extremes like having two, eight and twelve year old Protestants being elected bishops in order to get the territory into the religious camp. Complications arose when some important areas became Protestants of the Reformed type which worried the Lutherans. Thus in the Lutheran areas they would allow neither the Catholic Mass nor Calvinistic worship and in their areas the Calvinists reciprocated. Much bitterness went back and forth and at times each side was not sure if they did not prefer the Catholics to the other. It would only be in the seventeenth century that both sides reduced the essentials to some kind of common ground and thus reduced the tensions.

ZWINGLI

Luther was only one of several independent reformers for "the Reformation did not all spring from Luther, it sprang from those conditions of the Church and those states of mind which made Luther possible."[9] Thus Zwingli represents the reformer who was a contemporary of Luther but who disclaimed any dependency on him. Zwingli in fact was much more influenced by Erasmus. He was a Swiss pacifist and patriot who was more rigid than Luther and felt that nothing was religiously valid unless specifically mentioned in the

Bible. Therefore in his Swiss city of Zurich he removed relics, organs, pictures and smashed religious objects of art (something Luther would not have done) thus paving the way for English Puritanism. Like Luther he rejected the Mass as a sacrifice, papal authority and clerical celibacy. In 1525 he abolished the Mass and replaced it with a simple Communion Service (primitive simplicity versus ecclesiastical superstition). However, Zwingli was unable to get all of Switzerland to accept the new faith and political alliances were thus formed. In time matters went badly for Zwingli: he could not agree with Luther about the eucharist, he was excluded from the Meeting of Augsburg and the League of Schmalkald. By 1531 he had formed an economic blockade against the Catholic cantons and war was imminent. Zwingli, the pacifist, entered battle and was killed. Peace was arranged and each canton was permitted to determine the faith within its own boundaries. Thus the new faith received a measure of toleration but remained a minority religion.

CALVIN

Calvin, a Frenchman who at twenty-four had left the Catholic Church, was one generation removed from Luther. Thus he grew up in an environment quite concerned with the religious issues Luther had raised. He had his starting point, therefore, not in the crisis of conscience like Luther but in the religious upheaval created by him. It was Calvin's task to bring order and system to this upheaval and become the mentor of the Presbyterian and Reformed churches. Calvin had fled from his persecuting France to Geneva in Switzerland which had become a haven for such religious refugees. Geneva was already Protestant due to men like Zwingli, Bucer and Farel.

Calvin had already written his famous *Institutes* which gave Protestantism its much needed systemization and had developed his teaching on Predestination. This teaching was based on the absolute majesty of God and the logical conclusion that man is saved by grace alone. God, in the words of Calvin, "ordains some to eternal life, the others to eternal damnation." No one knew for sure who was who but there were certain fallible signs of the elect: acceptance of the Gospel, the reception of the Lord's Supper and the decent lives men lived. In due time Calvin forged Geneva into a system which indeed became militantly determined to see that men fulfilled these three signs of election. Again, papal authority was replaced by state or civic authority. There was little that was democratic in Calvin's ideal community and the State Board or Consistory as it was called controlled the town in godliness.

The Consistory met weekly to consider matters such as blasphemy, dancing, to check on the obligatory church attendance. Worldly songs met with punishment, theaters were closed and gambling forbidden. In six years the Consistory excommunicated more than 1,300 persons. Heresy was most intolerable and when the erratic Spanish Unitarian, Michael Servetus fled to Geneva for Calvin's protection Calvin had this denier of the Trinity burned at the stake "in the name of the Father and of the Son and of the Holy Ghost." "This act makes the blackest page in Protestant history"[10] and did not promote the unpopular Calvin any. Calvin lacked Luther's flair and warmth and good humor. He did not enjoy nature and married out of principle, not love. It was he who gave the uncompromising color to Protestantism, stressing that the road to heaven was straight and narrow. He gave Protestantism its hard-working, no-nonsense ethic and inspired the early Calvinists that they were the elect of God. Such Calvinists, so inspired, became fearless and hard-working for life was short and much remained to be done for God. Like the monks of old they often fell into the same problem: they were successful and soon became prosperous, middle-class citizens.

Yet it was Calvinism, not Lutheranism, which would become widespread. Lutheranism always remained a somewhat German phenomenon and never went beyond that country except to Sweden. To this day Wittenberg holds no place in history or in the popular mind comparable to Rome or Geneva. It was Calvinism and its Reformed churches that became international and free of the patronage of the princes. Men were drawn to the Calvinist discipline rather than to its doctrines. The Calvinist became the hard-working, fearless rear guard of Protestantism and created a spirit that worked well with political agitation and expansion. The lay people were taken with the novelty of collaborating in the running of their churches; they grew close together and formed strong (and at times fanatical) proselytizing groups. The clergy, thanks to the Academy of Geneva founded by Calvin in 1559 were trained and capable in contrast to the ignorance and apathy of the Catholic clergy. Calvinists grew bold, spread the faith and met death with great courage. It was their blood, shed by Catholics and other Protestants alike, that kept the Reformed faith moving.

SPREAD OF REFORMATION

As we just mentioned the Reformed pattern of church formation took the lead in Europe rather than the Lutheran (considered too popish by many). This meant having the eucharist as a memorial, an austere worship ritual, moral discipline, a drive to get every man to read the Bible and a religion free from any subjection to the state (though the state should work on behalf of religion). Yet for the new faith to succeed it had to involve itself with politics, for to the medieval mind the ruler still determined the religion of his subjects. Thus the drive was on to convert the ruler, depose him for a more favorable candidate or get him to legally permit the new faith co-existence. In most places force and attempts at deposition prevailed. The cause of religion was joined to the cause of politics—and vice versa.

SWEDEN AND THE NETHERLANDS

In Sweden there was the usual tension of hostility between Church and ruler and the Reformation there was a political effort at imperial consolidation. In 1523 the king's newly appointed chancellor filled his mind with Lutheran ideas. By 1525 a decree was issued ordering all Church income to go to the crown and by the following year all clerical matters were placed under the king's jurisdiction. Catholic rebellion was crushed. In 1529 a Protestant was appointed to the important see of Uppsala and by 1544 all Catholic practices were purged. In 1575 a new king made up a new liturgical order and even went so far as to open secret negotiations with Rome. In 1592 the Catholic Polish king, Sigismund succeeded to the Swedish throne but was opposed by his Protestant uncle. This uncle called a meeting, condemned Catholicism as well as the teachings of Zwingli and Calvin and adopted a form of Lutheranism as the state religion. Thus initial political dissatisfaction ended up with Sweden allied with Reformation ideas. In 1604 all Catholics were deprived of offices and banished from the realm.

In the Netherlands the merchant people were prosperous and educated and so Reform ideas spread quickly among them. The ruler was the Catholic king of Spain, Philip II. Political resistance to Philip became identified with religious dissent. In 1566 a mob broke stained glass windows, desecrated churches and sacked monasteries pushing the country towards civil war. In 1568 William of Orange, former Catholic, former Lutheran and present Calvinist, became the leader of the anti-Spanish forces and thus automatically leader of the pro-Protestant party. The result was civil war that with the help of England brought about a divided country: the Calvinist northern section (which one day would become Holland) and the Catholic southern section (which one day would become Belgium).

POLAND AND FRANCE

Poland was a more religiously pluralistic society and the arm of the government was not used to establish any religion. Protestants were not persecuted in Poland but just withered away. Moreover there was really no political issue at hand for the nobles in general were content. They already possessed considerable power over the Catholic Church and the king. They had no special grievance to which the new faith could attach itself. Protestantism did come to Poland and some of the lower nobility espoused it and even the king petitioned the pope for a married clergy and a vernacular Mass but was refused. The king and the people remained loyal to the Church and so "The Reformation in Poland failed because Protestantism was unable to make its political case."[11]

In France the king had too many privileges and controls over the Catholic Church to relinquish that Church lightly. Therefore if Protestantism was to make headway it had to align itself with and become a political issue. Protestantism had come to France by way of Luther and Calvin's writings but it had its own native reformers as well who were actively stirring up disunity at the precise time the king needed national unity to face his many problems. Besides the king was suspicious of the new faith; he had seen some of its political excesses elsewhere. So in 1540 he acted; he made heresy a matter of state suppression. A new king in 1551 for the next twelve years persecuted the French Protestants or Huguenots as they were called and made glorious martyrs out of them.

When this king died his fifteen year old son ruled through Cardinal Guise. It must be noted that the Guise family was staunchly Catholic while the rival Bourbon family was pro-Protestant. The Huguenots therefore jumped headlong on the Bourbon side and into the political maneuverings that would bring them to power. After Cardinal Guise the real ruler and regent was Catherine de Medici. Faced with so many hostile voices on all sides she became surprisingly tolerant and in 1562 permitted the Huguenots to hold services outside the fortified cities. Even with this concession however hostilities between Huguenot and Catholic broke out and religious warfare raged for the next nine years. Catherine tried again to heal the breach by marrying her daughter to Henry of Navarre of the Bourbon house, a Huguenot and heir to the throne. One of those attending this wedding was an Admiral Coligny, a Calvinist, who had considerable influence over Catherine's royal son and who moreover was seeking an alliance with Protestant Elizabeth of England. Catherine apparently planned to have the Admiral assassinated (he was wounded not killed) and fearing a religious backlash for this action decided to murder all the Huguenots who had gathered for the wedding. Thousands of them were slaughtered on what has become known as the Massacre of

St. Bartholomew's Day. When he heard of the event at Rome Pope Gregory XIII sang a song of thanksgiving in the Sistine Chapel.

The martyrs of St. Bartholomew's Day and other martyrs went to their deaths singing songs and becoming symbols of resistance to the living. Pro-Protestant and antiroyalist tracts began to appear and tensions were growing. At this point a new factor entered the political picture. The last Valois king died without children. Actually he was assassinated in retaliation for having the Guise family leaders assassinated. On his deathbed he pronounced Henry IV, Bourbon and Protestant leader to be his successor. Henry IV turned out to be more Frenchman than Protestant. He knew he could never rule a basically Catholic country from Catholic Paris so he promptly converted to Catholicism supposedly commenting that "Paris is well worth a Mass." The Protestants were aghast. However King Henry did not forget them. On April 13, 1598 he issued the famous Edict of Nantes, a milestone in religious toleration (for the time) and granted religious liberty to the Huguenots. In that one decree a thousand years of one faith were undone and now more than one faith was officially tolerated.

This Edict permitted religious freedom to the Huguenots only in certain towns and fortified cities. To this extent they were separated from the mainstream of France and somewhat independent. Such an arrangement was all right for a while but later the monarch was becoming so absolute in France that he could not tolerate such independence. Cardinal Richelieu, the real ruler of France, saw that the Huguenots were really a state within a state and was determined therefore to deprive them of their fortified cities. He attacked their strongholds and reduced their castles (most of the castle remnants seen in France today testify to the Cardinal's work). However the Cardinal confirmed their religious freedom and the Huguenots thus submitted and became quite loyal to the crown.

We might carry the story ahead a little and observe that the Edict of Nantes would be revoked under Louis XIV. The Church in France had regained real strength and was becoming independent of Rome. In 1682 the great preacher Bousset drew up the famous Gallican Articles proclaiming the King superior to the pope and the French Church possessor of its own inviolable liberties. Louis, of course, reveled in this and felt that with the Church in his pocket the whole land should once more have one unifying religion. In 1685 he revoked the Edict of Nantes with terrible vengeance on the French Huguenots with the result that some two hundred thousand exiles fled to Switzerland, Berlin, Holland and North America.

SCOTLAND

Scotland too went to the new faith by way of politics. In that country it came to be the pro-France Catholics of the government versus pro-England antigovernment Protestants. Entering this political climate was the arrogant and rude John Knox who was totally convinced that God had called him to proclaim the Protestant message in Scotland. He became chaplain to a group of nobles who assassinated the Catholic power, Cardinal Beaton, causing Knox to flee to England and Geneva. Meanwhile the queen, Mary Stuart, Queen of Scots, had married the Catholic king of France in 1558 thereby agitating the Protestant political factions. The violently anti-Catholic Knox returned to Scotland to urge that country to disobey Mary. In retaliation in 1559 Mary issued laws against the new faith but Knox carried Scotland to the brink of civil war by his opposition to her. Finally the English government stepped in (Elizabeth could not afford a Catholic pro-French Scotland) and sent assistance. In 1560 Parliament adopted a confessional statement made up by Knox and passed several laws against Catholic practices. Mary, Queen of Scots, having been accused of murdering her Scottish Catholic second husband was forced to abdicate in 1567. She fled to England where she gave herself to the protection of her cousin Elizabeth. She foolishly plotted to seize the throne and Elizabeth had her executed. This unusual woman and her intrigues, several husbands, her relationship to Queen Elizabeth has always made for high drama and to this day countless movies, plays and television serials have depicted her life and death. In any case, in due time because of Knox's influence a Calvinistic type of Protestantism became the religion of Scotland. There is only one more country to consider, the England that produced Queen Elizabeth, and that is a story by itself.

NOTES

1. Martin Marty, *op. cit.*, p. 206.
2. Hans J. Hillerbrand, *Christendom Divided*, p. 288. Corpus of New York, Westminister of Philadelphia, Hutchinson of London. 1971.
3. Owen Chadwick, *The Reformation*, p. 25. Penguin Books, Baltimore, Maryland. 1964.
4. Historian Norman Cantor gives five reasons why the Reformation did not occur earlier (1) the absence of the printing press (2) the long depression that sapped men's energies from active reform (3) the weakness of the papacy (4) a fear of the social reactions that might result from widespread heresy (5) royal governments previously were too distracted with other matters. cf. his *Medieval History, The Life and Death of Civilization*, The Macmillan Co., New York. 1968.

5. Martin Marty, *op. cit.*, p. 208.
6. Owen Chadwick, *op. cit.*, p. 57.
7. Hans Hillerbrand, *op. cit.*, p. 42.
8. *Ibid.*, p. 127.
9. Owen Chadwick, *op. cit.*, p. 76.
10. Martin Marty, *op. cit.*, p. 246.
11. Hans Hillerbrand, *op. cit.*, p. 265.

XV

Dissent: Radical and Established

REFORMING THE REFORMERS

Before we take a look at the color and drama of England's road to Anglicanism we must take some time to look at a movement we mentioned in chapter IV of this book, the Radical churches. In every reform movement there are always those who want to reform the reformers. Such were the Radical Protestant sects that arose at the time we are considering and which proved to be such an irritant to Luther. The Radicals—sometimes called "Believers"—were often rooted in the medieval mysticism and particularly enamoured of what they considered the simple "Golden Age" of the apostolic era:

> Ernestness, witness, covenant (signing their names), discipline, mutual aid, simple pattern of worship—these are the hallmarks of the believing people. The tragedy of Protestantism is that when such groups did emerge in history, Luther and his colleagues could see nothing in them but enthusiasts, fanatics, and rebels. This prejudice has not been completely overcome to this day.[1]

The Radicals had the habit of going one step further with Luther's principles: if man is saved by faith alone, they asked, why baptize infants who cannot give faith? If Scripture was the sole guide and the Spirit was needed to interpret it, did this mean in the last analysis that the inner Spirit is more important than the written word? Freedom from all externals made them impatient with all forms of organized religion. Thus they threatened religious principles and, because of some extremes and stupid actions, civil stability as well. For this both the government and established religions (Catholic and Protestant) persecuted them.

The major radical group was known as the Anabaptists (or rebaptizers). They did not believe in infant baptism and were dedicated to restore the Church to scriptural purity. They did not have one body of teaching but branched off in many directions. Some of their extensions were quite susceptible to lunatic leadership. Men like Thomas Munzer had led the disastrous Peasants' Revolt in Germany (the one Luther was involved in). A man called John Batenburg believed that the unconverted must be killed, that polygamy was right (it was in the Old Testament) and that he himself was Elijah the prophet. A group of Anabaptists got political control of the town of Munster, decided to turn it into the New Jerusalem and therefore proclaimed polygamy, the extermination of the ungodly and (a favorite theme) the imminent Second Coming of the Lord. They led raids on nearby towns, ran naked through the streets. In 1535 they were finally invaded and slaughtered. The whole episode had the net effect of setting back any religious toleration besides giving the radical sects a bad name. At the Diet of Speyer in 1529 both Lutherans and Catholics agreed to kill the Anabaptists. The Anabaptists had to flee and in so doing broke up into several groups. One group, known as the Hutterites settled in Moravia to live a communistic life. Their work, industry and honesty won them a good reputation and wealth. There came the time when they had to flee Moravia for the wilds of South Dakota in 1874. Another group called the Mennonites withdrew into very simple living patterns and their exclusivity went so far as to make them divorce an unbelieving spouse and excommunicate the unworthy. They split into factions and their descendants are to be found in the Pennsylvania Amish who to this day do not wear buttons since they are ornamental.[2] A third group gave rise to the Unitarians who revived the old Arian heresy in denying the Trinity. We might recall that Michael Servetus was one of them. So also was a man named Sozzini who gave Unitarianism its real form and body of doctrine. There were other groups too numerous to mention, many of them unbalanced and always proclaiming the Second Coming. England for example was so rife with them that generations of Englishmen would always harbor suspicion for religious enthusiasm of any kind.

We might mention that one of the English groups survived to become the Society of Friends, or the Quakers. Its founder, George Fox (1691) at nineteen was one who sought God in the fields and within himself. Around 1648 he became an evangelist preaching common radical messages such as the repudiation of oaths, military service, a suspicion of external forms and the inspiration of the Spirit Who could speak to the humblest peasant. The silent prayer meetings of the Mennonites and the writings of the medieval mystics influenced Fox into feeling that no external guide, no ministry, no authority was needed for there was always the "inner light" to teach men. This "inner spirit" led him and his followers into eccentricities. Fox, for example, would not take off his hat (at the direction of the inner spirit); he used the pronouns thee and thou to all men, he never said "Good evening" nor would he use the names for the days and months of the year, only numbers. He interrupted services and one of his converts allowed himself to be worshiped as the Son of God. What eventually saved Quakerism from such fanaticism and extinction was Fox's own maturity in being able to distinguish the practical from the absurd and his luck in running into a Mr. and Mrs. Fells who gave him refuge and common sense. Fox married the widowed Mrs. Fells and proceeded to organize the Quakers. By 1670 the Quakers found stability while holding on to their quietism and teaching of the indwelling light.

The Radicals or Believers' Churches have continued to this day and the average Catholic has little knowledge or appreciation of them. The Catholic convert, Msgr. Ronald Knox, in his book *Enthusiasm* describes their origin:

> You have a clique, an *elite*, of Christian men and . . . women, who are trying to live a less worldly life than their neighbors; to be more attentive to the guidance . . . of the Holy Spirit. More and more, by a kind of fatality, you see them draw apart from their co-religionists, a hive ready to swarm. There is provocation on both sides; on the one part, cheap jokes at the expense of over-godliness, acts of stupid repression by unsympathic authorities; on the other, contempt of the half-Christian, ominous references to old wine and new bottles, to the kernel and the husk. Then while you hold your breath and turn your eyes in fear, the break comes; condemnation or secession, what difference does it make? A fresh name has been added to the list of Christianities.[3]

Such a list in the United States includes the Hutterites, Baptists, Quakers, Church of the Brethren, Methodists, Disciples of Christ, the Plymouth Brethren, Mennonites and others. Some of these sects would startle Catholics by arguing, as we pointed out in chapter IV, that they are descendants of a long line of "heretics" who have always kept the torch of Christianity alive while the corruptions of the organized church grew. Yet, they too, like their more "established" Protestant counterparts have fallen into divisions. Denominational handbooks list in the United States alone twenty-seven Baptist, four Brethren, three Disciple, eight Plymouth Brethren, nine Quaker, fifteen Mennonite and twenty-two Methodist bodies. All these are sharply divided among themselves along ethnic and doctrinal lines.

Still, as Msgr. Knox points out, if these sects have erred they have done so on the side of enthusiasm and that might be preferable to erring on the side of indifference. We might also note a parallel in the turmoil of the 70s in the Catholic Church. Groups such as the Jesus People and the Pentecostals are precisely such enthusiasts looking for a more basic and fundamental Christianity. Whether they will find it, whether they will survive and whether they will break away is another matter; but they have a kinship with radical Christian enthusiasts of the ages.

ENGLAND

England is the most simon-pure example of the religious issue being determined by the ruler. There was, of course, the chronic anti-Roman antipathy towards papal taxations, foreign appointments, etc. England was the home of Wycliffe and his Lollard followers; an English Bible by Tyndale was there and so were the ideas of Erasmus but these elements were not determining. Henry VIII, like other rulers, took advantage of the Church's influence. Henry could use highly placed churchmen like Cardinal Wolsey to control Church property and keep the clergy in line. He was not ready therefore to cast off the Church. As a matter of fact when Lutheranism reached his realm he wrote a treatise against it earning from the pope the title "Defender of the Faith."

Yet the break with Rome came from Henry himself. In

1527 he sought a divorce from his wife of seventeen years and for the next five years his divorce was to occupy his mind. His wife, the aunt of the emperor, Charles V, had borne him only one daughter. His Tudor family had fought too hard for the throne to lose it by default of a male heir. Thus Henry sought a divorce on the grounds that for a few months his wife had been the wife of his deceased brother and the papal dispensation for him to marry her was invalid. He should therefore be free to marry Anne Boleyn. The whole consensus of legal and ecclesiastical opinion was against Henry and the pope himself hesitated to reverse one of his predecessors acts, not to mention the hesitancy in incurring the wrath of the emperor, Henry's nephew-in-law.

By 1529 Henry gave up trying to persuade the pope and turned to pressure tactics. He resurrected old laws to harass the clergy and force them into recognizing him as the national head of the Church. In 1532 he made Parliament pass a law forbidding the annual payments to Rome. Abetted by Thomas Cromwell (whom he later beheaded) in 1533 Henry restricted appeals to Rome. In 1534 all the pope's rights were transferred to the king and the Act of Supremacy was passed by which the king was declared supreme head of the Church in England in everything. As such there was a quick divorce trial presided over by Archbishop Cranmer (warmly recommended by Anne Boleyn) and a week later Henry married Anne.

To support his break with Rome Henry needed theological underpinnings. Protestant tracts began to appear in England but Henry insisted that the propaganda be only antipapal not anti-Catholic and he killed those who offended the faith. It came to be a strange choice in England: death to the Protestants who dissented from Catholic dogma and death to the Catholics who dissented from the Act of Supremacy.

John Fischer and Thomas More were unjustly beheaded because they would not submit to the Act of Supremacy. The following year, 1536, Henry, always in need of money, dissolved the English monasteries and by 1540 the centuries-old monasteries ceased to exist. Trumped up charges were made against the moral lives of the monks yet "whenever the time came to confiscate the glebes of a monastic house, its monks were charged with gross immorality and then were pensioned as if they had been altogether respectable."[4] True the English monasteries had lost much of their vitality but their suppression caused major social problems in the discontinuances of many hospitals, orphanages and almshouses; in the plight of former monks, nuns and teachers. In England as elsewhere the suppression of such monasteries was a long-range mistake, for the Protestant rulers of Europe, "in their need for money, missed a unique opportunity of converting these charitable resources to truly charitable ends like education, hospitals or the relief of the poor. It would not be so severe a charge if it could be shown that the endowments were diverted to truly national ends. Some of the endowments were so diverted. In other cases, the effect of the dissolutions was to put money and land into the hands of the lay lords."[5] From the scholarly point of view many fine libraries and works of art got scattered all throughout England and many were forever lost.

ENGLAND UNDER EDWARD AND MARY

In 1547 the king of the Six Wives died leaving behind him a hybrid Church: a Church without the pope, Catholicism without Rome, but no Protestantism for in 1539 Henry had issued the Act of Six Articles decreeing punishment for anyone denying Catholic doctrines concerning the Mass, celibacy, etc. Under his sickly nine year old son Edward religious matters changed. By 1548 the vernacular was ordered to be used in the Communion service and in 1549 the famous *Book of Common Prayer* (compiled mostly by Cranmer) was issued, a book of lovely prose, ambiguous theology and half-Catholic ritual soon to offend the radicals, Puritans and other rigorist dissenters. After six years of Edward's rule Protestantism was in England, yet not very deeply: the masses of the people were unconcerned by it all.

Mary Tudor, the daughter of Henry's first wife and the wife of Catholic Philip of Spain came to the throne in 1553 at the age of thirty-seven. She who had been rejected by her father, shunted aside all these years, was determined to restore Catholicism. She was in many ways noble, idealistic and pious. Her failure was that she did not know the temper of her people, she was hasty and impatient. Had she lived long enough and been more prudent she could have restored Catholicism on the proved basis that a nation went along religiously with its ruler. For the few years she did reign she brought England into conformity with Rome.

> One marvels that the English, if they loved Rome should have permitted the Protestant Reformation, and if they loved the Protestant Reformation should have been willing to return to Rome. Evidently they did not greatly care what happened to monks, whether priests were married or celibate, and whether the Mass was in Latin or in English. Rather than incur civil disorder, they were ready to return to the old ways.[6]

Mary through Parliament did restore Catholicism to England. Henry's Act of Supremacy was repealed and heresy persecutions begun. In this Mary

> . . . Showed herself thereby a true child of the age, for religious diversity was, for sixteenth century man, a pill too

bitter to swallow. Diversity seemed to entail the disruption of order which was feared as much as the possibility that the dissenter might infect others with his heretical venom. Since criminal law was severe, and capital punishment an all-too common matter, the Marian persecutions were in a way neither particularly unique nor ruthless. The number of victims was less than three hundred, but was substantial in a country that for more than two decades had experienced gradual alienation from Catholicism.[7]

Mary's big mistake was not just the burning of the rabble rousers or unpopular figures but of men of repute and integrity like Archbishop Cranmer. In short, Mary created Protestant martyrs and forged the association in the minds of the English between ecclesiastical tyranny and Rome. Englishmen began to associate loyalty to country with resistance to a half-foreign government. Books like John Foxe's *Book of Martyrs* told tales of the chilling tortures and brave resistance of Mary's victims and was second only to the Bible in popularity. Unfortunately there were no gifted Catholic leaders left on the scene and so, after reigning only five years, Mary died leaving the throne to her half-sister, Elizabeth.

ELIZABETH

What Elizabeth's religious convictions were no one will ever know. She preferred a celibate clergy and the Real Presence in the eucharist. The Protestants, she claimed, drove her further than she wanted to go. But realistically there was no doubt that this daughter of Anne Boleyn, considered illegitimate on that account by the Roman Church, must be Protestant. In 1559 she was not the head but the "governor" of the English Church. *The Book of Common Prayer* was restored with some changes especially those making the Lord's Supper something between the teaching of Luther and Zwingli. The Catholics understandably were not pleased and their lot was made most difficult when Pope Pius V excommunicated Elizabeth in 1570 and released her subjects from obedience to her—one of the greatest blunders in the whole Catholic reaction. This act in effect made traitors of Catholics. Added to this was the fact that Jesuits were infiltrating into England and the Catholic, Mary, Queen of Scots, was plotting to seize the throne. All this forced Elizabeth to persecute the Catholics thereby arousing the hostility of France (which she placated) and Spain (whose famous Armada she defeated).

The Jesuits were not the only ones sneaking back into England. English Catholics trained on the Continent and armed with pamphlets and the English Catholic Douay version of the Bible returned to re-Catholicize their native land. Many priests, almost two hundred of them, were apprehended and killed including such famous names as the Jesuit Edmund Campion. The Guy Fawkes Plot of 1605 to blow up Parliament, unknown to the Catholics of England, became associated with Catholic activity. Soon the Queen's ministers were seeing treacherous Catholics all over the place. A papal brief did arrive assuring Englishmen that they could obey the Queen. Certain Catholics did become more radical politically but they were few and there was never any serious danger to the crown from Catholics. "That this Catholic political threat was ever serious may be doubted,"[8] but it was never absent from the minds of those who thought it so.

More furious than the Catholics over Elizabeth's religious settlement were the radical Puritans. In their eyes the Church in England had too much popery in it: vestments, having bishops, etc., upset them. In reaction the Anglicans, as we might call them now (though the term did not come in until 1836) began to argue that bishops were indeed authentic expressions and by 1590 it began to matter very much to the Anglicans that their bishops be in the line and succession of bishops of the Middle Ages. Scholarship of the time was in fact revealing that the office of bishop was around in the early Church (much to the chagrin of the radicals). There was even a distinct move on the part of the Anglicans to appropriate the best of Catholic devotions and traditions. Meanwhile Elizabeth in 1593 passed a law forcing dissenters to leave the country.

THE STUARTS AND CROMWELL

Elizabeth, the unmarried Queen, was the last of the Tudor line. Now came the Stuarts whose flirtations with Catholicism would be their undoing. Under the Stuarts also the cry arose to curb the powers of the king. The first Stuart king, James I, gave in to Puritan demands by authorizing the King James version of the Bible. On the other hand he offended those same Puritans by asking for money, by favoring Anglican practices in Calvinistic Scotland, permitting games on Sunday and negotiating to marry his son to a Spanish Catholic princess. The chronic fear of a Catholic restoration was raised. James was succeeded by his son, Charles I in 1625. He, in the minds of the people, was even more associated with the Catholics. He married a Catholic. Then there was his Archbishop of Canterbury, William Laud. Laud insisted on uniformity of the Anglican liturgy, vestments, the surplice (which became something of a symbol) and so forth. And he backed up his wishes with punishment. He used the Star Chamber, a kind of Anglican Inquisition, to induce uniformity. He only succeeded in aggravating the radicals: the Congregationalists, the Baptists, the Quakers, the Unitarians, the Puritans and a hundred other radical sects so numerous at this period.

Since Scotland and England were now joined in the United Kingdom Laud's efforts extended to that country as well. Riots broke out in Scotland and war was imminent. King Charles made a temporary treaty while he obtained money for an all out offensive. Parliament however was not ready to allocate him money unless he redressed certain religious grievances. Charles disbanded Parliament. He was defeated by the Scots and forced once more to recall a now Puritan Parliament. This Parliament had Archbishop Laud unjustly executed. The king had the nerve to try to arrest some of the Parliament leaders so civil war broke out between Parliament and king.

The leader of Parliament's forces was Oliver Cromwell, strict Puritan and firm believer in Holy War. He handed the king's forces several stunning defeats and ultimately Charles fell into his power. Cromwell could get no firm commitment from the devious king and the king could not fathom Cromwell's basic honesty. Finally Cromwell purged Parliament of all Presbyterians, pronounced Charles guilty of treason and had him beheaded in 1649. (Charles who believed in the episcopal tradition helped the Anglican ultimately to win out over the Puritan ways. His death made him a hero and martyr persecuted by fanatics.) Cromwell next turned to Catholic Ireland which had conspired with English and Scottish loyalists to restore the Stuarts to the throne. He treated Ireland brutally with much slaughter and deportation of priests. Then he proceeded to push the Catholics into the least productive areas of Ireland and parceled out the rest of the confiscated land to English Protestants. In time this group created "the Ascendancy," that is, a Protestant aristocracy that was to govern the island, deny the civil rights of the majority Catholics and ultimately in the early 1970s to produce the Catholic-Protestant bloody confrontations.

In any case, having defeated the Scottish Presbyterians Cromwell became England's virtual dictator. Under him Catholics, Anglicans and Unitarians were not allowed to worship publicly but were tolerated. Quakers were imprisoned for not paying fines but were allowed toleration. Blasphemy was punished by tortures but not death and *The Book of Common Prayer* was suppressed. Actually these enactments were rather tolerant for those times. To pay for his wars Cromwell had to resort to selling Church land and levying taxes. He imposed a military rule and imposed government censorship under John Milton poet and advocate of free speech. Cromwell died in 1658 and King Charles II was summoned to rule. With him returned a conservative Anglican Church though he was always suspected of Catholic leanings. In 1685 King James II succeeded Charles. James was a Catholic. He gave tolerance to others but he did favor Catholics and his son was born a Catholic. This alarmed his countrymen and so William of Orange in a bloodless "Glorious Revolution" came and took over.[9] William was a Calvinist and under him laws were passed in 1689 whereby Presbyterians and others had to subscribe to certain religious articles and only Protestants by law could ever sit on the English throne. Catholics and Unitarians were forbidden. Puritans fled. Some went to Holland and some of the Puritan "saints" and many "strangers" boarded the *Mayflower* for the New World.

THE THIRTY YEARS' WAR

We have seen that while individuals did not have religious liberty territories did. Mostly the northern European countries had adopted the new faith while the southern countries stayed Catholic. By 1618 in a complicated set of circumstances the Thirty Years' War of religion broke out; as always such wars were intimately bound up with politics and economics. It began in Bohemia, a part of the German empire, which had given toleration to Lutherans but not to Calvinists who thus fought the arrangement. The Bohemians thus disregarded the Peace of Augsburg, brought in another king to replace the Catholic emperor, Ferdinand II, and war broke out. The Bohemians were crushed. The Danes intervened and were repulsed. The Swedes came into the war under Gustavus Adolphus. He felt he must protect all Protestants against the Catholics and thus as a Lutheran he assisted his religious enemies the German Calvinists. On the other hand, if the emperor's war were successful he would make Germany once more united under one faith and neither the pope nor France could tolerate that. For the pope it was the perennial fear, ever since the German Ottos, of German interference. For France it was politic to keep Germany religiously divided. Thus Catholic France, under Cardinal Richelieu, with the pope's approval, supported the Lutheran Swedes to prevent a united Catholic Germany, demonstrating once more the subordination of religion to politics. The whole war was ended by the significant Treaty of Westphalia in 1648. This treaty established the religious lines of modern Europe. Both Catholics and Protestants received a measure of toleration in each other's territories and Calvinists were given an equal footing in the Empire with Catholics and Lutherans. The pope, relieved on the one hand at the failure of a united (and now wrecked) Germany, was provoked on the other at the anti-Catholic clauses in the treaty and the concessions to the Protestants. His feeble protests gave ample evidence that from this point on the papacy was no longer even considered in the political settlements of Europe anymore and no one paid any attention to him—especially the growing absolutist monarchies of Spain and France, the former now broken and poor and the latter emerging from the war as the most powerful nation of the time.

The era of the Thirty Years' War and of the peace of Westphalia is highly important in the history of modern Europe. The Thirty Years' War itself was the worst but the last of the so-called religious wars. While it began as a fight between Protestants and Catholics, its chief stakes were ever economic and political, and it closed a major conflict between Hapsburg and Bourbon dynasties, both nominally Catholic but chiefly concerned with statecraft. That a Protestant prince of Brandenburg should give assistance to the Catholic emperor and that a cardinal of the Roman Church should incite Catholic France to aid German Protestants were clear signs of a noteworthy transfer of interest, in the first half of the seventeenth century, from religious fanaticism to secular ambition. The Thirty Years' War paved a rocky road toward the eventual dawn of religious liberty.

The Thirty Years' War likewise prepared the way for the emergence of the modern state-system of Europe, with its formulated principles of international law and its definite usages of international diplomacy. Modern diplomatic usages had originated among the Italian city states early in the fifteenth century and had been adopted early in the sixteenth century by the monarchs. . . . Yet the modern state-system could not emerge as long as one European state—the Holy Roman Empire or the dynastic empire of the Hapsburgs—claimed to be, and actually was, superior in power and prestige to all other states. What the Thirty Years' War did in this respect was to reduce both the Holy Roman Empire and the Hapsburg empires to a position certainly no higher than that of the national monarchies of France, Sweden, England, Spain, or that of the Dutch Republic. Indeed, from the negotiations and treaties of Westphalia truly emerged the modern state-system of Europe, based on the novel principle of the essential equality of independent sovereign states, though admitting of the fact that there were great powers as well as lesser powers. . . .[10]

OBSERVATIONS

From 1517 to 1648, some one hundred thirty years, the religious face of Europe (and America) was changed. Religious pluralism was now in and with it the hostility and polemics which would last for the next three hundred years. Then some Christians—not all, for some do not believe in a visible church at all and others see in sectarianism a sign of vitality—began to feel the disgrace of disunity of those who, after all the anger and violence was said and done, had much in common. A new phase would enter, an attempt at mutual understanding between Catholic and Protestant and the open admission of blame. The decree on Ecumenism of Vatican II would state bluntly:

> From her very beginnings there arose in this one and holy Church of God certain rifts . . . but in subsequent centuries more widespread disagreements appeared and quite large communities became separated from the full communion of the Catholic Church—developments for which, at times, men of both sides were to blame. . . . Catholics must joyfully acknowledge and esteem the truly Christian endowments from our common heritage which are to be found among our separated brethren. . . . Nor should we forget that whatever is wrought by the grace of the Holy Spirit in the hearts of our separated brethren can contribute to our own edification (chapter 1, articles 3 & 4).

There were many things that Protestantism has brought to the edification of the world. It gave impetus to religious instruction and the centrality of the Bible. Many a sincere Protestant would work his day around the Bible, reading it frequently, knowing large sections by heart. It was Protestantism which took sanctity out of the exclusive hands of the religious, the monk and the friar and said that it was common commodity for the common man. It was Protestantism which gave a dimension of unity and spirituality to family life. Luther himself had no intention of marrying but when a whole nunnery closed down and all nuns were placed in homes except one, he married her, not out of romance "but out of a sense of duty"[11] and with her he became the forerunner of the Protestant parsonage. Protestantism gave its laity participation and to Christianity in general a suspicion of too much reliance on external forms.

In many ways the whole Protestant Reformation came down to the question of freedom of conscience versus authority and it is the rare Catholic who can appreciate the sincere Protestant's stance on this.[12] As the average Protestant has (or has had) a caricature of the average Catholic bowing in blind submission to an avaricious pope who told him what to think and how to vote, so the average Catholic has (or has had) the image of the average Protestant as totally amorphous, a self-appointed pope, anti-Catholic and possessing a morality as fluid as the times. In the same way, neither one has ever really appreciated that, at the beginning at least, the desire of the Reformation was to reform, not break away from the Church. The really full theological differences did not come until relatively late and even at that the theological differences need not have brought separation. After all, as we have noted, one of the crucial points of Luther, that on justification, was not initially a Catholic dogma but still allowed for free discussion. It was the heat of controversy which called for the emotional words urging the more daring, the heretical.

Rather than theological the Reformation was a religious matter, a concern to renew and even redirect the Church. It was basically a matter of spirituality, a getting back to the Church which many corruptions, superstitions and externals had obscured. There was a desire for new forms of piety. There was genuine hope that what the Protestants initially said could be taken into the Church just as the Church tolerated many dissenters (such as Erasmus) and forms (such as the religious orders). That is why most of the people who thronged to Luther and supported his cause did not consider themselves in opposition to the Church. They might be against the clergy and against Church privileges but not really against the Church. That stance and the mood of separation came much later, but at the moment the Reformation was a prodding for change. And here, in the words of Lutheran historian, Hans Hillerbrand, the Church was to blame:

> If anywhere, the fault of the Catholic Church in the schism we call the Reformation lies here—not in its neglect of reform or in its toleration of abuse, but in its failure to afford the notions of Luther a full hearing . . . Such was the setting that caused the reformers to be dismayed and then turn adamant. The case can be made that they emphasized their insight only after they had become persuaded that they had not been heard. . . .[13]

Then it was that they rejected infallibility and papal authority for the reformers felt that they would rather be heretics than be untrue to their notion of the gospel. So, once more, the real issue at stake came to be that of authority: the Church or the individual, the pope or conscience. Luther, in fact, continued to insist in all his later writings that he was not contesting the authority of the pope as such, but rather the abuse of that authority.

> . . . The Reformation was above all a fundamental crisis of confidence in the authority of the Church's teaching office.

It was for this reason that a different emphasis was placed, in Protestant teaching, on the meaning and function of the apostolic office. What was stressed above all was that the gospel, as bearing witness to the saving event of Christ, always transcended the institutions of the Church and that all ecclesiastical institutions were there to serve the gospel.[14]

PLUSES AND MINUSES

It is interesting to note, of course, how many of the items considered so important by the reformers have been adopted by the Church of Vatican II. The Church now permits the sharing of the chalice. Parish councils and the pope's synod of bishops reflect congregational overseeing. The use of the vernacular which always distinguished Protestants from Catholics is now part of Catholic worship. Scriptural studies and scripture reading among Catholics and Protestants are no longer distinguishable and joint Bibles have been published. Clerical celibacy is once more a debating point within the Church. The simplification of rites reflect the initial drive of the reformers for simplicity in worship. In many ways, then, the demands of the Reformation have found their way, four hundred years later, into the Catholic Church.

On the other hand Protestantism has had its share of troubles and has bequeathed certain problems to its followers. Many of the things the reformers rejected in the first flush of reaction their spiritual descendants are reappraising today. For example, in reaction to the magical approach that Catholics often seemed to place in the sacraments, the reformers stressed that the sacraments had no objective reality apart from faith. Yet, illogically, they continued for four hundred years (except for the Baptists) to baptize infants who could not make an act of faith. This is why some Protestant theologians are beginning to admit some objective reality to the sacraments as the Catholics have understood them.

Another thing: Luther taught the priesthood of all believers and freedom of each individual conscience: "Therefore I declare that neither Pope nor bishop nor any other person has the right to impose a syllable of law upon a Christian man without his own consent." Yet he was too much a child of his times. He could not be democratic in his churches. He would not give the lay congregation any authority and when confronted with a plan for a congregational type of church rule he rejected it. Nor would he ever accept the congregation choosing its own pastor.

Perhaps the reformers' biggest disappointment was in reference to their famous "Scripture Alone" as the basis for Christian knowledge and belief. For Luther and for the other reformers it was a case that

> They miscalculated in their assumed ease of united affirmation on the basis of New Testament authority. Protestantism was never to overcome its difficulties in this respect; it appealed to the Scriptures, but men of different birth and land and tradition and experience read them differently. . . . If every man was to be his own judge, if every man was to be of the universal priesthood, standing before the Scriptures as his own pope—what would prevent the growth of as many churches as there are men or factions or parties? The experience of Europe in the half-century following 1517 certainly seemed to thunder corroboration.[15]

Or again, as Lutheran Hans Hillerbrand puts it:

> The hopeless and apparently insoluable division [of Protestantism] called into question the basic Protestant affirmation that Scripture was clear and self-evident, and that men of goodwill could readily agree on its meaning. Luther, who had first voiced such sentiment, was to learn its weakness in

his controversy with Zwingli over the interpretation of Communion. His increasingly rigid view of Scriptural interpretation may well have been influenced by his dismay over the inability of men, even men of goodwill, to agree on the interpretation of Sacred Writ.[16]

Finally Luther's alliance with the German princes did not render the best service to Lutheranism. The princes of course were ready to listen to Luther in his attacks on Rome. Religion could be brought under national control and Church wealth appropriated. With such princes leading, with the emperor preoccupied elsewhere and with the absence of any vital Catholic leadership the Reformation easily moved ahead in Germany. It persisted for it had no particular hardships to endure. In fact so political did the religious issue become that the Catholic emperor could get Lutheran princes to war on their co-religionists much as later on Cardinal Richelieu would have Catholic France side with Protestant Sweden against Catholic Spain.

As the old order fell before Lutheranism there arose the question of who should fill the authority vacuum and the princes were the most likely candidates. Many of them in fact acted as did the Catholic bishops of old. Frederick appointed parish visitors. This system of state visitation tended to become institutionalized and thus the appointment and removal of ministers became dependent on the state. Even the ministers' salaries were paid out of the income of secularized Catholic property. "Under such circumstances Luther's dictum that the minister should be the mentor of the magistrate sometimes was difficult to realize."[17] In fact "by the time of Luther's death the secular leaders were well poised to assume spiritual functions and make the church in many respects a lackey in their temporal pursuits."[18] Right up to modern times the closeness of Lutheranism with the state had unhappy results:

> The oldest, largest, and in a geographical sense most catholic Protestant body, Lutheranism, has suffered most in times of catastrophe and suppression. Sorely tried in its German stronghold by the First World War and post-war disillusion, it was handicapped by a long tradition of accepted paternalism on the part of the state. Never working out a detailed approach to church-state religions, it held largely to a doctrine of acquiescence, always uncertain when the moment would come when one must forget penultimate for the superior: "We ought to obey God rather than men." Much of Lutheranism in Germany was therefore quiescent in the rise of Hitler. The extreme element rallied around the Nazi puppet, Reichsbischof Mueller. Some theologians tragically sold themselves to the German Christian Movement.[19]

THE ECUMENICAL SPIRIT

Whatever the ultimate problems for Catholicism and Protestantism alike the fact is that Western Christendom was permanently divided and its position in society unalterably changed. The great political significance was that no longer would the Church, any church, have control over the state as it did in the Middle Ages. In fact, it was more the other way around and religion for some powerful monarchies (for example, England) became a department of state. As we shall see in the next chapter, men were still of the medieval mindset whereby they thought that political and religious uniformity were intertwined. The Catholics in their Counter-Reformation cleaned house and drew up lines against the Protestants. The Protestants drew up lines against the Catholics.[20]

Today as we know, however, is the age of ecumenism, the age of undrawing those lines. Likewise no knowledgeable Catholic or Protestant thinks any longer that ecumenism means to convert the other to his side. Today ecumenism means rather that both are seeking unity in Christ whatever that might mean, wherever that might lead. Both have a common Christian tradition and now that much of the in-fighting has calmed down each can look at what the other is really saying with less passion and more charity. A full discussion of some of the fruitful harmonization that has taken place between Catholics and Protestants is beyond the scope and purpose of this book. Yet we might take a few pivotal examples to demonstrate how far the dialogue has gone. For instance: the Roman Catholic explanation of the Real Presence was summed up in the scholastic term of "transubstantiation," a term which to many Protestants smacked too much of philosophy, too much of unbiblical rationalization.[21] When the Catholics explained the intent of this doctrine, namely, that God really does something and that Christ really is present in the Lord's Supper, then Protestants saw that this was *their* intent as well and most of them could give agreement. For instance, when a joint committee of Roman Catholic and Lutheran theologians met in 1966-1967 the Lutheran conclusion was as follows: "It becomes clear to them (the Lutherans) that the dogma of transubstantiation intends to affirm the fact of Christ's presence and of the change which takes place . . . when the dogma is understood in this way, Lutherans find that they also must acknowledge that it is a legitimate way of attempting to express the mystery. . . ." Most Catholics are surprised to find out that most Protestants believe in the Real Presence and that many of them can accept the Eucharist as Catholics mean it. This is why on July 7, 1972 guidelines were issued by the Secretariat for Christian Unity permitting, under certain strict conditions, Protestants to receive Holy Communion in a Catholic Church.

Protestants too have come to recognize that there is no really pure distinction between the Bible and tradition, that "Scripture Alone" does not operate in a vacuum but in the context of *their* tradition. As Lutheran Michael Rogness expresses it:

> The fact of the matter is that although Protestants claim "Scripture Alone" as the source of their doctrine, the historical tradition of each Protestant church has been decisive in determining its doctrinal outlook. For about 400 years Lutherans have accepted the *Book of Concord* documents as their doctrinal statements, that is, writings from their north German situation which they believe accurately define biblical doctrine. The "39 Articles" of the Anglicans and the various catechisms of Reformed churches are all doctrinal statements growing out of particular historical traditions and circumstances. Every Protestant church must acknowledge that it is shaped doctrinally by its tradition, and it ought not to fall into the temptation of imagining that its tradition is the only one striving to be loyal to the Bible.

> The irony is that a Protestant who is immovably loyal to his church's tradition and refuses to budge one iota from his church's inherited doctrine has surrendered the basic Protestant principle of *sola scriptura*. He has fallen victim to precisely that sin of which he accused the Roman Catholics, namely becoming trapped in his own tradition, failing to see that biblical truth might demand a new kind of proclamation than the thought forms of past centuries. To be truly Protestant is to be not only true to one's heritage, but to allow our doctrinal concerns to be molded by the Bible's message for today's world.[22]

Even on the basic issue of justification one of Protestantism's leading theologians, Karl Barth, in commenting on Hans Kung's explanation said, "All I can say is this: If what you have presented in Part Two of this book is actually the teaching of the Roman Catholic Church, then I must certainly admit that my view of justification agrees with the Roman Catholic view."[23] In fact, it has been remarked about the Council of Trent which we shall see in the next chapter, that if its decree of justification (beautifully and economically set forth) had been decreed at the Lateran Council at the beginning of the sixteenth century the Reformation would not have occurred.

Disunity is a luxury in the 1970s where the question is not "What is the most valid form of Christianity?" but rather, in the light of fantastic technological advance, "Is Christianity valid at all?" In the light of a threatened planet, the possibility of nuclear war, genetic control, organ transplants and interplanetary exploration partisan differences in Christianity are obscene. The minds of both sides which accept "Jesus Christ, the same yesterday, today and forever" (Hebrews 13:8) must join forces to make him credible to the modern world.

NOTES

1. Donald F. Durnbaugh, *The Believers' Church:* The History and Character of Radical Protestantism, p. 4. The Macmillan Company, London. 1968.
2. The Amish in the United States in May of 1972 won the right from the Supreme Court to keep their children from the "ungodly" compulsory high school education.
3. R. S. Knox, *Enthusiasm*, p. 591. Oxford at the Claredon Press. 1950.
4. Roland Bainton, *op. cit.,* p. 288.
5. Owen Chadwick, *op. cit.,* p. 109.
6. Roland Bainton, *op. cit.,* p. 290.
7. Hans Hillerbrand, *op. cit.,* p. 202.
8. *Ibid.,* p. 223.

9. William of Orange sought to regain control of England by first establishing control over Ireland. Meanwhile Protestant Ulstermen at Londonderry successfully fought the deposed King James who had arrived in Ireland. The following year William came and defeated James at the Battle of the Boyne rejoicing Ulster's "Orangemen."

10. Carlton J. H. Hayes, *A Political and Cultural History of Europe*, p. 274. Vol. I. The Macmillan Company, New York. 1932.

11. Bainton, *op. cit.*, p. 272.

12. We should not take our impressions of Protestantism from the insincere or ignorant Protestant any more than they should take their impressions of Catholicism from the insincere or ignorant Catholic.

13. Hans Hillerbrand, *op. cit.*, p. 287.

14. Concilium, p. 72, volume 64. 1971.

15. Martin Marty, *op. cit.*, pp. 225 and 228.

16. Hans Hillerbrand, *op. cit.*, p. 290.

17. Roland Bainton, *op. cit.*, p. 270.

18. Martin Marty, *op. cit.*, p. 244.

19. *Ibid.*, p. 350. We have mentioned some of the positive contributions of Protestantism. It would go beyond the scope of this book to mention its negative aspects yet we might focus on one radical facet. There are those who contend that Protestantism has brought us to the cold, mechanical, ruthless world of today. Its passion for godliness, cleanliness and right ordering (observed in the severe, plain and precise Puritan churches of New England) has been the basis for the "manifest destiny" for the Protestant white man to become imperialist; for the dominance in America of the WASP superculture which has suppressed the ethnic soul of the masses; for the conception of the alienated and computerized society. Thus Jewish writer Norman Mailer: "American Protestantism has become orientated to the machine, and lukewarm in its enthusiasm for such notions as heaven, hell and the soul. The Catholic Church can still not divorce itself as much from one of the indispensable notions of Hip, that particular one which is now unhappily codified by saying that we have a body (Catholics would say soul) which is growing at every instant of existence into more or into less. . . ." Protestantism, Mailer contends, "is not so much a religion as a technique in the ordering of communities, able to accelerate the growth of the scientific spirit. . . ." (*Advertisements for Myself*, Signet, N.Y. 1959)

   Indeed there is the celebrated thesis of Max Weber that Protestantism is the basic ethic behind the growth of capitalism and ruthless industrialism. Catholic writer, Michael Novak, adds his critique: "Perhaps no belief about man is more deeply Catholic than that: a fundamental and radical trust in the goodness of creation, however wounded, bloodied, flawed. It is (in Catholic eyes) the Protestant who quintessentially announces the depravity and corruption of nature, culture, and man himself—and then, paradoxically, announces with the utmost cool extravagant plans for organizing the world reasonably, sinlessly, and spotlessly. The Protestant is forever confessing his contriteness, and then exalting his own acceptance of his 'responsibilities' for changing history. . . . To the Protestant, creation is apparently 'redeemed' only through being mastered. Protestant countries tend to be avid for modernization; Catholic countries are 'backward'." (*The Rise of the Unmeltable Ethnics,* Macmillan Co., New York, 1972; p. 290.)

With such criticism from many quarters, no wonder Lutheran Martin Marty says, "The Protestant era may, indeed, be coming or have come to its end."

20. Unfortunately, division would always plague the Protestants because they tended to become rigid and themselves could not tolerate diversity. The only way to have a tolerable alternate interpretation of the Bible was to start a new sect. Catholicism, on the other hand could subsume many diversities within itself. It even had the escape valve of monasticism "which allowed those dissatisfied with the standard of ecclesiastical practices to go their own way and yet remain within the Church. Such possibilities did not exist in any of the Protestant churches, where a break was necessary to assert a different religious or theological position." (from Hans Hillerbrand, *op. cit.,* p. 291.)

21. For a very sensitive and sensible commentary on the whole question of transubstantiation see John Macquarrie's fine book, *Paths in Spirituality,* p. 88ff. Harper and Row, New York, 1972.

22. Michael Rogness, *op. cit.,* p. 58.

23. Hans Kung, *Justification,* p. xx, Thomas Nelson and Sons, New York. 1964.

XVI

Catholic Reform

SOURCES OF REFORM

Prior to and during the Protestant Reformation the Catholic Church was beginning to reform itself. Later on this reform took on some of the characteristics of an offensive (which could hardly be helped) against Protestantism but it still had its own independent wellsprings. Catholics, in the company of (at that time) their fellow Catholics like Luther, Calvin, Zwingli and others, had always complained against Church abuses. There was no local national meeting that did not bring the matter up. Hostility to the Church was indeed a characteristic of the fifteenth and sixteenth centuries. Dante had put cardinals in hell and Erasmus depicted St. Peter driving some popes from the gates of heaven. Art and literature had ridicule for the grasping prelate or immoral pope. We have seen Catholic monarchs trying to bring the Church into their national ambitions. There was, then, much pressure *within* the Church for reform and the Church was able to tap its wellspring of spiritual vigor that lay deep underneath.

There was the revival of Thomism for one thing, a revival that equipped the Church for its intellectual renewal. Cardinal Cajetan who debated Luther early in his career was a noted commentator on St. Thomas. There were many devotional books in the Catholic tradition, the most influential being *The Imitation of Christ* from the Netherlands. There were the writings of the mystics: Peter Canisius (based on Tauler, a fourteenth century mystic), St. Peter Alcantara and the famous duo, St. Teresa of Avila and St. John of the Cross who are only two towering figures among a whole mass movement of Spanish spirituality. There were the writings of the Franciscan Spiritualists, the example of the Carthusians and a still living spirit of St. Francis.

Each country had its outspoken Catholic reformers whose names regretfully are unknown to the average Catholic of today. There was the great Cardinal Ximenes in Spain who fostered a kind of religious purity based on blood and who therefore, in his vision of things, permitted the genocidal practices against the Moors and Jews. In France there was Jean Standonck who in 1499 organized a college to train priests. In England Colet tried to do the same thing and in addition there were Reginold Pole (Cardinal), the Bishop John Fischer and the better known Sir Thomas More. Italy had its Savonarola, the pious Bishop Gian Matteo Giberti who assiduously visited his parishes and reformed their liturgies; there was Cardinal Sadoleto who gave up his tenure at Rome. In Poland there were outstanding prelates such as John Laski and Peter Tomicki.

RELIGIOUS ORDERS

In spite of a general decline several religious orders were being renewed and others were being founded. The Franciscans branched off into an Observant Order for more purity of life. The Carthusian Order influenced many laymen who added their considerable support for Catholic renewal. There was the new Theatine Order which was very influential in attracting holy men and forming future worthwhile bishops. There were the famous Oratories, the best known being that of the gentle St. Philip Neri. There were the Barnabites founded by laymen in 1533 who were known for their open air meetings in the cities of northern Italy. A group known as the Somaschi were noted for their examples of practical charity. The Capuchines did much to hold the masses to the Church.[1] Maria Longo founded the Capuchines to restore the spirit of St. Francis. St. Angela Merici founded the Ursulines in 1535, one of the earliest teaching orders of women. Finally there were the shock troops of the Reformation, the Jesuits.

The Jesuits were founded by Ignatius Loyola, a contemporary of Luther and one who also had an inner struggle but who found his answer within the Church. He found his answer in inner meditation. He wrote his world renowned *Spiritual Exercises* and got his new order approved by Pope Paul III. The Jesuits made their first great impact on Italy and their first colleges appear there: Bologna, Messina, Palermo, Rome. In Ignatius' native Spain they encountered the jealousy of the Dominicans; in France they were not at first very successful and did not penetrate England until the middle of Queen Elizabeth's reign. But they grew in number (there were one thousand members by the time Ignatius died, and 13,000 five years later) and through their excellent schools for the sons of the nobility and kings, they became very influential. They became in fact associated with the Catholic courts often to their peril; in the future their influence would be resented, fearful legends would grow up around them and one day the whole order would be suppressed.

THE DELAY OF A COUNCIL

All of these outstanding people and movements were only one element in not only pressing for reform but in pressing for a general council that might achieve reform effectively and universally. But for many reasons, often beyond the control of the popes, no council was called until it could no longer be denied. For one thing, when the affair of Luther broke, communication with Rome was poor and the popes did not detect either the enormity of what was happening or therefore the need for a council. Secondly, Luther's new ideas were still being assessed and there was not, at first, a consensus that they were radically opposed to Catholic doctrine. Thirdly, the popes, as always, were too engaged in Italian politicking to be bothered with a council. Fourthly there were tremendous outside distractions. Henry VIII was pressing for his divorce. France did not want a council lest it suddenly clear up the Protestant Reformation by bringing a Catholic settlement to Germany and France did not want a united Germany. Fifthly, the popes of the times simply did not reign long enough. Whereas the Emperor Charles V ruled Germany for almost fifty years, the seven popes of his time ruled on an average of seven years. Pope Clement VII had to deal with King Henry's divorce and witness the sack of Rome in 1527 by Charles V's Spanish troops. He did not want a council lest he be deposed for he had been born out of wedlock and his election had been tainted with simony. Finally, there was always the fear of conciliarism: another council might raise the question again of the superiority of a general council over the pope.

It was the pope following Clement VII who was destined to call a council. This was Paul III who made his teenage grandson a cardinal and gave his disreputable son the dukedom of Parma and Piacenza. Yet, he also raised to the cardinalate such men of quality as John Fischer, Contarini, Caraffa, Sadoleto, Pole and Morone. And it was this pope, much to the dismay of the emperor, who called a council at last. The emperor who always wanted a council felt it would be inopportune now and feared that the council would firm up Catholic teaching thus preventing a sorely needed unity in Germany with the Protestants (remember Charles still needed the Protestant princes to fight the Moslems). In 1536 Pope Paul III[2] appointed a commission to study Church reform and they came up with the startling document, *The Council of Cardinals on Reforming the Church.* It became famous as the most direct and blunt condemnation of abuses ever written by a papal commission. So strong was the document that even Luther published it in German with scurrilous margin notes. In fact the document's very frankness of Church abuses prevented its public use and so not many of its striking reforms were put into effect. Yet this document did mark a change in outlook and induced reform.

Finally in May of 1542 the bull was issued summoning the council. Since Germany and France were currently at war both sides forbade its bishops from attending. At last, on December 3, 1545, three years later, the first session was held. Only thirty-one bishops attended[3] and none of them from really Protestant territories: in fact the majority were Italian. All the sessions (there were three main sessions stretching over eighteen years due to enforced recesses) had a majority of Italians. Of the two hundred seventy bishops attending one time or another during those eighteen years one hundred eighty-seven were Italian, thirty-one Spanish, twenty-six French and two German (many actually preferred to stay at home to take care of matters). Of the two hundred twenty-five who signed the final Acts of Trent one hundred eighty-nine were Italian.

There were, however, men of high caliber at the Council of Trent, theologians, religious and bishops. During the first eight meetings of the first session the Council set the tone for doctrinal conservatism. This precisely was what the emperor feared: a retrenchment of Catholicism which would prevent dialogue with his German Protestants. In the second series of meetings some few Protestants appeared but offered little more than the Augsburg Confession plus a few impossible notions as to what the Council was all about to begin with. In this second session the Council defined transubstantiation and reaffirmed the sacraments of Extreme Unction and Penance. In 1552 the Council was broken up by political matters (the Council Fathers feared capture by the French), a recess that lasted ten years. The final and third series of meetings was recalled in 1562. By this time the Spanish contingent was working to make a national hierarchy and talking about the divine rights of bishops (and therefore their independence from the pope). At this session the question of offering the chalice to the laity was defeated, the Mass was reaffirmed to have a sacrificial character and was to be celebrated in Latin. This latter point, namely the use of the vernacular plus the question of celibacy caused some heated debate (not to mention political considerations) but the very divisions of the Fathers failed to provide a consensus which would change these issues. The Council also placed tradition along side of Scripture as a source of revelation. This was done in reaction to the reformers' insistence on "Scripture Alone."

Actually, the Council of Trent did an excellent job. Its decrees were models of clarity and directness and were not as hostile as they sounded to the Protestants of the time.[4]

"The decrees of Trent were framed with care; their language was designed to allow more liberty of opinion than their Protestant critics believed. The care with which they were framed has only been fully evident during the twentieth century."[5] A general well being came from Trent and practical actions such as the catechism, the reform of the missal and breviary and, above all, the establishment of seminaries. Modern Catholics have generally been more impatient with Trent than modern Protestants because they have failed to see the difficult political circumstances surrounding this Council and have failed to appreciate the care that went into it. More seriously, Trent for Catholics has suffered from its interpreters who did not teach the nuances and refinements built into its decrees.

Of course the Council of Trent was not perfect. Its defensive attitude towards Protestantism led to some short-sightedness (later to be corrected by Vatican II). For example the Council, in spite of the current biblical interest, failed to encourage biblical studies. Nor did the Council encourage the laity to read the Scriptures or provide a scripturally oriented catechism. In fact, the old Baltimore catechism many older Catholics of today remember reflects almost entirely Trent's preoccupation with precise doctrinal statements as a counteraction to the Reformers' teachings. In a newer, modern ecumenical era the Baltimore catechism, which did good service in the past, has had to give way. The Council of Trent failed to encourage teachers to go into the natural philosophies and sciences but rather set a conservative tone for many centuries, a certain close-mindedness to science; such again was a reaction to the Reformers who, it was felt, went awry in unguided speculation. Finally, Trent while reflecting much previous tradition did make additions and defined matters that were not up to that time universally held throughout the Christian world. Perhaps it was a

mistake in some cases to close matters which were still speculative and under discussion at the universities. The conservative cast given by Trent provided the basis for the suppression of ideas. The barbs of the next century by someone
like Voltaire and the reopening of old questions at Vatican II
in our own century would be potent reactions to this condition. Yet as A. G. Dickens points out:

> These strictures are easy to make in the context of our own
> society, which so long ago decided to pay the price for free-
> dom of thought; they will give little offense at a time when
> Catholics themselves are increasingly critical of Tridentine
> habits of thought. Yet in its own period-context, Trent cor-
> responded with the demands of many men, who may well
> have been right in believing that a far larger measure of
> doctrinal definition had become a critical necessity for Cath-
> olic survival. And even those who judge Trent to have defined
> too sweepingly, and to have reacted too automatically against
> anything remotely savoring of Protestantism, may still think
> that the sheer weight of its intellectual achievement entitles
> it to a place of honor in Christian history. The canons and
> decrees remain one of the greatest monuments of committee-
> thinking in the whole history of religion. Given their general
> purpose and outlook, their technical perfection and consist-
> ency are worthy of the highest admiration. In form and lan-
> guage they are models of clarity and care; they are serv-
> iceable documents well abreast of the modern idiom of their
> day; whatever their debts to scholastic theology, their lan-
> guage is uncluttered by the scholastic habits which had so
> little relevance to the needs of simple priests and literate
> laymen. To study them can be a fruitful, almost a moving
> experience, and this even for readers who normally inhabit
> very different worlds of thought.[6]

REFORMING POPES

We have seen that it was finally Pope Paul III who called
the Council. He was succeeded by a series of reforming

popes who did as much as anyone to interpret Trent strictly and lend their sometimes fanatical house-cleaning crusade to the Council itself. Paul was succeeded by Julius III who continued his reforms. He was succeeded by Pope Paul IV who at 79 scattered the reforms of Trent like wildfire. He was the one who as Cardinal Caraffa had advocated reform through fighting the Protestants in contrast to Cardinal Contarini who favored conciliation and concession. Contarini met with the Protestants in 1541 and obtained considerable agreement with them despite skepticism from the absent Luther, the annoyance of his pope, Paul III, and the hearty disapproval of Cardinal Caraffa. This meeting came to naught because of French political fears (of a united Germany). Contarini died under suspicion of collaboration with the Protestants and Caraffa's hard line approach became the alternative. This was the Cardinal who got Pope Paul III to establish a Roman Inquisition. Now at last he himself was pope, Paul IV. He had no mercy. He bore down on permissions and dispensations and the nominations of bishops. On one day he rejected fifty-eight nominations—all that were proposed. He was ready to use torture and punishment. In Rome itself he filled criminals with terror, sent wandering monks to the galleys or to prison and in 1559 invented the Index of Forbidden Books, an indiscriminating list mercifully modified later by Trent.

He was succeeded by Pius IV, a man of no outstanding qualities, three illegitimate children and concern for this family. Fortunately one of his nephews, made a cardinal at twenty-two, was St. Charles Borromeo, the bishop of Milan who was destined to become a shining light of reform. This was the pope who summoned the final sessions of Trent in 1562 (no one really wanted to reassemble during the wild reign of the previous pope anyway). Pius IV was succeeded by the grim St. Pius V (d. 1572). He supported the Roman Inquisition, stamped out any vestiges of Protestantism in Italy, cured financial abuses in the Curia, supported the fierce persecutions of the Spanish Duke of Alba in the Netherlands, aided Charles IX of France to stamp out the Huguenots and ordered such heretics killed. His biggest blunder, as we have seen, was to excommunicate Queen Elizabeth in 1570 and urge her subjects to disobey her. His successor was Pope Gregory XIII (d. 1585) who rejoiced that Henry of Navarre, the Protestant king of France, became a Catholic so that he could have an ally against the Spanish. The next pope, Sixtus V (d. 1590) set up the papal Congregations we know today to take care of Church matters. He also revamped the city of Rome in a huge urban renewal. All of these popes of the Counter-Reformation had one thing in common: a determination to clean house, to renew the Church no matter what the cost.

AFTERMATH OF THE COUNCIL

In the long run the Council of Trent was only as effective as the Catholic kings and princes wanted it to be. The rulers hindered Trent's reforms to the extent that they wanted to dominate and nationalize the Church. Diplomacy and concession had to creep back in. Especially with Philip II of Spain the Church had difficulty. He protected the Church on the one hand and was determined to rule it on the other. Philip controlled his clergy, forbade his subjects to appeal to Rome and from his territories in Naples pressured the pope to accede to his wishes. Much of the papal activity of the time consisted in efforts to offset Spanish Hapsburg domination. Yet, outside of the political entanglements the time after Trent did bring several results.

One we might mention is that since the Council of Trent besought the pope to confirm its decrees (which he did in 1564) it implicitly recognized his primacy. Conciliarism, for the time being, had been put to rest. The papal monarchy was reenforced to the extent that the pope was able to do without a council for the next three hundred years. Even then when such a council was called (Vatican I) it wound up declaring the pope's infallibility. Trent thus elevated the papacy to the role of absolutism and isolationism which was to last until Pope John XXIII.

Futhermore, as we have noted with the reforming popes, conservative trends set in, an intolerance, a certain hostility towards uncontrolled learning and a suspicion of science. The case of Galileo and his condemnation in 1633 are a good example of an obscurantist spirit that fell upon Catholics and Protestants alike.

> The pile of books condemned by Protestant censors reached as high towards heaven as those condemned by Catholic censors. The defenders of orthodoxy were slow to realize that where they once cut manuscripts to pieces, the printed book was bound to escape their clumsy scissors. Pope Urban VIII and his advisers who condemned Galileo (it has been said by Giorgio de Santillana) were not so much oppressors as the first bewildered casualties of the scientific age.[7]

Still, for all the censorship, scholars managed to speak out and move ahead. The Roman catacombs began to be discovered in 1578 and in 1584 the pope set up a printing press for Oriental literature. In one of the great contributions to civilization Pope Gregory reformed the calendar in 1582 (naturally the Protestant countries were among the last to accept this: England, not until 1752). Nevertheless a certain control remained and it was only those countries which broke away from their religious restrictions that made cultural progress, namely, the Netherlands and England. Interestingly censorship was least enforced in the Netherlands so that country published books nowhere else permitted. Also, in spite of more respectable scholarship witchcraft and witch hunting began to flourish again in the Protestant countries especially in Germany and England, the latter influencing the witch trials among the Puritans and Congregationalists in the famous Salem witch trials in Massachusetts.

ASCENDANCY OF MORAL CONCERNS

Another result of Trent was that it so fashioned dogma and was so definitive about it that it more or less closed off doctrinal speculation. The focus among Catholic theologians therefore began to shift to moral questions and concerns. Besides, did not Trent in its pronouncements on the sacrament of Penance insist that sins be confessed according to number and kind? Soon whole new schools of moral theology arose complete with many theories and systems on sin and its divisions. The use of confession increased. Manuals assessing the gravity of sin, advising to the confessor, and offering complex moral cases were popular. Texts were written that weighed the moral implication of every human action. Nothing was too big or, unfortunately, too small for the attention of the casuists: how much meat one could eat on a Friday before it was a question of mortal sin; how much of the Mass one could miss before sin set in; if lipstick broke the eucharistic fast or chewing gum; if lipstick rendered invalid the anointing on the lips at the sacrament of Extreme Unction (Sacrament of the Sick); whether pregnancy was an excuse for missing Mass; whether the fasting time from midnight was computed on natural time, man-made time, local time or universal time; whether sexual thoughts were mortal or venial, etc. During the centuries after Trent there were endless discussions (and manuals) on so called moral minutiae, the net effect of which was to produce the sin-conscious, scrupulous mentality that was the lot of many a Catholic prior to Vatican II.

The beautiful medieval formulas for absolution gave way to the legalistic, declarative forms of the present day wordings. Certain sins were taken out of the priest's hands and were reserved for the absolution of the Holy Father or the bishop. The priest moved from the role of community reconciler and representative to that of judge. The confessional became, not the locale of the encounter with Christ in the spirit of the Prodigal Son, but it became the place of tribunal where one's case was heard, tried and pronounced upon. Attention was given to the "five steps" in order to make a good confession: examining one's conscience, being sorry for one's sins, having a firm purpose of amendment, telling one's sins to the priest and being willing to do the penance the priest gave one. Elaborate rules were devised for dealing with forgetting a sin, deliberately keeping one hidden, forgetting one's penance, what to do about it, etc. The legal moralist replaced the prophetic figure.

Needless to say the reaction to all of this was either a morbid preoccupation with sin or a reactive laxism. As we shall see later there were some very disedifying public quarrels among casuists and religious orders and others over what was right and wrong. The Jesuits acquired a reputation for moral laxity and the Jesuit confessors could reputedly find a reason for whatever one wanted to do. Purists such as the Jansenists and others tended towards a stricter code. No one really gained from the frequent public and offensive debates that followed.

THE MASS

In reaction to the reformers, the Church after Trent continued to emphasize those devotions most under attack. This meant the veneration of the saints, particularly devotion to the Blessed Virgin Mary, and the adoration of Christ in the Blessed Sacrament. More and more, in reference to the sacrament of the Eucharist, the trend towards distance and away from participation which we have noted before, continued. No longer was there even any thought that the laity had a part to play. On the contrary, since the reformers had made a big thing of the priesthood of all the faithful, post-Trent Catholicism felt it was necessary to emphasize the distinction between priest and people. Mass was the one public place that this could be taught. The people came to watch the priest "effect" this great drama. Mass was shrouded in mystery and the laity were to stay at a distance preparing their hearts by acts of faith, hope and charity for that great moment of the Mass, the elevation of the Host and chalice. At that moment they were to bow their heads and strike their breasts in profound adoration. Popular prayers such as the rosary were thought to be the best acts of piety during Mass. Missals were not permitted to the people and indeed in 1661 the Roman Latin missal was forbidden to be translated into the vernacular under pain of excommunication. Missals in Europe in the vernacular did not appear until 1897. As far as the United States goes there was no vernacular missal until 1927, the St. Andrew's Daily Missal put out in St. Paul, Minnesota. Others followed such as Father Lasance's missal, the St. Joseph's Daily Missal and the Maryknoll missal. The biggest impetus given to missal use in our country came with World War II when Father Stedman produced those pocket-sized missals that the soldiers took all over the world with them. Only since World War II did the missal in the United States become commonplace and small beginnings made at participation. The decree on the liturgy in Vatican II has been an effort to undo the thrust unconsciously caused by Trent.

POPULAR DEVOTIONS

Meditations on Christ's passion and death continued to play a large role in Catholic piety. The Rosary with its Joyful, Sorrowful and Glorious mysteries was encouraged. Receiving Communion was more frequent after Trent but it was still looked upon as an "extra," something the truly devout would do out of devotion but something not necessarily connected with the Mass. In fact, Communion was often received after Mass or outside of it. The tabernacle grew in importance, especially after having been fixed to the altar. The adoration of Christ in the Blessed Sacrament, visits to the Eucharistic Lord, were considered the high point of devotion. The parish church existed to house the tabernacle. Forty Hours was a high point of the eucharistic devotion and Benediction was far and away more important than the Mass.

THE BAROQUE PERIOD

The slow but steady recovery of the Church began to manifest itself not only in such devotions but also in its architecture and music. A note of triumphalism appeared and the baroque made its appearance. It became a sign of the Catholic counter reformation. At first the baroque style was cautious and restrained but later broke out into some glorious

and some wild fantasies. It was the Church Militant in stone
and plaster, a genuine sign of genuine faith.

The last stone of the dome of St. Peter's was put in place in
1590, a few months before the death of Sixtus V. The long
period of austerity and consolidation was almost over, and in
that decade were born the three men who were to make visible the victory of the Catholic Church: Bernini, Borromini
and Pietro da Cortona.

How had that victory been achieved? In England most of us
were brought up to believe that it depended on the Inquisition, the Index and the Society of Jesus. I don't believe that
a great outburst of creative energy such as took place in
Rome between 1620 and 1660 can be the result of negative
factors, but I admit that the civilization of these years depended on certain assumptions that are out of favor in England and America today. The first of these, of course, was
belief in authority, the absolute authority of the Catholic
Church. This belief extended to sections of society which we
now assume to be naturally rebellious. It comes something of
a shock to find that, with a single exception, the great artists
of the time were all sincere, conforming Christians. Guercino
spent much of his mornings in prayer; Bernini frequently
went into retreats and practiced the spiritual exercises of St.
Ignatius; Rubens attended Mass every morning before beginning work. The exception was Caravaggio, who was like
the hero of a modern play, except that he happened to paint
very well.

This conformism was not based on fear of the Inquisition,
but on the perfectly simple belief that the faith which had
inspired the great saints of the preceding generation was
something by which a man should regulate his life. The mid-
sixteenth century was a period of sanctity in the Roman
Church almost equal to the twelfth. St. John of the Cross,
the great poet of mysticism; St. Ignatius of Loyola, the
visionary soldier turned psychologist; St. Teresa of mystical
experience and common sense; and St. Carlo Borromeo, the
austere administrator—one does not need to be a practicing

Catholic to feel respect for a half-century that could produce these great spirits. Ignatius, Teresa, Filipo Neri and Francis Xavier were all canonized on the same day, 22 May 1622. It was like the baptism of a regenerated Rome.[8]

Indeed the seventeenth century has been rightly called a century of saints and spiritual vigor. There were, in addition to the saints mentioned above, Bossuet, Fenelon, St. Jean Eudes, Peter Canisius (Jesuit missionary, reformer, founder of colleges, preacher and author of a famous catechism), Jeanne de Chantal, Cardinal Berulle, Jean Jacques Olier, founder of seminaries and St. Vincent de Paul (d. 1660) who inspired retreats, disseminated humane ideas and founded the Ladies of Charity and its numerous offspring of the Sisters of Charity. One of the most influential saints was St. Frances de Sales (d. 1622). He began modern spirituality. He was a friend to the Jews, conciliatory towards Protestants and founder of his famous Oratory. He gave to the laity their rationale to seek and practice sanctity in the world. His famous book is, of course, the *Introduction to the Devout Life,* one of the most widely read spiritual books in the seventeenth and eighteenth centuries and is still periodically reproduced today. Scholarship moved ahead with men like Suarez and St. Robert Bellarmine. In 1592 the first Congregation of Christian Doctrine was founded (mother of our modern CCD programs).

THE BEGINNINGS OF TOLERANCE

We have seen plenty of evidence of intolerance and suppression in the wars of religion that ended with the Peace of Westphalia in 1648. Intolerance existed between Catholic and Protestant, between Protestant and Protestant, between Christian and Moslem and Jew. Catholics had their Inquisition, Calvinists had their Consistories and the Anglicans had their Star Chamber. As time went on each side saw some good in the other. Cultural exchanges were made such as Protestants composing Catholic Masses, Catholics who sang Lutheran hymns. Devotional literature was exchanged. Protestants of the immediate times could not shuck off their Catholicism easily. Many still continued to bless themselves, celebrate Palm Sunday and honor statues. Only gradually did cultural differences grow, such as a sterner Sunday as inspired by the Puritans, the destruction of musical instruments and objects of religious art giving way to bare churches. Yet in the aftermath the Protestants picked up simple music (though by no means universally or willingly) and gave birth to the chorale. Catholics on their part, as we have just seen, played up the old devotions and added new ones such as the Angelus, etc. They focused on the altar while the Protestants focused on the pulpit. In spite of this, toleration was setting in for the simple reason that too many countries were now having several denominations within their boundaries. A whole series of persecutions and killings could not go on forever. Simple expediency of living together, the desire for a unified country—all tended to bring about a measure of toleration in due time. While the medieval mind could not conceive of a people and its ruler having different religions, freedom of conscience, as we know it, was coming into its own in the seventeenth and eighteenth centuries. It was even receiving theoretical foundations in writings like the pioneer Sebastian Castellio whose book of 1550 favoring toleration was highly influential.

For Catholics there was no doubt a different Church after Trent. Some Protestants have been quick to point this out and even mark Trent as the beginning of modern "Roman" Catholicism in the sense of a Roman-directed Church, in the sense of being one of several denominations. There is some justification for this as we have seen. A stricter party line was in order in contrast to the more free wheeling speculations permitted in the past. An uncontested papacy, monarchial and absolute, resulted in contrast to the more pliable and contestable maneuvers of other bishops and kings. A more universal conformity to what Rome would henceforth decree in contrast to local customs and traditions resulted. Italian-Roman coloring would dominate the Church in contrast to international influences before Trent. All this, once more, would be contested and to some degree overturned by Vatican II.

THE MISSIONS

We do well to close this chapter on reform and renewal with a word about the great missionary activity of the Church at this time. When the Catholic Europeans went to settle the New World (before the Reformation got going) they did so with the medieval presumption that the faith as well was to be propagated. Colonists were not only planting colonies but churches as well. The long list of Portuguese and Spanish holy names in the Americas attest to this fact: San Francisco, Los Angeles, Corpus Christi, San Antonio, St. Augustine—to mention just a few on the mainland United States. Soon schools were built and the first university in the New World was that of Mexico and the first diocese that of San Domingo in 1511.

All Europeans looked upon their colonizing as a holy crusade. This was especially true of the dominant power and discoverers of this time, the Spanish. They set out to civilize and evangelize the heathen and they brought to the task the fierce crusading spirit honed to a fine edge through centuries of conflict with the infidel Moslem in their own country. Their forced conversions, their exterminating tendencies, their exploitation of the heathen Indians in Mexico and Latin America must be seen in this light. In 1519 when Cortes landed in Mexico the native population was some fifteen million. By 1575 only about two million were left. The Portuguese, Dutch and English were to prove no better when their colonizing began.

Yet there were several outstanding voices against such cruelty who fought mightily for the interests of the natives. One of these was the first priest ordained in the New World in 1519, the Dominican, Bartholomew de las Casas. He spent his whole life getting legal protection for the Indians and reminding his fellow Spaniards that Indians were human beings and must be treated as such. His persistence and work laid the foundation for international justice and law. Moreover, "it is to the credit of the popes of the Counter-Reformation that they steadily condemned the doctrine of slavery for the Indians."[9] St. Peter Claver, curiously unappreciated, worked among the negroes and opposed the slave trade in Columbia. Another spokesman for the underdog was the great Archbishop of Peru, Turibio (later canonized) who passed laws to defend the rights of the Indians and Negroes and who even educated them. The most famous of all aids to the Indians were the Jesuit reservations known as the Paraguay Reductions which provided protection for the Indians (from the white men) schooling and a measure of civilization. (Later through jealousy they were suppressed.) Civilization meant, of course, becoming Spanish and mass baptisms were as much geared to make the Indian Christian as Spanish.

THE EAST

We have already alluded to the work of St. Francis Xavier in the East. Here we must now emphasize how the missionary experience in the East was entirely different from that of the Americas. Here the Catholic missionaries ran into the great Eastern religions such as Hinduism and Buddhism. In India and China the missionaries were stunned to find genuine virtue, mysticism and asceticism. They began to acquire a respect for these religions and therefore held back on the heavy handed mass forced conversions such as occurred in the Americas. The more daring and insightful missionaries allowed the continuance to their converts of those Eastern practices not incompatible with Catholicism. In Peking there was the famed Jesuit Matteo Ricci who learned Chinese, dressed in mandarin clothes, studied Chinese science and presented Christianity as the fulfillment of what the people already knew from Confucius. As might be expected, he was not without his shocked conservative critics. His successor, Father Adam Schall, became an even greater scientist at the Chinese court and even its Minister of State. By 1650 there were Christian congregations scattered throughout the main Chinese cities (however, there were no Chinese priests yet).

In Japan the same respectful approach was used but Christianity was doomed when Dutch and Spanish ships came on the scene. The fears were raised that Western imperialism was at hand. In 1614 Christian missionaries were expelled from Japan and there began the worst persecution in all of Christian history. In some twenty years over 40,000 Christians were martyred. By 1638 Japan was officially closed to foreigners. Thus if by 1614 there were some 300,000 Christians in Japan by 1697 there were hardly any left. We make passing mention of another great missionary, the Jesuit Robert de Nobili who in India adopted the Brahman way, dress and life style and liturgy. He too was denounced by jealous conservative Catholics and hauled before the Archbishop of Goa. Counter-Reformation conservatism perhaps did most harm in the area of the missions. Daniel-Rops in his volume *The Catholic Reformation* gives a telling example:

> If there was one country where the missionaries had made the mistake of trying to impose the framework and methods of European Catholicism upon native converts, that country was India. . . The Archbishopric of Goa, with its suffragan bishoprics of Meliapur and Cranganor (not to mention Macao in China), presented a handsome facade behind which there was little spiritual reality—dioceses administered on European lines, and more Portuguese than Hindu. In 1559, however, Catholicism won a notable success: the 200,000 descendants of the "Christians of St. Thomas" in the region of Cochin, who were subject to the heretical and schismatic Jacobite patriarch of Mesopotomia, but who retained vivid memories of a visit paid to them by St. Francis Xavier, determined to submit to the Holy See. Unfortunately, they were soon led to regret their decision by the stupidity of a few Western missionaries who wished forcibly to latinize the age-old Syro-Chaldaic, and to forbid them to pray in the popular tongue of Malabar. The resulting tension produced a new schism in 1633.[10]

In 1622 Pope Gregory XV created the Congregation of the Propaganda or the Society for the Propagation of the Faith to assist the missions. However, many Catholic missions were destined to disappear before the colonial ascendancy of the Protestant Dutch and English.

We might add a postscript which will conveniently introduce us to the next chapter and a new era. Missionary activity gave Christians new and disturbing thoughts. For the first time they travelled to new parts of the globe. There they met strange animals. Were they on the Ark? Did the Indians descend from Adam and how did they get all the way over there? People were living somewhat happy lives and those in the East, as we have seen, virtuous ones. Was, then, Christianity unique? Men's minds were stretching beyond the narrow confines of a Europe. Explorations were being made. Scientific discoveries (such as those of Galileo's) were reshifting the Christian world view. A certain skepticism was on the horizon, the beginning of a dark period which has been dignified by the name of the Age of Enlightenment.

NOTES

1. In spite of the fact that the Catholic world was stunned when its vicar general became a Protestant in 1541.
2. This was the very same pope who approved the Ursulines, Barnabites and the Jesuits. He took an interest in the oversees missions, enriched the Vatican library and appointed Michelangelo as the chief architect of St. Peter's.
3. The Council of Chalcedon had some 630 participants, Vatican I over 700 and Vatican II over 2,000.
4. The decrees, the soul of brevity and completeness, were largely the work of the Augustinian (fittingly, the same order as Luther's) Seripando.
5. Owen Chadwick, *op. cit.*, p. 276.
6. A. G. Dickens, *The Counter Reformation*, pp. 132, 133. Harcourt, Brace & World, Inc. 1969.
7. Owen Chadwick, *op. cit.*, p. 300.
8. Kenneth Clark, *op. cit.*, pp. 174, 175.
9. Owen Chadwick, *op. cit.*, p. 328.
10. H. Daniel-Rops, *The Catholic Reformation*, pp. 292, 293. E. P. Dutton & Co. Inc. New York. 1962.

XVII

Reason and Reaction

THE ENLIGHTENMENT

While men were fighting the wars of religion, each side trying to defeat or dominate the other, there was going on a revolution far more reaching, far more threatening to all religion regardless of denomination. It was a revolution in thought, in emphasis, in science. The seventeenth and eighteenth centuries were witnessing men whose works and ideas laid the foundation for the modern age. It was the age of the philosophers like Descartes, Spinoza, Leibnitz, Locke, Montesquieu. It was the age of scientists like Newton, Linnaeus, Lavoisier, Boyle, Fahrenheit, Halley (Halley's comet), Adam Smith. It was the age of writers like Pope, Milton, Defoe, Swift and Fielding. These men, and many others like them, helped in one way or another to shift the world's spiritual axis from heaven to earth. They helped to create a scientific mentality. They created a thirst for knowledge and a keen desire to throw off all restraints and traditions of the past in following wherever knowledge would take them. This was the age too when men had discovered new worlds, new cultures, new peoples. Men who were filled with disgust at the vices and follies of Europe would profess to see in the pagan savages (the "noble savage" as the

immoral and later demented Rousseau would call them)
more goodness and nobility than the Christian European.

What was happening was that men like the great genius
of the age, Isaac Newton, were demonstrating that the universe was not a haphazard puppet on divine strings, but one
of fixed, universal immutable laws. The universe was an accurate, programmed clockwork with discoverable and know-
able laws. It was not a world ever open to divine intervention. Rather the world was infinite, self-sufficient, dynamic
and as closed to divine intervention as it was open to rational
inquiry. Naturally, all this sudden shift, this radical reorder-
ing of the world raised some terribly important questions.
If, for example, the world was running on precise and immutable laws, did God have a part to play? Did, as a matter
of fact, fixed laws allow for miracles? If there is a common
natural law governing all, does this apply to men as well? If
it does, does that mean that beneath all the religious sects,
beneath the beliefs of the Protestants, Jews, Catholics, Moslems and American Indians there lies a natural common
universal law applicable to all men ? Does this further imply
that morality therefore rests on a much broader foundation
than Christianity?

Could not reason even sit in judgment on religion itself?
Must not religion and its teachings and its miracles come
under its scrutiny? Was, in fact, revelation even necessary?
With reason to figure out everything there was no *need* for
God to reveal. It was a waste of time, superfluous. And why
should religion have anything to say about politics? If there
is a sub-Christian natural law it is to that men must look for
reasonable conduct among all men, Christian and non-Christian. There is no need for divine guidance in political matters.

It must be said that the early scientists like Newton were
reverent toward religion and were anxious to reconcile re-

ligion and science. But later others less reverent raised the questions above. There arose deliberate challenges to traditional religious beliefs. An all out war began on religion, superstition, and intolerance of all kinds. The natural must be substituted for the supernatural and reason must be the measurement of all things. Thus began the Age of Enlightenment, or the Age of Reason or, if you will, the secularization of the world which continues to the present. In many ways therefore the Enlightenment was more opposed to Catholicism than the Protestant Reformation for it obviously struck at the very roots of revealed religion in denying the authenticity of the Scriptures and the very existence of the supernatural. Now that man had gotten hold of his natural reason the notion of progress was born, progress freed from the gross "superstitions" of the ecclesiastical Middle Ages. Be it noted here that by the time the Enlightenment was over, having reached its extreme expression in the French Revolution, Christianity would have slipped from the world's center stage, become separated from secular and civil life; all religion would become, not an affair of the state (a radical departure from tradition), but a very private affair of free citizens.

DEISM

The results of all the preceding attitudes—that reason and natural law were co-partners in discovering the validity of everything whatever—was Deism. Deism was a compromise between the God of Christianity and the Law of Reason. It held that while a man can reasonably believe in God (for reason argued back to a Prime Mover, an Uncaused Cause) this God was not Personal. He is rather the God of the Newtonian laws, a Divine Architect who, like a watchmaker, wound up the world and lets it run according to the immutable laws He built into it. God is thus enabled to withdraw from the scene and let reason run the planet. Thus Deism was a natural religion.

Deism and its foundation, the Enlightenment, had its start in England but found its home base in France. The French took Deism to its logical course. Voltaire, the perfect example of the perfect scientific skeptic, was its chief exponent.[1] He wrote profusely, though his works are not read today. More than any other he made Deism, cynicism and religious skepticism respectable. Voltaire led the attack against Christianity, mocked miracles and inveighed against all superstition. He spearheaded much of the enlightened reforms which are still our mental equipment today, such as popular education, humanitarianism, freedom for slaves and anti-war movements. Voltaire contributed to the famous Encyclopedia of Diderot which was a compendium of all knowledge of the time and shot through with deistic principles. But organized religion continued to be his target to the point where it became an obsession. There is no doubt that Voltaire and his co-deists did much to discredit religion. As historian Philip Hughes puts it:

> The French deists and atheists availed themselves of every possible literary weapon, and they secured a hearing in thousands of minds where no serious work of theology or apologetics would ever gain entry. The Jansenist had been a solemn and serious opponent and could be fought off, intellectually, and without any great difficulty. But the mockery of these new foes, the pioneers of the modern popular assault on traditional faith and conventional morality, could not be met with the weapons of learning. They had the first laugh, and the crowd that laughed with them was already beyond the reach of the dialectic. For the hour when the crowd turned to reflect, the movement provided a great compendium

of knowledge, the first Encyclopedia, and there the civilization of the eighteenth century found a kind of universal popular educator by which to initiate itself into all the sciences and general history, and so written that at every turn the universality of human knowledge was made to tell against religion, and especially against the Catholic Church.[2]

Most of the intellectuals of Europe and America fell under the deist spell. Thomas Paine scoffed at the devil and Ben Franklin and Thomas Jefferson held deist ideas. Alexander Pope and the historian Gibbon promoted deism in their works. Deism became the official religion of the fast growing Freemason lodges which spread rapidly throughout Europe and America. Ben Franklin and George Washington were such members. (Some Freemason lodges abandoned deism for atheism, were heavily anticlerical and anti-Catholic and the refuge for former Catholics. This explains the Church's condemnation of them.)

THE ENLIGHTENED DESPOTS

Many of the rulers of Europe were dedicated to the Enlightenment and almost rivaled each other in inducing liberal reforms. They were bent on ideas of toleration, popular education and freedom from the traditions and superstitions of the past though in the process they trampled on a lot of freedom. Many of their countries, as we know, had several religious sects. This fact, plus the skepticism of the times, indifference to dogma and the desire of such religious minorities for a place in the sun led the enlightened rulers to be champions of religious toleration. They lost any enthusiasm for maintaining any organized state religion. Anti-Protestant laws in France and anti-Catholic laws in England began to be relaxed. The Inquisition was considerably curbed in Spain and even Pope Benedict XIV, an enlightened and witty pontiff, was praised by Voltaire for his tolerance for tolerance was reasonable. Hand in hand with such toleration went the enlightened people's desire for humane treatment of all minorities, not only religious but racial. Negro slavery began to be assailed. The Quakers condemned slavery as early as 1696 and in 1761 forbade their members to engage in it. In America, a society for the abolition of slavery was founded in Philadelphia in 1774 by an enlightened physician, Dr. Benjamin Rush. Many enlightened Fathers of the American Revolution such as Washington and Jefferson, even though they themselves owned slaves, hoped it would disappear.

All these things were positive legacies of the Enlightenment. The rulers who sought these ideals could not, however, achieve them without the cooperation or the subordination of the Church. Thus, while enlightened rulers did not seek the Church's annihilation they sought to control it, to purify it of "unreasonable" elements and bring its clergy, in the interests of its over-all programs, into the status of civil servants. We might note here what we shall mention below, namely, that many of the Reformed Catholics (Catholics anxious to reform the Church following the spirit of Trent) were in agreement with the rulers' aims and each used the other for their ends. In any case, the Church was very much in line for the attention of any despot who considered himself enlightened.

AUSTRIA

Austria, under Maria Theresa (defeated rival of Frederick the Great of Prussia), pursued a moderate policy of enlightenment such as popular education, and so on. She however protected the Church. Her son, Joseph II felt no such compulsion. He introduced compulsory education, granted religious toleration, took over seminaries, put the clergy under civil control, suppressed some monasteries, regulated the holydays, determined what prayers were to be said, what songs to be sung, forbade the rosary and determined the number of candles to be lit on the altar for Mass. He was bent on making the Catholic Church a national one by putting the bishops under his care and resisting all papal decrees. (This is called Febronism or Josephism; we shall meet its French counterpart called Gallicanism.) In 1782 Pope Pius VI made an unprecedented journey to Vienna to get Joseph to reverse his policies but to no avail. With such overkill Joseph only succeeded in triggering reaction and ultimately his work was undone, but for the time being he helped keep the Church impotent. It was the same story in Spain, Denmark, France and Portugal. There was not one single Catholic country where the Catholic Church was free to live its own life.

FRANCE

France, the home of Voltaire, merits our special attention for in the age of enlightenment in France would be found the stuff of the French Revolution and the Church's role in it. Louis XIV, the Sun King, had made France the cultural and social arbiter of the world. He was the perfect absolute monarch even in religious matters. We have seen how he revoked the Edict of Nantes in the interest of national unity, but once having a uniform Church he must, of course, control that Church. There were the Four Articles of 1682 but they are not as important as the spirit they engendered known as Gallicanism. This was a spirit which in essence wanted the Catholic Church and wanted the pope but rejected his central control from Rome and his claims to infallibility. In short, papal power was to be ineffective in France. Every school in France, every seminary, was required to convey the spirit of Gallicanism. But it was not just the anti-papal spirit that was present. There were some resentments over the Church's wealth, over its almost full control over education and charitable institutions. Most irritating was the fact that in the nation's financial stress, the Church did not pay taxes nor even offer to help carry the financial burden. France was full of other conflicting forces.

For one, there were those Frenchmen who did not want Gallicanism and the curtailment of the pope's power. They were called the "Ultramontanes" which literally means those who looked "across the mountains" to Rome for guidance. Among the Ultramontanes were the Jesuits. And the Jesuits were powerful. They were mentors to the sons of nobles, confessors to kings and princes. They were a bit too prone to hobnob with the nobility and too accommodating morally. They gained the reputation for finding legal loopholes to permit doubtful moral actions. Then there was the rest of the clergy. As in other countries, both Protestant and Catholic, they were sharply divided into higher and lower clergy, the latter living in ignorance and abject poverty and the former living as well endowed nobles. Many of the upper clergy were so much the children of the Enlightenment and so free-thinking that even tepid King Louis XVI said about a certain candidate, "No, the Archbishop of Paris must at least believe in God." The upper clergy, which meant largely the espicopacy, was too tied to the monarchy, too much the home for the nobility.

JANSENISM

Then there were the Reformed Catholics and the Jansenists. The Reformed Catholics were the spiritual ancestors of the leftwing Catholics after Vatican II. They were radical, progressive and wanted the Church to move ahead with Trent's reforms, free itself of the monarchy and reduce its wealth. The Jansenists started out as Catholics dedicated to the ideals of Trent also. They too wanted to get back to the older and stricter practices of the Church and advocated the equality of all bishops with the pope. They were Pietists (which we shall describe below) in that they wanted more simplicity, less theology, a greater dependence on God's grace and less dependence on the sacraments, ritual, the cults of the saints, and a severer, stricter moral code. They were in short a kind of Catholic Calvinists. Politically they consistently were for more state authority and less church authority, more modern and secular administration. In this they were allied with the aims of the state. The Jansenists were condemned at various times and in 1713 the papal bull *Unigenitus* made it official yet Jansenism continued to flourish. It was found even at Rome among the cardinals which explains why it held on so long.

Needless to say the strict, papal-decentralizing Jansenists had for their arch-enemies the Jesuits. As long as the Jansenists served Louis XIV's ambitions against the Church they were unmolested but when Louis made peace with the pope (for reasons of expediency) he began in the interests of unity the persecution of the Jansenists. Still the Jansenists continued to draw people. To the nunnery at Port Royale came some famous names such as the Abbot St. Cyran (who popularized the Netherlands-born Jansenism in France) and Blaise Pascal. The hostilities between Jansenist and Jesuit continued. The Jesuits were able to obtain from the weak Louis XV that no one could receive the last rites who did not accept the Jansenist-condemning bull *Unigenitus*. This became a matter involving the French Parliament and the infighting kept alive in men's minds the association of the Jesuits with political maneuvering and moral laxity which was much exploited by the Jansenists. The Jansenist movement finally died (except for some "old Catholics") but not without causing much agitation in the Church.

The victory over Jansenism had other results which we shall examine in the next chapter. For one thing the whole affair showed that the reforms demanded by the Jansenists and the Reformed Catholics were not possible without the support of Rome. This had the result of driving many towards the French Revolution which was in the offing. This explains why many of the progressive members of the clergy went over to the Revolution. "After the disappointments with Rome and with enlightened absolutism it was widely felt that the ideals of Reform Catholicism could only be realized with the help of the Revolution and in close alliance with the democratic movement."[3] We might anticipate somewhat and remark here that such an alliance was to crumble because of the excesses of the French Revolution. Catholic Reform became associated with such excesses and revolutionary terrors. Thus it perished, Rome emerged victoriously conservative and in 1794 was strong enough to condemn both Jansenism and Reform Catholicism without fear of reaction.

QUIETISM

There had been another heresy afflicting the Church in France which we must mention. It was called Quietism and it too was a Pietism attitude, a reaction to the rationalism and formalism of the times. It was propounded by a Spanish priest, Michael Molinos, who taught that man must suspend all of his human power and become passively resigned (quiet) to what is good and evil. Temptations and the sins that resulted must be simply accepted since they were, for the moment, God's Will. Man must be passive and even vocal prayer was unnecessary. Famous French bishops took sides here. One was Fenelon who favored Quietism and the other Bossuet who opposed it. Quietism was condemned in 1694 but the movement left a suspicion on the entire contemplative life.

Thus, there was France: the seat of the Enlightenment, the home base of the devastating Voltaire. There was the Church upset by Quietism, stunned by Jansenism and dishonored by the infighting between the Jesuits and Jansenists. The whole position of the Church in France is best summed up by Philip Hughes when he writes:

> In this France, where Catholicism lay helpless, racked with the Jansenist controversy, cut off from Rome by its Gallicanism, shackled by its long connection with the State, oppressed by a hierarchy too often incompetent and not infrequently worldly, a France whose ruling classes were more and more given over to immorality, the mockery of Voltaire, in a single generation, put the Church in the position of the defendant, Catholicism was summoned to explain what right it had to live. Hated, derided, it was henceforward, for the best intellect of France and therefore for the intellect of the world, an infamy, and not to be endured.[4]

SUPPRESSION OF THE JESUITS

One of the indirect results of the Enlightenment was the suppression of the Jesuits. There were many reasons why this happened. There was the Jesuits' undue influence over the nobility and royalty and this in itself caused much jealousy. They were associated with the pope's interests; they were among the "ultramontanes" who looked to Rome for leadership rather than the state. To this extent they were antiroyalist and dangerous to national interests. Besides, in an age of toleration the Jesuits as champions of a monolithic church were considered hostile to tolerance and freedom. There were the continued hostilities of the Jansenists and others who thought the Jesuits' moral teaching lax. Finally the Jesuits were at times too affiliated with the politics of the times and also at times they tended to overplay their hand. Many powerful enemies could not but plot their downfall.

The attack on the Jesuits began in Catholic Portugal. There a strong, very able and self-seeking minister named Pombal saw that the Jesuit influence on the royal family might obscure his own. Pombal came up with some flimsy evidence that the Jesuits were somehow involved in an assassination attempt on the king by a jealous husband whose wife the king had slept with. In 1759 he confiscated their property and expelled them from the country.

In France besides the usual enemies of the Jesuits such as the Jansenists and Calvinists, was the king's (Louis XV) mistress, Madame de Pompadour, the real ruling power, the "minister in petticoats." What happened was that the king's Jesuit confessor had chastised him over his affair with Pompadour and so she was determined to have revenge. The occasion of her action was the financial failure of the Jesuits' mission on Martinique due to the loss of cargo to English raiding ships. The creditor tried to recoup his money but the Jesuits claimed that they had no responsibility for this loss. In any case, the Society appealed to France's highest court and a hostile Parliament was glad to have a pretense to investigate all Jesuit activities. Their decision was that the Jesuits should be expelled. In 1764 the weak Louis XV signed the decree. Pope Clement XIII protested but could do no more. Next, Spain followed suit by expelling the Jesuits in 1767 with great suddenness and surprise. Next the kings of Naples and the duke of Parma, Spanish relatives, followed suit. By 1769 all of the Catholic rulers were demanding the suppression of the entire order. The pope held out. He tried to conciliate. He even made Pombal's brother a cardinal. Pressure still continued to mount and there was even the threat from the Bourbon powers of an invasion of the papal states. Finally on July 21, 1773 Pope Clement XIV gave in and the Jesuits were suppressed. Father Ricci, the General of the order was imprisoned where he died a year after the pope. Ironically the non-Catholic rulers refused to publish the bull of the pope thereby keeping the Jesuits in existence in their countries. One was Frederick II of Prussia and the other was Catherine the Great of Russia. Moreover, we might note that the pope was forced to suppress his most ardent supporters and most vocal upholders of a centralized papal power as against the state power. By repressing the Jesuits the pope in effect was telling the world (or at least those who were anxious to read into his act) that he repudiated the former teaching of the supremacy of the Church over the state.

PIETISM

Pietism is the name for the general reaction that people gave to the tiring infighting among the various denominations, the heavy theologizing, the cold rationalism. It took many forms. We saw it in Quietism and Jansenism in Catholic France. But in the Protestant countries it took place as well and in the form of revivalism it was a Protestant phenomenon. Among the Lutherans in Germany Pietism got a strong hold. A man named P. J. Spener created Pietism there which took the form of a personal religion, one where dogma and doctrine were less important and the interior life of the spirit was more important. Under another remarkable Lutheran Pietism spread. This was Count Zinendorf. It was under him that Pietism broke away from its native Lutheranism. He associated himself with some Moravians and they migrated to Pennsylvania to found the city of Bethlehem. They became known as the Unity of Brethren or the Moravian Church. Pietism in Germany was very popular yet it had such drawbacks that it eventually disappeared. For one thing it became too subjective and introspective. It did not keep spiritual vitality and intellectual vitality in balance and so became theologically sterile. It tended to become too emotional. There is an interesting sidelight to German Pietism which historian Roland Bainton points out: "The suggestion has been made that when Pietism kindled the emotions of many in the nation and the Enlightenment diminished the intensity of faith, emotion was transferred from God the Father to the fatherland. It is at least plain that the romanticists who saw a special divine afflatus in the German soul had been reared in the Pietist tradition."[5] We have already taken note of George Fox the founder of the Quakers. He too was a Pietist.

Pietism was bound to break out in England for much the same reasons that Jansenism got a foothold in France. The Anglican upper clergy were infected with enlightenment ideas, the church became more and more tied to the state and so "became politically useful and theologically insignificant."[6] The upper Anglican clergy lived as well to-do nobles while the lower clergy languished in poverty. It was under these circumstances that an Anglican priest, John Wesley, founded the Methodist church. John was one of nineteen children. He was ascetic and was impressed with the Pietism of the Moravians. He decided to regenerate society through individual preaching. No one ever wandered more throughout village and town to preach the word than Wesley. He never left the Anglican church for he was determined to purify it, yet his successors broke off into the Methodist Church. He urged piety, sobriety and chastity. He had a great concern for the working man, the very person neglected by the German Pietists—and this would make a difference in time to come. Wesley's Methodists shared pietistic concerns with the English Evangelicals who also reacted to the tepidity of the Anglican church but who remained within it. They were very humanitarian and fought the battle against slavery, founded schools for children and established missionary and Bible societies.

Before we leave England we might mention the status of the Catholics there. The Catholics in the eighteenth century were a small minority. With the overthrow of the Catholic king, James II, (which Louis XIV's revocation of the Edict of Nantes in France stimulated) they lost their ability to influence national affairs. Yet in the minds of their countrymen they continued to be a political threat. In due time, however, Irish immigration swelled their numbers and by 1791 (the very year Wesley died) it was generally thought safe to grant privileges to Catholics and free them of many legal disabilities. In another forty years the English Oxford Movement would see a revival of Catholicism, a "second Spring" to use the phrase of its most illustrious member and convert to Roman Catholicism: John Henry Newman.

ENLIGHTENMENT AND THE CHURCH

In general it is evident that the Enlightenment dealt the Church in particular and religion in general a severe blow. The Enlightenment succeeded in exposing the Church as a force that shackled men's minds. It made Christianity not something to be despised, not something without function, but rather totally irrelevant to the modern world. And the Church had no men of note who could effectively refute its adversaries. It was forced into the embarrassment of suppressing its own spokesmen, the Jesuits. It did not have a Catholic John Wesley. So the Church retreated into the less satisfying realm of authority, into identifying itself more and more with the old order of things. This meant that the Church would not and could not come to terms with the new learning. Protestants were already wrestling with enlightenment ideas and succumbing to its onslaught. The Catholic Church tended to retreat from the new science. It used censorship and old fashioned apologetics which were out of touch with the science of the times. By not coming to terms with the new scientific discoveries which raised such havoc with the Bible and revealed religion the Church merely postponed the inevitable confrontation. This would happen in the nineteenth and twentieth centuries when the movement called Modernism would force the Church to take a second look at what science and critical studies were saying about Christianity.

But more was at stake than the Church's failure to come to intellectual terms with the Enlightenment. As we have hinted before the Enlightenment only added to the general disintegration of the old European unity which was centered in the Church. Feudalism had declined, the centralized monarchial powers were in the ascendancy and were busy depriving the Church of its international character by weakening the bonds that held their nations to the Holy See. The Italian Renaissance had rejected the barbarism of the Middle Ages and was looking for cultural purity. The Germanic Reformation was seeking Gospel purity. The Humanists were castigating the Dark Ages.

Even though piety in the seventeenth century was remarkable religious skepticism fostered by the philosophers of the Enlightenment was growing and "the greatest religious genius of the century, Pascal, was already acutely conscious that it was this easy-going, light-hearted skepticism, and not Protestantism or metaphysical error, which was the great danger that Catholicism had to face."[7] Of course, as it so often happens, the actual aim of the Enlightenment turned out to be a far cry from the toleration they preached. The real aim of the enlightened skeptics was to replace one unity by another: to substitute the universal reign of science and reason for that of religion and authority. There was no real sympathy for political or social revolution for the men of the Enlightenment were squarely on the side of vested interests, on the side of property and order. The Enlightenment, like the Renaissance, was an elitist movement, allied with the powers that be and determined to give the people only what was good for them. As Voltaire admitted, "We have never pretended to enlighten shoemakers and servant girls. . . ." It is ironic, for example, that they succeeded in getting the Jesuits suppressed only to substitute themselves as "confessors" and advisors to the rulers of Europe.[8]

Up to this point the rulers and their advisors shared a common faith. Now, of course, the enlightened philosophers felt that Christianity was good for the lower classes but not for the elite. The net result was to sow discord and beget division between the upper and lower classes. Thus the common man turned away from the sweet reasonableness of Voltaire and to a new star on the horizon, Rousseau. He was the one who took the high flown liberal ideas and clothed them in religious terms and popularized them for the masses. He vocalized the thoughts of the individual against society, religious sentiment and intuition against the rationalism of the philosophers, the poor against the rich. He filled men's minds with the idea of democracy not as a mere system but as a way of life for everyone. Thus it was that the abstract, elite, enlightened rationalism met head on with the strong romantic feelings of Rousseau. The result was the French Revolution.

Meanwhile we must admit to some signs of quiet religious vitality among the people during this era in spite of its being ignored by the philosophers. The Age of Voltaire was also the age of Wesley, Tersteegen (a Protestant mystic and religious poet), St. Paul of the Cross, the founder of the Passionists, St. Margaret Mary, St. Leonard of Port Maurice and the great St. Alphonsus Liguori who founded the Redemptorists and whose spiritual writings, verses, music and sympathetic moral theology guided the hearts of many. There were the Moravians and Pietists in Germany, the Methodists in England and the Great Awakening in America. There was the building of the great Catholic baroque monasteries. In fact, "Nothing shows the divorce between the bourgeois rationalism of the Enlightenment and the religious traditions of popular culture better than the figure of the beggar saint Benedict Joseph Labre (1748-83), who lived the life of a medieval ascetic and miracle worker in the age of Gibbon and Adam Smith."[9] Yet, all in all, the eighteenth century was not a good one for the Church. But all was not over. The French Revolution was about to begin. The Church would be further shaken, recover and retreat into the deepest suspicions of liberalism and democracy which came forth from that turning point of modern history.

NOTES

1. Enlightened as he was, however, Voltaire was antisemitic. In his book *The French Enlightenment and the Jews* Rabbi Arthur Hertzberg says, "An analysis of everything Voltaire wrote about the Jews throughout his life establishes the proposition that he is the major link in Western intellectual history between the antisemitism of classic paganism and the modern age."
2. Philip Hughes, *op. cit.*, p. 222.
3. Karl Otmar von Aretin, *The Papacy and the Modern World*, p. 20. World University Library, McGraw-Hill, New York, 1970.
4. Philip Hughes, *op. cit.*, p. 222.
5. Roland Bainton, *op. cit.*, p. 354.
6. Age of Enlightenment, Life-Time Books, p. 32. New York. 1966.
7. Christopher Dawson, *The Gods of Revolution*, p. 13. New York University Press, New York. 1972.
8. Indeed, there are those who maintain that it was the Enlightenment which set the world on its rise to dehumanizing power control. By downgrading true medieval culture the Enlightenment turned aside forces which might have prevented modern day economic and cultural alienation. Thus Lewis Mumford in his book, *The Myth of the Machine* writes: "Our current views of both the terrestrial and the mechanical New Worlds have been falsely colored by the opaque religious prejudices of the eighteenth-century Enlightenment. Thinkers like Voltaire and Diderot, judging medieval institutions by the decayed survivals of their own day, took for granted that the Middle Ages were a period of besotted ignorance and superstition; and in their desire to throw off the influence of the Established Church, they converted the High Middle Ages, one of the great moments in European culture, into a neo-Gothic horror story, assuming that no serious progress had been made in any department until their own period. This anti-Gothic obsession resulted not only in the devaluation of medieval achievement but also in the wholesale destruction of buildings and institutions that, if preserved and renewed, might have helped to humanize the rising power system." (p. 6)
9. Christopher Dawson, *op. cit.*, p. 34.

XVIII

Liberalism and Conservatism

THE FRENCH REVOLUTION 1789-1799

Before we get into the immediate story of the French Revolution we must first realize that we are dealing with an idea, an ideology, almost a religion. The Enlightenment had had its effect. Men were prepared to jettison Christianity (at least those of the intellectual elite) and replace it with a new enlightened, humanitarian, natural religion. There was an almost mystical enshrinement of humanity in the Freemason lodges. The "Rights of Man" were to be upheld. All those kings, popes and bishops who had enslaved man must go. The appeal was for freedom, democracy and equality. It was a real spiritual program, a genuine ideological force that was at the bottom of the French Revolution and all the succeeding revolutions that were inspired by it. Just as Communism in its early days presented itself as a true religion, with its hierarchy and promise of spiritual regeneration and liberation, so too the French Revolution was based on a precise ideology which was to change the world. (Like the Russian Revolution it was conceived in a blood bath, had its purges, fell far short of freedom and wound up with a dictator.) We must keep this in mind as we turn now to the immediate factors that unleased the revolution in France.

There was always in France as elsewhere the chronic agitation for reform, both of Church and state. People wanted the Catholic Church to remain the established Church, of course, but they wanted it renewed and reformed. The interesting thing to note is that Gallicanism had done its work well for in all their aspirations of reform the people and clergy looked, not to the pope, but to the king.

There were many matters in France that cried out for relief. The cost of wars was heavy; taxes were galling and oppressive. More annoying was the fact that there was such a wide gap between the life styles and wealth of the lower clergy and peasants and the nobility and upper clergy. In France the upper clergy and nobility owned one fifth of the land. The old caste divisions of clergy, nobility and commoner were irritating—especially since by this time the enlightened aristocracy had become vain social parasites at the royal court living on the shallow resources of a bankrupt state (so that it is no wonder that they fell like a rotten tree at the first struggle and resigned their rights and privileges without a whimper). The middle-class bourgeoisie were getting restless. These, we recall, were the very ones imbibing the ideas of the Enlightenment from Rousseau and who were chafing at the moral restrictions of the Church on their commercial interests. For the Church right down to the eve of the Revolution was opposed to the new capitalist philosophy and commercial view of life which had triumphed in Protestant England and Holland. The Church was an irritant with its ideals of poverty and its condemnation of the greedy and competitive spirit which the new commercial society was acquiring. Yet this middle class, precisely because of their interests in capital and commerce, was the real power and was ready to throw off the Church. Ultimately just as capital and commerce played the real role in the Puritan American Revolution so they would be radical factors in the French Revolution.[1] On top of all this the kings of the time were incompetent. Louis XV was pleasure loving and dominated by his mistresses. It was Madame Pompadour who urged the expulsion of the Jesuits. It was she who got France into the financially disastrous Seven Years War. Louis XVI was no improvement. He was lazy and untalented. The one man who might have saved France from bankruptcy was his minister Necker but the Queen, Marie Antionette, had him dismissed. Of course, in France's grave financial straits the nobles and upper clergy could have shared the tax burdens but they were unwilling so Louis had no choice but to call on the Estates General which had not met for one hundred seventy-five years.

The three orders of the Estates General met at Versailles: the clergy, the nobility and, numerically superior to both combined, the commoners. Originally each order was supposed to vote as a separate bloc which meant that the first two related orders, the clergy and the nobility, would always outvote the commoners' bloc two to one. But this was not to be. Many humble parish priests were there as delegates to the clerical order and they insisted on voting with the commoners. After much maneuvering it was agreed and a National Assembly was formed with each member having an individual vote. This was most significant. It meant that the higher clergy and nobility had been defeated by the parish priests of France by this blending of the three orders into one vast democratic assembly where the commoners had the most members. Though reform of state and Church was at first the aim, revolution was in the making. The king tried to cower this National Assembly but the people of Paris who identified with it rose up and stormed the fortress of the Bastile on July 14, 1789 and Paris became the seat of the Revolution.[2]

REVOLUTION AND THE CHURCH

The National Assembly set out to construct a new government and they did it with a vengeance. When their work was finished they declared that they had undone fourteen centuries of abuses in three years, that the Constitution they had made would last forever and their names would be blessed by all mankind. Yet in just a few months their work was wrecked and their leaders exiled or imprisoned. "They had destroyed what they could not replace and called up forces that they could neither understand nor control."[3] Most of the members being influenced by the Enlightenment wanted to abolish class privilege and distinction. Financial stability was to be obtained through the seizure of Church lands. This was done and the priests were to receive a stipend from the government in place of land-producing income—though the class that actually profited from all this stripping of the Church was the capitalist class who made fortunes in the purchase and resale of Church property. Next monasteries were disbanded except for those engaged in running orphanages and the like. Then the dioceses were rearranged by the government and the novelty was introduced whereby the government would make bishops and notify the pope later. Even the French kings had not done this; they would nominate men to be bishops but always sought papal confirmation. So far the parish priests were agreeable with these changes for such arrangements could only improve their lot. However they were soon to learn that if the state were paying their salaries the state could and did interfere in the realm of doctrine. The aged pope, Pope Pius VI, wrote and told Louis XVI not to approve the new laws but Louis did so for the pope's letter came a day too late. Soon the clergy saw themselves being reduced to mere civil functionaries. They, along with the Reformed progressive Catholics wanted to integrate the Church into a new pattern of society and to make the Church and state a harmonious unity. Now they were being required to take an oath supporting a new Civil Constitution which did not accept Catholicism as the state religion.

About a third of the lower clergy took the oath and only about four of the bishops did. It was easier for the bishops to refuse for they had to go into exile, rather comfortable for most of them, which was closed to the lower clergy. There was much confusion about this oath and a word or directive from the pope would have been most helpful but the pope delayed too long. In any case, there were now a divided clergy, the "Romanist" clergy (those who refused to take the oath) and the government approved constitutional clergy (those who did). Only the latter were able to perform weddings, give the sacraments, etc. Rioting, often involving sacrilege, broke out. Matters took a turn for the worse when Louis XVI tried to flee his country after the pope had condemned the Civil Constitution in 1791. In effect the king had broken with the Revolution, the pope was against it and this made the Romanist clergy suspect. Especially after the new kingless government became involved in a war with Catholic Austria were the Romanist priests regarded as a fifth column. To offset this danger a new oath was imposed on the clergy in 1792. Those who refused were to be deported. Those too ill to be deported were to be imprisoned where many were killed. Death, deportation and exile reduced the number of clergy obedient to the pope. The whole Church-state relationship was deteriorating quickly. There was practical schism. As Carlton J. H. Hayes summarizes it:

> The ecclesiastical policies of the National Assembly were perhaps the least effacious and the most fateful achievements of

the Revolution. Yet it would be difficult to perceive how they could have been less radical than they were. The church appeared to be indissolubly linked with the fortunes of the "old regime"; the clergy comprised a particularly privileged class; and the leaders and great majority of the Assembly were filled with the deistic or skeptical philosophy of the "Enlightenment." In November, 1789, the church property was confiscated. In February, 1790, the monasteries and other religious communities were suppressed. In April, absolute religious toleration was proclaimed. . . . In December, the Assembly forced the reluctant king to sign a decree compelling all the Catholic clergy in France to take a solemn oath of allegiance to the "civil constitution."[4]

The remaining constitutional clergy, those who took the oath in obedience to the state, did not long enjoy their privilege. A newer and more radical leadership had taken over the Revolution, an enlightened leadership which sought to de-Christianize religion. This leadership made marriage, not a sacrament, but a civil contract. Clerical marriages were made legal and so also the remarriages of divorced persons. By 1793 any clergyman who did not agree with such legislation was deported. Meanwhile the marriages of priests were actually encouraged. Austria and Prussia were threatening war in order to protect and restore the king of France. A mob reacted to such foreign threats by imprisoning the king and executing him in January, 1793. Soon France was being invaded from all sides.

SUBSTITUTES FOR CATHOLICISM

The deported French bishops and other clergy could not but hope for victory for these invaders. Their open encouragement only served to make the French home government more anticlerical. In 1792 and 1793 an effort was made to throw out the whole package of Christianity. In the spirit of Voltaire, violent denunciations of the Catholic faith were made. There was the destruction of vestments and statues. On November 10, 1793 in Notre Dame Cathedral a Feast of Reason was held. An actress, a "Goddess of Reason" was enthroned to preside over an orgy. Images were smashed. Donkeys were paraded wearing bishops' mitres. Churches were closed. Yet while such Church-hating men like Hebert and Marat were urging violent anti-Catholic measures, others like Robespierre and Danton saw that it was a fruitless venture. Some lessening of the anit-Church laws was obtained. Robespierre, when he came to power as a virtual dictator, substituted for the God of Reason the shade more personal Supreme Being and in 1794 himself conducted a ceremony in honor of the Supreme Being. But Robespierre was soon beheaded in the Reign of Terror which sent thousands to the guillotine. By 1795 under the rule of a dictatorship of a five man Directory some toleration came in though anti-Catholic measures were still being carried out. It was at this time that the Abbey Church of Cluny was leveled to the ground as were the lovely cathedrals of Arras, Liege, Cambrai and Bruges.

By 1795 permission was given to the Romanist priests for partial use of some of the churches if they made a full act of submission to the laws of the government. Many refused. Two years later they were required to take the "Oath of Hatred" against the monarchy. Refusal meant deportation. Still failing to get rid of Christianity a new religion was invented in 1796 whereby hymns to Nature were sung along with readings from the pagan philosophers, the Koran and the Gospels. Still, the people flocked to the priest offering Mass even though the priest was under a limit of time imposed by the government. Yet, for all of the harassment the faith lay deep in people's hearts. Many were impressed by the fidelity of those at home and those in exile. It was only natural, of course, that those exiled clerics were repulsed by the Revolution and longed for the restoration of the monarchy. This is important to remember when, later on, we see how the papacy would look with suspicion on revolutionary ideas and liberalism for its initial contact was with the excesses of the French Revolution. "If some of the Romanists were more preoccupied, in their exile, with the fate of the monarchy than with the fate of the Church, if some of the bishops were blind adherents of the *ancient regime,* and if many of the constitutional clergy dishonored their calling, it is right that the sacrifice of the devoted, during a period of extreme trial, should be remembered, for without it the remarkable revival of the Church in France, in the following century, is unintelligible."[5]

PIUS VII

One of the failures of the papacy in the French Revolution was that it did not clear up in the minds of the clergy where their duty lay. The clergy, divided into constitutional and Romanists, were unable to present a united front. The papacy hesitated too long and was too indecisive. The old pope, Pius VI, delayed too long in condemning the Civil Constitution of the clergy. He did sympathize with Louis XVI and the political aspirations of the French deportees, but this only made the lot of the loyal clergy in France that much harder. On the other hand the power of the papacy in general was at a low ebb and besides the spirit of Gallicanism had led the clergy to seek redress from the king rather than from the pope. Yet, in spite of all this, there were a few perceptive men who felt that if Rome could ever give a clear cut directive to the Church in France, that directive could solve many problems and give a unity to the nation so sorely needed. In fact, a French general occupied Rome in 1798 and carried off the eighty-two year old pope to Siena and then to Florence. The Austrians tried to rescue him so "citizen" pope had to be taken to France. The aged invalid, paralyzed in both legs was dragged over the snow covered Alps. He got as far as Valence where he died. A conclave met in Venice in a place set aside by the Holy Roman Emperor who hoped to obtain a pontiff agreeable to himself. In 1800 Pius VII was elected but this choice did not please the emperor who refused to let him be crowned in Venice or pass through northern Italy to Rome. The new pope had to travel by slow boat where four months later he entered Rome.

NAPOLEON

Meanwhile the ruling Directory of the Revolutionary Government in France had been overthrown by one of its generals, Napoleon. He became France's dictator or First Counsel. More than anyone else by his European conquests he spread the ideals of the French Revolution[6] over the Europe he conquered. The whole feudal system and the classes of society on which medieval Christianity rested were permanently swept away under him. Even when he fell from power other countries took up those ideals and fanned the liberalism that would be so threatening to the papacy. For the present, however, Napoleon had to deal with the Church. One of his first acts was to allow the Romanist priests full freedom in religion. Napoleon knew the depth of Catholicism and saw that the persecution of the Church was a source of internal weakness. He must therefore reestablish the Catholic Church to fulfill his own ambitions. His own cynical frame of mind was summed up in his words: "My political method is to govern men as the majority of them want to be governed. That, I think, is the way to recognize the sovereignty of the people. It was by making myself a Catholic that I won the war in the Vendee, by making myself a Moslem that I established myself in Egypt, by making myself an Ultramontane that I gained men's souls in Italy. If I were governing a people of the Jewish race I would rebuild the Temple of Solomon."

At the beginning Napoleon quieted down the anticlericals of northern Italy.[7] Next, he had to settle with the new pope, Pius VII. Pius was ready enough to yield on the material property of the Church: he wrote it off as a loss in France, but in matters spiritual he proved difficult. His famous and notable minister of state was Cardinal Consalvi who had to work with the redoubtable Talleyrand, Napoleon's minister of state. The result of their negotiations was the famous Concordat of 1801 (which lasted till 1905). The Catholic religion, while not the state religion, was allowed to be practiced openly but with some government regulation. All new bishops were to be nominated (and the old ones had to resign) by Napoleon but the bishops were to be invested only by the pope who had the option to invest them or *refuse* to do so and who even afterwards could depose them. We must take note of the grand novelty here. For the first time in the Church's history there was no state intermediary. The pope and the pope alone could invest or refuse to invest bishops. He and he alone could depose them. No governmental intervention was to be a part of this. We can see that this gave the death blow to Gallicanism in France and its equivalent elsewhere when this Concordat was copied by other countries.

By this Concordat of 1801 a different Church came into being (the one modern Catholics know). The bishops were no longer to be allied with the government. The negotiating party was the bishop and the pope and his curia as in the United States today. Henceforth there was no other authority in religious matters than Rome. Local hierarchies were discounted as they now had to look to Rome, not to the government, as had been done since Constantine. We recall that always the ruler had rights over the episcopacy: Constantine, Charlemagne, the Ottos, Henry IV and Louis XIV. Even when Gregory VII humiliated Henry IV at Canossa and won the right to invest bishops he still had to invest those bishops nominated and approved by the king. Even in the great centralization move under Innocent III and the other jurist popes the national rulers rewarded their loyal followers with the bishopric. Now the bishops were directly under the pope. He was their superior, not one among equals with special privileges. He could even deprive them of their office. All state mediation had been revoked. Surely this was one great triumph for the pope's able secretary, Cardinal Consalvi, who participated in the Concordat. He surely knew that in fighting for an international centralized papacy he was bucking the trend towards separate national independent states, yet he felt that local nation churches were too much of a danger for the Catholic Church.

The rest of the Concordat stipulated that the lower clergy were to be nominated by the bishops. No longer were priests to be presented for ordination by lay sponsors. This too tightened up the chain of power right up to the pope. As historian E. E. Y. Hales puts it so well:

> One result of lasting consequence to the Church in Europe, and ultimately to the whole world, which flowed from the reorganization involved in the Concordat, was the appear-

ance of a new centralization within the Church itself. No longer were the lesser clergy nominated by private patrons, they were nominated by the bishops, and any promotions they gained they would owe to those same bishops. . . . This strictly hierarchical organization which is characteristic of the Church today, is doubtless now a source of strength; but it is interesting and perhaps significant to notice that, in its modern form, it dates from the Napoleonic Concordat with Pius VII, and that it owes something, at least, to Napoleon's determination not to allow too much independence to the local curés [parish priests]. For he knew very well that the curés, in 1789, had launched the Revolution.[8]

Finally, by the terms of the Concordat, churches and cathedrals were to be restored and the state was to pay clerical salaries (which was not to the pope's liking). Thus the Constitutional Church of the Revolution disappeared. Napoleon chose not only most of the old Romanists to be bishops but also a big minority of Constitutionalists. There was some bitterness among the exiled bishops which caused something of a schism since they would not deal with an "anti-Christ" Revolutionary like Napoleon. The Concordat which was destined to be copied by many another country helped put the Church back on its feet again not only in France but in its dependencies such as Belgium, the Rhineland and part of Germany and Italy. The Concordat showed, moreover, that the Church need not be tied to the old regime but could survive under Napoleon or any form of government if it were left alone.

Yet, Napoleon was minded to get concessions. Unbeknown to the pope he published with the Concordat the "Organic Articles" which in effect were designed to regulate the affairs of the Church in the spirit of Gallicanism (which incidentally, he made mandatory in all the schools and seminaries in France). Napoleon insisted on one liturgy and one catechism and no feast days and a civil ceremony prior to the church wedding. On the other hand, Napoleon was so pragmatic, so concerned that the Church should teach obedience to the state that it was to his advantage to see that it was efficient. Napoleon even forced the Constitutional clergy to make their obedience to Rome.

NAPOLEON AND PIUS VII

In 1804 Napoleon was given a new title of Emperor (a title not likely to please the other rulers) and wanted the pope to come to Paris to crown him. The pope was in a bind. Such an act would be an affront to the legitimate Bourbon king in exile, Louis XVIII, not to mention the insult to the Holy Roman Emperor. Nor did he much like to give the crown to France which had just handed the Church such persecution. Cardinal Consalvi felt however that there would be more advantages in going so the pope started out. In the forest of Fontainebleau he was "accidentally" met by the hunting Napoleon which was Napoleon's way of paying the pope homage in private rather than in the public limelight of Paris. At Notre Dame cathedral Napoleon, who had just quickly married Josephine in a religious ceremony (there had only been a civil one) and who would not go to confession or receive Communion refused to receive the crown from the pope but placed it on his own head.

Despite criticism, the pope's going to France was a measurable success. The people in the streets of Paris pressed in on him with unbounded adulation. His visit helped the French to look once more to Rome. He helped show that he was not tied to the old regime. But then real friction came in. Napoleon on his own instituted the feast of St. Napoleon (a doubtfully authentic saint). He rewrote the catechism inserting his name frequently as the object of loving obedience and veneration for the school children. The last straw was that as he began to conquer all of Europe he made himself King of Italy, kept the northern papal states and wanted the pope to close the shipping ports of the remaining papal states to the British (he was trying to starve out the British during his war with them). The pope refused and even asked for his northern papal states back. In 1809 Napoleon simply confiscated the pope's territories and a general arrested the pope and snatched him away. For forty-two days the pope traveled and arrived at Savona. He was a prisoner and Napoleon did not allow him communication with the outside world. But the pope had a trump card. It was necessary that he invest the newly appointed bishops in their sees and he refused to do so. Pius was cajoled, threatened, drugged, but he held out. And this encouraged the clergy. In 1812 Napoleon had the pope removed to a prison in Fontainebleau (south of Paris). During this secret journey the pope almost died. He was to stay there while Napoleon made short work of the Russians and then come back to deal with the pope. But Napoleon came back in defeat with his remnant army disbanded. He had to raise a new army. He needed a settlement with the Church and sent envoys to the pope. Then Napoleon himself went to see the prisoner and he stayed six days. No one knows what passed between them. There were rumors of hair pulling and dish smashing. In any case the pope agreed to invest the bishops in return for his freedom to exercise his powers in France. Napoleon abused the concession, gave out a new concordat and the pope promptly issued a denial. Napoleon imprisoned him once more. But within two years Napoleon was defeated and the Bourbon king, Louis XVIII was restored. The pope was driven in triumph to Rome at the very moment Napoleon was being secretly driven to his exile in Elba. Yet, even after all of the indignities done to him the pope wrote on Napoleon's behalf asking consideration and easement of his trials on Elba. Napoleon died on May 5, 1821 on the isle of St. Helena. There is a story that he was slowly poisoned by his jailer. With supreme illogic the French soon forgot his ambitions, the devastation of property and the enormous loss of life he wrought all over Europe. His memory soon became the "Napoleonic Legend" and this legend soon became powerful enough among Frenchmen to seat another Bonaparte on the French throne in the future.

AFTER NAPOLEON

A new spirit of liberalism had been unleashed by the French Revolution and spread by Napoleon. Liberty, Equality and Justice, although much abused during the past years, were potent forces which were abolishing class distinction and opening the way towards a new democracy. Between the years 1815 and 1870 the Church was in a position to adopt these more liberal tenets and to harmonize her old policies with them. That the Church did not do so has brought it considerable chastisement from future historians. Yet the context of the times did not warrant such a move. Rome, in 1815, was besieged with so many problems, so much devastating aftermath of the Revolution that it was looking for stability and peace in order to find solutions to many problems. For one thing, since Pius VII was in prison for five years a large number of sees throughout France and its dependencies were vacant because he had withheld his approval. The pope's cabinet, the Curia, could not exercise many ordinary duties since the ecclesiastical archives had been removed from Rome to Paris. Then after Napoleon in the Peace of Vienna many territorial adjustments were made which vexed Rome. The traditional Catholic Rhineland fell into the hands of Protestant Prussia as did parts of Catholic Poland. In Italy a general was trying to build a kingdom south of Rome while Catholic Austria (under conservative Chancellor Metternich) had occupied the northern papal states to keep an eye on the south. Revolutionary forces were throwing out not only Spanish rule in South America but the Catholic Church associated with it as well. Rome was in no mood to embrace liberal ideas. Conservatism reigned there as it did politically in Russia, Austria, Sweden and Holland which extolled "law and order" governments.

Besides the political preoccupations of the time there were the spiritual. Monasteries had to be reopened. Religious orders had to be restored. Influenced by his new secretary—Napoleon had Cardinal Consalvi dismissed from that job because he refused to be present at Napoleon's second marriage (he was reinstated after Napoleon's fall)—Pius VII restored the Jesuits in 1814. Seminaries had to be renewed. War had taken a fearful loss of young men and there was a severe shortage of priests. With all of these things on his mind, the pope tended to deal with the old monarchies, the old regime, at the Congress of Vienna. Rome by no means gave sanction to such monarchies in principle. It remained neutral. Yet for the life of the Church to resume law and order had to be reestablished. To many people and to the Church the horrors and excesses of the revolutionary forces underscored the need for the old traditional monarchies as the restorers of stability. The Church, of course, was under no illusion. It had suffered a great deal from the kings but was inclined to feel that they were not as dangerous as the revolutionaries. This prevailing attitude brought back the Bourbons to France and Spain and other princes elsewhere.

It was with these monarchs that the pope through Cardinal Consalvi had to deal at the Congress of Vienna.

CONSALVI AND THE PAPAL STATES

Rome made no attempt to recover its properties confiscated all over Europe during the Revolution and Napoleonic era; it only insisted on recovering its own papal states. Most of them, thanks to Consalvi, were restored and were allowed to keep some of the reforming changes in administration introduced by Napoleon when he held them. Consalvi, the most able diplomat of the time (even beyond the astute Talleyrand) had no position of strength to bargain from except the almost universal admiration for Pius VII who had withstood Napoleon and whose integrity and strict neutrality induced the other great Powers at the Congress of Vienna to restore the papal states to him. But this was not solely due to admiration. The restoration of the papal states was more due to mutual jealousies and fear among the great powers. Neither the British nor the French wanted Austria or each other to get the papal states and it was therefore due to their insistence and diplomacy that they were returned to the neutral pope. We shall see shortly how the papal states became a severe bone of contention when the liberals wanted to unite Italy. It is pointed out here that this problem had its immediate origin, not in papal domination, but in European politics which restored the papal states to the pope as the lesser evil.

There were compelling reasons at the time why Consalvi wanted the papal states. For one thing the northern papal states were an economic necessity if the pope's office was to function. Another thing was that Austria already had taken over Venice and Milan and controlled other duchies.

Since the pope was not ready to get out from under France only to fall into the hands of Austria, possession of the papal states seemed the best protection at the time. Yet we say, "at the time" for we have observed before that increasingly the papal states were more a hindrance than a help. When Pepin had given the pope these lands it was a necessity for it gave the pope some temporal independence from warring barbarians in Italy. The papal states were a good buffer for subsequent encroachments as well. Yet by the fifteenth and sixteenth centuries, as we have seen, these states became a liability. They kept the popes in the role of Italian sovereigns rather than spiritual leaders. It made them Italian princes involved in Italian politics and thus confined their truly catholic view. As new nations arose and took over Europe the papal states had even less value as a source of protection and independence for we have seen how easily the major powers or dictators could take them over. It would have been better had the pope surrendered them before they were wrenched out of his hand by Italian patriots in the 1870s. But this is hindsight. For the reason given above Consalvi felt that the keeping of the papal states at the moment was of an advantage to the papacy.

ROME'S ANTILIBERALISM

We have noted how the kings and the Church tended to become suspicious of liberalism. To them it meant havoc and excess, political and religious upheaval. The result was, as far as the Church was concerned, that where liberal movements and liberal revolutions took place, they did so without the approval of the Church. And at this time there were several countries where Catholics and liberals got together to throw off the government or obtain freedom. Still, Rome disapproved and even opposed them. England, for example. What had happened there was that by 1800 Ireland and England were joined, the Parliament of Dublin was dissolved and the Irish members could sit at Westminster. The king however insisted on privileges over the Irish Catholic Church since he was supreme head of the English Church. He wanted to be able to veto clerical appointments and censor communications with Rome. The British Catholics were ready to accept this but not the Irish Catholics. They, led by Daniel O'Connell, did not want their Church subjected to a Protestant Parliament which had so long oppressed them. O'Connell therefore waged a successful nonviolent campaign, got elected to Westminster, despite his ineligibility as a Catholic and got a seat in Parliament. The government gave in and in 1829 removed all the disabilities which had prevented Catholics from taking part in public life. There was here a great victory for the Church from this alliance of Catholics and liberals but the victory was achieved without cooperation from Rome.

The same thing happened in the Netherlands where Catholics and liberals fought side by side to obtain freedom. The Church not only did not cooperate but even negotiated with the opposition. What had happened was that Belgium with a great Catholic majority was joined to Protestant Holland under the kingship of a Protestant king who proceeded to discriminate against his Catholic subjects. The liberals and the clergy joined forces to effect the revolution of 1830 by which Belgium gained its independence.

Poland was another example—the most notorious—of papal rejection of a liberal cause. For years the Poles, thanks to the Jesuits, had remained Catholic. But Poland was partitioned among the powers of Europe: Prussia, Austria and Russia. In 1825 Czar Nicholas I wanted to unite his territories into one land with one sovereign, one law and one faith. He abolished the Greek churches in union with Rome and tried to bring the Polish Catholic Church into the Greek Orthodox camp. He intercepted the pope's letters. Yet, in the face of all of this, everyone was astounded when the pope during the Polish revolt against the Czar in 1830 counseled the Polish clergy to tell their people to submit to Russia. After the Czar crushed the Polish revolt the pope sent a letter to the bishops urging their submission to legitimate authority. Liberals everywhere were dismayed at the pope's lack of support for the oppressed Catholic Poles and his support for the absolutist policies of the Czar. Rome had failed to assist the Catholics in England, Belgium and Poland. It cast a pall over the whole democratic and liberal movement.

Because Rome was so hostile or indifferent to democratic liberal ideals the Church soon ceased to be a formative influence on the age. The Church was reduced to upholding the old order of things and producing citizens obedient to the lawful monarch. This was the sort of attitude that led to a certain passivity, made the Church a useful tool of despotic kings and occasioned Karl Marx's famous remark that religion is the opium of the people. We might mention here also that this political conservatism of the Church had its counterpart with theological conservatism. We must remember that with the Enlightenment and the wars the religious orders had suffered a great deal and Catholic or papal universities had been replaced by state universities. This meant that manpower was short and that the formal teaching of theology would be relegated to isolated seminaries separated from the larger intellectual communities much to the harm of the Church. The defects of an isolated religious training apart from the university led to the great efforts of Cardinal Newman of England to found a Catholic university and to the achievement of the bishops of America to establish one in Washington, D.C.

In any case, the net effect was that Rome cut itself off from the intellectual influences of other countries like Germany, England and Holland and fell back onto the most sterile area of theology, Italy. Such political and theological conservatism led succeeding ages to issue a long series of condemnations, excommunications and the suppression of various theological schools. The newly shored up papacy became the sole arbiter of what was theologically correct (in a departure from the ages where theological ideas were freely exchanged) and all unfamiliar thinking was uprooted. Or perhaps it would be more true to say, driven underground only to reappear in Modernism (which we shall see shortly) and in the notions of Vatican II.

RELIGIOUS REVIVAL

In spite of the severe efforts to eradicate religion during the French Revolution there was a revival of religion. In spite of the frankly antireligious onslaught of the Revolution in France, in spite of the attempts at control of the Church in places like Austria and Germany, in spite of the fact that the Enlightenment had infected the upper class prelates, religion revived or rather, in the hearts of the masses of people, remained as strong as ever. Many clergy, after all, had met death with honor and heroism. There were those who denied the old religion but there were also those like the Abbe Pinot who mounted the scaffold like a priest going to the altar in his vestments and saying "I will go unto the altar of God." The masses celebrated in secret, the devotion of the Romanist clergy went far to give religion a great deal of prestige. Since the Revolution was the outcome of the

Enlightenment many people had second thoughts. Many recovered their faith in Christianity. Those classes of people we call the Romantics were inspired by a new spiritual revolution. They all turned in admiration to medieval Catholicism and its great unifying role. Many of these romantics such as the Schlegels, Clemens, Brentano and others found their spiritual home in the Catholic Church. The greatest orator of the time, the Dominican Lacordaire gave his dramatic sermons extolling Catholicism because of its social and moral contributions to civilization and thousands who had lost their faith, such as the aging Talleyrand, returned to the Catholic faith.[9]

Along with this religious revival and this desire to return to the traditions of the Church was the attempt, made by such men as Lacordaire, to reconcile the modern liberties with the Church in spite of the papacy's conservative reaction. There were those, in fact, who looked to the papacy itself as the one stable guardian of both orthodoxy and political stability (remember, for example that the Jansenists and the Reform Catholics were allied in changing the Church). It was clearly shown that nothing could succeed unless the popes were for it. The papacy came to be seen as a force in international order. Some went so far as to feel that if any government from now on were to succeed there must be a union of Church and state but with the papacy dominant. Such were the super-ultramontanes.

LAMENNAIS

Among the super-ultramontanes was a famous name, the Abbe Lamennais. He was an upholder of papal centralization and hostile to the resurgence of Gallicanism in France. On the other hand he saw that the ideas of the French Revolution though tarnished were not disappearing. He also observed that the monarchy to which the Church was hitching itself was only another form of despotism. The Church, he held, should be free of any state association. Then, as Lamennais witnessed the struggles of the Irish, the Belgians and the Poles he began to be converted to democracy and carried his ideas further. In 1819 he called on the Church to ally itself with all peoples striving for independence for the Church would flourish better in a liberal social order. The pope therefore should not engage in concordats with kings but put his faith in the people directly. In his celebrated phrase there should be a "free Church in a free state."

In 1830 he began his little review *L'Avenir* the most important Catholic journal of the century (though it lasted only a year). He advocated freedom of conscience, religious worship, instruction, opinion, open assembly and popular elections. He was enamoured of what was happening at that very moment in the United States. There there was no connection between church and state. In fact, because there were so many competing Protestant churches the United States forbade any established church. So, argued Lamennais, let it be in Europe. Let all churches compete privately for men's allegiance. Let them run their own affairs free of the government.

Lamennais, who was highly thought of by some in Rome, felt that if he could get to speak with the pope he would listen and embrace his teaching. But Lamennais, of course, had his enemies. And then there was the pope. Pope Gregory XVI was an honest, reactionary, conservative monk who ran the Church like an Abbot ran his monastery. He was the pope who disliked trains, who failed to back the English and Belgian Catholics and who backed the Russians against the Catholic Poles. He was perhaps willing to concede to

America the things Lamennais said but in America there was no Gallicanism, no prior traditions to state interference. He could not see the same arrangement in Europe. Gregory, an advocate of strict, hierarchical obedience was not about to give credence to wild revolutionary statements like "power to the people." Anyway, Lamennais and his two famous companions, Montalembert and Lacordaire, went to Rome but were coolly received. He had a polite audience with the pope, left Rome in 1832 not expecting approval right away but not expecting condemnation either.

Lamennais was stunned when the pope issued the encyclical *Mirari Vos* condemning out and out his teachings. There were words such as these: "From this poisonous spring of indifferentism has also flowed that absurd and erroneous doctrine or rather, the delirium, that freedom of conscience is to be claimed and defended by all men." In 1834, at the time when his contemporary countrymen, the Cure of Ars was drawing souls to God and Bernadette Soubirous was beginning her visions at Lourdes, another encyclical came out condemning liberal ideas. Lamennais lost faith in Rome. He left the priesthood and the Church. He died in 1852, bitter, unreconciled to the Church and so poor that he was buried in an unmarked pauper's grave. Thus had Rome laid the groundwork for the even more antiliberal *Syllabus of Errors* of Pius IX and the road to the Catholic ghetto.

It goes without saying that Lamennais' ideas are acceptable today and indeed that most countries run on them. Yet they were too novel for the pope who, like most of his contemporaries, Catholic and Protestant, could not conceive of a government by the people, a free press, toleration and the disestablishment of the church and state. Unfortunately, in condemning democratic ideas Pope Gregory used such strong language that he offended even those well disposed to the Church. As for those hostile to the Church, it only made them make the association of liberal with anticlerical. To fight for freedom was automatically to be against the Church. No wonder that the Church would have to wait a long time to shake off the image of being friend to tyranny and foe to freedom. Only with Pope Leo XIII (d. 1903) and Pius XII (d. 1958) would the papacy begin to understand and espouse, very cautiously to be sure, the social and scientific problems of the time. Only with Vatican II would it officially and openly embrace the liberal aspirations of mankind.

On the other hand, the Church would remain a cautionary force against tyranny in the name of revolution and reason. The Church would be wary of any system that merely substituted one repression for another, that would denigrate religion as peripheral. If the inner moral persuasion of man is not motivated by religion then he must be manipulated by external forces. This is why external control and conformity become primary objectives of totalitarian governments. Any government that tries to make religion absent (as in the Soviet Union) or practically irrelevant (as in the United States) must necessarily resort to more control by force (as in the Soviet Union) or manipulation (as in the United States). Arnold Toynbee says of the era we have just covered: "The Revolution's supreme paradox was that, in the act of deposing the traditional Christian 'Establishment,' it opened the way for an atavistic return to pre-Christian religion: the worship of collective human power which had been the religion of the pagan Roman Empire and of the Greek city-states which the Roman Empire had incorporated. This worship of human power is about ninety per cent of the religion of about ninety per cent of the present generation of mankind. Shall we succeed in shaking it off? And, if we remain enslaved to it, whither will it lead us?. . . ."[10]

NOTES

1. Actually the American Revolution was inspired not by constitutional questions, but by commercial and capitalist considerations. The original quarrel began over taxations, over the fear of losing the frontiers gained by the Yankees and others to the British crown. There was not an especial fervor for the "Rights of Man." Witness the tarring and featherings, the rank discrimination against minority groups, mob rule. We forget that the liberal and cultured life of Jefferson at Monticello and of Washington at Mount Vernon was made possible by the existence of Negro slavery. It was only later that the myth of humanity and the rights of all men got intertwined into the American Revolution and became a source of admiration to the French. Its real origins rest in the commercial and capitalistic desires of the average man.
2. One of the things that makes the French Revolution so difficult to unravel is the great number of names that flit off and on stage, as it were, and disappear without a trace. The reason is that for about ten years there were no great men, except perhaps Robespierre. There were no leaders except the self-seeking opportunists. Then of course, as we shall see, they got a leader in 1798—with a vengeance: Napoleon.
3. Christopher Dawson, *The Gods of Revolution*, p. 63.
4. Carlton J. H. Hayes, *op. cit.*, p. 612.
5. E. E. Y. Hales, *The Catholic Church in the Modern World*, p. 50 Hanover House, Garden City, New York. 1958.
6. It deserves more than a footnote, but Napoleon terminated the Holy Roman Empire. In July of 1806 he cleaned up the feudal remains of some more than 303 independent sections of Germany. He consolidated them into 38 sections, into the federation of the Rhine. From the Church's point of view this left only five bishops and there was the imminent danger of a National German Church forming. This never materialized due to the efforts of men like the Redemptorist priest, St. Clement Hofbauer.
7. In France itself Napoleon reformed the legal system, patronized the arts and improved education. His colonial enterprises were not too successful. He unloaded the "Louisiana Purchase" on the

United States in 1803 because of his imminent war with England. He repressed his critics and royalists and killed the young Bourbon prince.

8. E. E. Y. Hales, *op. cit.*, p. 62.
9. This new apologetic, of seeing in Catholicism the preserver of civilization and being capable of assuming the new liberal ideals was taken up by the famous writers, Chesterton and Belloc.
10. Introduction to Dawson, *op. cit.*, p. xx.

XIX

The Age of Pius IX

LIBERAL TO CONSERVATIVE

In 1846 the ultra conservative Pope Gregory XVI died. A compromise candidate was elected, a young man of thirty-four who was destined to have the longest reign in the history of the popes. This man was Pius IX[1], and he it was, as we shall see, who set the tone for the Church until modern times and gave the image of the papacy that the modern Catholic knows. Pius was a man of much personal charm though of no great intellect. He was also a home grown product in that he had never been outside the papal states but once. This drawback, as it would turn out, did not prepare him well to deal with the world problems unleashed by the French Revolution that confronted him.

At the beginning there was promise. He became the instant darling of the liberals by granting amnesty to thousands of his predecessor's exiled enemies. He even lit the streets of Rome with gas and displayed many other liberal trends. His name was on everyone's lips. Now the big question was whether Pius would show such a liberal spirit in politics. There were several revolutions in the making, not the least of which was the one in Italy itself. We might recall that the conservative Austrians had stationed themselves in the northern papal states to offset the liberal revolutionary forces in southern Italy. Which group would the pope back? At first the pope seemed to side with the liberals for he set up a form of representative government right in his own papal states. This alarmed the conservative Austrian chancellor Metternich who occupied another papal state, but the pope forced him to withdraw. For this papal act the liberals' admiration knew no bounds and Catholics and Protestants alike heaped praise on the pontiff. But not for long.

Pius IX granted other liberties in the papal states and even gave to Rome its own elective government, freedom of the press and a constitution with the power to veto his own proposals. This last step went a bit beyond where he wanted to go in temporal matters and put him in a dilemma. Suppose, for example, that the papal states voted to oust Austria altogether? Could the pope go along? If he did, could he thereby condone the inevitable war between his Catholic children? Could he afford to support a war against his prime mainstay, his protector in time of crisis? This was the dilemma that broke Pius' liberal image. He refused, as he had to, to bless any popular liberal cause against the Austrians. He was immediately booed by the liberals everywhere and his huge popularity dwindled as quickly as it had arisen. When in fact an invading army had been routed by the Austrians the pope's lack of support was blamed for the defeat.

PREMATURE ITALIAN REVOLUTION

Reaction to the pope showed itself in more and more liberal demands by the Romans. A series of Roman leaders could not bridge the growing gap between papacy and the city. Unfortunately the one leader moderate enough to please both pope and the Romans was murdered by Italian army volunteers, an event which did not seem to concern the Romans much. This was the end of the rapport between pope and liberals. Before long tension reached a point where a mob surrounded the pope's palace. On November 24, 1848, dressed as a simple priest he escaped to southern Italy (near Naples). In his absence a new assembly in Rome summoned Europe's leading revolutionary, the non-Roman and anti-clerical Mazzini and one of the world's great guerilla leaders, Garibaldi. Pius called for assistance. At first the Catholic powers were slow to move (mired in old jealousies and competition) but finally Louis Napoleon of France ousted Mazzini. Pius was restored to Rome in 1850 and it can be imagined that he wanted no more representative government in his states. This, unfortunately, was Pius' personal experience with liberal politics. Equally unfortunately he had to deal not just with liberals but the most extreme kind who were anticlerical and ". . . it is hard to believe that he could have collaborated for long with the more extreme Italian liberals like Mazzini and Garibaldi. Their religious positions were irreconcilable, and Pio Nono was above all a man of religion."[2] The net effect was to make Pius forever suspicious of liberalism. He did not condemn it as such but he had become scared of what he saw. Under the influence of his ultra conservative secretaries of state such as Lambruschini and Cardinal Antonelli Pius came to see nothing good in any liberal Catholic movement.

THE PROTESTANT COUNTRIES

We have already noted how through the efforts of Daniel O'Connell of Ireland a Catholic Emancipation Act was passed in England in 1829 removing most of the political disabilities for Catholics. Irish emigration continued to flood England. The time came to consider the restoration of the Catholic hierarchy there (for Catholic England had been a "missionary" country ruled by Apostolic Vicars). Most agreeably to England Pius IX in 1848 was preparing for such a restoration when the Italian Revolution broke out. When later in 1850 Pius sought to resume negotiations regarding England he met an entirely different mood. Because of the suppression of the Roman revolution Pius was now detested by Englishmen as a tyrant. All the old hatreds of the "foreign and immoral" pope nourished during the days of the Reformation revived. It was the least happy moment to think of restoring the Catholic hierarchy. Riots broke out in England. Pius was burned in effigy. Galling restrictions were placed on the proposed Catholic restoration. The pope, for example, could not choose dioceses which were already Anglican. It was very bitter for English Catholics to forego historical places like Canterbury, York, Lincoln and Salisbury which played significant parts in Catholic medieval history. Saints names and titles already used by the Anglicans could not be used by the Catholics. Catholic public processions were banned and the clergy could not wear their clerical clothes in public. Yet, in spite of all these restrictions (many of which were soon not enforced) the Catholic hierarchy was restored. Cardinal Wiseman was made its leader and slow but steady Catholic progress was made.

The same routine occurred in Holland where Pius restored the hierarchy there in 1853. Again there were the outrages against Catholics which even toppled the local government, but in time affairs settled down. The same was true in Prussia where the Church was permitted freedom. In fact, it turned out that the Church was freer to fulfill her mission in Protestant Holland, England and Prussia than in the

Catholic countries especially in Hapsburg Austria and Gallican France.

IMMACULATE CONCEPTION

When Pius IX returned from exile in 1850 he attributed his restoration to the intercession of the Blessed Mother to whom he always had a great devotion. He was therefore disposed to listen to the petition both from the people and from his theological commission to define her Immaculate Conception. While in exile he had asked the bishops for their advice and the replies were favorable. On December 8, 1854 the dogma was proclaimed. Devotion to Mary thereby received a great spur. Less than a hundred years later another pope, Pius XII (1950) would proclaim the doctrine of the Assumption. Yet, the interesting thing with Pius IX was that he acted on his own authority in proclaiming the Immaculate Conception even though he consulted the bishops. Alone he proclaimed the dogma. This had the effect of giving a certain elevation to his authority. The proclamation of the dogma of infallibility some twenty years later was the logical heir to what he did in 1854.

LOSS OF THE PAPAL STATES

Despite the premature revolution of 1848 in Italy the liberal spirit still flourished though to the pope liberalism was now equated with rebellion. The liberal spirit found its nationalistic outlet in the Risorgimento or the movement for the unification of all Italy. Naturally this implied the absorption of the papal states and the end of the Church's control of education, marriage and the abolition of all monasteries. All eyes were turned towards the state of Piedmont whose leader, Victor Emmanuel II, had an army which might be able to expel the Austrians. Pius IX might have gone along with a program of Italian unification for he had urged Austria to leave Italy provided that the Church would be left in peace. But there was every indication that the government of Piedmont was anticlerical. In its own territory it had abolished Church courts, feast days, clerical immunities and the like. Under the very able minister, Cavour, a proposal was made to suppress monasteries not engaged in "useful" work. What upset the pope was that there were no negotiations on these Church matters; they were done unilaterally and portended a further anticlerical policy.

We mentioned that unification implied the absorption of the papal states. Actually, some of the papal states in the north had had a taste of the better, more democratic and more efficient government of Napoleon. They were not happy to be back under the old antiquated regime of the pope. The educated classes resented that Canon Law had weight in civil matters and that the courts might impose fines and even imprisonment for eating meat on Fridays. Such states were already on the edge of revolt. Most of the papal states were run poorly, though not as badly as current propaganda made out. The pope tended to look on them as his little papal family. There were initially some attempts to find an honorable place in any Italian confederation for the papacy but Lambruschini and Antonelli blocked any attempts to reform the economic and political situation and would not hear of the papal states being incorporated into the Italian confederation.

In July of 1858 a secret meeting was held between Cavour and Napoleon III to liquidate the papal states. Together they did manage to drive out the Austrians. The vacuum let the northern papal states invite Victor Emmanuel in to take over—which he gladly did and Napoleon, with some misgivings, allowed. The pope saw that obviously he could no longer rely on Austria or France to protect his property. He decided to raise his own international army in spite of the protest of his secretary of state, Antonelli, who saw this as a move which would annoy France. True France allowed a take over of the northern papal states but had no intention of letting Rome fall to the nationalists; and Antonelli did not want France to feel the pope's loss of confidence.

In 1860 Garibaldi arrived in Sicily and advanced to Naples. Cavour did not want Garibaldi to advance too far or to make all of Italy his republic so with his Piedmontese troops he headed south to forestall him. To go south he had to invade the papal states, "to restore order" as he put it. The international papal army was soon routed and the papal territory was reduced to a little strip of land. So far France had stood by but was still determined not to let Rome fall. Yet, as we shall see, France was engaged in war with Germany and was forced to withdraw her troops from Italy. The Piedmontese army thus entered Rome and the papal states disappeared forever. The new government went out of its way to be respectful of the pope. It was seeking recognition from abroad and could not afford to estrange the Catholics in Italy and elsewhere. The pope was given the rights of a sovereign and could maintain his own postal and diplomatic services. In hindsight, the pope was best rid of his temporal territories which had sapped the time and energy of many popes in past centuries. But to Pius IX it was a disaster and one which he must protest. He made himself a voluntary prisoner of the Vatican refusing to recognize the new government.

THE SYLLABUS OF ERRORS (1864)

To understand the disastrous Syllabus we must remember that the pope just lost the papal states to forces who felt that they were doing what they did in the name of progress, liberalism and civilization. The same catch words were being used by revolutionaries in France and elsewhere. The pope and his advisors came to see political issues in black and white. To them to be a liberal was to be anti-Church—and this in spite of the fact that some liberals were quite good churchmen such as Prime Minister Gladstone of England (a devout Anglican) and the Italian author Manzoni who wrote the most famous novel of the time, *The Betrothed.* But for Pius reaction to liberalism (as he understood it) was elevated to a theological principle and in the Syllabus issued in 1864 he condemned a whole hodgepodge of theological and political statements. Its eighty propositions condemned progress, liberalism and modern civilization. Most of the Syllabus was taken from previous encyclicals and therefore had to be read in their light (which few did). The Syllabus carried the signature of Antonelli, not Pius, but many thought that it was an infallible pronouncement even though Bishop Dupanloup tried to demonstrate it as a work to be seen within its Italian setting.

The Syllabus succeeded Gregory's *Mirari Vos* as the papacy's clearest rejection of the times. Its language was intemperate and couched in universal terms when in reality the pope was thinking of the local Italian scene. What were Protestants and Catholics to think of a pope who condemned liberalism, a free press, freedom of conscience, civil rights and even modern civilization? Prime Minister Gladstone and President Lincoln were perplexed to say the least. Those less favorable to the pope gave the Syllabus the widest publicity. In its context, as we have tried to point out, the Syllabus was not really that bad but few knew of the context and the effect was disastrous. Lamennais' old friends in France, Lacordaire and Montalembert, were disturbed and the Syllabus led Montalembert to end his campaign (which he shared with Frederick Ozanam) for a "free Church in a free state."

The Syllabus also put the brakes on others in the Catholic intellectual movement and widened the split between Catholic conservatives and Catholic liberals. In Germany the great Catholic historian Dollinger was depressed and his famous pupil in England, Lord Acton, left the pursuit of Church work (not the Church as Dollinger finally did) and turned to secular history. The whole Catholic intellectual movement received a stunning blow from the Syllabus—although it must be added that it pleased the ultramontanes such as Louis Veullot, W. G. Ward (who said he would like an infallible encyclical every morning to read with his paper) and Cardinal Manning of England. In any case, the popular mind saw in the Syllabus an infallible teaching indicating that the Church was opposed to modern liberties. In this light it is easy to see why the campaign to promote papal infallibility raised such alarm. If the pope who had just condemned modern liberties and reasserted the superiority of the Church over the state was declared infallible, where would that leave modern governments and their subjects? Infallibility could only increase political tension.

VATICAN I

Even though the Piedmontese army was at Rome's gates the pope insisted in convening a General Council of the

Church. The previous council of Trent had to define its dogmas to counter another Christian alternative. Now, with the onslaughts of the Enlightenment, Christian revelation itself was being denied. The Church had to define itself anew for a new age. It had to look at its relationship to the state and the new democratic governments. Then, too, there was much agitation about papal authority and all kinds of talk, promoted by the ultramontanes, about papal infallibility. In fact, the conservative Jesuit weekly *La Civilta Cattolica* said that when the Fathers met at Vatican I papal infallibility would spontaneously be acclaimed and so would the Syllabus of Pius IX. The liberals were especially distressed with this linking of the disastrous Syllabus with infallibility making the latter seem like another bulwark against modern democracy. There were other things too that bothered the liberals. They disliked the very conservative tenor of the hasty dogmatic constitutions proposed for discussion. Even more, the liberal bishops disliked the contempt the conservatives had for Protestant thinkers. The liberal Crotian Bishop Joseph Strossmayer at one of the early sessions protested against attributing all of the Church's ills to Protestantism. He reminded his listerners that after all rationalism had found its home in Catholic France. Many Protestants had good will towards the Church he said. The conservative majority listening to this soft talk about Protestants became so noisy that order had to be called and Strossmayer warned to go easy on his praise of Protestants. The bishop defended his right to be heard but was shouted down with cries of "He is another Luther! Throw him out!"

This was the background when the large crowd of bishops and news correspondents descended on Rome. There were some 744 bishops attending one time or another in the Council's seven months existence and, thanks to modern travel, forty-six came from the United States. Among the various committees set up was the "Requests Committee" which provided for any free suggestions from the bishops not officially on the Council's agenda. It was through this committee that the unscheduled topic of papal infallibility was introduced. No one was really surprised for the subject was already highly charged and discussed before the Council ever met. There was as a result a strong pro-infallibility majority and a strong anti-infallibility minority at the Council. In fact, the topic was not only introduced but even pushed before the other topics in line to be discussed. The pope himself let it be known that he favored the subject and favored it from the ultramontane point of view. The secular press was making much copy out of the subject.

We mentioned the minority anti-infalliblists at the Council. We must remember that most of them were not opposed to the doctrine as such. They were alarmed over its inopportune timing. Some felt that it would set back Protestant-Catholic relations. The French bishops were against it because it was too proximate to the hard line Syllabus. The American bishops felt that any definition of papal infallibility would hinder conversions in the United States. The greatest thinker of the day, Cardinal Newman (who was not invited to the Council) rightly felt that any definition at this time was premature and unnecessary—and too much of a flag-waving sop to the ultramontanes. With his characteristic insight he wrote, ". . . What have we done to be treated as the faithful never were treated before? When has a definition *de fide* been a luxury of devotion and not a stern painful necessity? Why should an aggressive and insolent faction be allowed to 'make the heart of the just sad, whom the Lord hath not made sorrowful' ".[3] He was irritated because the ultramontanes were pushing the infallibility dogma for personal and political reasons. He felt that the ultramontanes would use infallibility to enforce the Syllabus and that, besides (in an insight used at Vatican II) the whole community of the Church should be consulted: "We do not move at railroad pace in theological matters even in the nineteenth century. We must be patient and that for two reasons, first in order to get at the truth, and next in order to carry others with us. The Church moves as a whole; it is not a mere philosophy, it is a communion."[4] Others felt that infallibility would be terribly misunderstood. It might imply mind-control by the pope, the abolition of all liberties, that all words from the pope, even the most off hand utterance, might be construed as infallible, etc. The German theologians thought the matter indefinable anyway and feared more Roman centralization. Some bishops were not impressed with the low level of the theological background of the Spanish and Italian bishops who were pro-infallibility. Dollinger, Newman, Lord Acton, Kettler (the founder of Catholic Social Action), Bishop Dupanloup, Montalembert, and other notables all opposed the definition. Ultramontanes like Cardinal Manning, Veullot, Ward, and others were for it. They and their sympathizers, particularly the ultramontane press, spread critical and inaccurate stories implying that those who were against the definition of papal infallibility were not quite good and loyal Catholics.

The debates on infallibility went on in May and June of 1870. Voices were raised over the fact that nothing was said about the power of the bishops; that each bishop was autonomous in his own diocese and his authority was derived from God and not the pope (which is the view held today). Pius IX disagreed and got the Council to declare that the pope had full power in jurisdiction all over the world—an important step in the further centralization of the papacy (though the bishops' role was to be taken up later: Vatican II as it turned out). Some of the minority bishops, some sixty of them, rather than embarrass the pope by voting negatively, left Rome before the day for voting came.

Finally the day arrived. It was July and a dark summer thunderstorm came up making St. Peter's so dark that the pope needed a candle to read the pronouncement on papal infallibility which had been overwhelmingly approved by the 535 bishops present. Only two voted "nay" and afterwards came forward to profess their belief. One was Bishop Fitzgerald of Little Rock, Arkansas. Later on the wits commented how the Little Rock submitted to the Big Rock. Meanwhile the Franco-Prussian war was getting serious. France, as we have seen, pulled its troops out of Rome. The Italian army moved in and Pius had to suspend the Council indefinitely. Vatican I had never been officially reassembled and in a sense Vatican II can be considered its termination.

The final decree on infallibility reads like this:

> The Roman Pontiff, when he speaks *ex cathedra,* that is, when exercising the office of pastor and teacher of all Christians, he defines with his supreme apostolic authority a doctrine concerning faith or morals to be held by the universal Church, through the divine assistance promised to him in St. Peter, is possessed of that infallibility with which the divine Redeemer willed his Church to be endowed in defining doctrine concerning faith and morals: and therefore such definitions of the Roman Pontiff are irreformable of themselves and not from the consent of the Church.

That last clause still causes difficulties but it was inserted at the last moment to be a death blow to conciliarism, not to imply that the pope could define something in opposition to the whole Church. We might note also that the definition of the pope's infallibility is linked to that of the Church's infallibility and that has never been defined.[5] People reacted differently. Once the definition was given, Cardinal Newman, for example accepted it and in his famous *Letter to the Duke of Norfolk* explained the definition satisfactorily to many. On the other hand the German Dollinger could not accept it. He resisted, was excommunicated and died outside the Church.

RESULTS OF THE DOGMA

Many trends, started before Vatican I, were confirmed as a result of the dogma of infallibility. For one thing, the old scholasticism in the spirit of St. Thomas had been revived by the Jesuits. After Vatican I this neoscholasticism not only became more conservative but also the dominant school. Other schools of theology were looked on with suspicion, especially the stimulating German schools. We might recall that after the destruction of the Catholic universities during the wars of religion joint Catholic-Protestant theological faculties were founded in the universities. Among these were Tubingen, founded by Drey and Mohler (modern theologian Hans Kung is from there), Munich which housed the greatest Catholic historian of the day, Dollinger, and Bonn. Such German experimentation and thought were considered too liberal by Rome which wanted to protect Catholic theologians from Protestant "contamination" (an attitude not entirely absent today). With chastisements from Pope Gregory XVI, Pius' predecessor and the pronouncement of papal infallibility such liberal German schools declined and the German conservative, neoscholastic schools were in the ascendancy. It was the same with liberal Catholic thought in France and England. The proclamation of infallibility was a victory for the neoscholastic conservative forces and

Thomism was on its way to becoming (as it did under Leo XIII) the "official" theological system of the Church until modern times. Intellectual vitality dried up and soon there were no intellectual links between the papacy and the liberal middle class. Rome alone became the source of theological decisions. No new theological trends could get off the ground without Rome's approval. This meant that the curia became more powerful for it was this official papal cabinet which often spoke in the pope's name. The curia was notoriously conservative and saw to it that no new theological experimentations were approved or honored. This attitude explains the theological explosion at Vatican II: a hundred years of repressed thoughts forced their way to the surface.

Politically, we have already noted how the papacy looked on any Catholic political party as potential national bodies which might separate themselves from Rome as the national hierarchies had done so often in the past. Rome always felt that Catholic liberals might join the state against itself. After Vatican I the liberals found themselves in a position of less influence than ever before. They witnessed their cherished dreams practically condemned by Rome (one result of the excesses of those ultramontanes who identified the Syllabus and infallibility). In such countries as France and Germany political issues could not help but involve Catholics, yet Rome did not and would not give any support to them. In Italy Catholics were forbidden to vote or take part in political life which left the vacuum for the anticlericals to fill. In Germany Bismarck's *Kulturkampf* tried to pry Catholics from Rome but only succeeded in creating a Catholic liberal party which Rome was forced to recognize. Neither France nor Belgium nor Germany could influence Rome on social questions and Rome retreated more and more into itself.

Rome—the pope and the curia—took on the aura of standing apart from the world, the last citadel of truth. It thus backed the old kingships and frowned on any social reforms as being suspect. Catholic liberal reformers such as Buchez in France (the father of French trade unionism), Gorres in Germany, etc. had to go it alone. So while some Catholics were working hard for social reform and democracy, most Catholics, because of the attitude of the papacy, withdrew from the field. In such isolation no one could really impress on Rome the real problems in the Church. The Church's image became that of the closed corporation, one hostile to democratic freedom and to the world at large. Pius placed the Church in the ghetto and it was not until Pope John XXIII that it emerged.

CULT OF THE POPES

Among Catholics Pius IX enjoyed great prestige. He was admired for being persecuted by the Italian liberals. He was a man of great personal charm. He represented to the ultramontanes the one stabilizing force in Europe after the excesses of the French Revolution and Napoleon. Extremists began to look on him as almost an eighth sacrament. The Jesuits in their conservative newspaper would describe the pope in such bold words: ". . . treasures of revelation, treasures of truth, treasures of justice, treasures of charismata, coming from God are deposited on earth in the hands of a man, who is their sole dispenser and guardian . . . this man is the pope . . . and in respect to us he would seem to be Christ, if he were himself and visibly here below to govern the Church."

After Vatican I the mystique of the pope grew even more. Groups were dedicated to his cause. The revival of Peter's

Pence gave him financial independence. The almost mystical awe that modern Catholics associate with the pope began with Pius IX. He was accessible to all. He was the first pope to give many audiences to groups and individuals. He introduced the *ad limina* or regular episcopal visitations to Rome. He conferred widely the papal title of monsignor and saw that the Roman liturgy was generally adopted everywhere. By making himself the "voluntary prisoner of the Vatican" in reaction to Victor Emmanuel's seizure of Rome he won the sympathy of many.

ASSESSMENT OF THE AGE

The biggest failure of Pius IX was not to read the signs of the times. He treated Catholic liberals as less than loyal and favored the conservative ultramontanes. This is not to imply that liberals of every type were guiltless. As is usual with some liberals they tended to naivety. Some felt that if man once had the chance to be educated, to free himself of all authority then progress was inevitable and the millennium would arrive. Most governments of the time were conservative and so were most Catholics. Pius was a child of his time and could not be expected to suddenly drop centuries old traditions to embrace the new liberalisms whose more radical excesses he had experienced. He and his successors were faced with rapid change and tremendous challenge. As Robert Cross puts it:

> The problem [of reconciling the Church with a new era] is most severe in periods of rapid cultural change like the nineteenth century when traditional policies are satisfactory to neither the cautious nor the confident. Through the preceding century, the rationalism of the Enlightenment had been reconciled, to the satisfaction of most Catholics, with the

trusting faith demanded by Christian orthodoxy. But the problems presented to the Church by Newton, Locke, and Voltaire were trivial compared to the challenges of scientists like Lyell, Darwin, and Virchow, of philosophers like Benthan and Spencer, of historians like Strauss and Renan. The collapse of the old regimes during and after the French Revolution also drastically affected the Church. Catholic leaders, accustomed to dealing with anointed monarchs, were confronted with governments conceived in revolution, and dedicated to the rights of man and the sovereignty of the people. Social relationships were also in flux. Moral theologians, therefore, had to turn to such novel problems as the ethical responsibilities of factory owners and industrial laborers. Parish priests had to learn how to care for a flock not scattered over a countryside, but jammed into urban tenements. And the immense migrations from country to city, from nation to nation, even from continent to continent, taxed the ingenuity of bishops to build diverse classes and nationalities into a unified Church.

In the face of these confusing developments, the prevailing confidence of eighteenth-century Catholicism gave way to fear and suspicion. Catholics began to demand greater vigilance in distinguishing and defending the City of God from the City of Man.

. . . The Society of Jesus, which in the eighteenth century had supplied many spokesmen for the Catholic rapprochement with modern tendencies, now took the lead in combating the age. . . . Catholic doctrine should be taught in its full stringency, allowing no concession to the predilections of the age for 'liberty of conscience.' . . . Many who preached in this way were avowed traditionalists, who refused to acknowledge that they advocated the slightest modification of historical Catholicism to fit the new circumstances of the age. . . . By 1860, these activist conservatives had almost unanimously subscribed to two such developments: the increased centralization of the Church under a papacy of unlimited power; and an intensified devotionalism.[6]

Still, he should have noted that education was taking place rapidly in Europe and he would have to deal with this transformation of minds and increase of knowledge in ways other than suppression. Nor was he helped by his curia which boasted no intellectuals nor the church in Rome which was at a low theological ebb. Much of his thoughts have been disregarded today. Vatican II has reversed much of what he taught. The decree of Religious Freedom for example has virtually reversed Pius IX's policy as expressed in the Syllabus of Errors. It was Vatican II which adopted much of Newman's thoughts which so distressed the ultramontanes of his time: "It is Newman's profoundly historical mind which places him in the tradition which has finally reached recognition in the Second Vatican Council; and it is that historical attitude which commends this Council to English-speaking peoples today."[7] Perhaps the best conclusion to the age of Pio Nono is expressed by the historian von Aretin:

> The history of the papacy from 1831 to 1878 is a story both significant and depressing. Except for the short interlude from 1846 to 1848, the papacy grew ever more confident in its antagonism to the age. This reactionary attitude became an inherent part of the church and ultimately prevented it from exerting any kind of positive and formative influence.
>
> The reign of Pius IX certainly had its impressive aspects. But his many widespread condemnations affected such varied issues as liberalism, pantheism, naturalism, absolute rationalism, indifferentism, communism, secret societies, bible societies, freedom of worship, free speech and many more besides. Ultimately Pius made no contribution to the social problems of human society nor to any of the great issues of his age.[8]

Yet, to be fair, there is another school of thought concerning the Church's reaction to the times. The nineteenth century was indeed a time when all churches lost confidence in themselves and were faced with the choice of withdrawing from the modern world or accommodating themselves to it. Pius IX, as we saw, chose the former and has come in for much criticism. Most Protestant churches chose the latter and they have in recent times come in for their share of criticism as well. The result of their marriage to the age was a decline of creedal certitude and moral fervor. As historian R. R. Palmer puts it:

> Church attendance among Protestants became increasingly casual, and the doctrines set forth in sermons seemed increasingly remote. Protestantism traditionally trusted their own private judgment and regarded the clergy as their own agents, not as authoritative teachers placed above them. Protestants also had always set especial emphasis on the Bible as the source of religious belief, and as doubts accumulated on the literal truth of Biblical narratives there seemed no other source on which to rely.[9]

Interestingly, those historians who hold such a view maintain that, of the two choices of withdrawal or accommodation, the Catholic Church under Pius IX and his successors in the long run made the wiser choice. In their eyes Catholicism by so doing resisted better the secularism of the times and was insulated from the disasters of the twentieth century. In striking contrast to a critical point of view therefore

> . . . many secular historians, accepting the premise that Christianity and culture truly were incompatible in the nineteenth century, regard the strategy of ultramontanism, however reactionary it might appear, as eminently sensible and astute. Through the trials of the period the Catholic Church, unlike its Protestant counterparts, remained true to itself and occupied a powerful defensive position from which it could reemerge as a political and social force when the energies of modernity had played themselves out in the catastrophe of the twentieth century.[10]

NOTES

1. Pius IX was commonly called "Pio Nono." The term could be one of endearment. It could also be one of distain for "nono" means "grandfather" referring to the pope as being old and doughty. That is the way his enemies used the term. Modern liberals who enjoy taking pot shots at Pius IX insert a hyphen to indicate his intransigency: "Pio No-No."

2. Alec R. Vidler, *The Church in an Age of Revolution*, p. 148. Penguin Books, Baltimore, Maryland. 1961.

3. Quoted in *Prophets and Guardians* by Meriol Trevor, p. 117. Doubleday and Co., Garden City, N.Y. 1969.

4. *Ibid.*, p. 118.

5. It is interesting to note that the hundredth anniversary of the proclamation of the dogma of infallibility was passed over in silence by Rome; surely a symptom of the unfinished questions raised by Vatican II and the post council upheavals.

6. Robert D. Cross, *The Emergence of Liberal Catholicism in America*, pp. 2 to 5. Quadrangle Paperbacks, Chicago, 1958.

7. Meriol Trevor, *op. cit.*, p. 110.

8. Karl von Aretin, *op. cit.*, p. 120.

9. R. R. Palmer, *A History of the Modern World*, 2nd edition, p. 603. New York. 1960.

10. David J. O'Brien, *The Renewal of American Catholicism*, p. 80. Oxford University Press, New York. 1972.

XX

The New Governments

THE WORLD SCENE

As we move into the twentieth century we must give a quick survey of the world scene and the reactions of the popes of the time to it. The popes we have in mind must be considered as a unit because their reigns together form a pattern of the Church's activity during these times. The three popes are Leo XIII (1878-1903), Pius X (1903-1914) and Benedict XV (1914-1922). It was these popes who had to deal with a rapidly changing world in which the Church was playing a less and less important part.

OVERSEAS EXPANSION

The end of the nineteenth and the beginning of the twentieth centuries were the periods of what is called the "Europeanization" of the world. Every new nation so scrambled for more outside territory that soon the overriding concern was for a "balance of power" so that one would not be more powerful than the other. By 1914, for example, the British Empire took in one fourth of this earth's land and one fourth its population, including India, Hongkong, Cyprus and parts of Africa. Spain was in far away Cuba but had to give it independence and to cede Puerto Rico and the Philippines to the United States as a result of the Spanish American War of 1898. Japan, as we have seen, was opened by the missionaries, closed to foreigners and then reopened in 1854. In due time Japan became industrialized, Europeanized and imperialist. She engaged in the Chino-Japanese war of 1894 and obtained Korea and Formosa. Britain forced China to admit her in the Opium War and soon other Western states tried to parcel her up. By the early 1900's three-fifths of the entire area of Asia was ruled by the European powers including the United States. By 1914 Europe owned almost all of Africa.

The result of all this imperialist fever was a new and intense spirit of nationalism and economic competition and rivalry. Nations tried to outmaneuver each other and were even "arming for peace." Historian Carlton Hayes gives a good descriptive picture of the atmosphere that was building up to World War I.

> In 1913 the international situation was extraordinarily perilous. Recurrent crises in Morocco and in the Near East had cost every Great Power some measure of prestige. Germany had been outplayed in the Moroccan crises by France and Great Britain. Yet France had been forced to cede African territory to Germany, and Great Britain to yield predominance in the Ottoman Empire. Russia had been outplayed in the successive Near Eastern crises by Austria-Hungary and Germany. Yet Austria-Hungary had been flouted by Serbia and held in leash by Italy and Germany had to face the fact that instead of exercising an hegemony in Europe, as she had done in the days of Bismarck, she was now "encircled" by a ring of potentially hostile Powers.
>
> . . . Naval rivalry was in full swing. . . . Imperialistic rivalry . . . was intensified for all these Powers . . . Nationalism in an aggravated form, was everywhere rampant; it was dictat-

ing to governments an emotional, rather than a reasoned, be-havior; and, quite triumphant now in the Balkans, it threat-ened speedily to become so throughout east-central Europe.[1]

INDUSTRIAL REVOLUTION

A part of the three popes' lives was another revolution besides the political ones taking place; that was the industrial revolution. After the 1830's mechanized machinery and industry spread quickly. Fulton made his steamboat in 1807; there were the Bessemer steel furnace, the Gattling machine gun (1862), the telegraph of Morse (1837), dynamite (1867), submarines (1875), the wireless (1895), the refrigerator, the sewing machine, the bicycle, the diesel engine, the automobile and the airplane (1905), and many more. The importance for the Church and for society was, of course, the introduction of the factory system and the rise of a new propertyless, moneyless class, the proletariat, who had only his labor to sell and who was easy victim for exploitation. Then, too, the governments abandoned the old liberal self-determination for national priorities and national conformity. Nations were in competition in industry and capital as well. More significantly for the Church, as each nation sought to consolidate its identity and to subordinate all interests to the state, the Church was obviously something to be likewise brought under state control—or at least made impotent so as not to stand in the way of "progress."

INTELLECTUAL REVOLUTION

Science was advancing and even trickling down to the average person. Advances were being made in natural history, botany and geology. The earth's surface was being studied as never before. Perhaps the high point of intellectual and popular awe was the great theory of Darwin who shook the world with his explanation of evolution and shook several religions in their interpretation of the Bible. The result of all the new knowledge culled from anthropology and archaeology and the other sciences was to bring into vogue the educated skeptic. Philosophers like Huxley, Haeckel and Spencer formulated materialistic theories. Schopenhauer and Nietzsche (d. 1900) wrote extolling the will and the natural instinct of man with his consequent trampling on the weak and the survival of the elite. Such thoughts were eagerly received in an age of growing militarism, imperialism and nationalism. Karl Marx (changed from the Jewish Mordecai) issued his famous *Communist Manifesto* in 1848.

As we have indicated the new discoveries of man's origin and the age of the earth and such affected deeply biblical studies and religion. Strauss wrote his *Life of Jesus* denying the supernatural nature of Christ and the possibility of miracles. Renan in 1862 published a *Life of Jesus* also portraying Christ as a kind of self deluded prophet and Christianity as a myth. Religion among the intelligentsia was falling into disrepute. Among common men the industrial revolution and the new city life were loosening their ties from traditional religious affiliations. The states became indifferent to all religions and the new nationalism itself was a kind of religion. It was this nationalism that would accuse a denominational Christian (especially the Catholic) of being less than a good citizen.

This, then, was the world inhabited by the Church in the early 1900's. It was a world of contest: the Church was alternating between resistance and accommodation to the new governments; the anticlerical governments were bent on subduing and emasculating the Church in their drive for the self-determination, nationalism and imperialism which would lead to World War I. It was to be a contest between the Church's conservative theological approach to the new discoveries in scholarship and those men who sought some kind of rapport with the modern world. We must now see how the Church and its popes acted in such times.

FRANCE

After Napoleon the monarchy had been restored in France but did not last long. Louis Philippe succeeded the king, acquired for France Algeria but could not withstand the many factions against himself. Many, particularly the clergy, wanted the restoration of the Bourbon monarchy. In 1848 a revolt forced Louis Philippe to flee to England and a Second French Republic was founded with Louis Napoleon as its president, but in 1851 he established a new empire with himself as Napoleon III. We have seen, however, how he was entangled in Italy's unification attempt. He allowed himself to be pulled into the venture in aiding Victor Emmanuel but when the latter was victorious Napoleon's fears of a united Italy returned. He tried to withdraw and work out a compromise which would leave Italy divided. The Italian patriots were duly outraged and forced Napoleon to recognize their work. He lost much prestige at home because of this and even more when he failed to take over Spanish Mexico and lost to Bismarck in the Franco-Prussian war of 1870. A Third Republic, born of humiliation and defeat in the war of 1870 with Prussia, replaced him which was liberal, imperialistic and anticlerical.

ANTICLERICALISM

Rome's attitude at the time of all this was definitely pro-monarchy and Pius IX who was reigning was, as we have seen, deeply suspicious of any liberalism or democracy such as the Third Republic of France represented. The new government retaliated with anticlerical measures. The Jesuits were expelled, a divorce law was published and education was secularized. The new pope, Leo XIII, was quick to see the problem. He perceived that the Church's persistent backing of the old monarchies such as in France and hostility to the newer liberal democratic forms of government had to change. His task was to show Catholics that they could live in a liberal world without sacrificing their Catholic principles. He asked French Catholics to support the Third Republic. Leo shocked many of the French clergy with this sudden turnabout even though he was at pains to affirm the old union of Church and State as an ideal. But Leo's words came too late and his approach failed. Many of the French clergy could not be expected to turn from ardent monarchists to fervent republicans. They continued their hostility and suspicion of the Third Republic. Conservative groups resisted the pope and met and prayed for his enlightenment. Thus were Catholics divided in France into conservatives and liberals. But the worst was yet to come.

The conservative French Catholics made two major blunders. First of all they backed the ill-fated General Boulanger who tried to take over the Republic and establish a dictatorship. Secondly, they, along with many of their liberal Catholics, were on the wrong side of the sensational Dreyfus affair. Dreyfus was a Jewish officer in the French army who was accused of selling military secrets to the Germans. Although found guilty he was proved innocent later by further investigation.[2] The army, riding a wave of nationalism and antisemitism, was against Dreyfus; however so too were the Catholics and their nationalism and antisemitism were as strong as any. The Catholic press shared in the antisemitism and presumed the guilt of Dreyfus. The leading Catholic paper of the day, *La Croix* said, "Dreyfus is an agent of international Jewry which has decided to ruin the French people." This blunder cost the Church a great deal of prestige and promoted a new wave of anticlericalism: "Because the Catholic Church, and especially a large number of militant priests and monks from such orders as the Assumptionists, had taken an active and verbally violent part in the bitter campaign to deny justice to Dreyfus and discredit the troubled Republic, the Church now had to face the consequences."[3]

In 1901 the government suppressed all religious orders driving many into exile. Under Emile-Combes over 13,000 schools were closed. By 1904 the French government had broken off relations with Rome and finally in 1905 the final step was taken. Church and State in France were officially separated. The "eldest daughter of the Church," the heir of Clovis and Charlemagne since the eighth century, now broke away. To many contemporaries it must have seemed gloomy indeed. They had witnessed the fall of papal Rome and now Catholic Paris was no longer Catholic. Church property was handed over to a lay board but this was so outrageous that the board was permitted to have Catholics on it. Nevertheless, the Church lost control over her own buildings and churches. With this in mind, Pius X who was now pope[4], although he condemned the separation, edified the whole world by simply renouncing all Church buildings to the

State. The Church rented out her own old and glorious cathedrals for Mass.

It was not long before the Church in France recovered. With the separation of Church and State the pope was at least free to run the Church without intervention. Bishops were consecrated. Money was raised and new seminaries, churches, hospitals and schools were built. Anticlerical attitudes continued to be taught in the state schools yet the Church moved ahead nourished by new devotions to the Blessed Mother and the Sacred Heart. In fact, the great Sacred Heart Cathedral completed in 1912 is a monument to the revival and was built in reparation for the crimes of anticlerical France.

ITALY

As we have noted with Pius IX the situation in Italy tended to color the popes' outlook for the rest of Europe and America. There the government was anti-Catholic. Religious orders were dissolved, clerics were forced into military service and the government even attempted to seize the funds of the Church's Propagation of the Faith. Feast days were abolished, education secularized, religious processions were banned and clerical criticism of the state was punishable by law. Pius IX reacted by forbidding any Catholic to take part in such an anticlerical government as voters or office holders. Leo XIII unwisely held to the ban against the wishes of his more perceptive advisors. He even resorted to politicking by trying to get Bismarck and King William II of Prussia to abandon Italy as an ally and to side with France. This could hardly please the Italian government. Thus the warfare continued and each side lost no opportunity to harass the other. The government held jubilees and public events designed to embarrass the pope. When Pius IX's body was being transferred in solemn procession to the cathedral of San Lorenzo in 1881 fanatical crowds abused the procession and almost threw the pope's body into the Tiber. Many a time Leo was ready to flee Rome. On his part he countered with harassment of his own. He made a flourish of church festivals and played up the Holy Year of 1900 losing no opportunity of telling visitors to Rome of the persecution by the Italian government.

Pius X began to relax somewhat the ban on Catholics taking part in the Italian government. However he would permit no Catholic political party to form because he and his conservative curia were much concerned that the laymen be submissive to the Holy See and take its political orders from them. They did not want any threat of independent action from the laity nor that the laity should be strong enough to deviate from the party line of the curia. Pius condemned the writings of anyone who suggested otherwise and sought to protect seminarians from similar dangerous ideas by forbidding them to read newspapers. Even the beginnings of Catholic Action founded by Leo XIII and furthered by himself was meant simply to be an organ of the hierarchy, not an independent movement. Pius' successor, Benedict XV, was likewise unhappy with the anticlerical Italian government but found it wiser not to take any offensive against it. During World War I he remained strictly neutral so as not to offend Catholics of the varying sides. Afterwards in 1919 he did permit Don Sturzo to found a People's Party and finally withdrew entirely the ban forbidding Catholics to take part in politics. The whole Italian situation was behind the continued suspicion of any democratic government and the ban on Catholics to share in them. The papacy could not make distinctions from country to country and felt that it could not condemn democracy in Italy and, for example, support it in France.

GERMANY

When the new anticlerical, nationalistic government established itself in Italy this was but the forerunner of several similar forms of government throughout Europe. Each nation, as we have indicated, became highly nationalistic and imperialistic and to that degree anticlerical for clericalism was a threat to nationalism. Moreover the Enlightenment had done its work and the Church had lost many members among the intelligentsia. A whole new working class was being raised in an increasingly secular world and the new nationalism was not about to tolerate any check to its conscience from any Church anyway. In Germany this feeling of nationalism was especially marked. Prussia had just defeated France and the chancellor, Bismarck, was seeking to absorb the other German states into a new Germanic empire or Reich with Prussia at the helm. Of course, German Austria had been the dominant power heretofore but Bismarck defeated Austria in 1866 and put it in an inferior position. The new Germany became in effect an expanded Prussia with its headquarters at Berlin. By 1870 the only resistance to German pride (racial and intellectual) was the Catholic Church (the Lutherans, always tied to the state, were delighted with Protestant Prussia's leadership).

Since the new Germany (the "Second Reich"; Otto I was the head of the First "reich" as Hitler would call his empire the Third Reich) had about one third Catholics, Bismarck knew he must dominate them and control the Church much as Napoleon did. By 1872 he had passed the Falk laws subjecting all schools to the state, expelling the Jesuits, putting the clergy under state control, etc. Fortunately Germany possessed a remarkable Catholic leader named Windthorst who led a Catholic Center Party which was able to offset some of the *Kulturkampf* of Bismarck. Still Bismarck had his effect and by 1875 millions of Catholics were deprived of the sacraments since thousands of priests had been sent into exile or imprisoned. However, by 1878 Bismarck began to retreat for political reasons and some of the offensive laws were relaxed. He was making no headway against a loyal clergy and laity or against the skillful work of Windthorst's Center party. In 1881 the new emperor, Kaiser William II came to the throne. He needed the Church's support against the socialists and thus dismissed the "iron chancellor" under whom the Church had suffered so much.

Another feature in Germany was that after Bismarck's time model Catholic associations began to appear and flourish. Catholicism grew strong again. Leaders like Bishop Kettler, the father of social action, created strong workers' associations. The Germans received Leo XIII's social encyclical *Rerum Novarum* with enthusiasm. Yet, under Pius X and his conservative curia, the old suspicion of Germany returned. We have seen that intellectually Germany was superior to Rome even in Pius IX's time. Protestant-Catholic faculties taught in the universities there. It was the home of the suspected Dollinger. Rome revived its suspicion of German scholarship and approach to modern times. The books of a certain Hermann Schnell who tried to wed Catholicism to German modern culture were put on the Index for example. Rome—and some German bishops themselves—did not like the independence of the German associations, did not like the interdenominational character of the trade unions or the fact they were not controlled by the clergy.

Catholics, with Pius X's example, split on these issues and only the outbreak of World War I prevented further polarization.

BRITAIN, SPAIN, PORTUGAL AND AUSTRIA

We recall that in 1850 the Catholic hierarchy was restored in England. In spite of this there was no noticeable "second spring." The Catholic population grew mostly through the birth rate and Irish immigration although there were impressive conversions among the intellectuals. Yet many lapsed in spite of Cardinal Manning's hope that Vatican I would present a compelling Catholic Church. A lingering anti-Catholicism and the materialism and secularism of the day took its toll. However as would be usual in the Protestant countries the Church fared better with its schools. In England, Holland and Scotland the state assisted the parochial schools and worked out solutions to problems which still vex the United States. In 1927 the anti-Catholic measures were revoked and Britain even kept representation at the Vatican.

The main problem with Spain and Portugal was that the Church and state were united and therefore as governments fell so did the Church. Succeeding governments likewise were thus anticlerical to the extreme and passed humiliating anticlerical measures. In Spain the king fell from power in 1931. The ensuing republican government carried out anti-clerical measures with such ruthlessness that it provoked a reaction which supported General Franco who in the 1936 bloody civil war took over. In Portugal religious orders had been suppressed by 1901 and by 1914, after the king was expelled and the republic proclaimed, there came the official separation of Church and state. After World War I Salazar took over and the life of the Church was able to be resumed. In Austria, the old Catholic mainstay, there was a *Los von Rom* (Freedom from Rome) movement. But a lot had happened to Austria. From head of the German confederation we saw that she was reduced to a secondary place. She was expelled from the papal states and northern Italy. After World War I it was reduced to almost nothing and Vienna became a capital almost without a country as her provinces fell to the communists.

SOCIAL PROBLEMS

Much of the Church's relationship to France and the other countries revolved around two major points: the first, the social problems brought about by the Industrial Revolution and secondly, recognition of the new democracies. We have seen how profoundly the Industrial Revolution spread and it is commonplace to acknowledge the social ills it brought and the plight of the landless workers. The problem for the Church was that Pius IX had foolishly prohibited the Italians to take part in the new republican government of Italy and frowned on Catholic political activity in any country. Associations of workers of any kind were suspect. Leo XIII, however, saw the pressing social problems and permitted organizations such as those of the French industrialist Leon Harmel who allowed his workers to organize and who led them on pilgrimages to Rome.

In 1890 Leo felt it was time to issue an encyclical on the working man for the question was becoming more urgent. He had certain encouragements to do so. In the United States, for example, Cardinal Gibbons in 1887 defended the Knights of Labor as a legitimate association and in England Cardinal Manning had so successfully intervened in the docker's strike that they carried his picture with that of Karl Marx. So Leo issued his famous *Rerum Novarum* wherein he stressed the working man's right to private property (as against the socialists), the right to form associations and to receive a just wage.[5] He spoke out against exploitation and unchecked competition. He warned against extreme socialists (i.e. communists in his time) and other societies hostile to both state and religion. Also, significantly, Leo laid the foundation for a different relationship between Church and state. It came down to the position that the Church was not committed to any particular form of government (a blow to the monarchists) as long as it was free to function. In 1885 Leo came to accept the independence of Catholic political parties who could act on their own (something his successor did not like). In short, Leo was trying to live with the fact that the new democratic governments were here to stay, that the old regimes were dead or dying and that Catholics must recognize these facts. However, if the Church was somewhat ambivalent about its attitudes towards the new democracies it was, under Pius X and his successors, of definite mind when it came to the new modern scholarship.

MODERNISM

We have noted how the theology of St. Thomas had been revived under Pius IX. Under Leo XIII Thomism was made the basis of study in seminaries and colleges though by no means exclusively. Still, the ever conservative curia (especially under Pius X) took encouragement to use Thomism (as they conceived it) as an absolute norm and even as a weapon with which to persecute differing systems. Leo did other things which disturbed the curia. Though basically conservative he did try to conciliate the Church to modern times. He supported scholarship, opened up the Vatican archives and encouraged historical research. Most of all he set guidelines in his encyclical, *Providentissimus Deus* for studying the Bible. The Bible in particular was under much scrutiny. There was such an explosion of knowledge in archaelogy, geography and critical scholarship that men were looking at the Bible in a new light. Scholars were questioning the traditional stories. They wanted to know if the Bible were true, if it could be reconciled with science. They wanted to know about Jesus himself. Who was he? What, if anything, did he teach? Did he or Paul really invent Christianity? Leo's encyclical tried to guide such questions. He even set up a Biblical Commission for this purpose, but the conservative curia soon used the commission as a means to stifle scholarship and keep scholars on the straight and narrow path.

Certain men were impatient of such restraint. They felt that the Bible must be treated as any other secular work and interpreted as such devoid of any supernatural quality. These were men who fell into "modernism" which started about 1890 and ended in 1910. Actually, modernism was more of an attitude than any precise system of thought. Basically it was the attitude to urge the Church to come to terms with the modern world. Such modernists ". . . had first been struck by the incompatibility between many traditional tenets of Catholicism and the findings of modern scholarship, and they had felt bound to use scientific and historico-critical methods of study and to follow argument wherever it led . . . What they had attempted to do was, while remaining sincere and loyal Catholics, to forward such a revision and fresh presentation of the Church's teaching as would acclimatize it in the modern world."[6]

There were three famous names associated with modernism although there were many others in several fields of discipline (such as Murri, the father of Christian democracy in Italy and Fogazzaro, author of the famous book, *The Saint*). First there was Alfred Loisy (d. 1940). Loisy was a scholar in Old and New Testament studies and was knowledgeable about the new scientific methods applied to the Bible. In 1902 he published his book *The Gospel and the Church* indicating that Christ came to give, not any truths to mankind, but a "spirit," a religious movement; that Jesus was only one point in a development and that as times change so also can dogma. Then there was George Tyrrel (d. 1909) a Protestant, turned Catholic, become Jesuit. He also proposed that the Church's theological system needed overhauling and that dogma was not the container of immutable truth. Finally, there was Baron von Hugel who was a kind of international go-between. He introduced Tyrrel to Loisy writings and sent articles back and forth to various friends.

PIUS X'S REACTION

Pius X who became pope in 1903 was politically naive and soon came under the influence of his conservative curia. They held up to him the ghost of some kind of conspiracy, originating in Germany (the old suspicion of German thinking again). Pius reacted by his encyclical *Pascendi* in 1907 which condemned many of Loisy's statements though not mentioning him by name. In so far as Loisy and Tyrrel had, unknown to each other, written articles under assumed names the pope was convinced that there was some kind of international conspiracy and his language was almost violent in his denunciations smacking very much of the tone of Pius IX's Syllabus. The modernists cried "foul" for the modernism described by Pius existed nowhere but in his mind. They were right for modernism, as we have said, was no one concept or teaching but an attitude. Pius crystallized that attitude in several propositions and called it modernism and condemned it. To this extent the pope had a point:

> It was undoubtedly the merit of biblical modernism that it called attention to the law of development of dogma and the need of including the historical method in dealing with the texts of Scripture. But its principle was to leave entirely out of account the supernatural and inspired character of the scriptural testimonies, and also the interpretations suggested by tradition and the magisterium of the Church. Further, historians are now becoming more and more alert to the fact that the notion of history used by Loisy and many of the modernists was dependent on the positivist notions of the end of the nineteenth century, which are today undoubtedly outdated in many respects.[7]

Loisy and Tyrrel would not submit and both were excommunicated. Von Hugel stayed for he had seen indeed that some new thinking was necessary for the Church in the modern world but within the tradition of the Church and not in opposition to it. The results of Pius' extreme denunciations, however, were disastrous. His encyclical had the effect of intellectual witch-hunting. Catholic scholars backed down on their investigations. Pioneer scholars like the famous Pierre Batiffol and Pere Lagrange had to narrow down their biblical studies and writings. A "reign of terror" set in and modernism became a catch-all word for all that the pope (or his curia) thought was harmful from modern scholarship. Professors were removed from teaching on the slightest indication of modernism. No theologian of note was safe from the curia's suspicion. An oath against modernism was made obligatory for all professors, teachers and priests—which no one had any trouble in taking since the term itself was so nebulous. Even this was not enough. The conservative Catholics were still determined to uncover all "modernists" wherever they were lurking. A secret service organization was set up with some thousand agents to keep files on professors, teachers and even bishops. When some of these files fell accidentally into German hands in 1915 they thought they had uncovered some international espionage ring. Catholic journals were suppressed and a veritable censorship was in force. A protest from the German cardinal got the professors of theology at the German universities excused from the oath.

We recognize today that such a vehement over-reaction by Pius to modernism and its severe suppression was due to the grip that the conservative Catholics and curia had on the pope and the Church. There was no question that many of the modernists were too much blinded by current fashions of thought and that some of their views could not be reconciled with traditional Christianity. Yet the Church could have handled the situation more calmly without panic and not have scared off the scholars who could have helped the Church understand the problems that sooner or later it would have to come to terms with. Meriol Trevor in her book *Prophets and Guardians* puts it well:

> The usual defense of Pius X and his advisers is that they were acting on behalf of the "little ones" whose faith was threatened by the Modernists. Christ's warning, addressed to those who mistreat children, was taken by ecclesiastical rulers to include adult but simple members of the Church. But were Loisy's exegetical studies a terrible danger to the fishermen of Brittany? Would Blondel's philosophy, almost incomprehensible to his friends, upset the peasants of Provence? If the little ones were the bourgeois capable of reading books of criticism, was a condemnation the best way of answering the questions raised? If it was necessary to crush

Modernism in order to preserve the faith, what sort of faith, what sort of faithful were envisaged? When Cardinal Richard censured *L'Evangile et L'Eglise,* Loisy's sales doubled. After Tyrrell was dismissed from the Society of Jesus, his books commanded a wider public than before. People wanted to know what the fuss was about—they always do. Suppression of criticism and of new ideas, never easy since the invention of printing, was quite impossible by the beginning of the twentieth century. No one in authority would admit the questions, let alone provide what could have subdued Loisy's influence—better answers than his. Persistent refusals to face these questions surely meant that it would become harder for educated Catholics to remain believing Christians. And if Rome was willing to jettison the educated in order to preserve the faith of the simple, it was shortsighted not to realize that as more and more received education, so the problems would be revived on a wider scale and would not be less difficult to solve for the passage of time.[8]

Pius thus did set the tone which would prevail until John XXIII. Pius XII, for example, was in the tradition of Pius X when in 1950 he issued his encyclical *Humani Generis* condemning many propositions of the "New Theology." Although no one individual was named many theologians were removed from their teaching positions.[9] We can sense, then, what happened at Vatican II. Under Pope John's more congenial attitude the lid was taken off and the world was surprised at the sudden expression of thought, differing opinions and the theological questionings that followed the Council. It is not without merit to suggest that the explosion of Vatican II was in direct proportion to the suppression begun in the time of Pius X.

THREE POPES

We saw that the new democratic governments were anticlerical and not one failed to go through the obligatory motions of expelling religious orders, closing monasteries, taking over the schools, etc. This helps explain the reaction and resistance of the popes and many Catholics. Yet, as we have seen, Leo made an attempt to come to terms with the new governments and the new social ills of the age. His social encyclical mapped out a program for practical attitudes and action. It encouraged labor unions and associations as long as they were open and not hostile to religion. Leo almost condemned the Knights of Labor in America (the predecessor of the A.F. of L.). It had many Catholics in it and was established for collective bargaining. Yet Leo at first thought it was of the secret revolutionary Freemason type. He almost condemned it and only the explanations and courage of Baltimore's Cardinal Gibbons saved it. Leo did fail in his attempts to restore even partially the papal states and he failed in preventing a clash between the Third Republic of France and the Church. Yet he established Thomism as the official theology of the Church, established the Biblical Commission, opened the papal Catholic University in Washington, D.C., filled the college of cardinals with capable and sincere men including Cardinal Newman to whom he had given the red hat as a sign of his (Leo's) coming to terms with the progressive thought represented by Newman.

Pius was a political and diplomatic failure. It was under him that Church and state were separated in France and modernism was condemned. It was under Pius that strict control from Rome became a high art and modern thought was repressed. It was under him that the papacy and curia reached its high point of power and control and witch-hunting took over. It was under him that Theodore Herzl, the key Zionist figure was refused the Church's approval for the founding of the State of Israel. In the famous incident of Herzl's interview with Pius's secretary he was told that before the pope would declare himself for the Jewish people they must first be converted. Since they were not about to do that Pius said, "We cannot favor this movement." Yet Pius succeeded in the areas he knew best: in the Church's internal and spiritual realm. He restored Gregorian Chant in 1904, reorganized the seminaries, reformed Canon Law and curtailed the power of the Roman congregations. He revised the breviary, encouraged daily communion and permitted first communion at the age of seven. He was canonized by Pius XII in 1954.

Benedict XV was pope for only eight years and was the one who had to guide the Church during World War I. Naturally he was accused of favoritism by each side. He gave the papacy new prestige by the great works in alleviating the suffering in war and assisting prisoners of war. He was willing to accept the new governments and saw the resumption of diplomatic relations between France and the Vatican. At the war's end the rampant anticlericalism of Italy prevented the papacy from any voice in the treaties or any part in the League of Nations.

> As one surveys the period of the First World War and its aftermath one has the impression that even less than in the days of Napoleon did the governments of Europe pay any serious attention to Rome, that Benedict was even less likely to achieve anything to influence Clemenceau, or Lloyd George, or President Wilson, than Pius VII had been to influence Napoleon or Metternich. Napoleon had tried to bend the Church to his service, but at least he had recognized its power. And at the Congress of Vienna, unlike the Conference of Versailles, a papal delegate had not only been present but had been offered the presidency.[10]

Yet, as so often happens during times of great disasters such as World War I, the Church's enemies saw much to admire:

the priests in the trenches, the nuns in the hospitals, the important part that the Mass and the sacraments played in the life of the Catholics. Lost (though not altogether) were the fears of the divided allegiance and lost also was the violent brand of anticlericalism of the previous hundred years.

NOTES

1. Carlton J. H. Hayes, *op. cit.*, p. 566.
2. In 1905 the appeals court acquitted Dreyfus of all charges and re-instated him in the army. He was promoted to major, decorated with the Legion of Honor and died in 1935.
3. William L. Shirer, *The Collapse of the Third Republic,* p. 70. Simon and Schuster, New York. 1969. For a good summary of the whole sordid Dreyfus affair see the first chapter of this book.
4. Actually, at the time Cardinal Rampolla was the favorite to be chosen pope, but the Austrian emperor had the Polish cardinal exercise an old veto over this choice. Thus the vote shifted to Cardinal Sarto, Pius X. One of his first acts as pope was to abolish the privilege of veto.
5. Pope John XXIII expanded Leo XIII's notions concerning Church-State relationships in his encyclical *Pacem in Terris* and repeated much of Leo's basic teaching of *Rerum Novarum* in his *Mater et Magistra.*
6. Alec R. Vidler, *op. cit.*, p. 180.
7. Sacramentum Mundi, vol. IV, p. 103. Herder and Herder, New York.
8. Meriol Trevor, *op cit.*, p. 80.
9. Actually, the references were to the French writers of the times: Henri de Lubac, Jean Danielou, Yves Congar—all names held in high esteem today (Danielou is a cardinal).
10. E. E. Y. Hales, *op. cit.*, p. 249.

XXI

The Church in the United States

SPANISH BEGINNINGS

Much of American Catholic religious history has yet to be explored. In this chapter we propose to give a resume of the activities, challenges and attitudes of the Catholics who came to America and the men who led them. Catholics, of course, were the first to come to the New World. These were the Spanish Catholics who preceded the French and English by almost a century. In 1513 Ponce de Leon set foot in Florida and Balboa gazed at the Pacific Ocean. In 1541 de Soto explored the Southwest and in 1562 de Ayllon saw his settlers attend Mass along the Chesapeake, some eighty years before the English Protestants settled at nearby James-town. In 1605 the oldest capital city in the United States was founded, Sante Fe (Holy Faith). All along the southern rim of the United States, from Florida to California Spanish Catholicism was planted. The many Catholic names that exist today testify to their presence: St. Augustine, Florida, San Antonio, San Francisco, Los Angeles, Corpus Christi and the like. The distinctive Spanish architecture still graces the southwestern coastline.

Since in Spain Church and state were united it meant that exploration was intimately bound up with the spread of the faith. Columbus himself remarked that among the aims of his voyage was that of seeking ways by which men could be converted to the Faith. Colonization and conversion were two sides of the same coin for the Spanish. As happened in the mother country there was the inevitable conflict as to the spheres of influence and jurisdiction between Church and state as to where the one left off and the other began. This conflict was most pronounced in the treatment of the Indians. The civil administration tended to exploit the Indian plying him with liquor and forcing him into slavery or taking over his land. The churchmen were squarely on the side of the Indians. The Spanish theologian, Francisco de Vitoria delivered his lectures at the University of Salamanca in 1539 which laid the foundation for a humane international law. He declared that the Indians were not to be taken as slaves, that they should handle their own disputes according to their own customs, that their property should not be taken from them except in fair trade. He went so far as to say that neither the emperor nor the pope were masters of the universe and even if they were this would still not deny the rights of the Indians to hold property. In fact, Spain should administer the Indians only till such time as they could handle matters themselves. We have already seen in another chapter how Bartholomew de las Casas was a pioneer in getting fair treatment for the Indians. It was his influence along with others that made Pope Paul II in 1737 declare, "The said Indians and all other people who may later be discovered by Christians, are by no means to be deprived of their liberty or the possession of their property, even though they be outside the faith of Jesus Christ."

The French followed the Spanish, mainly the Jesuits and Franciscans, with men like Verrazano (an Italian in French service) exploring the North Atlantic seacoast, Cartier sailing up the St. Lawrence; and there are the still famous names of Champlin, Joliet, Marquette, Duluth, La Salle, etc.—all French missionaries. They too were fired by the faith. Many of them were men of high culture, honored at their universities at home; yet they left such prestige and comfort to live, suffer and die among the Indians often with the most horrifying and excruciating tortures such as the famed Isaac Jogues and his companions. The French attitude towards the natives was not to forcibly convert them like the Spanish or exterminate them like the English, but to treat them as brothers. The historian Boltin praises them as "a force which made for the preservation of the Indians as opposed to their destruction, so characteristic of the Anglo-American frontier." The exploits and hardships of these men make the most glorious pages in the history of the Church's missionary activity. Many of their efforts proved in vain, but their blood watered the faith; their efforts gave some measure of civilization to the Indians as they taught them how to weave, tan leather, and tend cattle. Their efforts produced the early dictionaries and the first maps of the new country.

Eventually, the Spanish and French missionary and political enterprises receded in importance as England was victorious in the colonial wars. Protestant England thus gained the ascendancy and the Spanish and French disappeared as a political force and their missions remained to survive as best they could. In time to come the Jesuits would be suppressed and this would hurt considerably the missionary thrust. By 1763 Spain would cede Florida and England in turn would gain all the territory east of the Mississippi from France. America was on its way to becoming, not a Catholic country with Spanish or French culture, but a Protestant country with the distinct Anglo-Saxon culture of the WASP (White, Anglo-Saxon-Protestant).[1]

In fact, from the very beginning so identified did America become with Protestantism that the two were interchangeable terms. The result was twofold. One was that non-Catholic historians invariably regarded the nation as Protestant and so American history has been written, until modern times, from a Protestant bias. In an essay entitled "The Problem of the History of Religion in America" Sydney E. Ahlstrom spoke of the sum total of American church history (until recently) as an "uncritical Protestant celebrationism" written from a point of view that was "proud, nationalistic, stridently Protestant." H. Richard Niebuhr was only echoing prevalent opinion when he wrote in his book *The Kingdom of God in America,* "Doubtless Roman Catholicism had made important contributions to American life yet both history and the religious census support the statement that Protestantism is America's only national religion and to ignore that fact is to view the country from a false angle."

The second result, as we shall see, is that many Protestants took as an article of faith that therefore the Catholic Church, with its strong central control could never adapt to American conditions. Again, that is why Protestant historians in the past took little interest in Catholicism; for them it was still a foreign appendage beyond the "normal" or "natural" alliance of the nation and the Protestant religion. This explains why many American Catholic leaders identified getting into the mainstream of America with getting into and imitating the dominant WASP culture. Let us now turn to the origins of this Protestant ascendancy.

THE ATLANTIC SEACOAST

The dominant English brought to the Atlantic colonies a deeply ingrained hatred of anything Catholic. They had memories of their homeland's "Bloody Mary", a Spanish Armada and the inept Guy Fawkes Gunpowder Plot which tried to blow up the King and Parliament to advance the Catholic cause. Catholics were thus hated not only for their "popish" religion but for their attempts at political domination (although, as we saw, the serious attempts at such were more in the minds of the English than in reality). The thirteen colonies were so vigorously anti-Catholic that it was a real challenge for the handful of Catholics to cling to their religion at all. The rival predominant denominations, the Anglicans in Virginia and the Puritans in Massachusetts, agreed on one thing: their hatred for Catholics. They both passed similar laws against Catholics and so did the other colonies, all of which amounted to a serious case of overkill since there were such a small number of Catholics around at that time. Yet, because of the eventual political victory of the colonies in securing independence from England it was to be the Catholics of the colonies who would share the future Church.

The small band of English Catholics had come to America for the same reasons as the Puritans: to worship freely and get out from under the English penal laws. It was under the leadership of an English Catholic convert, George Calvert, who became the first Baron of Baltimore that in 1643 Maryland was founded. He had originally planned to settle in Virginia but as a Catholic he was not welcomed there. It was this Baron Baltimore who made Maryland a colony of religious toleration for all faiths. In April of 1649 the Baron issued an Act of Toleration putting in writing what was already in practice: religious toleration for all (his famous phrase "the free exercise thereof" was to be found a century and a half later in the Constitution). Soon a Puritan faction from Virginia toppled his government and obtained control.

In 1654 they repealed the Act of Toleration and outlawed Catholics in Maryland. They condemned ten Catholics to death, executing four and plundering the houses of the Jesuits forcing them to flee. In 1691 Maryland became a royal colony and the Church of England was established by law in 1692 towards which Catholics had to pay taxes. Until 1781 Catholics were not permitted to participate in public life.

In New York in 1682 a Catholic governor had been appointed. The next year he also issued a guarantee of religious freedom joining Baltimore, Penn and Roger Williams as leaders in religious toleration. However in 1689 a Calvanist overthrew his regime and began a reign of terror against Catholics. In 1693 the Church of England was established in New York with all of the usual anti-Catholic laws. So it was in every colony. It is worth mentioning, however, that in the two cases in the colonial period where Catholics were (briefly) in control it was they who issued acts of religious toleration.

THE CARROLLS

Anti-Catholic prejudice slackened during the Revolutionary War (as it would during the Civil War). Catholics were needed to fight and their loyal and noble conduct, especially the dedication of the priests and sisters, went a long way to break down the barriers. Then too Frenchmen from France (such as Lafayette) were assisting the colonies and it would not do to have overt bias in the presence of such allies. On the other hand, the bias was quite active in the case of Canada. England had just granted the French Catholic Canadians religious freedom. The outcry in the American colonies was bitter and vocal. The Continental Congress itself in no uncertain terms denounced Catholicism to the King of England and chastised him for giving freedom to a "religion that has deluged your island in blood and disbursed impiety, bigotry, persecution, murder and rebellion through every part of the world." The Congress turned right around and asked Canada to help them fight against England! Catholic Canada understandably refused to trust themselves to such bigots who persecuted their fellow Catholics in the colonies; they preferred to remain neutral with England which gave them religious freedom.

It was not only the Revolutionary War that brought relief to Catholics but also the predominant family of the Carrolls. They were to the 1700s what the Kennedys were to the 1900s. Charles Carroll was a signer of the Declaration of Independence and almost our first President and a member of the aristocratic colonial establishment. His patriotism was unimpeachable and he happened to be a Roman Catholic (though possibly not a very practicing one). The Carrolls demonstrated that one could be a Roman Catholic and a good American at the same time. The magic Carroll name made it a natural that Charles' cousin, John Carroll, an able and talented man, should become the first bishop of the United States in 1789.

EARLY COLLEGIALITY

If we recall that Catholics and their clergy were in the country since the 1500s and that there was no bishop until 1789 we will rightly be surprised to suddenly realize the import of this. It means that for some one hundred and fifty years there was no administration of the sacraments of Confirmation and Holy Orders. It means that all during this period the Church in the United States was ruled by what we must call a presbyterate. The local clergy under their local superiors ruled. Rome was far away and besides Rome hardly considered the new country as more than barbaric. In 1757 it is true Rome made a bishop in London the overseer for the American Church but he too was far away and his jurisdiction virtually ceased when England went to war with America. Not that the American clergy wanted a bishop around anyway. The Protestants were so hostile that they did not want to risk further harassment by having a "foreign" bishop sent over to take control.

Finally, the matter could not be put off any longer. Rome, still thinking in European terms, inquired of the government (through Ben Franklin) its opinion about the first American bishop and Congress, to the perplexity of Rome, replied that it did not have competence in such matters. By this time, of course, due to the sheer multiplicity of denominations, expediency had forced Congress to enact the First Amendment forbidding the establishment of any one religion (which pleased the minority Catholics no end)—though some states still kept established Protestant churches till the 1800s.

John Carroll was the natural choice. Still he insisted that in democratic America he must be elected by his peers. Thus it came about that the first bishop of the United States, and later on his two assistant bishops, were elected by the clergy. Unfortunately this initial bit of democracy did not persist and Rome took over. Still, the entire one hundred and fifty years' experience gave the bishops of the United States a strong independence from Rome from the start. It was this same independent spirit that led the Third Provisional Council of Baltimore in 1837 to protest their loyalty to the pope, but only in spiritual matters. They boldly said, "We do not acknowledge any civil or political supremacy, or power over us, in any foreign potentate or power, though that potentate might be the chief pastor of our church." Even before Carroll's time general chapters had been held and the clergy decided all legal, liturgical and disciplinary matters themselves. Carroll only continued that tradition as did the half dozen Provisional Councils held over the next twenty years:

> In each case, all the bishops of the country were present, and their legislation was binding on the Catholics of the entire nation. These were not merely meetings to discuss problems; they were legislative assemblies. . . . There is no other national church within the Roman Catholic communion which met so regularly and legislated so widely.[2]

We might move our story ahead a little here to demonstrate the continued independence of the American hierarchy from Rome. For example, the bishops resisted papal representation in America. They opposed the semi-official visit of Archbishop Bedini in 1853 (whose appearance in the land occasioned violent anti-Catholic demonstrations) and it was only with reluctance that they accepted the Apostolic Delegate in the 1800s. In 1864 Pius IX's Syllabus was received coolly nor would the bishops publish his appeal to enlist members for a papal army to expel the Italian nationalists from Rome. Unlike their European counterparts, the American bishops did not consider the papal states as necessary to the papacy. The bishops were generally opposed to the definition of papal infallibility proposed at Vatican I. They were far more interested in defining episcopal authority because of their own collegial background. This issue was not treated because the Franco-Prussian War dispersed the Council but it was raised and defined at Vatican II which reflected American thoughts on the subject. Such bold independence on the part of his hierarchy is a revelation to the modern American. He has known only a submissive hierarchy. This was because, after Vatican I, Rome's hold became stronger. Also more American boys went to Rome to study for the priesthood and it was these boys who inevitably became bishops. They brought with them the attitude of looking Romewards for answers. So, by the 1900s

> . . . The role of the Apostolic Delegate increased, and the American Church became more and more used to having its problems solved by Roman Congregations. The crises over Americanism and Modernism threw a cloud over the more daring excursions of independent thought. . . . Vital contact with the past, the past of the Maryland missions, John Carroll, the conciliar and collegial tradition was largely lost . . .[3]

THREE PRESSURES

No appreciation of the Church in the United States is possible without a profound recognition of the three basic pressures it had to contend with. First of all, as we have already noted, the Church was taking shape in prejudiced English colonies. Catholics were therefore made to feel as foreigners and less than American. They were reduced to the role of second class intruders while the Protestants took for granted that America was Protestant and Protestantism was America. This factor alone goes a long way in explaining the reaction of some American bishops in unceasingly and vigorously protesting how truly American they were. The second major factor to remember is that the Catholic Church in America was a Church of the immigrants. In the 1800s and especially after the Civil War a veritable deluge of foreigners swept over the country. Most of them were, of course, Catholic and this posed an enormous problem for the struggling Church: how to Americanize such foreign Catholics and prove their loyalty to the United States. Finally we might recall that during the nineteenth century there were revolutions taking place in Europe. It was the age of Pius IX, the fall of the papal states, the Third Republic of France, the deep and abiding suspicion of democracy, freedom and modern civilization so criticized in Pius' Syllabus. It was the age of a strong ultramontane reaction, an increase of Roman centralization, the drive for uniformity and the unresolved problems of church-state relationships. It was on the anvil of these three pressures—American Protestant hatred and fear of Catholics, the high waves of immigration and a suspicious and uncomprehending centralized Rome—that the liberal American Church was forged.

EARLY RIVALRIES

America was blessed with extraordinary leadership during the early years. John Carroll was an ardent patriot of an aristocratic family. His election as America's first bishop was a great help. He was liberal minded as we have seen in his insistence to be elected by his peers. He pleaded for a vernacular liturgy back in 1787. A contemporary of his was the very remarkable John England of Ireland who in 1820 was appointed as bishop of Charleston, South Carolina. South Carolina was too small for this man's influence. He soon made his influence felt all over and became an instant American super-patriot. He loved the country, espoused every liberal cause and lost no opportunity to get in the mainstream of American life. It was he who made up a constitution for his dioceses, established parish councils and began the first Catholic newspaper, *The United States Miscellany.* He was an ardent ecumenist, spoke in non-Catholic pulpits and in 1826 was the first Catholic priest to address Con-

gress.[4] He was a giant away ahead of his time. He even began his short-lived "American" seminary.

We put the word "American" in quotes to point up a deep
conflict and rivalry within the hierarchy. There already was
a seminary, the one founded in Baltimore by the French
Sulpicians. That was the problem. John England thought
the French too foreign. The French bishops, on the contrary, thought of John England and the immigrant Irish as
late-comers who threatened to make the Church less American and more Irish. The French felt that as they were here
well over a hundred years that they represented the true
American heritage. They and their French Sulpicians were
more cultured, better educated and more in the tradition
of the old Maryland Catholics. They felt that they should
predominate and carry on the leadership; that they should
protect the American way of life from the foreign tendencies
of the Irish bishops. They were not therefore happy with
John England and the growing Irish dominance of the
hierarchy.[5] The Irish in turn, becoming very predominant
through immigration, began to resent being ruled over by
the French clergy with their strange accents. Some Irish congregations went so far as to get their own clergy and frequently such clergy were troublemakers expelled from Ireland seeking their fortunes in the New World.

The Irish and the French were not the only ones with such
conflicts. The immigrant Germans resented the ministrations
of an English or Irish clergyman. The problem of lay-trustee-
ism arose to plague the Church. This was the system by
which the laymen not only ran the administration of the
parish (which the more liberal bishops such as England were
all for) but they attempted to hire and fire their clergy.
Even John England would not tolerate this. In fact it was

his strong personality that settled this nasty business that had been an embarrassment for some thirty years.

PROTESTANT REACTIONS

Those Catholic immigrants alarmed the Protestants no end. Their fear of cheap labor and job layoffs agitated their traditional hatred and fears. On January 2, 1830 a group of Protestant ministers therefore launched the anti-Catholic weekly *The Protestant*. It purveyed all of the exaggerations and horror stories possible. The results of such inflammatory nonsense were evident in a rather mild incident that took place in Philadelphia. There Bishop Kenrick submitted a quietly respectful request to the city fathers asking that Catholic children be not forced to use the King James version of the Bible. The result of this was to bring fearful rioting and destruction of church property. In Massachusetts, incited by the harangues of the Reverend Lyman Beecher (father of Harriet Beecher Stowe, author of *Uncle Tom's Cabin*) a mob burned down the Ursuline convent. Stories of ex-priests and escaped nuns such as the widely believed fiction of Maria Monk made the rounds. Not all were as passive as Bishop Kenrick of course. Bishop Hughes of New York warned that if any Catholic churches were burned in his diocese he would not prevent retaliation and he had a mob of willing Irishmen to back him up. There were no incidents in New York. It was this same Bishop Hughes who finally broke the monoply of the Protestant groups in New York by seeing that no state aid was given to the public schools which were inculcating Protestant religious principles. Inadvertently he set up the precedent of no aid to any school teaching religion and thus laid the foundation for the chronic school aid problems that plague Catholics to this day.

The Protestants kept up their attacks. In 1854 a national organization known as the Know-Nothings supported to a large measure by the Protestant ministers appeared dedicated to issuing endless anti-Catholic pamphlets, books and newspaper articles. Again, it was the loyalty and dedication of Catholics of the Civil War that took the steam out of such open bias. Catholics fought on both sides and conducted themselves loyally. The conduct of the Catholic chaplains and sisters again merited high praise. President Lincoln said, "Of all the forms of charity and benevolence seen in the crowded wards of the hospitals, those of some Catholic sisters were among the most efficient." And, to the astonishment of many, the Catholic bishops from both North and South continued to hold their meetings and never let their differing political views shatter their spiritual unity. After the war prejudice again came to the forefront. In 1887 a new organization was founded by some ninety-four Protestant ministers, the American Protective Association (The A.P.A.) which was dedicated to keeping the United States American and Protestant.

THE CHURCH OF THE IMMIGRANTS

The status of the Catholic immigrants was indeed difficult. They discovered that in their new land their status was often lower than that of the Negro slave. Harassed with chronic anti-Catholic bias they were often faced with the practical choice of renouncing their religion in order to advance socially and economically or retaining it and thereby accept a permanent status of inferiority. The immigrants tended to move into the cities (giving American Catholicism its distinctive urban character) and there they settled in their ghettos trying to preserve their nationalities and religion. Since they thus withdrew from the mainstream of American life they acquired a certain inferiority. It was this mass of people that the Church had to Americanize and indeed it was most effective in doing so. The parochial school was established to meet the immigrant needs. In 1884 the bishops meeting in Baltimore made the parochial school mandatory and by 1900 there were some 4000 of them in existence. Georgetown University had already been erected in 1791 and in 1809 Mother Seton founded the first native community and opened a school for girls in Emmitsburg, Maryland. Her Sisters of Charity became the first source of teachers for the new Catholic schools. The Church's school system in particular did more than anything else to assimilate the immigrant. Historian Henry Steele Commager puts it this way:

> It might, indeed, be maintained that the Catholic Church was, during this period, one of the most effective of all agencies for democracy and Americanization. Representing as it did a vast cross section of the American people, it could ignore class, section, and race; peculiarly the church of the newcomer, of those who all too often were regarded as aliens, it could give them not only spiritual refuge but social security.[6]

Orphanages, hospitals and Vincent de Paul societies were begun. The unsung heroes, the parish priests, did yeoman's work in guiding and assisting the bewildered immigrant. The Church's ministrations were especially needed as Protestants abandoned the lower classes and the cities and became a middle class religion (something the Catholic would be guilty of in the 1960s). On the other hand Protestants were happy that the Church stayed with the crude and unruly lower classes. Someone had to control the mob:

The business tycoons, the real spokesmen for America in this era, saw the problems with cold realism. "Look at the millions of foreigners pouring into this country," the Canadian-born James J. Hill said, "to whom the Roman Church is the only authority they either fear or respect. What will be their social view, their political action, their moral status if that singly controlling force should be removed?" . . . Political leaders were also grateful. Mark Hanna was supposed to have said that the only two safeguards against anarchy in the United States were the Supreme Court and the Roman Catholic Church . . .[7]

AMERICANISTS VERSUS THE CONSERVATIVES

As the Church moved towards the end of the nineteenth century and into the twentieth, divisions arose in the American hierarchy not so much along lines of nationality but along the lines of ideology. They were divided into conservatives and liberals. The conservatives felt that the Church should not assimilate itself into the mainstream (for we have not here a lasting city anyway); that it could make no headway against Protestant bias which saw to it that the public schools were in reality Protestant schools, who threw the pope's gift of a block of marble to be used for the Washington monument into the Potomac River and hedged them in at every turn. Pious, quiet, isolated citizens preparing for another world was the role of the Catholics. Such conservative bishops were represented by Ryan of Philadelphia, Elder of Cincinnati, Gilmour of Cleveland and especially Corrigan of New York and McQuaid of Rochester.

On the opposite side were the liberals, called the Americanists. As their names implied they were totally dedicated to American culture, supported the public schools, reached out to Protestants and firmly believed in America's posture of complete separation of Church and state. Such were

Bishops Keane, Spalding, Ireland and Gibbons. Gibbons was especially important for he became a cardinal in 1886 and was *the* churchman in America. He had worked in North Carolina where he became acquainted with the Protestants, preached in their churches and made many converts. He wrote the famed *The Faith of Our Fathers* based on American analogies. As leader of the Catholic Church for some forty years he did more than anyone else to mediate between the Church and the country. He was in demand as a speaker, was consulted by presidents and did much for the church-state relations. At his jubilee in 1911 people of all faiths gathered to honor him including President Taft and ex-President Roosevelt. He was a good balance to his more outspoken Americanists, Ireland and Keane and a hard pressed diplomat in trying to control the conservatives and the liberals.

KNIGHTS OF LABOR

For very good reasons Rome had always been suspicious of secret societies. In Europe they had frequently been revolutionary and anticlerical, but in America the many societies were harmless enough (with the exception of a few anti-Catholic masonic lodges) such as the Knights of Pythias, the Sons of Temperance and the Ancient Order of Hibernians. Since they posed no threat the Americanist bishops felt it would be futile to condemn them and to do so would only invite new hostilities. The conservative bishops saw it otherwise and prodded Rome which finally did condemn a few of the secret societies such as the Knights of Pythias and the Odd Fellows. Gibbons would not publish the decree until forced to do so. The real issue, however, in which Gibbons triumphed was the matter concerning the Knights of Labor, a workingman's organization and forerunner of the

A.F. of L. The conservatives wanted that condemned also but Gibbons spoke strongly out to Rome. He won the day and became the hero of the working man. Four years later Gibbons was vindicated when Leo XIII came out in *Rerum Novarum* defending the rights of workers to organize.

APOSTOLIC DELEGATE AND CATHOLIC UNIVERSITY

The conservatives and Americanists clashed also over the establishment of a Catholic University. The problem was one of location and curriculum. Each wanted it in his own diocese. Messages went back and forth to Rome trying to either squelch or keep alive the idea. Finally the issue was settled and it was erected at Washington, D.C. with Bishop Keane as its first rector. The Americanists also opposed the appointment of an Apostolic Delegate. For one reason, it was the heyday of anti-Catholic organizations which would make much capital out of a foreign bishop coming to rule the American Church. Besides, the bishops felt they could handle things by themselves. We might recall that the last time a delegate from Rome visited the United States (Bishop Bedini in 1853) Protestant riots followed him wherever he went. Rome, however, had its way and Archbishop Satolli came as Apostolic Delegate. At first he was on the side of the Americanists but in a few years he did a strange turn-about and when he went back to Rome he was instrumental in having Keane removed as rector of Catholic University and influential in Leo XIII's condemnation of "Americanism."

APPROACHES TO PROTESTANTISM

The Catholic liberals and conservatives, as might be expected, had highly different views about Protestantism. The conservatives, smarting under the tradition of the Know-Nothings and the A.P.A.'s were always deeply suspicious of the Protestants and felt that distance from them was the best policy. The liberals, on the other hand, were always ready to reach out and admit the virtues and some of the truths they possessed. The conservatives wanted a rigid interpretation that "outside the Church there is no salvation" and their only consolation in the days of high bigotry was their conviction that, in the final run no Protestant would be in heaven. The liberal Americanists and the newly founded Paulists (founded by convert Isaac Hecker) felt otherwise and would stretch the saying widely. It was the Paulists who in 1904 established the first house at Catholic University to train priests for the special mission to Protestants. They even went to preach in the streets. The liberal bishops accepted all invitations to speak in "Protestant" territory. Bishop Keane spoke at Harvard in 1879 (although Bishop McQuaid refused to let him come in and speak in his diocese at Cornell University). In 1893 the Americanist bishops attended the great Ecumenical Parliament in Chicago.

APPROACHES TO SEPARATION OF
CHURCH AND STATE

The conservative American Catholics were wary of church-state separation. They saw that the Protestants were dominant, the public schools Protestant and Catholics discriminated against. They saw the separation as an aberration, a departure from centuries of tradition and boding no good for the Church. The Americanists, needless to say, saw it otherwise. They felt that the medieval union of Church and state was only an "accident" and not essential and they lost no opportunity to tell their Protestant neighbors that the Church had no design to unite Church and state. They could point to Carroll of Maryland and Donegan in New York who had issued the first acts of toleration which were repealed by the Protestants. They were content with the freedom of the Church to do what it wanted in America in contrast to the European situation where Concordats and traditions hindered the Church at every turn. Ireland could characteristically exclaim that a Catholic could "go forward, in one hand bearing the book of Christian truth, and in the other the Constitution of the United States." The Protestants themselves were not always convinced of this and felt that the Catholic took political orders from his clergy and ultimately from the pope.

One of the ticklish situations came for the Americanists when the pope demanded public support for his regaining of the papal states lost to Italian unification. Leo XIII again stated that the Church's possessing temporal properties was the best safeguard to the Church's independence. The Americanist bishops could not agree less. The American conservative bishops could not agree more and they and their followers like the Jesuits, almost made the temporal territory of the papacy an article of faith. The Americanist bishops, under Gibbons simply ignored the pope and wrapped up his wishes in harmless rhetoric and outright disagreement. It was due to the liberal leadership that forthright support for the temporal powers of the pope was not forthcoming from America.

THE SOCIAL ATTITUDES

The early approach to the social problems of the country is summarized by historian Robert D. Cross when he writes:

The transition was particularly difficult for a Catholic priest. The clerical education of a traditional Church prepared the young man to deal with social problems as they had been known to the Church for centuries. The discipline of an authoritative Church was better designed to preserve unity by continuing traditional actions than to promote innovation. Where prelates of liberal conviction were installed, it is true, liberal priests enjoyed greater sanctuary from outside coercions than did Protestant ministers mortgaged to the approval of their middle-class congregations. But since it was logical for the Church to place conservatives like Archbishop Corrigan where immigrants were most numerous, those priests who found conditions in the eastern cities an incentive to reform activities usually had to fight a running battle with tradition-minded superiors. Moreover, in most areas, unless a priest chose to conduct a one-man campaign, he had to join nondenominational reform movements, which too often in the past had been hostile to the Church. The greatest incubus to Catholic reform, however, was not organizational, but the widespread religious belief that human enterprise was presumptuous.

To the Catholic conservatives, the most proper response to social difficulties was devout passivity. . . .[8]

It was the Americanist bishops who moved the Church from this "devout passivity" to embrace social reform. They led the way to cooperate with non-Catholics and moving people towards active charity and the rights of workers. It was Gibbons we recall who prevented the Knights of Labor from being condemned.

THE SCHOOLS

The conservatives were against the public school system and felt that holiness was better than learning, especially in a "godless" school system. The Americanists, on the other hand, were for universal education and the public school system for all its faults. They were even for the education of women:

> On no point of educational theory were Catholics more sharply divided than on the desirability of providing the training more and more American women were demanding. Appalled as many of the liberals were by the more brassy demands for women's rights, and anxious that the traditional womanly virtues should not be lost, they felt certain that, if society was to be reformed, women's capacities for enterprising moral action could not be neglected. Christianity, they insisted, had always stood for the fullest realization of women's potentialities. . . . Most liberals believed that the education typically given by the convent school was too rigid, preparing girls only for the seclusion of the nunnery or the home. For young women as for young men, education should not close the door on the opportunity for any moral career.[9]

The conservatives of course responded that a woman's place was in the home. The public school system and the financing question of aid to private schools was and has remained a vexing question. The anti-Catholic forces of the time of course would brook no aid to Catholic schools. Various plans were tried and various experiments with public schools which the conservatives disapproved. However the liberals scored a point when Leo XIII backed up a liberal (short-lived) school experiment by Bishop Ireland.

HERESY OF AMERICANISM

Perhaps nowhere did the Americanists and the conservatives disagree more basically than on the issue of accommodation to America. The Americanists were wary of the contemplative life and were for the more active and enterprising (American) virtues. They looked with suspicion on too much devotionalism as taking away the energies better spent on up-and-doing activities. They firmly believed in individual freedom and liberty. They thought that laymen should have more of a part in the Church and more participation in the liturgy. They much preferred Isaac Hecker's new American Order of active and liberal Paulists to the ultra-conservative Jesuits whom Bishop Ireland attacked. Imprudently the Americanists in their super patriotism took to lecturing their European brethren on the merits of America causing renewed attention and suspicions. European conservatives, always abetted by Corrigan and McQuaid, began to add up the problems: the attacks on the religious orders, the Germans' unhappiness with Irish domination, a life of Father Hecker with its disastrous preface by Abbe Klein which seemed to extol the active virtues and the inner spirit at the expense of the contemplative virtues and the traditional Church structures, etc. In brief, to some Europeans the Church in America seemed little more than liberal Protestantism backed by the Masons. A catch-all term was invented. It was called the heresy of "Americanism."

Before long liberal Denis O'Connell was relieved of the rectorship of the American College in Rome. Bishop Keane was removed from the same position at Catholic University. Finally in 1899 Leo XIII came out with his letter *Testem benevolentiae* on "Americanism." It was mild and cautious and did not mention names, but it was directed at Baltimore and the slap at the Americanists was unmistakable. It warned against "Americanism," rejoicing the conservatives and the Jesuits. Gibbons of course protested that no such heresy existed but the cloud was there. In time, we might add, the Americanists did recover. In 1900 Keane was made bishop of Dubuque and Denis O'Connell became the rector of Catholic University. Rome, however, would not bestow the cardinal's hat on any of the Americanists. Instead it gave it to the moderate Bishop Farely of New York and the reactionary conservative, William O'Connell of Boston.

CONTRIBUTIONS OF THE AMERICANISTS

We must recognize the stature of men like Gibbons, Keane, Ireland and Spalding. They were men of strong personalities and by their actions and insights they forged a liberal American Church. Probably many of the clergy and laity were conservative but these Americanists led them well in building bridges to the American way of life. It must be admitted, however, that the Americanists had one thing going for them: they generally had the backing of the pope. Leo XIII was no flaming liberal but he was more open to democracy than his predecessor. True he almost condemned the Knights of Labor but he stopped short of it. His rebuke of "Americanism" was mild and courteous. But he was open to the Americanists and received their letters and personal visits, and even where he did not agree with them they in turn credited him with being misinformed rather than being in basic disagreement.

Yet, it must be noticed that the victories of the Americanists were not as long lasting as might be hoped in many cases:

> The decade 1900-1910 which succeeded the final failure of the Americanist attempt to harmonize Catholicism with American life appears to have been one of retrenchment significant of the spirit of conservatism which had emerged from the struggle victorious.

> True enough, John Keane had been elevated to the rank of archbishop, and Denis O'Connell was made the rector of Catholic University, but John Ireland was never to wear the cardinal's red hat which he desired with such unbecoming ardor, and in American public life Catholics were to hold positions of influence or authority which, in proportion to their numbers, could hardly have been fewer and farther between. Intellectually, Catholics also were remiss, compel-

ling the British observer D. W. Brogran to remark: "In no Western society is the intellectual prestige of Catholicism lower than in the country where in such respects as wealth, numbers, and strength of organization it is so powerful."

The Catholic laity was an anonymous, amorphous mass. Ireland and Gibbons might sing the praises of the American way of life from sunup to sundown, but the fact is that it was the conservative prelates who had the layman's ear. They had convinced them of the "contaminations" of "pagan" America, and had virtually herded them into a mental ghetto. . . . Catholics . . . seldom entered the national arena. In the field of social justice they were a cipher. And this, again, is because the layman had almost no standing. Having been indoctrinated with the seige mentality characteristic of the Council of Trent, they regarded themselves, to extend the military metaphor, as the ordinary soldiery, while the priests were the captains, the bishops were the colonels and the archbishops were generals. Generally speaking, for a layman actually to *do* anything without orders was not only unthinkable but perhaps even insubordinate. And this habit of mind, it seems, is directly attributable to the fact that the bishops actually did not trust the laymen.[10]

Still, it must be remarked that the Americanists have finally won in important areas for their thinking has not only prevailed in the question of religious liberty as defined at Vatican II (and proposed by Father John Courtney Murray, S.J., an "Americanist") but also in the area of granting to the laymen the position that is rightfully theirs.

ON ITS OWN

In 1908 the Church in the United States ceased being official missionary territory and was given status as an independent Church. Stability was setting in. Catholic population was rising although there was a certain amount of fallen aways especially in the country areas. The Church was a Church of the cities, where the immigrants settled. It was weak in the country areas, in the South and West and in rural districts. No, the action was in the big cities like Chicago and when in 1921 Congress began to restrict immigration the Church got a chance to collect its breath. Meanwhile another native religious order had been founded, that of the Maryknoll Fathers in 1912. Chicago hosted the international Eucharistic Congress in 1926. The monastic life came to America in 1875 with the Poor Clares and in 1848 some French Trappists had settled in Kentucky. The liturgical movement moved ahead in the 1920s and 30s. In 1919 a central organization which was to assist the bishops came into being, the National Catholic Welfare Conference. Cardinal Gibbons had died in 1921 and shortly after his death another anti-Catholic group was formed, the Ku Klux Klan. Actually it was a revival of a secret society founded after the Civil War in the South. The Klan was anti-Negro, anti-Semite and anti-Catholic. It was dedicated to the protection of womanhood and the ascendancy of white Protestant America. However it allied itself with the Scottish rite of Masons in 1922 and was responsible with the masons for getting the state of Oregon to pass the law forcing parents to send their children to the public schools. Fortunately the Supreme Court struck down the law. After this and an unsuccessful similar case in Michigan the Klan went into decline until the 1960s Civil Rights Movement stirred it into action once again.

During the 1930s America was entertained or enraged by two figures on the social scene, one very prominent and the other little known to the public. These figures were the Rev. John A. Ryan and the Rev. Charles E. Coughlin. Catholic social principles while having a good tradition with men like Gibbons, Keane and Leo XIII's *Rerum Novarum* never received the emphasis and spread among Catholics that they deserved. Catholics in particular remained indifferent to the social teaching of their church and the issues were confined to a few interested men like John A. Ryan. More than anyone else he kept the social questions alive, wrote his famous book *Distributative Justice* and agitated to the end of his life for social reform. Naturally he met with suspicion from the conservative members of the hierarchy and other Catholics. He was constantly being accused of being a socialist (Coughlin dubbed him "the Right Reverend New Dealer") but he was backed by the formidable Archbishop Curley of Baltimore (later the two split over Roosevelt's New Deal policies).

In 1926 Father Coughlin began his famous radio broadcasts. In five years he had a huge following and soon began to turn to political issues. He was an early supporter of Roosevelt but later turned bitterly against him. He went so far as to pick a candidate to run against him. He called Roosevelt a communist and in 1938 he turned antisemitic. A move was started to ban his magazine *Social Justice* from the mails and the Postmaster General finally persuaded his archbishop to silence Coughlin. In 1942 Coughlin went off the air obeying his bishop and thus ending a most colorful radio career.

CONTEMPORARY TIMES

In 1948 another anti-Catholic organization came into being, the POAU (Protestants and Other Americans United). It was a result of Paul Blanchard's book *American Freedom and Catholic Power* wherein he revived the old saw that Catholicism was hostile to American democracy. He received a wide hearing and his book was on the best seller lists. The famous McCollum case which outlawed religious instruction in a released time program in the public schools made further inroads against what was considered the separation of church and state and the Catholic Church's desires to force its will on the majority of Americans. The POAU issued a manifesto to all the old charges about the Church wanting to infringe on the state and NCWC's chairman, Archbishop McNicholas of Cincinnati had to comment once more:

> No group in America is seeking union of church and state; and last of all are Catholics. We deny absolutely and without any qualification that the Catholic bishops of the United States are seeking a union of church and state by any endeavor whatsoever either proximate or remote. If tomorrow Catholics constituted a majority in our country, they would not seek a union of church and state. . . . The signers of the Manifesto assume that their attempt to have the Supreme Court reverse its decisions is a patriotic virtue, but that it is criminal for others to seek an interpretation of an amendment of the Constitution. . . .

That the tradition of anti-Catholic bias continued was brought home forcibly in the campaign of America's first Catholic president, John F. Kennedy. Ted Sorensen, Kennedy's speechwriter, lawyer and confidant reported that well over three hundred anti-Catholic tracts had been distributed to more than twenty million homes. There were countless mailings, chain letters, radio broadcasts, television attacks. Sorensen said that one publication found it hard to decide whether Kennedy's election was a popish plot or the communist conspiracy but felt that there was not much difference. One theme persisted, according to Sorensen, and that was that the pope would soon be governing America. Kennedy had to meet with the Methodist ministers in Houston, Texas to try to convince them that his religion and his partiotism were not in conflict. In the long line of able Catholic Americans, he had to defend himself. Still, the suspicions lurked and the anti-Catholic campaign continued:

> But nativism's death was a reluctant one and in its last dying gasp it cost John Kennedy (according to the Survey Research Center at the University of Michigan) some five million votes. . . .

> After the convention and as the election campaign itself roared on, the prejudice continued. The POAU predicted that if the United States ever became 51 per cent Catholic, Protestants would be treated as second-class citizens and damned souls. A Protestant minister in Boston would say, "Like Khrushchev, Kennedy is a captive of the system." Norman Vincent Peale remarked, "Our American culture is at stake. I don't say it won't survive but it won't be what it was. . . ." Dr. Ramsey Pollard, the president of the Southern Baptist Convention, pointed out, "No matter what Kennedy might say, he cannot separate from his Church if he is a true Catholic. All we ask is that Roman Catholicism lift its bloody hand from the throats of those that want to worship in the church of their choice. I am not a bigot." And this same believer in free American elections also said, "My church had enough members to beat Kennedy in this area if they all vote like I tell them to." One wonders what would have happened if a Catholic bishop had said the same thing. . . .

> The Reverend Harvey Springer, a cowboy evangelist of the Rockies, offered a solution: "Let the Romanists move out of America. Did you see the coronation of Big John? Let's hope we never see the coronation of Little John. How many Catholics came over on the Mayflower—not one. The Constitution is a Protestant Constitution. . . ."[11]

After some four hundred years of Catholics being in America the old distrust still remains and the old complaint of Catholics trying to impose their doctrine or ways on America is still very much alive and the distrust is renewed whenever a new issue comes up. In the 1970s the abortion issue became the school issue of the 1950s and Catholics still had to plead their cause. A good example is Russell Shaw's letter to the pro-abortion *New York Times* on June 5, 1972:

To the Editor:
The progression of thought in your very interesting May 26 editorial "Church and State" flows with irresistible logic up to a point. But at that point, I am afraid, the logic breaks down and rhetoric takes its place.

You observe that religious leaders have a right and a duty to expound their point of view and to attempt to persuade others of its rightness. You acknowledge that it is not "improper" for churches to seek to convince legislators of the correctness of their views so that they will be embodied in legislation. You recognize further that every public official brings with him to office a set of values which might loosely be termed "religious."

But then, in a sudden leap of alarmism ("it is dangerous to a free society"), you cite the impropriety of "the use of the state's power to impose religious laws and doctrine." Granted the impropriety—no one would deny it—how does the abuse to which you advert relate to the premises you have so carefully and correctly stated?

Quite simply, it does not relate, and the reference to imposition by the state of "religious laws and doctrine" is no more than a straw man. No one, including the leadership of the Roman Catholic Church, is suggesting that governmental power be used to impose denominational beliefs and practices on the populace. To suggest otherwise merely obscures an already complex issue.

Many religious groups in our society exercise their right to speak to public issues and seek to influence legislation in line with what they conceive to be sound public policy. In doing so, however, they are not attempting to enlist the authority of the state to enforce creedal positions. They are seeking rather to make operative through the political process their convictions as to what will best realize the good of society.

Many other groups besides churches do the same. Legislators, judges, public officials and ultimately the people make the final determination whether to accept or reject as public policy the positions they advance.

The danger in your argument is its implicit suggestion that, whenever the social consensus as articulated in law coincides with a religiously based view of man and society, we are thereby in a situation where "the state's power (is used) to impose religious laws and doctrine."

The absurdity of this becomes apparent when one considers that, carried to its logical extreme, it leads to the conclusion that because a religious group regards, say, reckless driving as immoral, the state should do nothing to prevent or punish reckless driving (otherwise it is using its power to "impose . . . religious doctrine"). This may be an extreme example, but no more extreme than the position expressed in your editorial.

To be sure, the state should not take orders from the churches, but neither should it so wall itself off from them that religiously inspired views, alone among the many expressions of ideology and opinion in our society, are refused a hearing and denied embodiment in law and public policy even when they are judged by democratic consensus to be in the best interests of society.

Separation of church and state, as much desired by the churches as by the state, is not served by denying religiously based beliefs a role in the formation of public policy precisely because they are religiously based.

Russell Shaw
Director
United States Catholic Conference
Washington, May 26, 1972

In McNicholas' pronouncement, Kennedy's defense and Shaw's letter one can hear the refrains of John Carroll, John England, Bishop Ireland and Cardinal Gibbons and a host of others who from the beginning of the Republic have tried to defend the Catholic Church's right to be in America and its status as American.

THE KENNEDY YEARS

The Kennedy years were the (brief) high point for American Catholics. A few decades before with the cumulative impact of Roosevelt's New Deal, the CIO, wartime wages and the G.I. Bill of Rights American Catholics for the first time entered the middle class. Then with the election of and the subsequent universal affection accorded Pope John XXIII, the generally favorable attention given to the Vatican Council by the media and the election of America's first Catholic president, isolation and aloofness, long associated with American Catholic life, were brought to an end.

Yet, ironically, the very forces unleashed by the two Johns made the Catholic victory short lived and, as we shall see, cast new criticisms at the policies of Catholic liberals. Catholicism, of course, was gaining ground before Kennedy came on the scene. The parochial school controversies and the upheaval of the McCarthy era were stirring them up. There were the beginnings of critical self-examinations of American Catholic cultural and intellectual life spearheaded by John Tracy Ellis who wrote his celebrated essay on the subject in 1954. From that challenge there soon came questions of the liturgy and, above all, the role of the laity in the Church.

THE EFFECT OF THE COUNCIL

The Vatican Council too challenged some of the most cherished ideas and securities of the Catholic population. Heretofore since Catholics were treated (and often thought of themselves) as strangers in a Protestant country, they had concentrated their efforts on those features of their religion that most distinguished them from Protestants. As a framework of strong identity there were the Friday abstinence, compulsory worship on Sundays and the six holydays of obligation, a fixed moral code giving clear and unambiguous rules on sexual and marital questions and so on. All these things were challenged by Vatican II.

As a result there was, for many, much optimism after the council. Many new-breed Catholics—Greeley, Thorman, Novak, Leo, Hoyt, Callahan—celebrated its achievements even though most of them wound up later decrying certain excesses and failures. But for the moment things were moving. Representative structures were established, national episcopal conferences gained real power and on the local level parish councils were set up. A newer theology replaced the static, legal definition of the Church with the more democratic sounding "People of God." Ecumenism made contacts with Protestants respectable. A new openness was in and the laity were mandated their place in the Church.

Yet all these changes were to prove disappointing to many. For instance, liturgical reforms, aimed at revitalizing community life, found few communities receptive and brought forth no great spiritual or social awakening. When freedom of conscience had been given by conciliar decree to non-Catholics Catholics felt justified to apply the same right to themselves. They began to pick and choose among long-accepted Church teachings, ignore what they wished (as in the well publicized instance of birth control) and still consider themselves as Catholics. Episcopal collegiality weakened papal centralization and the stress put on the laity's role in Church matters and liturgy blurred the priest's role and produced for some an identity crisis. In short, the new sense of direction, of freedom and responsibility in the Church did not, as hoped, move Catholicism to a new unity of action and moral posture. Rather it occasioned deep and serious divisions within the Church which were bound to increase. "Few would have realized a decade before how serious were the forces which were at work around them. None would have believed that by 1970 news of priests leaving their rectories for married life would be commonplace, that a self-proclaimed Catholic resistance movement would be engaged in a nonviolent war with American government, that monasteries would sponsor conferences on women's liberation and that the leader of an important lay organization would use obscenity in a discussion with bishops."[12] Frightened Catholics, both clerical and lay, retreated into the old securities while disillusioned liberals faced crises of faith and conscience.

AN EMPTY VICTORY?

But there was one final irony left for American Catholics. After finally getting recognized as a genuine part of American life and their right to be full, accredited Americans—suddenly their own members and many of their most revered leaders at home and abroad began raising questions about America itself. The Council Fathers had for instance remarked in the light of their new notions of the Church that size, power, wealth, schools, church buildings, etc. were really not sufficient measurements of Catholic progress. Rather the question was: did the Church—and the Church in America—proclaim the Gospel? Did it take seriously its commitment of service to all men regardless of creed and color? Had the American Church in its pursuit of WASP approval, had it imitated America's gross concept of success and sold out its own soul?

Was the America that Catholics sought so long to emulate worth emulating after all? Was America that moral that it should be imitated? Suddenly, faced with the brutal assassinations of its best leaders, a vicious, unpopular war, the alienation of its youth, ugly, blood-spilling racism, the newly publicized plight of the American Indian, the nation did not seem that great to many. Apparently America was not the home of the noble and the free but a land of violence and oppression. And so, "A Church remade in the American image, the goal of Catholic liberalism for over a century, now seemed to many the basest form of blasphemy."[13] As historian David O'Brien remarks:

> The America Daniel Callahan had described in 1961 as characterized by freedom, openness and democracy was replaced by an image of America as militarist, racist and oppressive. Even the most casual observer could not help but notice the rapid changes which occurred in the 1960s, from the enthusiasm of new opportunity and reform of 1960 to near despair of 1967 and 1968. The America of John Tracy Ellis and John Cogley, much less than that of Ireland and Hecker, disintegrated in the reign of Lyndon Johnson. At the very moment when America gave its complete acceptance to Catholicism as a part of the natural order of the

nation, the nation appeared no longer a safe haven for the
Christian conscience.[14]

What he is saying is that perhaps the Americanist bishops
and their spiritual clerical and lay descendants had been too
optimistic, too hasty:

> While it is surely too early to argue that the mass of Ameri-
> can Catholics seriously question the moral validity of the
> nation, it seems true that for many Catholics America can
> no longer simply be taken for granted. It is events, and the
> conflicts they occasion, which have brought this about, not
> the superior wisdom of scholars maturing amid the trials of
> the 1960s. It must be clear that the Americanist heritage,
> which seems so sordid today, was a humane and honorable
> stance that reflected the best aspirations of the Catholic com-
> munity. Nevertheless, it was a position confined in its vision
> and limited in its critical edge. Expressing as it did the self-
> consciousness of the Catholic community, it too frequently
> was shaped by the dialectic of argument with conservative
> Catholics and anti-Catholic Americans with the result that it
> lacked a critical sense of the character of the religious situa-
> tion in America and of the dynamics of American society
> itself.[15]

As matters now stand American Catholics, like the rest of
the Catholic world, must struggle with that most basic of all
questions: "What is the Church?" They must live in hope
while they learn to accommodate themselves to a plurality
of structures. They must engage in the continuing process
of a Church, once preserved in medieval power and influence
and enshrined in authority and monarchial structure, redis-
covering its dynamism as servant, messianic sign and prophet
to the world. American Catholics now have a clearer mandate that they be not a reflection of but a witness to the very
America they have ever sought to emulate and have never
ceased to love.

NOTES

1. In our day, according to some, the WASP dominance is on its way out. See books like Michael Novak's *The Rise of the Unmeltable Ethnics*. The Macmillan Company. New York, N.Y. 1972. The classic work on Protestant dominance is Ray Allen Billington's *The Protestant Crusade*, first published in 1938 and reprinted several times since.
2. *Catholicism in America*, edited by Philip Gleason. Chapter, "The Distinctive Tradition of American Catholicism" by James J. Hennesey, S.J., p. 38. Harper and Row, New York. 1970.
3. *Ibid.*, p. 44.
4. Father Gabriel Richard was a congressman and functioned in that capacity. His speeches were those of a congressman.
5. The positions of the French and Irish are still disputed. The Notre Dame school of American History, represented by Thomas T. McAvoy, holds the French view as given in the text. The Catholic University school, headed by John Tracy Ellis, contends that it was the Irish who were the true purveyors of the American tradition.
6. John Tracy Ellis, *American Catholicism* (Second Revised Edition), p. 105. The University of Chicago Press, Chicago. 1969. See also the updated classic *The Uprooted* by Oscar Handlin. Atlantic Monthly Press Book. 1973.
7. Robert D. Cross, *op. cit.*, p. 34, 35.
8. *Ibid.*, pp. 106, 107.
9. *Ibid.*, pp. 132, 133.
10. Robert Leckie, *American and Catholic*, pp. 262, 263. Doubleday and Co. Garden City, N.Y. 1970.
11. Andrew M. Greeley, *The Catholic Experience*, pp. 281, 282. Doubleday and Co., Garden City, N.Y. 1967.
12. David J. O'Brien, *op. cit.* p. 140.
13. *Ibid.*, p. 73. So confused is America over its moral status that the nation's Bicentennial in 1976 is having trouble getting off the ground. Boston (the first choice) and Philadelphia have refused to host it. The churches are in an equal quandary: "The churches are confused by the new situation in which they find themselves in American culture, and by the new theological developments within and among themselves. The Protestantism that inspired the older American culture and civic religion is bewildered by the revolutionary changes that are taking place in the culture in which it was once at home. Roman Catholics, who have 'arrived' in

American culture on the wave of their revolutionary development
since Vatican II, find it difficult to know what to do with their
new-found liberation. . . . For both church and nation the Bicentennial is a painful challenge. . . . For the church it is a *karios*
in which it is forced to reassess its place and function in American
culture, to recover its theological integrity, and to become a
prophetic witness and priestly servant to a nation in distress. . . ."
From "The Church in the World" by E. G. Homrighausen in the
January, 1973 issue of *Theology Today,* p. 411.
14. *Ibid.,* p. 167
15. *Ibid.,* p. 72, 73. There are several books on the contemporary
American Catholic scene which will prove most helpful about
matters in the latter part of this chapter. O'Brien's book quoted
several times is the best. Others include the less scholarly but
more engaging *Bare Ruined Choirs: Doubt, Prophecy, and Radical
Religion* by Garry Wills. Doubleday & Co., Garden City, New
York, 1972. *The Decline and Fall of Radical Catholicism* by
James Hitchcock, Herder and Herder, New York, 1971, and
Catholic America by John Cogley who himself helped much of
contemporary liberal Catholicism. Dial Press, New York, 1973.
There is also the award winning scholarly book, Sydney Ahlstrom's
A Religious History of the American People, Yale University Press,
1972 (though for a dissenting review see *Worldview* magazine,
April, 1973, p. 49).

XXII

Towards Vatican II

AFTERMATH OF A WAR

The end of World War I had many frustrations, not the least of which were those of the Germans themselves. We should realize that in that war the allies had never set foot in Germany nor marched into Berlin demanding surrender. The German people had been kept in ignorance about their military defeats and were unaware that Von Hindenburg himself had insisted on surrender because their armies were exhausted. The Germans, on the contrary, thought that they had been betrayed through the machinations of the communists, the liberals, the Jews, the socialists, etc. They found it particularly hard to sign a document that indeed was untrue: that they and they alone were guilty for the war. They were stunned when they were saddled with a most humiliating peace treaty containing impossibly vindictive financial arrangements which bequeathed to the allies the future embarrassment as to how to collect or lessen the burden. France went so far as to invade the Ruhr valley's rich mining region for payment. This only served to solidify German morale and hostility. Many unworkable financial plans were offered and only a general economic depression wiped off the debts all around with hardship to all and leaving each nation unsatisfied and bitter. The seeds for World War II were in many respects planted in the peace terms of World War I. In spite of the fact that unrestrained imperialism and nationalism had led to World War I, nationalism continued to grow after the war. The map of Europe was redrawn and several nations emerged along national lines. The more democratic governments came into more vogue and yet, ironically, more and more countries succumbed under the iron hands of dictatorships. They posed a problem both to the world and to the Church.

THE POPES AND THE STATES

The monarchies which were former if troublesome allies of the papacy were now defunct for the most part. The aftermath of the war left the papacy with the challenge of dealing with each situation as it came along. We have already seen how the popes were wary of any political organizations of Catholic laymen. When and where they did permit Catholic associations, they called them "Catholic Action" and such groups were to be totally and exclusively under the control of the hierarchy and free of politics. They were forbidden any autonomous, independent action. This proved to be a major defect with the rise of the totalitarian powers. If a Catholic did not belong to a Catholic Action group and was forbidden to act independently, he often did not know how to deal with a Hitler or a Mussolini. Without firm directives or the strength of unity with his own free political parties he tended either to collaborate or resist. The popes by acting unilaterally with the heads of such regimes left no guide lines for the man in the street.

We might observe at this point that the results of forbidding any independent lay social action was to identify social harmony with the official concerns of the institutional Church. Leo XIII said as much when he wrote, "Let it become more and more evident that the tranquillity of order and the true prosperity flourish especially among those people whom the Church controls and influences." This meant that any Catholic social action was subordinate to concrete ecclesiastical interests and often abstract Christian principles, especially in reference to those outside the Church, were ignored. That is what led philosopher Sidney Hook to write, "In any crucial situation the behavior of the Catholic Church may be more reliably predicted by reference to its concrete interests as a political organization than by reference to its timeless dogmas." Guenter Lewy in his book *The Catholic Church and Nazi Germany* commented similarly that "the Church's opposition was carefully circumscribed. It was rooted in her concern for her institutional interests rather than in a belief in freedom and justice for all men." It would be an uphill struggle for the lower clergy and laymen, excepting those driven to radicalism, to take the social issues from the hierarchy's exclusive organizational preoccupations.

THE CONCORDATS

The popes did, in fact, act unilaterally with the various heads of state by making Concordats or agreements with them. By this means the Church obtained certain legal freedoms (often confined to the paper they were written on). The Concordats were a government-to-government diplomatic arrangement preserving the rights of the Church on the top level. The biggest defect of the Concordat manner of dealing with governments was that such an agreement did not take into account the needs of the ordinary Catholics, was made without their consent and bound them to a course of neutrality or inaction. In short, legal safeguards were granted to the Church but on the everyday way of living, acting, surviving and resisting there was no plan, no agreement. This meant that in practice a Hitler could gladly sign a Concordat with the Holy See (which he did) and then blithely go ahead and do what he wanted (which he did). The Church felt bound to the Concordat even when it was violated. It could protest but had no other means of enforcement which it could have had if the laymen were gathered into strong organizations. The Concordats proved to be more of a burden to the Church since they tended to substitute high level arrangements for daily Catholic participation. The papacy failed to see that the new regimes of Hitler and Mussolini were not merely indifferent to religion but hostile to it. Hitler and Mussolini never got around to a full-scale persecution of the Church because of World War II, but the anti-Christian Communist regime of Stalin did and that proved the danger of working with totalitarian governments by Concordats.

ITALY

In Italy the democratic government was faltering. Pius XI on his election was anxious to come to some kind of agreement with the government but he did not include the new People's Party of Dom Sturzo in his plans. If he had there would have been a strong party to support the old government. Since he did not Italy was susceptible to the many forces that wanted to take over after the war. Such forces included the communists, the socialists and the fascists of Mussolini. Mussolini, rising on the wave of division and depression, became Italy's prime minister in 1922 and obtained dictatorial powers. He quickly initiated much needed reforms, suppressed dissent and established a fascist dictatorship in 1925 with himself as "Il Duce." As did the wily Napoleon, Mussolini realized that to solidify Italy and to get the support of the masses he must make some peace with the Catholic Church. He toned down some of the anticlerical laws and in 1929 concluded the Lateran Treaty and Concordat with Pius XI. By the Lateran Treaty the papacy was given the sovereign state of the Vatican and Lateran palaces and Castle Gandolfo outside of Rome in return for the pope's recognition of the Kingdom of Italy. In addition the Concordat stipulated that the pope was to be paid about one hundred million dollars as payment for the seizure of the papal states and property in return for the Church's neutrality in the political affairs of Italy.

After the agreement of 1929 Mussolini went ahead to harass the Church anyway and so in 1931 Pius XI in an encyclical took issue with the oppressive measures of Mussolini. Yet Pius still kept the Catholic Action groups out of politics and forbade the clergy all political activity. By 1937 Mussolini's government was becoming even more dictatorial though the Vatican kept to its loose alliance (though not identity) with it. As the more pagan aspects of Mussolini's regime appeared, especially after his association with Hitler, the Vatican and Mussolini drifted further apart. Towards the end of his life Pius was beginning to denounce Mussolini.

GERMANY

In Germany after the war King Wilhelm II had fled to the Netherlands and so the German Weimar Republic came into being. Some progress was made especially in getting payments for the war reduced. Business picked up and Germany was admitted into the League of Nations. But all was not well. There were many pressures from the old line conservatives and communists. The former was successful in getting the old conservative von Hindenburg elected president of the Republic. Meanwhile another socialist party was gaining in strength. This was Hitler's Nazi party. His party became so strong that it could no longer be ignored. Hitler's real opportunity came when a series of economic depressions in 1929 shook the country. Von Hindenburg appointed von Papen as Prime Minister. He in turn, in order to achieve anything, needed Hitler's support thus bringing him more into the limelight. Von Papen was unsuccessful in his policies and so in 1933 von Hindenburg appointed Hitler as chancellor.

It was only a matter of time before the Weimar Republic gave way to the Third Reich and a revolutionary dictatorship was established. Immediately a drive was put on to oust the Communists. All dissent was crushed, the Jews were persecuted and several German states were brought under one government and united under the single Nazi party. To further crush dissent Hitler launched his infamous purge of 1934 whereby some of von Papan's associates and certain Catholic labor leaders lost their lives. The notorious concentration camps such as Dachau were started at this time. After von Hindenburg's death Hitler was voted in as President and Imperial Leader of the Third Reich. By tireless propaganda and his secret police (SS) Hitler tightened his hold on the country.

Hitler even made a concordat with the Vatican. Up to this time the Catholic bishops had forbidden the people to join Hitler's party because of his anti-Christian attitudes and racial intolerance but with the Concordat they withdrew this stricture. Again, it was a question that the Catholics, like many other Germans, were alarmed at the Communists and recognized that Hitler was the only one strong enough to subdue them. Although many did not like Hitler's atheism or militancy, many Catholics and the hierarchy thought that under the influence of von Papen and von Hindenburg, he would be calmed down. Anyway, the Vatican's Secretary of State, the future Pius XII, signed the Concordat with Hitler which was more to his benefit than to the Church's. Hitler now had an agreement with the Vatican to parade before German Catholics. He also had the prestige that went with it to parade before the world. He never intended, of course, to keep the agreements of the Concordat. During the years of 1933 to 1937 the Vatican protested his disregard of the Concordat. Again, it was a case that upper level negotiations were binding on the moral side, disregarded by the ambitious, immoral side and useless to the everyday man who had to live in the ambiguity of an agreement by his leaders without participation by himself.

Finally in 1937 Pius XI issued his sensational encyclical in German *Mit Brennender Sorge* (with burning anxiety) condemning outright the Nazi regime. The hierarchy did not come out with any similar statement and much of the reason lay in the fact that Rome was too centralized and always suspicious of any independent move by the German hierarchy. Besides in spite of the encyclical Rome did not want them to jeopardize the Concordat. The German hierarchy and the pope, now Pius XII, were trying hard to appease the Nazi regime. Perhaps this appeasement reached its extreme in the fact that neither the hierarchy nor the pope protested the extermination of the Jews. This became something of a scandal. Pius XII thought that any public protest would be useless for his protest would not really have changed matters and in this he was probably right. Besides he was trying to remain neutral. Above all he was convinced that the real enemy of the future was Soviet Russia. He did not want to break completely with Germany which he knew would have to be enlisted in defense of any Russian takeover of Europe. Pius' attitude has brought much criticism, some very extreme and unfair such as that represented by Rolf Hochhuth's play *The Deputy*. Perhaps the real blunder is not that Pius did not issue a strong statement on Jewish persecution for the reasons listed above, or that he put political consideration above such a grave moral issue, but that after 1945 the Vatican concealed the truth:

> At that time an open explanation of the reasons that lay behind his conduct would have been widely welcomed. But Pius XII never publicly voiced any regret or explanation, acting indeed as though there had never been any collaboration with fascism or any special consideration shown towards the Nazi regime.[1]

The Vatican did on April 4, 1973, reveal something. It revealed that at least the pope's aides knew of the Nazi slaughter of millions of Jews. Archbishop Roncalli, then Apostolic Delegate in Istanbul (and later Pope John XXIII) reported to Pius XII's substitute Secretary of State, Monsignor Montini (later Pope Paul VI) about the killing of the Jews in Nazi-occupied Eastern Europe. Presumably Monsignor Montini relayed this information to the pope. Other official documents from secular sources also indicate that Pius repeatedly received reports of mass killings of the Jews in occupied Poland. There are of course more Vatican documents not yet revealed and the world may not know for a long time to come the real story of the silence of Pius XII.

FRANCE AND OTHER COUNTRIES

After the war there were several factions vying for governmental control: the communists, the socialists, the democrats and the monarchists. The papacy rejected communism outright and was wary of socialism. It never came out forthrightly in favor of democracy and tended to favor the monarchy. In fact, resistance to the government brought the anti-Catholic measures of 1924. During World War II when the Nazis occupied France Pius XII recognized the Petain regime but he also negotiated with DeGaulle. The Church's collaboration with the Vichy regime brought protests from DeGaulle.

Spain, after World War I, was still a constitutional monarchy. Yet a disastrous defeat of Spain in Morocco in 1921 led to a revolt against the king. The king thus permitted and encouraged the dictatorship of Primo Rivera in 1923. Rivera ruled till 1930. In a new election Zamora headed the new Republic as its first president and a strong anti-Catholic majority caused severe anticlerical measures to be passed. In 1932 the Jesuits were expelled and the schools confiscated. In 1933 all church property was transferred to the state. New elections brought some relief to the Church which in turn infuriated the Communists and others and led to an insurrection during which many churches were burned and priests were terrorized. Anarchy was beginning to sweep the country. Suddenly in 1936 a general from the Spanish army in Morocco, General Franco, landed at Cadiz. He established a government with himself as dictator. A fierce civil war broke out and Franco emerged as victor in 1939. In 1941 agreements were made by the Church with Franco and Catholicism in 1953 was restored as the established religion.

Across the water in Mexico a radical revolutionary movement called for complete Mexican nationalization. This meant the expulsion of every foreign influence in the interests of the native Indian culture. Naturally, the Catholic Church felt the full brunt of persecution. In 1926 laws were passed forbidding the Church to own property and conduct schools. All foreign clergy were expelled and the Mexican clergy had to register with the government. For three years out of protest and in agreement with the pope the bishops and priests conducted no religious services in Mexico. Finally in 1929 a truce with the government was reached and the laws were more leniently applied. However, in 1931 a new and more vigorous anticlerical government came in and religious persecution became widespread. Under a new president in 1934 this persecution abated and Church services were tolerated.

AFTER WORLD WAR II

The Second World War had really been a continuation of the first. The League of Nations had grown more impotent and almost ceased to function by 1938. France feared Germany. England distrusted France and was soft in its approach to Hitler. Germany was still smarting over the terms of the treaty. Japan had entered Manchuria in 1931 and Germany began to rearm in 1935, the same year that Italy seized Ethiopia. In 1939 Italy seized Albania and Hitler seized Austria and Poland. Russia had at first been on Hitler's side since she always distrusted France and England anyway. Therefore Russia signed a nonaggression pact with Hitler in Moscow in 1939. With such support from Russia Hitler felt free to march into Poland and on that occasion France and England declared war. The rest is terrible and costly history.

After the war the U.S. and the Soviet emerged as the two most powerful nations. As Pius XI and XII foresaw, communism became very strong in Italy and France. The Communists continued to swallow up Catholic countries and they skillfully persecuted or maneuvered the Church. Missionaries were expelled as their atheistic campaigns moved ahead. Oppression followed in Poland, Czechoslovakia, Rumania, Yugoslavia and Hungary—wherever communism became the ruling power. It was no wonder that communism became the all-pervading, preoccupying concern of the Church. No wonder the Church saw communism as the implacable foe and took a rigid and uncompromising stand against it.

PIUS XI AND XII

Pius XI and Pius XII were authoritarian figures. They both issued several encyclicals giving rise to the controversy as to the exact authority of such letters. There was a distinct danger that these texts would be quoted as final authorities and that twenty centuries of Tradition and Scripture itself would be ignored by those who felt they needed an easy text for their particular points of view. Pius XI tried to isolate Catholics as did his predecessor, Pius X. In 1929 he had forbidden coeducation and interdenominational schools. It was he who canonized the Little Flower, St. John Fischer, Thomas More, the Cure of Ars, Albert the Great and John Bosco.

It was during Pius XII's long reign that World War II took place and the spread of communism. We are too near the events yet for an objective judgment of his reign both as to his political and ecclesiastical effects. Here we might mention a few of the items of his pontificate. Pius XII tried to keep peace between Mussolini and the Church and Italy out of World War II but was unsuccessful. After the war Italy was in political turmoil. The communists took advantage of this and made strong gains. There was, of course, always the possibility that the monarchy might be restored to Italy but Pius XII took no definite stand on this and in 1946 that form of government was rejected.

We have mentioned before how the Church became somewhat alienated from the rest of the world because of its narrow theology. At times Pius XII would take up some of the newer thoughts that emerged after World War II, especially those that originated in France—but he would not follow them through. For example, in 1943 he issued the letter *Divini Afflante Spiritu* which gave biblical scholars the freedom of inquiry. In 1947 in *Mediator Dei* he gave a great impetus to liturgical reform. He forwarded the missions. In 1939 he had issued a decree tolerating the honors paid to Confucius and the dead in China, honors which, we recall, Ricci had tolerated at the end of the sixteenth century but which Rome had condemned in 1704. During the war Pius gave immunity to a large number of Jews. He relaxed the regulations about fasting before Holy Communion, permitted evening Masses, revised the Holy Week liturgy and gave the world the "dialogue Mass." He gave permission for a number of married converts, ex-Lutheran pastors to be ordained.

Yet Pius, as we saw, was too political in not speaking out for the Jews' plight in Germany under Hilter. By 1950 he retreated somewhat into conservative positions again. He knew the Church had to open itself to what was going on—many of his speeches indicated this—but he could not break out of the mold of authoritarian teacher to permit this. He feared that things would go too far and get out of hand. So he retreated. He proclaimed the Feast of the Assumption in 1950, Marian devotions always being somehow linked with a kind of conservatism. He beatified Pius X and considered beatifying Pius XI thus giving support to the policies of these two conservative popes. In 1950 he issued the encyclical *Humani Generis* in which in a mild tone he rejected the new trends in theology and caused a smaller version of the intellectual witch-hunting that Pius X caused with his encyclical on modernism. He ended the priest-worker experiment in France. Pius XII was almost an absolute benevolent monarch. He ruled the Church by himself being too astute and experienced to let the curia take over. He pronounced on many things, some profusely some timidly. His was a one man rule and his contributions to the Church have yet to be assessed.[2]

PRELUDES TO A COUNCIL

In order to understand the brief reign of Pope John XXIII we must recall once more the ecclesiastical atmosphere of the times. The last four or five popes were authoritarian. Less than a hundred years before John XXIII infallibility had been proclaimed which seemed to put a stop to theological questioning. Some fifty years beforehand Pius X had cast a pall over all theological speculation. Yet, in spite of all this, small groups of churchmen were determined to ride out the tide of suspicion. We have noted how the Dominican Father F. M. Lagrange retired to Jerusalem to found there his famed Biblical school and prepare the next generation of scholars to face the problems so long ignored. Investigations were going on quietly at the universities such as Louvain in Belgium, Nijmegen in Holland, Frieburg in Switzerland, Innsbruck in Austria, the Catholic faculty at Tubingen in Germany and others. There was Romano Guardini (d. 1968) who promoted liturgical reforms; Jacques Maritain renewing Thomism; Erich Przyqara, Hugo and Karl Rahner; Ratzinger, Metz and Kung. In France there were Congar, de Lubac and

Danielou. In Holland there was Schillebeeckx. These men were helping the Church to return to the ancient patristic and biblical roots of the faith. They helped the Church (the papacy) to get out of its narrow vision of things, confined to the Western world, and see matters in more universal terms. They were awaiting an opportunity to come out into the open as it were. Still, they dared not. The Roman curia was keeping watch. Its continuous presence and its far-reaching control was a real factor in the Church. Xavier Rynne describes it thus:

> In the government of the Catholic Church over the course of the last two hundred years or so—at least since the French Revolution—the Congregations of the Roman Curia achieved a startling supremacy, so much as evidently to have given many members of these administrative organs the impression that, for all practical purposes, they were the Church. Bishops, priests, and faithful were dealt with as a sort of mass appendage to the Vatican. Many of these officials seem to have felt that they were the effective executors of absolutist papal power over the clergy and faithful, and their decisions should not only be law but that their opinions on doctrinal, moral and political matters were manifestations of papal infallibility. In the appointment of bishops all over the world, the creation and apportionment of dioceses, the surveillance of faith and morals, the authorizing and control of religious orders and congregations, the dispensing of Church funds for missionary enterprises, and the safeguarding of tradition and orthodoxy affecting every aspect of Catholic life, they gradually came to have the final say.[3]

JOHN XXIII

It was into this atmosphere that Pope John XXIII came. He was supposed to be an interim pope until the cardinals could come up with someone better to fill Pius XII's shoes.

Pope John was an old man, conservative and at the mercy of the curia who really ran things for the first few years. Under John a new warning was issued to New Testament scholars and Latin was reaffirmed as the language of the Church. Warnings were given against the new theologies. Yet, although John was conservative, he was open. He knew in his heart that the curia's hold would have to be broken. He knew that new thoughts could not be repressed forever. His own personal experience gave him a certain sympathy to what was going on. In 1925 he was the apostolic visitor to Bulgaria. In 1934 he was delegate to Turkey and Greece. In 1944 he was nuncio at Paris and in 1953 in Venice. While he was in France he had observed the experiments going on there with the priest-workers and he felt the impact of the new ideas. He knew something had to be done. That "something" was a council.

VATICAN II

Pope John's advisors were not happy with his announcement to call a council. John referred to them as "prophets of doom." When they saw that the pope was determined they got up a typical conservative agenda. But the pope, with his world wide experience, knew who was coming to the Council: that new forces and new ideas would turn things upside down. And he allowed it. In his famous opening speech at the Council on October 11, 1962, he gave positive encouragement to the new forces in the Church. Two days later when Cardinal Lienart proposed that the prepackaged, curia-dominated agenda be scrapped, the new spirit was unleashed amid thunderous applause. Renewal and reform were here to stay.

By the end of the first session of Vatican II it was obvious that a great change had taken place. No longer was the Catholic to be shielded from the rest of the world, something that the popes for the last two hundred years tried to do. The ideas were too strong. Pius XII might thus stand more condemned not for his silence in the face of the Nazi regime but for his hesitation to come to terms with the world. He was aware that this was a growing necessity but he was timid. He failed to meet the needs of the times which he himself knew. Under John all this changed. John knew that the laity had to be brought in. He knew that the Catholic Church concerned the eastern as well as the western half of the globe. He unleashed a whole new spirit of openness. He was even willing to dialogue with the communists and get the Church from a preoccupying and exclusive vision of that evil. A few months before he died in 1963 he received Khrushchev's son-in-law at the Vatican. In his encyclical *Pacem in Terris* he also condemned communism but also argued for peaceful coexistence. With John the anticommunist attitude has been modified somewhat and the door has been left slightly opened for future dialogue. It was also Pope John who at long last in his encyclical *Mater and Magistra* pronounced in favor on democracy. John moved the Church away from local Italian politics to consider the rest of the world. Under him the papacy's outlook was no longer seen through Italian political glasses. After many centuries the papacy was at last free from Italian politics. A new age was dawning and once more in her long two thousand year history the Church was entering a new phase, encountering new challenges and adapting to new ways.

AFTERMATH OF A COUNCIL

We have made note at the end of the last chapter on the Church in America that both conservatives and liberals were disappointed after the council. Initial optimism degenerated into division and confusion. Renewal and reform have never been easy. The old Church was one of order, authority, ascending structure and precise dogma, a universal and unerring organization for all men—and fearful must be those people who did not enter it, at least implicitly, before they died. The new Church by contrast is one of confusion, democracy, fluidity, speculation; it considers itself more as an erring pilgrim which may not be universal at all but merely contain the "remnant" to witness to the world at large. The clergy are not the Church and the pope is not the Church and the Church itself, according to the documents of Vatican II, is not the Kingdom of God. The practical difference between the old and the new is not unexpected: inefficiency, less respect for formal guidelines and authority and decentralized chaos. But the Church in the long run, as history seems to show, has far less to fear from deviation than from rigidity, far less from dynamism than from institutionalism, far less from service than from self-service, far less from witnessing than from self-preservation. In any case, while "the prophets of doom" have scored some telling points, Pope John's spirit is still detectable, that spirit of renewal, reform and adaptability which have been so historically consistent in the long journey of the Pilgrim Church.

NOTES

1. Karl Otmar von Aretin, *op. cit.*, p. 214.
2. However, books like Malachi Martin's *Three Popes and the Cardinal* are of little help being so one-sided (Farrar, Straus and Giroux, New York, 1972). Better are the books of Carlo Falconi.
3. Xavier Rynne, *Vatican Council II* (one volume), p. 18. Farrar, Straus and Giroux, New York. 1968. An entertaining if slightly prejudiced account of the speeches at Vatican II. The best one volume around.

XXIII

An Epilog:
Past, Present and Future

THE PAST

Now that we have reached the end we must pause, as we did half-way through the book, to reflect on what we have seen. We must take a brief look at the past, the present and the future of Catholics and the Church. Concerning the past there are a few conclusions that can be comfortably drawn. For one thing there is no educated Catholic who can say about some favorite devotion or ritual (or concept), "That's the way it always was!" On the contrary, he now knows that variety has been more the rule than uniformity. Now he knows that there have been great variations as to the role of the pope, the liturgy of the Mass, clerical life-styles and popular devotions. He knows, for example, that the eucharistic devotions such as Benediction go back only to the fourteenth century, that the small, round, white host we know today goes back only to the eighth century, that the Nicene creed was included universally in the Mass only in the eleventh century, that the rosary is a fifteenth century product and First Communion at seven years of age is a twentieth century novelty. He knows now that there were

513

many schools of theological thought, a variety of ministries and variations in the sacraments. He has seen in these pages the progress of political and ecclesiastical centralization and he is witnessing today the painful process of reversal. Once more, the average educated Catholic cannot say about too many things in his Catholic Church that "That's the way it always was!"—except that "Jesus is Lord!"

Concerning the past there is also this conclusion: the Catholic must learn to feel a great deal of pride as to his heritage, both cultural and spiritual. During these times when he has heard so much criticism he must renew his perspective. A Catholic should feel at home with Ignatius, Irenaeus, Augustine, Anselm, Gregory, Catherine, Francis, Thomas and Theresa. He should see in his local bishop the end product of a long line that stretches back to apostolic times. He should be able to visit or see in the movies the monasteries which bequeathed to him his ability to speak and read and write. He should be able to listen to Gregorian chant or Palestrina and be thrilled. He should be able to run his fingers over the sculptures at Chartres and remember how peasant and lord carried its stones on their backs for the greater honor and glory of God. He should be able to stand before a page from the Book of Kells or a Carolingian manuscript, before a Giotto, a Botticelli, a Michelangelo, a Rubens or an El Greco and contemplate the Catholic vision that guided their art. He should feel a deep kinship with the entire Christian community as he stands around the altar breaking the same Bread and drinking from the same Cup that the Apostles and fellow Christians throughout twenty centuries have eaten and drunk. He should recite with pride the ancient creeds and celebrate the various liturgies and devotions which have nourished millions of people before him. He should feel a part of the whole world where Catholic missionaries have penetrated and which they have watered with their blood. He should feel a part of the countless unknown reconciliations, the works of charity, the numerous schools, hospitals and orphanages that have been (and still are) a part of his Catholic heritage. He does not have to be a Romantic to sense brotherhood with a great Western civilization that has changed the world. He must be able to recite with awe the long litany of countless saints who have been the glory of the Church and its products even in its darkest days. There is a past that lives. There is a Catholic past that has touched every corner of the globe. There is a Catholic influence that is some part of every human being on earth today. The past of the Catholic Church is all too human, but the Church is a community of human beings, and in spite of this, great moments have been reached and many have seen and praised "the wonderful works of God" (Acts 2:11).

THE PRESENT: CONFUSION

Concerning the present, it is superfluous to say that the Catholic Church is indeed going through a time of confusion, crisis and turmoil. But if there is anything we have learned as we read this book it is this: yes, the Church of Vatican II is different, but—the Church of Constantine was different from the Church of the Fathers. The Church of the Barbarian was different from the Church of Constantine. The Church of Charlemagne was different from the Church of the Barbarian. The Church of the Popes was different from the Church of Charlemagne. The Church of Trent was different from the Church of the Popes. The Church of Vatican I was different from the Church of Trent. Nor were the transitions from one "style" of Church to the other made without considerable pain and hardship. The aspirations, the greatness, the pretensions, the mistakes of each type of Church has had to give way. This accounts for the styling of the modern Church by Vatican II as a "Pilgrim." The concept is that of movement, journeying, change. Ours is a "process" Church as people today speak of a "process" theology.

As in every age, people today are asking where all the changes will end; they are weary of all of the "instant" cures that have been offered, tried and failed. They are distrustful of the latest panacea whether it be group sessions, pentecostalism, cursillos, lay organizations, nuns' and priests' federations, new catechisms, and so forth. They are suspicious of the "expert" theologian and the latest liturgist and wish they would all go away. They are hostile to those answers that try to solve problems that took centuries to arise and which will not give way to six month's solutions. For many there is a failure of nerve about the whole concept of renewal and reform. Yet as Michael Novak says in his book *All the Catholic People:*

> . . . We are the Catholic people. We are no other. For better or worse, there lie the deep and ancient roots of our identity, which it is difficult to shed. Every day people "leave the Church," and every day the inner erosion of that imagination and instinct which constitute belonging to a people proceeds a little further in innumerable other modern persons. Still, those in whom a Catholic imagination and instinct are strong cannot escape by leaving the institution or by trying to make themselves modern. The "invisible religion" of American society has lost as much of its credibility as has the Church.[1]

THE PRESENT: CHALLENGE

For the present there are two challenges. One is for the individual Catholic himself. He must regain a sense of appreciation of his heritage, his past, as we mentioned a while ago. But this appreciation is not the appreciation of looking at the fond memories in a museum; it is the appreciation of learning from and building organically from the past. To be a Catholic is to have a large and long "context" in which to assess the modern world. To be a Catholic is to evaluate the present in the light of the past, to be sensitive to what moved the people then—what were their inspirations, motivations and their spirit—that we might recapture such for ourselves. Again, Michael Novak catches the meaning of all of this (and the point of this book) when he writes:

> To be a Catholic is, for many conservative persons, to belong to an institution whose concepts, rules, dogmas, and offices have already been defined and remain only to be accepted whole. In my view, it is rather to belong to an historical people, to whom that institutional structure belongs and who must seriously reform it. A serious Catholic, I would argue, takes every historical dogma or practice of his people seriously, hoping to learn why it was that persons in earlier times (or yet today) found them illuminating and helpful. Such historical materials are not absolutes, but data, data to be understood, to be sifted and weighed and compared with other data. A serious Catholic wishes to ignore none of them and, on the other hand, to account for each. . . .[2]

The second challenge is for the whole Church. It is the ever chronic challenge that the Church must achieve relevance to the modern world and yet at the same time not be absorbed by it. This has been a failure of much of the liberalism of the present. Dan Callahan, a perceptive and liberal critic of the times has this to say:

> . . . I think one of the great weaknesses of the liberal Catholic in recent years is trying to be "with it," to be relevant, to prove they're as secular as everyone else. I think that in the end this becomes either a big cop-out or a sell out. The most important thing is for Catholics to try to be distinctive

> and to be different, to try to probe the things which led Ca-
> tholicism to be a major historical force in the past. . . .

What he is saying is what Philip Gleason stated so well, that
the main problem is to grasp "the dialectical relationship of
the demands and dangers of a situation in which the Church
must maintain identity without isolation and achieve relevance without absorption."[3] As Catholics adjust to entering
more solidly into the social justice field, into the world, into
the mainstream of society they and their Church must keep
the balance of identity and affirmation to what the Church
stands for after all. "The Church must fight for the earthly
implication of the heavenly values it affirms; it can never
again divorce God from the Negroes, the poor, those dying
in war, and the rest of humanity. But over and above that
witness to the temporal meetings of the eternal there must
be the assertion of the eternal itself."[4]

Actually, the picture is larger than the Catholic Church.
The whole problem of "relevance without absorption"
plagues every religious denomination in the age of materialism and national paganism. The Jewish community is having
its first real identity problem in history. Tolerance is about
to achieve what persecution never could: the disappearance
of the Jewish community. In America, for example, there
are about five and a half million Jews and their leaders are
mightily worried that they are about to be so absorbed into
a tolerant American society that they will disappear. For the
Christian community, Roger Shinn of Union Theological
Seminary says:

> For "men to fulfill their own human potential" means many
> things. In most societies it has meant considerable cruelty
> and snobbery. It meant something vastly different to Nebu-
> chadnezzar and Gautama Buddha, to Genghis Khan and
> Francis of Assisi, to Adolf Hitler and to Martin Luther King.

> Empirically speaking, 'humanity' is defined by everything
> men do. But through the Hebrew prophets and Jesus of
> Nazareth there came to mankind a revelation of what hu-
> manity is and can be. Like it or not, we have that on our
> hands and must live with it. Christians must not say that
> they alone understand "humanity." But they must say that
> what they know they cannot surrender or distort.[5]

It is only by a sense of history, by a sense of our own heritage
that we will escape, in spite of a highly sophisticated mass
media, the assimilation into secular society and remain to
transform it.

THE PRESENT: WITNESS

We mentioned just now "secular" society and indeed such
secularization has been the triumph of the Enlightenment.
Priestcraft has been replaced by psychiatry and social man-
agers.[6] To the degree that internal spiritual motivation has
been replaced with psychological jargon and mechanistic
coils and springs to that extent external control and manipulation has become more important and necessary. "The
whole tendency of modern life is towards scientific planning
and organization, central control, standardization and
specialization."[7] Religion has a relevance if for no other
reason than to challenge the manipulators of humanity and
the all embracing commercial spirit that has marketed sex,
polluted the air, uglified the landscape and filled the atmosphere with smoke and emissions in the interest of the Gross
National Product. The Church as the bearer of a sacred
tradition, the guardian of all the richness of the inner life,
the home of mystics and visionaries must be there to challenge all of this. Historically the Church has done this in the
past. In the past Catholic Christianity was the principle of

moral, cultural and spiritual unity of the Western world. Even hostile historians like Gibbon admitted that much. Even he conceded that the religious influences and "the growing authority of the popes cemented the union of the Christian republic; and gradually produced the similar manners and the common jurisprudence which had distinguished from the rest of mankind the independent and even hostile nations of modern Europe."[8] The Catholic Church, like its brothers in Protestantism and Judaism, faces a common challenge of "relevance without absorption," a commitment to rescue the world from secularism. Martin Marty comments in the last paragraph of his book called *Protestantism:*

> Neither the institutional or the cultural prospects for Protestantism seem very bright to an observer in the late twentieth century. Readers of this book can see how readily Protestantism became established, authoritarian, and un-self-critical. Though several hundred million remain, even the number of Protestant church members has been in relative decline in many nations where once it was high. The Protestant era may, indeed, be coming or have come to its end. Perhaps the spirit of prophecy will then need new embodiments, and the witness to a transcendent God will find new incarnations as Protestantism joins other religions that, as Tillich noted, are "threatened by secularism and paganism. . . ."[9]

To assume new embodiments of the apostolic message—this is the present challenge of the Church today as it was in the past.

THE FUTURE

What can we say of the future of the Church and even of society except that no one knows what it shall be? But the past reminds us of some things about the future. When Pius

XII died, for example, who could have foreseen Pope John XXIII and the Vatican council? Who could have foreseen even Vatican I when Pius VII was abducted and died a prisoner in 1799? Who could have foreseen that Modernism would not really go away, that in fact we are still struggling with its basic questions today and that Pius X's untimely condemnation and World War I were but an interruption to what had to be faced sooner or later?

What we do know is that the future belongs to those who are rooted historically in the faith and the tradition of the Church. Growth is always organic and it is the "organic" man and woman who will shape the Church of the future. And perhaps as Fathers Rahner and Ratzinger remind us the Church of the future will get smaller, become more a voluntary grouping with consequent greater demands on its members. The Church of the future may be something like the Church of the past, like the early Church: a minority in a hostile society, yet full of fervor, building community and centered around its perennial liturgy and affirmations that "Jesus is Lord!"

Since prediction is such a chancy thing perhaps we had better end with the insightful words of John C. Meagher:

> The church is forever engaged in the process of understanding the Christ of History through its life as Christ in History, going about his Father's business. Precisely how the church's encounter with the new world of reforming movements will affect its understanding of itself and the Christ of History remains to be seen. We can only know that such heady new wine is bound to stretch and reform the old skins. That is the way it has always worked. We cannot yet predict what more of the church's belief will eventually go the way of the apostolic expectation of a first-generation Parousia, nor what may be added through new spirits, as the church once learned to repent of her toleration of slavery. Our task is sim-

ply to go about this business faithfully, with as much mutual trust as we can summon.

Such faithfulness does not require us to repudiate the past in order to participate in the formation of the future . . . To be faithful must mean both to preserve and to create . . . There will be time for new harmonies to arise out of new discords as long as we remember that nothing less than the reverent appropriation of Christianity's whole experience can provide a sufficient basis for the discernment of spirits.

. . . as long as men can continue to believe in the Jesus of Faith, Christianity will endure. . . . In the meantime, the Christianity of our new worlds must continue, like the Body of Christ everywhere, to be about its Father's business: no good work need be compromised, no faithful witness need be restrained, and no man need be ashamed of the gospel of Christ.[10]

NOTES

1. Michael Novak, *All the Catholic People,* Herder and Herder, N.Y. 1971.
2. *Ibid.,* p. 44.
3. Philip Gleason, editor, *Catholicism in America,* p. 150. Harper and Row, New York. 1970.
4. Quoted in William Braden's *The Age of Aquarius,* p. 269. Quadrangle Books, Chicago. 1970.
5. *The Church in the Year 2000, The Commonweal Papers: 4.* October 31, 1969. "More Than Survival" by Roger L. Shinn, p. 148.
6. There are many books that treat of the whole culture-faith-technology problems of today. *The Making of a Counter-Culture* (especially the first chapter "Technology's Children") by Theodore Roszak is one. See several of the "futuristic" books.
7. Christopher Dawson, *The Historic Reality of Christian Culture,* p. 26. Harper and Brothers Publishers, New York. 1960. This whole short book is very insightful especially the first essay, "The Outlook for Christian Culture."
8. Quoted in Dawson, *ibid.*

9. Martin E. Marty, *Protestantism*, p. 256. Holt, Rinehart and Winston, New York. 1972. See also Robert Jay Lifton's *Boundaries: Psychological Man in Revolution*. Random House, New York. 1970.
10. John C. Meagher, "Creating a Christian Identity" in *Commonweal* p. 439. February 11, 1972.

BIBLIOGRAPHICAL NOTES

Since this is a popularization there is no need to list endless books that no one would read anyway. Perhaps the best direction I could give is to recommend the books listed in the footnotes at the end of each chapter. With one or two exceptions they are all well done and comfortable reading for the average person. However, I would make special mention of the following:

One of the best works on Catholic Church history is the series *The Christian Centuries, A New History of the Catholic Church*. There are two volumes out, *The First Six Hundred Years* by Danielou and Marrou and *The Middle Ages* by Knowles and Obolensky. Unfortunately the remaining three volumes have not been published (McGraw, Hill, N.Y.) and, according to a communication from the publisher, will not be. But the two volumes mentioned are excellent.

Next, I would recommend the six volume paperback Pelican series printed in Britain but obtained in this country from Penguin Books, 7110 Ambassador Road, Baltimore, Md. 21207. They are popularly written but they deal with Christianity in general and are not exclusively concerned with the Catholic Church.

There is the three volume work by Philip Hughes, *A History of the Church* published by Sheed and Ward. But these volumes are somewhat dated now.

Otherwise I know of no single volume history of the Catholic Church except Philip Hughes *A Popular History of the Catholic Church*, a paperback put out by the Macmillan Company, N.Y. (1946) but the average American reader might find it too cramped.

Finally, I would recommend any and all of the books written by Christopher Dawson. They are worthwhile for their depth and understanding of Christian culture in every age.

In related theological and renewal issues I would recommend any book by Karl Rahner, Schillebeeckx (at least their more popular books: they can get pretty heavy) and Andrew Greeley (of whom it is claimed that he has not one unrecorded thought). Also recommended are any books by Richard McBrien, especially *What Do We Really Believe?* (Geo. A. Pflaum, Dayton, Ohio) 1968; *Church: The Continuing Quest* (Newman Press, 1970) and *Who Is A Catholic?* (Dimension Books, Denville, N.J. 1971). Also, Monika Hellwig's *What Are the Theologians Saying?* (Pflaum Press, 1970) and my own *Renewal and the Middle Catholic* (Fides Publishers, Notre Dame, Indiana, 1970).

Index